1963

This boo

MEDIÆVAL CULTURE

IN TWO VOLUMES
VOLUME ONE

MEDIAEVAL CULTURE

AN INTRODUCTION TO DANTE AND HIS TIMES

BY
KARL VOSSLER

VOLUME ONE

FREDERICK UNGAR PUBLISHING CO.
NEW YORK

Translated from the German
DIE GÖTTLICHE KOMÖDIE
by William Cranston Lawton

First American edition published 1929
Reprinted 1958

Printed in the United States of America

Library of Congress Catalog Card Number 58-10378

PREFACE

This book is intended to open up to a wider circle of intelligent readers the comprehension of the *Divine Comedy*. The essential facts in the history of culture out of which the poem takes its rise must first be considered; then the poem itself in all its poetic originality, in its unique character as a work of art. In the first part the background of the poet in the religion, philosophy, ethical and political thought, and imaginative literature of the Middle Ages is discussed; in the second part, his work alone. Hence the second part can be enjoyed, perhaps can best be enjoyed, apart from the first, for the first part takes for granted a thorough familiarity with the poem; and those who do not feel that they possess this familiarity might very well begin by reading the second part first. The introductory chapter on Dante and Goethe may also be left to the last, at least by those who do not bring to the reading a considerable acquaintance with both poets.

But Dante sums up so many sides of his own age, and the study of his background carries us over so wide a field, that a work such as this may very well serve as a gateway to the study of mediæval culture in all its manifold activities. It is for this reason that I have submitted to the suggestion of others and permitted this book (which in the original is simply called *Die göttliche Komödie*) to go forth in its English dress under the more general title of *Mediæval Culture: An Introduction to Dante and his Times*. It is that in a real sense perhaps, but only as an afterthought and within definite limits, for my primary aim has been to bring home to the mind and heart of my readers the great poem of Dante itself.

The present work has been translated from the second German edition, which differs materially from the first, especially in the interpretation of the *Purgatorio* and the *Paradiso*.[1] I have been as sparing as possible in citing authorities, for I did

[1] The translation has been carefully revised by Professor Dino Bigongiari of Columbia University, who has given it the benefit of his wide knowledge of mediæval thought.

not wish my narrative to be swamped by references and foot-notes. Even the references which appeared in the original have been for the most part eliminated in this translation, since they were so largely concerned with German authorities. In place of these, my friend, Mr. J. E. Spingarn, has kindly prepared, for the benefit of studious but inerudite readers, a Bibliographi-cal Note which is intended merely as a guide to the literature available in English, but which indirectly, by reference to ample bibliographical material, points the way to the whole literature of the subject. I had hoped that he would write an Introduction to this translation, but he felt that a bibliography would be more useful to the reader. It would afford me great pleasure if those who speak the noble tongue which has produced the vast literature he has there recorded would give a friendly welcome to the pres-ent work.

KARL VOSSLER

CONTENTS

vii

CONTENTS

VOLUME I: THE RELIGIOUS, PHILOSOPHIC, AND ETHICO-POLITICAL BACKGROUND OF THE "DIVINE COMEDY"

INTRODUCTION

GOETHE'S "FAUST" AND DANTE'S "DIVINE COMEDY"

I. The Nature of Their Mutual Relation

One cannot speak to any cultivated German of Dante's *Divine Comedy* without reminding him of Goethe's *Faust*. To compare the greatest Italian and the greatest German poem has become a German habit since the days of the Romantic Movement, and is not without justification; not so much because of any actual similarity or of a common subject-matter as because of an internal and, for that very reason, profounder kinship between the two works. Not that the *Divine Comedy* had ever exerted a decisive or inspiring effect upon the form of *Faust*. It is in vain that the attempt has been made to find "the Dante in *Faust*."

The literary influences are trivial and external. At one prominent point, however, the inner kinship which unites all great creations of the human mind is powerfully revealed in the poem, and here—at the culminating point in each work—a mystical and loving greeting is proffered by the German to the Italian genius, by the modern to the mediæval artist.

> All things transitory
> But as symbols are sent:
> Earth's insufficiency
> Here grows to Event:
> The Indescribable,
> Here it is done:
> The Woman-Soul leadeth us
> Upward and on! [1]

Gretchen and Beatrice clasp hands. In both it is loving self-devotion, pure womanliness, which grips us and uplifts us to the stars.

But only in this final and symbolic significance do the two women meet. Elsewhere their ways run wide apart.

[1] Last lines of *Faust*, Taylor's version.

3

2. Diversity in Plan

If, to use significant round numbers, we select the year 1300 for the *Divine Comedy* and 1800 for *Faust,* five centuries intervene between the former and the latter. Within this period are included the three mightiest movements of modern history: the Renaissance, the Reformation, and the Age of Enlightenment. All three taken together signify a continuous and progressive liberation of the individual from the universal, or if we will from the Catholic, norms of the Middle Ages. In the Renaissance, the sensuous and artistic imagination asserted its proper rights: through the Reformation, religious and ethical feeling, and through the Age of Enlightenment, philosophic reason, gained a like victory.

The Faustian man emerges from this complete liberation, freed from the bonds of society, of the state, and of the church, with law and fate enthroned in his own breast, reaching out Titan-like into the infinite and superhuman.

Nevertheless—and herein the demands of a newer time announce themselves—Faust's boundless will overreaches itself, entangles itself in agonizing guilt. Only through renunciation and self-limitation is he slowly restored to the circle of useful social activity. When he puts himself at the service of human society, he is uplifted into the company of the blest. In so far as the conscious and voluntary return of an individuality, freed from fetters, to its historically determined pale may be characterized as romantic and reactionary, the second part of *Faust* is romantic and reactionary. But it is so not through aberration or weakness on the part of the poet, but rather because of the inevitable development of this mighty, epoch-making poem itself.

From the storm and stress of unbridled and all-sided exertion his pathway leads Faust to a consciously purposed social and moral activity. Faust's headstrong will is gradually purified and clarified, until at last he sees but a single goal before him: to win from the ocean a bit of land, and make it fruitful.

> I only through the world have flown:
> Each appetite I seized as by the hair;
> What not sufficed me, forth I let it fare,
> And what escaped me, I let go.
> I've only craved, accomplished my delight,
> Then wished a second time, and thus with might

Stormed through my life: At first 'twas grand, completely,
But now it moves most wisely and discreetly.
The sphere of Earth is known enough to me;
The view beyond is barred immutably:
A fool, who there his blinking eyes directeth,
And o'er his clouds of peers a place expecteth!
Firm let him stand, and look around him well:
This world means something to the Capable.
Why needs he through Eternity to wend? [1]

Therein lies a limitation, but not a constriction of the will; a subordination, but no sacrifice of free individuality. By setting definite goals before himself he does not break his own will; he rather purifies and strengthens it.

But if we interpret romanticism and reaction as remorseful self-destruction, mystical contrition, and weary homesickness for a Gothic mediæval refuge, then there is not a romantic or reactionary fleck in Goethe's poem. Remorse as a lasting condition, penance as an end in itself, weariness as a luxury, enfeebling self-contemplation—of all this, not a trace! On the contrary, just what rescues the hero and thwarts the Devil is the restless, never-wearying activity of the will. The same Titanic vigor which threatened to down him now exalts him.

To be sure,

> Still doth man err while yet he strives.

But:

> The man who ever toilsome strives,
> Him only can we save.

So the struggling will is the source of both evil and good. This double nature of the will is set forth by the Pater Profundus in an occult figure:

> Around me sounds a savage roaring,
> As rocks and forests heaved and swayed,
> Yet plunges, bounteous in its pouring,
> The wealth of waters down the glade,
> Appointed, then, the vales to brighten;
> The bolt, that flaming struck and burst,
> The atmosphere to cleanse and lighten,
> Which pestilence in its bosom nursed,—
> Love's heralds both, the powers proclaiming,
> Which, aye creative, us infold. [2]

[1] *Faust*, Part II, V, v, Taylor's version.
[2] *Ibid.*, vii, Taylor's version.

The highest form of the will is life-giving love, its basest aspect destructive hatred.

Viewed from this side, *Faust* reveals itself as the poem of the supremacy of the will, and the purification of the hero is accordingly accomplished through deeds, action, events, in the reality of everyday life.

The theme of Goethe's poem is the same as that of Dante's. It is, to use Kuno Fischer's words, "the fall and the redemption of Man." This identity in the fundamental idea "uplifts Goethe's *Faust* to the *Divine Comedy* and justifies the comparison with Dante." [1]

The treatment of the theme, however, by the mediæval poet is essentially different. The scene of the fall and of the redemption lies in the other world. The whole evolution of man occurs not in the tangible world of reality, but in a dreamlike vision. While *Faust* enfolds a human life from the fresh vigor of manhood to blind old age, the events of Dante's poem occur in the other world within the narrow limits of an Easter week. In short, the *Divine Comedy* is a vision, *Faust* is a drama.

But the vision is the favourite literary form of the Middle Ages. The noisy reality of life had for them only a subordinate value. Only when beheld through the veil of vision does existence acquire its full meaning.

> Merely a phantom
> Is all that is mortal.

Thus *Faust* voices the wisdom of the heavenly choir. It is not the wisdom of man in this world, which demands above all moderation, and utters the warning:

> A fool, who there his blinking eyes directeth
> And o'er his clouds of peers a place expecteth.

With Dante it is quite the contrary: for him, too, all transitory things on this earth are but phantoms. His sin had consisted precisely in this, that he took seriously and in earnest "present" things (*le cose presenti*) and allowed himself to be fettered by them. In sharp, curt phrases, Beatrice characterizes the moral condition of this sinner:

---

[1] K. Fischer, *Goethes Faust*, 5th ed., II, 178.

> Thou oughtest verily at the first shaft
> Of things fallacious to have risen up
> To follow me, who was no longer such.
> Thou oughtest not to have stooped thy pinions downward
> To wait for further blows, or little girl,
> Or other vanity of such brief use.[1]

But instead of uplifting himself after the first blow of misfortune, that is, after Beatrice's death, instead of following in the footsteps of her who was now dead toward the contemplation of eternal truths, instead of renouncing all earthly ties—

> And into ways untrue he turned his steps,
> Pursuing the false images of good,
> That never any promises fulfil.

Thereupon Beatrice complains:

> Nor prayer for inspiration me availed,
> By means of which in dreams and otherwise
> I called him back, so little did he heed them.
> So low he fell, that all appliances
> For his salvation were already short,
> Save showing him the people of perdition.[2]

Through the delusion of his reason came the fall: through its restoration, his redemption.

In such a process of purification, instruction, penance, scrutiny, and every kind of remorseful check upon the will, those ascetic practices which in *Faust* are hardly mentioned play a leading part. Viewed from this side, the *Divine Comedy* is the poem of the unfolding of truth.

Here lies the profound distinction between the two poems, a distinction which has its roots in historic conditions: in the one, the control and discipline of the will; in the other, the unfolding and elaboration of truth in the form of a vision. Kuno Fischer has expressed this contrast clearly, when he says:

Despite the similarity of their themes, the distinction between Dante and Goethe, between the mediæval and the modern poet, lies here: that for the latter, life itself is the mighty cleansing fire, the world itself is the great Purgatory; and the steps in the development of a noble nature are themselves the path to his redemption.[3]

[1] *Purgatorio*, XXXI, 55–60. The translations of the *Divine Comedy* are those of Longfellow, with a few exceptions.
[2] *Ibid.*, XXX, 130–138.
[3] *Op. cit.*, p. 189.

The distinction becomes clearer if we consider the political aspect of the two poems.

Compared to the eternal problems of the lone human soul, the controversy of the empire and the papacy becomes a mere masquerade. Goethe accordingly treats these antiquated powers humorously and ironically. But for Dante the world-empire and the Church constitute the great divine Vessel wherein the ideals of the individual calmly rest beside those of the community. Everything is contained within this Vessel, with nothing outside of it. And even if the entire structure has collapsed, yet it abides as an idea, and is to be measured accordingly. Therefore Dante treats the political conditions of his day with holy wrath, but the political future which the practical Faust strives to reconstruct in miniature on the border of the crumbled Empire is viewed by Dante with the nostalgic gaze of an enraptured prophet.

3. DIVERSITY IN EXECUTION

Of course such generalizations do not exhaust, by any means, the infinite variety of a great work of art. *Faust*, as well as the *Divine Comedy*, has other sides, other relationships.

It is not all action, not all exertion of the will, stormy activity and drama, that rise and fall in Goethe's poem. Indeed its lack of action and a corresponding undramatic quality have been pointed out by some critics. Much of its contents is merely imagery, symbol, intimation, instruction. Gradually Faust makes his way out of the fury of action, lets the whirl of life go rushing by him, and is no longer himself carried away by it. The poet by degrees assures him a freer foothold over and above passing events in his desire to unfold before his hero's eyes the world in its fullest extent. The youthful Faust acquired wisdom through suffering; grown old, he obtains it through contemplation. And what does he behold? Not always historical events, but often mere symbols or even allegories. His experiences become visions and so assume the artistic forms of the Middle Ages. What, for example, does the Helen episode offer if not a picturesque enrichment, an artistic rather than an ethical education of humanity? Even the last and mightiest thoroughly practical decision of Faust no longer arises out of the pressure of reality and through the application of will-power,

but springs, almost in jest, out of a discussion with Mephistopheles. In fact, this decision itself is in truth only a symbol.
Were it interpreted in a narrow, literal sense, it would show but
a wretched doom: Faust, the Titan, ending his life as a landed
proprietor and colonist.

The background and the scale of action have grown so large
that they can only be grasped by symbols and concepts. The
pictures become more and more transparent and dimmer; ever
more mysterious grows the connection of the incidents in the
drama. The colourful passions surging against the control of the
will have disappeared, and a mighty Reason now rules and illumines the poetic world of the Second Part. In it there is much
that can no longer be grasped intuitively and that reveals itself
only to the few who are familiar with the poet's philosophy. A
mystical ceremonial sanctifies the brilliant fantasy; the sounding
verses still glide on; but in the heart of the poem there is an ever
deeper and deeper calm.

So, then, *Faust*, which received its original form from a dramatic
impulse, deepens presently to thoroughly lyrical tones and closes
in a meditative pianissimo, interrupted by pensive pauses.

The *Divine Comedy* seems to follow almost the opposite path.
The plan and framework of the poem are scientific, and every
detail seems calculated in advance. The structure in its completeness, the noble proportions, and the mechanism of the poem,
will be intelligible to every one who has made himself familiar
with mediæval scholasticism. The much-admired consistency
and clearness, the so-called unity of structure, is rather archi-
tectural than organic. To attain it required rather a master
builder than a creative poet.

It may well have been all the more difficult to move freely
within these walls and circles. An unruly fantasy is here bridled
by an incredible mastery. A whole sea of imaginative visions
rages against the dikes of the general plan. But reason merely
indicates the direction in which strong-winged imagination rushes
on: and all personal suffering, feeling, and desire, all hatred, all
love, all earthly cares, are carried by it down into Hell or up into
changeless Heaven.

And not only the practical execution, but also the inner development of the poem and the evolution of the poet, pass—as
we shall see later in detail—from cleverness and rationality to a

sentimental and volitional mysticism. The final ennoblement of Man no longer lies in that illumination of reason which Beatrice, on the summit of the Purgatorial mountain, had demanded; it culminates in Love, and rings out in the words:

> But now was turning my desire and will,
> Even as a wheel that equally is moved,
> The Love which moves the sun and the other stars.[1]

Viewed from this new side, *Faust* no longer appears exclusively the poem of the control and discipline of the will; and the *Comedy*, also, goes far beyond the glorification and unfolding of human and divine Truth. In *Faust*, man, passionate and unpractically practical, grows calm in the contemplation of a deep harmonious connection between the natural and the spiritual world. In the *Comedy*, absorption in the inner life of man and in the future world leads to a complete elevation of character.

It may well have been the conditions of their respective ages which before all else made Goethe give to his work a practical foundation and a dramatic form, and Dante to his a scientific, theological foundation and visionary shape. But that neither became a prisoner within his plan, that each strove to move away from the pre-established goal, that the one transformed the vision into drama, and the other his drama into a vision, all this may have been made inevitable in the last resort by the peculiarity of their natures.[2]

4. SPIRITUAL CHARACTER AND KINSHIP

It was first necessary to disclose these natural peculiarities, in order that we might then see clearly to the very bottom the diversity and the similarity of the two works.

The differences strike the eye more quickly than the similarity.

[1] *Paradiso*, XXXIII, 143-145.

[2] Of course historical conditions also played a part. Fr. Gundolf has shown this excellently in his *Goethe*, Berlin, 1916, pp. 24-5: "Dante's world was a compact one . . . visible as a whole. . . . Goethe's was already shattered, not to be viewed as one, and its foundations had largely become insecure. Dante was able, from his central point, with a mighty grasp, to draw his world to himself, within himself. For Goethe, with like powers facing his own world, this was no longer possible. He had to find his bearings in this incoherent unlimited world; he had to seek out his own place, and the materials which he could use to depict and support his ego. So his entire creation, as compared with Dante's and Shakespeare's, seems somewhat experimental, tentative, and his laborious quest in *Faust* and in *Wilhelm Meister* . . . compared with Dante's unerring, calm assurance, was certainly a necessity, even though Goethe has made a virtue of it."

Dante's destiny, every incident, almost every word from him, every feature in his countenance, are austere and grim. But Goethe's life, his poetry, his scientific works, his whole personality, are pervaded by a gentle self-poised spirit. This simple sensuous beauty was denied to Dante. Repellent, defiant, haughty, he passed through the world. Everything that he had begun had remained fragmentary. Unhappy in love, pitifully shipwrecked in his political hopes and plans, interrupted in two ambitious scientific works, he throws himself, finally, with all the impetuosity and persistency of his will, upon his unique life-task, and never leaves it again until it stands forth living and perfect.

That which Dante, to be sure, pondered long, but finally, as we may assume, wrung from himself within a few years, Goethe could round out calmly and uniformly in the course of a rich life. That is why all in him flows on so clearly, plentifully, and naturally. The banished Florentine, on the other hand, had a grievous task to perform, over which he, as he himself says, grew lean.[1] The reader himself cannot help feeling the increasing effort. We follow with amazement, sometimes with stupefaction, the gigantic exertion of his inexhaustible powers. Dante, if ever man did, made Poesy come at his bidding. But Goethe's method of working was "never to force himself, and to idle through or sleep away all unproductive days and hours, rather than to attempt to create something, in such days, in which one could thereafter take no delight."[2] He regrets that Schiller—a man of will like Dante— "drove himself to his work when he was not at his best, and felt that his talent must at every hour obey him and be at his service. . . . But this injured his health, and was also harmful to his productions. . . . I have," he ends with the delicious naïveté of the child of nature, "I have all respect for the categorical imperative . . . but one must not drive it too hard."[3]

These radically different fashions of living, thinking, and working have coloured deeply both the poems. If one takes the philosophical passages of the *Divine Comedy*, e.g. the didactic bits, he feels everywhere the passionate energy of reason, a rapid and sharp incisiveness which may rise to the driest and harshest precision. If one takes the more stirring, lyric, dramatic, satirical passages,

[1] "So that it many a year hath made me lean," *Paradiso*, XXV, 3.
[2] Eckermann's *Conversations with Goethe*, March 11, 1828.
[3] *Ibid.*, January 18, 1827.

there is always in evidence a peculiarly Southern mingling of force
and sensitiveness, which with a phrase, with a single word, now
reaches out to the uttermost limits of passion and in the next
instant is forced back by the imperious will into the bounds of
decorum. It may have been this dæmonic intensity of passion,
accompanied and dominated by a relentless self-discipline, that
made Dante appear uncanny to Goethe, who always held himself
somewhat aloof from this terrible and lordly man. The unceasing
struggle between spirit and sensuality, between cold reason and
hot-blooded fantasy, must have appeared to him as something
Gothic and barbaric.[1]

Not that there is any lack, in Goethe's poetry, of vigorous life.
It, too, attains the highest levels of despair, of wrath, of horror,
and the uttermost glowing depths of love. But it reaches them
differently: not by a single leap, but in long and graceful curves.
A natural deception of the eye causes the steep mountain-heights
to appear loftier than the gradual and rounded peaks, and so it
comes to pass that Goethe, by contrast with Dante, has been
characterized as the poet of weaker and softer emotions. But it
is a question not of quantitative but of qualitative differences.
Dante is violent. Goethe is elastic. Two great personalities are
belied and discredited when each one is measured by the strong
points of the other.

It is much the same if one compares the truth contained in the
two poems. Here again we are not of the opinion that the one poem
is surpassed by the other in depth of thought. The searching
intellect of the Italian cuts and dissects his problems, the contemplative reason of the German turns and surveys them on
every side. Dante's scientific conversations with Virgil or with
Beatrice always end in a clear, complete, harmonious solution.
As often as Faust and Mephistopheles encounter each other,
there ensues a constant shifting of their positions so that the
controverted point is viewed from all sides but never completely
settled.

Furthermore, neither Goethe nor Dante was mentally fitted

[1] "He revered the mighty nature and the powerful soul of Dante but loathed
his ecstatic fervor, his stern wrath and his fanatic denunciations. He valued
and prized his artistic genius, his all-pervading intuitiveness and piercing scrutiny,
but abhorred the visionary horror of his dreamland. He appreciated, to the point
of imitation, the all-controlling creator of language, but was always repelled by
his systematized Gothic Catholicism and logical mysticism." Gundolf, *op. cit.*,
pp. 688–9.

for the rigours of systematic philosophy. As against the creators
of systems, Goethe agrees with Mephistopheles:

> For *Teufel*, *Zweifel*'s the only rhyme:
> So there I'm quite in place.

His attitude toward logical constructions may be best expressed,
therefore, in the words which Mephistopheles utters to the bach-
elor:

> Though bold ye seem and resolute,
> Ye never settle your dispute.

Precisely this bold and resolute appearance drew the eager Dante
into scholasticism and succeeded also in holding him captive there
for a while. But almost in spite of himself he is finally driven
back by his artistic and religious feeling to that mysticism in
which he had passed his dreamy youth. Not with the smile of
the doubter, like Goethe, but with the seriousness of the unsatis-
fied truth-seeker, he turns away from the school. But in mysticism, where the unattainable becomes actual, and the indescribable
is accomplished, the two draw near each other once more.

As for the rest, each seeks in his own fashion the highest satisfaction of the spirit. Goethe turns to natural science, where the
immanent divinity surrounds him with its eternal change. Dante,
the believing seeker and metaphysician, devotes himself to theological speculation and hopes thereby to accomplish the reconciliation between religion and science. It is interesting to see how in
Faust the scientific, and in the *Comedy* the theological, fancies—I
am tempted to say whimsicalities—break through, and here and
there mar the surface of the work of art.

In the last analysis, to be sure, each is no thinker or scholar,
but a poet. They desire to see before them an entire world in
harmonious completeness. But in truth a logical system, so far
as it is really logical, never can be complete and finished; it must
rather remain open, or become illogical, at that point where the
progress of later thinkers is to begin. A unified view of the universe can be attained only by the individual in his own soul.
What the understanding, induction, abstraction, refuse to him,
comes to him as a gift from the prophetic vision of faith. In just
this respect, Dante and Goethe are noble brothers in the spirit
in that they both have at last satisfied their craving for universal

order, for world-harmony and completeness, by finding it in the
loftiness of their own natures—not in philosophy, not in natural
science, not in theology. And therein lies also, for us, the highest
point of resemblance between the *Divine Comedy* and *Faust*.

Along with this similarity of aspirations there must doubtless
be a similarity in the fundamental character and imagination of
our poets.

As a common trait in their characters, I might point out that
inwardness which ultimately works exclusively for its own end.
Hence a complete renunciation of effect, a detestation of rhetorical
tinsel and brilliancy, a concealed, never-proclaimed doubt as to
the value of fame, an honest self-confidence, and an integrity of
spirit which, to use the phrase of Dante, dictates what the poet
writes. For this rare type of inwardness we have a much-used
word which nevertheless, if all its sensuous meaning be stripped
off, hits the mark. It is *greatness*.

Similar to the quality of the poets' characters is the nature of
their imaginations: inward and self-contained. Schiller, a profound critic, distinguishes between a naïve and a sentimental
tendency of the imagination. He has accorded to his great friend,
certainly with justice, a place among the naïve poets. It might
be questioned whether the art of Dante should also be so classified.
Certainly Dante felt far more painfully and keenly than Goethe
the contradiction between the ideal and the real. During his
life he never adjusted himself to this contradiction, and under no
circumstances did he reconcile himself to it or calmly endure it.
But neither is the less austere and more humane morality of Goethe
by any means so united or harmonized with his sensuousness as to
be called, in the full sense of the word, naïve. Nor was that what
Schiller meant by the word. An absolute naïveté is animal, and
if there is an animal humanity, it is made up of other individuals
than Goethe and Dante. Neither in their characters nor in their
actions could they reconcile themselves to whatever in the world
was base and hateful. Only in their poems and in their imagination has spirit been completely harmonized with nature. And
even there they did not drag spirit down to nature, but rather
uplifted nature to the spirit. Their art demands the noblest
type of naturalness. Gretchen and Beatrice are the gracious
manifestations of this ideal naïveté, the finest creations of naïve
idealization.

Only the obtuse pretentiousness of the late Renaissance could discover, in the bluntly naïve scenes of the *Inferno* and in the fragrant earthy odour of the whole *Comedy*, anything vulgar and improper. The late Renaissance, indeed—and that includes even Voltaire—was not naïve, and had every reason to sneer. Even at the present day many a sophisticated classicist thinks it clever and refined to cultivate an aversion to the crude barbarism of our *Faust*.

We must define with greater precision this lofty and intellectual type of naïveté, which in Occidental literature has perhaps shown itself only in Dante and Goethe. An ingenious essay by Wilhelm Dilthey on "Goethe and Poetic Fantasy" [1] will be helpful. Dilthey has placed by the side of Schiller's "naïve and sentimental artists" the "personal and impersonal poets." As examples of the former he accepts Goethe and Byron; of the latter, Shakespeare and Cervantes.

Poets of the first type [says Dilthey] live in their own environment and ideals, portray these in their works, using external experiences, historical events, traditions, and information of every sort, merely as means for the presentation of their inner selves. Goethe often described this process in his own case. . . . How differently have poets of the other class created their masterpieces! The mysterious power to endow with life the manifold images of individuals and of their destinies round about and within themselves, to discover occasions for their activities, to hear mighty words which they can utter—this is the work of their life. Their imagination is the scene of action where individuals imperfectly sketched by life are made perfect by art and where they in turn yield their place to other creations. The types of genius which underlie these two forms of creative power are united in every great poet, but no human capacity would suffice to develop them both completely. [2]

It is only necessary to remember how behind the verses of *Faust* there stands the entire figure and the innermost experience of Goethe, and how out of the lines of the *Comedy* Alighieri's dark, strenuous, earnest face uprises to point out this close relation of the work to the personality of the creator as the common trait of the two artists.

Most poets who are so completely subjective in their art control with the magic wand of their imagination only a small area of reality. They face the rest of life's domain inattentively,

[1] Dilthey, *Das Erlebnis und die Dichtung*, Leipzig, 1906, p. 137 sqq.
[2] *Ibid.*, pp. 199–200.

as though bewildered, with confused feelings, and in a sentimental mood.   Recall, for instance, the one-sidedness, the comparative narrowness, of the poetic outlook of Rousseau, Byron, Schiller, Heine, Leopardi, or Carducci, to name only the best of the poets that we have called "personal."

That a firmly self-rooted, absolutely subjective and personal mind, without losing in the least this inborn foundation, grasps and draws to itself all culture and the entire world, absorbs them, and recreates them again lifelike in a single work of art—this marvel, so far as my vision extends, has occurred only twice: in the *Divine Comedy* and in *Faust*.

Only we Germans then have a thoroughly personal, naïve, and equally eminent poet to set beside the great Italian.   And since *Faust* has come to be our loftiest and most cherished creation, and because we flatter ourselves that we are moderately familiar with it, we have a right to hope that we may approach the *Divine Comedy* with a prepared mind.

DEFINITION AND ANALYSIS OF THE PROBLEM

Comparison with *Faust* has helped us to indicate in outline its relation to the *Comedy*. But a comparison with a work of modern times does not suffice to make us familiar with one of the remoter past. Our knowledge can only become reasonably complete if it be examined, not only in retrospect, but in its origins also. Only from this two-sided study can historical comprehension arise. After surveying the work from the standpoint of the present, after having gained information from the actual significance of the work, the study of antecedent history reveals to us the mystery of its genesis.

But how far back does this previous history reach? If one speak literally, to the beginning of the world, back into grey infinity. However, as we are not to write the history of the world, but that of the *Divine Comedy*, a provisional understanding of its significance will aid us in fixing its limits.

The fall and the redemption of mankind, revealed in the form of a harmonious whole: that is Dante's task. All efforts of man to find himself spiritually in the unity of the universe therefore belong to this antecedent history of the *Comedy*.

Under simple and natural conditions this transcendent relation of the continuous spiritual unity of man, that is, of the universe as mind, leads over, or inward, or upward, or downward, or backward, to the Absolute. In this guise it appears as Religion. So the inward life of primitive man is encompassed in the concept of the religious. But if this unity be weakened through conscious cultivation of or favour shown to one or the other side of the mind, then the metaphysical relation to the universe may become one-sided, in one of two directions. For it may either be limited to reason, and then it appears as philosophy, or else restricted to the will, and it is then called morality.

Accordingly, the spiritual content of the *Comedy*, taken as a whole, has a religious antecedent history, but its parts have philosophic and ethical forbears. The *Comedy*, however, is not only spiritual in content but also in the last analysis spiritual in form as

17

well. As such it has also a formal, that is, a literary or artistic, history behind it.

Our study will then occupy itself first with the religious, next with the philosophical, then with the ethical, and lastly with the literary evolution of the great poem.

The political world, which has so prominent a place in the *Divine Comedy*, seems to be excluded from our analysis. But in Dante's day, and before him, political interests were so closely bound up with moral principles that they can only be treated as a particular phase of ethics. The separation of political and economic action from moral conduct has been made, indeed, in all times, by men of practical nature, but the peculiar value of political activity was first consciously brought out by Machiavelli.

Likewise, just as in the Middle Ages political science was still under the control of moral teachings, so the empirical sciences were still subject to philosophic and theological speculation, and cannot therefore reasonably claim separate treatment.

I: THE RELIGIOUS BACKGROUND OF THE "DIVINE COMEDY"

1. SYMBOL AND RELIGION

Only in the form of symbols can religious feeling express itself. Whoever renounces symbols stifles the expression of his religion, and not only the expression but the practice of it as well, and, finally, religion itself. Even the most modern man who holds himself aloof from all ritualistic ceremonial cannot, provided he has any religion, reject the symbol. He will, rather, ascribe to his entire life the symbolic value of a continuous and serious "divine service," so that no single moment of his whole existence can be deemed trifling or indifferent. Even so did Goethe—we must allude to him once more—wish to live.

The nature of the symbol demands serious acceptance and belief. A symbol remains vital only when its representation is accompanied by faith. As soon as belief deserts it, it sinks to a fanciful and empty form; it becomes a theatrical performance, and might far more fitly be abolished.

Linguistic usage again and again obscures this view, since it sometimes expresses the form of the symbol, sometimes form and content united. As form alone symbol is an empty husk; when a symbol is a thing of meaning, a form with content, it is no longer a mere sign for a holy object; it is that object itself. There is no third possibility. Luther was quite right, as against Zwingli: If the Last Supper is to remain a holy act, then the Host must not alone formally, but actually, betoken the body of Christ; that is, it must be the true body of Christ. The significance of a thing is the essence of the thing itself. So every rationalistic interpretation of a symbol, in so far as it separates form and content, is equivalent to destruction or desecration of that symbol. Existing churches all have good reason, but do not always have the necessary power and prudence, to defend themselves against these dangerous attempts.

It results, from what has been said, that man's belief—for this is what lends value and reality to the symbols—has the power to elevate everything that he can see and think of, and to make them religious, that is, holy things. From the idolater, who adores a mere bit of wood as divine, up to Goethe, to whom all existence throughout its natural and spiritual extent is holy, the power of religion affirms itself. It is the divine that through the centuries victoriously covers and permeates the world—and which perhaps in a remote future will unite a most profound intensity to its all-embracing extensity.

Let us endeavour to set the *Divine Comedy* in its proper place, as a landmark or milestone on this path of ideal development. Dante has brought the fall and moral redemption of man into such an intimate connection with the religious conceptions of a world beyond the grave that it becomes clear only when viewed from a lofty stage of religious life; that is, with a profound abundance of religious symbols. We have, therefore, a long ascent ahead before we can reach his height.

2. The Pre-Christian Belief in a Future Life

The conception of an Hereafter is one of the earliest utterances of religion. Such a world is either the realm of the dead or of the gods, or of both at once. Since the gods of primitive religions are imagined as present and visible, whether it be in the form of a fetish, or as active in natural phenomena and events, or as dead princes or heroes who have been deified, it will not be amiss if the thought of death and what goes with it—cults of ancestors and of the dead—be regarded as the most important starting-point of the belief in another world. Such cults are found among the lowest races: Kaffirs, Hottentots, Negroes, and Australians.

Certainly it is not fear alone but also love and hope that inspire us with a desire to prolong the life of our departed relatives and friends under new forms. For religious life begins only when the entire and undivided soul with all its emotions strives toward a higher unity. No single sentiment, no single mental power, can ever become the sole ground of religion. As we cling firmly to this truth, that is, that all religion, as we see it, lays claim upon the whole man in his entirety and unity, we must reject as perverse, one-sided, and petty every psychological interpretation of religious symbols or myths, and endeavour instead to set clearly before our eyes at all times the complete, undivided spiritual activity of individuals and of peoples.

THE EGYPTIANS

Among early civilized races the Egyptians are especially distinguished for their elaborate cult of the dead. The unlimited effort and care which they devoted to the preservation of the corpse shows that the continued life of the dead was thought of as closely connected with the burial place and conditions of the lifeless body. The bond between the mummy and the soul appears to have been loosened very slowly, and never to have been wholly broken. While in the earlier days the doom and journeyings of the dead were depicted in the most varied fashion, there gradually arose, under the influence of the Ammon-Râ theology, a uniform conception of the realm of the dead. It is the kingdom of darkness, an underworld with twelve divisions which is traversed during the night, in twelve hours, by the sun god, Râ or Rê. The dead man protects himself against possible perils by means of charms and amulets which are laid in the grave. Through magic, and a suitable provision of ladders, ships, servants, representations of which he finds in his grave, the dead man can assure himself of every possible advantage.

Nevertheless, there is no lack of evidence to indicate that the condition of the dead depends upon their moral character in life. In the famous Egyptian *Book of the Dead* (Eighteenth–Twentieth Dynasty) a scene of judgment in the other world is depicted. The dead man is led by the goddess of truth (Maât) before forty-two judges, and the throne of Osiris. His heart is weighed in the balance, and he must proclaim his innocence by recounting the sins of which he knows himself to be free. The later texts, indeed, even tell of a Hell with most cruel tortures.

But on the whole there is no complete development of the idea of retribution. Ever and again magic rends the net of justice. The strong man and the shrewd man can help themselves in the next world as well as in this. Rulers, when they die, join immediately the company of the gods. The conception of the Hereafter is therefore somewhat unsystematic and incongruous.

THE BABYLONIANS AND ASSYRIANS

In the Babylonian and Assyrian religion the fate of the dead appears much more uniform, relentless, and gloomy. Poor and rich, good and wicked, all lead the same helpless and miserable ghost-life in the underworld, which is represented as a city begirt with seven walls, with an immense palace where dwells the goddess Allatu. No ray of light pierces to its depth, no mortal can rescue himself therefrom.

Only the god of spring, Tammuz, who after each summer passes into the realm of death, is allowed to rise again out of the world of gloom. Only his friend Innanna or Nanai, or again Ishtar, the goddess of fruitfulness, follows him, sprinkles him with the water of life, and leads him forth once more. Here we have the first clear conception of a mystical descent into Hell.

THE ISRAELITES

The Israelites were a people of a practical and profoundly moral sense. They liberated themselves early and decisively from the sensuous representation of nature-gods and attained a loftier ideal of their divinity. Originally, to be sure, Jehovah appears as a nature-god, in fact, as the god of awe-inspiring natural phenomena: earthquake, storm, thunder, and pestilence. In still earlier times he must have been worshipped as an astral deity, especially as a moon-, perhaps also as a sun-god. The representations of his godhead were, however, fragmentary and in no wise clear. So the greatest prophets, especially the creator of national monotheism, Moses, succeeded in stripping off the remaining naturalistic features of this divinity, and substituted a firm ethical concept for this evanescent figure. Such a profound simplification is always the work of a single extraordinary man. Perhaps Moses originated the profound interpretation of the name Jahve, according to which it indicates not this or that divine individuality with these or those prominent characteristics or functions, but "He who is," not, however, in the sense of mere existence, but as an eager personality, of which man need make himself no image, because the Divinity is to be known solely by its actuality; it is to be recognized only in the help, punishment, or reward it metes out to mankind.

This god loses his original naturalistic character, enters through a treaty or compact ("Torah") into legal and definite relations with his people, and becomes a part of their history. They must accord him unconditional devotion, for which he assures them political freedom, power, and earthly prosperity. Through this strictly mutual agreement the ground is definitely cleared of all

sorts of magical practices and of every kind of caprice and favourit-
ism. Therefore, among all the gods of the ancient world, Jahve
is the first who can be called, in the proper sense of the word,
just. Cruelty, mercy, and forgiveness are excesses which he, to
be sure, now and again permits himself, but of his lasting goodwill
only the punctilious and conscientious son of the Law can be
assured.

The compact was made by the people as such, not by a single
man. Its benefits, therefore, will pertain to the political and
economic future of the whole nation. Jahve will destroy the
enemies of Israel. Thus religion arrays itself wholly under the
banner of earthly and national hopes, for the righteousness of
Jahve excludes the possibility of an extension of his divine favour
or punishment into fields which were not considered in the compact.

Nevertheless, there is no lack of forecasts, in this national
religion, of the complete destruction of this world and of an
eternal heavenly bliss in the next. There are in the old prophets
unmistakable allusions to a mythical cosmography and eschatology. Whether, and to what extent, the early popular traditions,
legends, and tales were native, or of Babylonian or Egyptian
origin, is not as yet positively determined. This much, however, is sure, that the prophets recast these mythical notions in
the true spirit of Israel, limited their meaning, and utilized them
to arouse political and ethical hopes.

Out of the remote destruction of the world as told in popular
tales, the prophets, according to their mood and need, created
an imminent national misfortune, a merited penalty for Israel;
with the colours of the happy Golden Age they depicted the
hoped-for release of the people from enslavement.

These views of the end of the world were intimately associated
with a mythical figure, demigod, a future king, the original
man, who was to appear as deliverer, champion and judge,
and prince of peace in Paradise. These representations waver
between human and divine heights and are gradually reduced to
the conception of the "Messiah" and the "Son of Man." They
probably came from abroad, but took on, at the hands of the
prophets and apocalyptic writers, a more Jewish, national, and
ethical character.

However marked the alien influence may have been, the religious feelings of Israel remain primarily practical and national

in character. It required political dissolution to enable the old national god to enter into direct relations with individuals. It required the harshest disillusionment before the ideal of divine justice could make room for the belief in divine mercy and love. It required, finally, the most abject enslavement before the persistent hope of the most unfortunate of peoples could rise from earthly redemption to spiritual salvation.

These requirements were fulfilled in the long periods of misery extending from the Babylonian exile to the birth of Christ.

THE PERSIANS

Like the Israelites, the Persians were a strong-willed, fundamentally moral people. In their case, too, divine teachers like Zoroaster or Zarathustra early lifted what was a nature-cult to the level of conceptual simplicity and lofty ethical ideas. But while the self-centred Israelites hedged themselves in a more and more rigid monotheism, the warlike and expansive Aryan nature of the Persians conceived of all existence as dualistic, as a great drama of truth and falsehood, of good and evil. "And at the beginning were the two spirits who existed as twins, and each for himself." "And when the two spirits met, they made as their first creation life and death; ordained that Hell should ultimately be for the wicked, Heaven for the righteous." "Of these two spirits the unbelieving one chose for himself evil, but the good spirit chose for himself righteousness, and elected unto himself those who by good deeds please Ahura Mazda." So related one of the old Gâthâ hymns of the Avesta.

Strife must finally come to an end, and dualism find its solution. Hence, in the Persian religion the end of things took on an extraordinarily clear and definite shape. Not only the multitude, but each individual, must reach a solution of the contradiction between good and evil. Every Persian is a combatant, an ally, in the great world-strife between Ahura Mazda (Ormuzd), the god of truth and light, and Angra Mainyu (Ahriman), the spirit of deception, of death and darkness. Out of this sharp contrast, which permits no mediation or middle ground, arises the moral energy of the Persian religion.

Hardly is a man dead when the unclean spirits seize upon the rigid corpse; the soul, however, requires three days to struggle out of the earthly sphere. It is conducted by Sraosha, the soul's escort; prayers and sacrifices of the survivors defend it, during its perilous journey to the other world, against the attacks of demons. Finally the soul arrives at the Cinvat bridge, which rises to heaven from a high mountain in the middle of the earth.

There Mithras, the austere god of justice, holds court and weighs the deeds of men. The evil actions, even when they are outweighed by the good, must be atoned for before leaving the mountain. Not until then can the soul approach the sundering bridge: he that is damned plunges into the abyss of Hell; the righteous man passes over unharmed. At the entrance to Heaven he is met by a radiant maiden who says: "O thou sprung from good thoughts, good utterances, and good deeds, I am thy true faith, thine own conscience." Through three courts, through the abodes of good thoughts, words, and deeds, the blessed one enters into eternal light.

But the final judgment will be at the end of time, after twelve thousand years have elapsed. Hostile nations, throngs of demons, monsters, will overrun the Persian realm. In three long periods the strife is carried on against the powers of darkness, until finally the Saviour (Saoshyant), he who completes the salvation of the world, is born of the seed of Zarathustra. The souls of the departed will receive their bodies again; the wicked will be set apart from the good, and during three days suffer torture in their bodies. Then a great fire will utterly melt the earth: the righteous man will feel it as if it were lukewarm milk, the damned as if it were molten metal. But at last all, purified and united, will praise the victorious glory of Ahura Mazda.[1]

THE GREEKS

The cheerful and sensuous side of the Greek religion has found its most beautiful expression in the imitative arts. Our study, however, demands that we turn our attention to the ethical, ascetic, mystical, philosophical, and gloomy features of Hellenism. For only when man lingers in earnest thought over the idea of death, and from the ephemeral nature of life draws moral conclusions as to how it should be spent, will his imagination be disposed to form definite conceptions of the other world. So it is not to be wondered at that even the plastic intuitiveness of the

---

[1] It is doubtful whether the hope that the damned finally enter the kingdom of glory is a part of the oldest doctrine.

Greeks contented itself primarily with indistinct and contradictory representations of the Hereafter.

In the Homeric poems we have three forms of future life side by side: Tartarus, where Kronos and the Titans dwell; the realm of Hades, to be sought perhaps in the extreme West on the shores of Okeanos, or perhaps beneath the earth; and the Elysian Fields—the Islands of the Blest. Traces are also found of an earlier belief that the dead are not confined to any definite place.

The condition of the dead also is variously conceived, now as a wretched shadowy existence without strength of body or vigour of mind, and again as a conscious continuance and a sorrowful persistence of earthly memories; neither are avenging deities and tortures absent from the underworld. There is Minos, the infernal judge, the Erinnyes, avengers of perjury, the terrible Gorgon and the infernal dog—figures which we find again in Dante, serving the purposes of a Christian Hell. The greatest criminals, Tityus, Tantalus, and Sisyphus, who especially aroused the wrath of the gods, endure special punishment. Beyond this there is no mention of retribution in the Homeric Hereafter.

In the post-Homeric age also, the conceptions of the realm of the dead are not connected with ethical values, but rather with the cult of Chthonic divinities and with the family. "Distinct beliefs concerning the life of the dead could not be derived from this cult and therefore have not been so derived. Here everything had reference to the relation of the dead to the living." [1]

Even the Eleusinian Demeter mysteries, although they promised the initiated a higher form of immortality, and perhaps also in their dramatic performances presented the kingdom of the dead, did not essentially further the belief in a future life. The imagination played with the subject, without elaborating it seriously. Typical examples of this are found in the Old Comedy.

The idea of a higher separate life of the soul can only attain clear expression, as the example of the Persian religion showed, where soul and body are contrasted with each other and where the conception of the world is dualistic.

The first in Greece to experience this contrast in their own persons were the worshippers of Dionysos. By dancing and drinking they put themselves in the orgiastic condition of ecstasy in which the soul deserts the body and becomes united with the

[1] E. Rohde, *Psyche*, Freiburg i. B., 1890, p. 256.

god. The Dionysos-cult came from Thrace, doubtless originating in the Orient, and was cultivated especially by the Orphic sects. These sects gave to their myths a higher significance and a dualistic character. Man, they taught, is made up of Dionysiac (divine) and Titanic (material) elements; or, as another and perhaps older tradition has it: the soul-element proceeds from Ouranos, the corporeal from Ge. The body appears as the prison of the spirit, and the release from this sensual and sinful existence is man's task.

The purification and atonement for inherited sin is attained, however, not by moral conduct, but through the mystic power of grace, and is reached through the intervening steps of the wanderings of the soul. The unpurified and uninitiated will lie in Hades in a foul pool, while the Orphics in eternal intoxication celebrate divine banquets. The symbolism in this system of retribution is quite transparent: the impure end in filth, the ecstatic orgiasts in a frenzy of delight. These dualistic and mystical conceptions were further developed, especially by the Pythagoreans, but never acquired prominence in the state religion of the Greeks.

Instead, they took on a lofty purity through Plato's dialectics and speculations, and were thereby rendered most effective.

The idea of immortality is at once the crown and the vital nucleus of Plato's theology. Out of the divine kingdom of Ideas springs the human soul, and like the Ideas, it, too, is without beginning or end. By its entrance into human life it comes in contact with the defilement of material things, is debased and sullied.[1] Through abstinence the soul can again become pure, and it can again uplift itself through dialectic and contemplation to its eternal abode. The spirit that possesses the highest "virtue," viz., the comprehension of the Ideas, will easily acquire all other merits. The denial of what is ephemeral is in itself and for itself virtue, immortality, and blessedness.

The next world is, for this contemplative soul, a realm of supersensuous conceptions. Every representation which we may form of it is but a symbolic makeshift, a contamination, an allegory, a deception. However powerful Plato's imagination,

---

[1] Matter, however, is not conceived by Plato as anything positive, but as τὸ μὴ ὄν ("that which is not"), which for him is identical with empty space.

however great the delight he took in devising eschatological myths, his entire imaginative creation was none the less relentlessly destroyed by his logic and refuted by his ethics. In him for the first time were united the most emphatic assertion of individual immortality and the most emphatic denial of a sensuous future life.

At this point the religious question of the Hereafter enters upon its philosophic stage. The figurative representations of the next world are now left to poetry. Though this complete separation is only temporarily realized by the most advanced minds, yet again and again Platonic criticism has prevented, or at least limited, all credulous, sensuous descriptions of the Hereafter. The realization that the future world is supersensuous and invisible passes on as a permanent acquisition and a philosophic leaven—now less, now more, effective—into the religion of Christendom. It is not improbable that the later Roman Church would have completely materialized her God and her Hereafter and petrified them in images if she had not been affected by the critical and mystical spirit of the Platonic philosophy. Had Plato not driven art out of his ideal state and discredited it for centuries thereafter, it might have become all-powerful in the Church and might again have set an idol in the place of the Idea.

Alighieri has the Greek philosopher to thank if it was granted him, without transgressing dogma, to mould and colour his Hell and his Heaven in his own fashion and with the utmost originality.

FUSION OF RELIGIONS AND THE LATE JEWISH HEREAFTER

It required a thinker like Plato to rid the Hereafter of its materialism, but the removal of national boundaries from the ideals of salvation could only come as a consequence of the thorough destruction of the old racial and political units. A world-empire must take the place of the national kingdoms. This transformation was accomplished in the period between Alexander the Great and the first Roman emperors.

The fragments of Alexander's empire never became true states. They were founded neither upon racial consciousness nor upon racial religion, but upon bureaucracy and administration. The satisfaction of religious needs was left to the individual. There arose everywhere religious associations, mystic sects, secret cults, theological unions, theosophic schools, and numberless mystery societies. Religions broke up and combined. Egyptian, Babylonian, Persian, and Greek cults were amalgamated; the isolated Jewish race was dispersed over the whole Hellenistic world.

Nevertheless, the connection was never lost between the Judaism of Palestine and that of the Dispersion. Nowhere else in the ancient world did religious unity so vigourously survive and so fully replace nationality.

So independent a growth of a religious community (synagogue) was made possible only by the fusion of national and religious ideals, accepted by the congregation and interpreted spiritually. So—to recall merely the most important incidents—after the nation as such was destroyed, the pious congregation appropriated the name of the "Chosen People," which thus acquired its special application to religion and to orthodoxy.

The Chosen People had had its definite political hopes. Jahve had promised his people that he would send them a mighty ruler from the seed of David, who would conquer the enemies of Israel and create a great empire. This expected world-empire, in the late Jewish religion, gradually changes to the kingdom of God, and the national Messiah becomes the Son of Man. The old prophetic energy rises to apocalyptic mysticism. Instead of a victory in battle, a Day of Judgment is announced on which not only the people but the whole world is to be judged. Instead of the national enemy, Satan or the Antichrist appears; the earthly Jerusalem makes way for the City of God, and the future of the nation fades into the Hereafter, with eternal happiness for the pious and eternal damnation for the unbelievers. This development of eschatology was accomplished gradually, and not in such fashion that the old was ever wholly crowded out by the new. There still remained, side by side, hopes national and ethical, ecclesiastic and religious, material and spiritual. Numerous intermediate stages in this process of amalgamation are indicated in the late Jewish literature.[1]

It is not our problem to arrange these evidences in their psychological or historical order, for we are interested rather in their fusion than in their development. In fact, if one seeks for his-

[1] A general description, which is, to be sure, rather theological than historical, is given by Paul Volz, *Jüdische Eschatologie von Daniel bis Akiba*, Tübingen, 1903. The best historical account is to be found in W. Bousset, *Die Religion des Judentums in neutestamentlichen Zeitalter*, 2nd ed., Berlin, 1906.

torical evolution in this change of attitude, there is a yawning gap at the critical point.

Neither the belief in immortality nor the concomitant contrast between body and soul, matter and spirit, Devil and God, appears to exist or even to be adequately foreshadowed in the old religion of Israel. According to the most recent investigations, it may be assumed with reasonable certainty that the Jews borrowed these beliefs from the Iranian religion, and that the contact occurred at Babylon and in the Babylonian lowland, about the beginning of the age of the Diadochi.

It is at any rate certain that the conservative representatives of Judaism, above all the priestly nobility, regarded the doctrine of future retribution and immortality as an unseemly novelty and refused to accept it. But the Pharisaic tendency was victorious, and the belief in the resurrection, as Josephus testifies, became the chief test whereby the Epicurean band of unbelievers was set apart from the pious.[1] The name "Epicureans" was already applied by Jews of the Hellenistic age to those who denied the doctrine of immortality. Dante uses it in the same sense.[2] And with the name the doctrine lasted for centuries that the unbeliever, even though born into the pious congregation, is not of it, and forfeits thereby his eternal salvation. The doctrine of the sole church that assures salvation, to which doctrine Dante, despite all that may be said, unconditionally subscribes, is chiefly a legacy of the Jewish synagogue. To be sure, piety hedged within a church will always eventually arrive at some such exclusive isolation as we find also in the mystical societies of the Greeks and again in Islam.

Like the belief in immortality, all dualism also, and above all the belief in the Devil and the acceptance of an organized infernal kingdom, are originally unknown to the Old Testament. "On the other hand, in no other religion are dualistic doctrines so entirely at home and so deep-rooted as in the Persian. From this point also the conclusion that the Jewish revelation is a borrowed one becomes imperative."[3]

Furthermore, upon the monotheistic foundation of Judaism,

---

[1] An unmistakable polemic of that time is to be found, for example, in Chapter 2 of the so-called "Wisdom of Solomon"; cf. I. Kautzsch, *Die Apokryphen des Alten Testaments*, Tübingen, 1902.

[2] *Inferno*, X, 13–18.

[3] Bousset, *Die jüdische Apokalyptik*, Berlin, 1903, p. 49.

the opposition of Devil and God could never be carried so far that the Devil could be set over against the old Jahve as an independent and uncreated spirit. He was regarded rather as a fallen angel, and through the doctrine of the Fall by sin, the rigid dualism of the Persians was softened in such a way that the Devil appeared not merely as the enemy, but also as a tool in God's hand, and as an avenging angel. The Jews were inclined by their religious nature and past history to overcome gradually the borrowed contrast of evil's might which had forced itself upon them in times of deepest humiliation.

If it breaks out with greater violence in Christianity, and especially in the Gospel of John, here, too, foreign forces have been at work. Only it is no longer Perso-Iranian influences, but Hellenic, especially Orphic and Platonic, doctrines that brought about a second period of belief in the Devil. It will always be difficult—in the present state of our knowledge, almost impossible—to define the limits of the influence on Judaism of the Iranian eschatology as against that of the Greeks; especially inasmuch as the Orphic popular belief, with its conceptions of the world's end and the Hereafter, has reached us either as it was recast by the speculations of the philosophers or else in insufficient and uncertain fragments.

In a quite general way, we may assume it as assured that Irano-Jewish dualism is marked by an ethical, strong-willed, and essentially optimistic mood, whereas under Greek influences it becomes ascetic, pessimistic, contemplative, and ecstatic. This latter becomes more notable in the time of Christ and later, the closest approach of Judaism to Hellenism being made by the theology of Philo the Alexandrian Jew (about A.D. 40).

The question of the sources of Jewish apocalyptic literature is made more complicated by a third difficulty. The contact of the Persian with the Jewish religion took place in Babylonian lands and through Babylonian influences. Unfortunately we know far less of the later Babylonian religion with which we are here dealing than we do of that of Babylon's Golden Age. Doubtless it was in Alexander's time already largely intermingled with Persian elements, so that it would be extremely difficult to distinguish the purely Persian from the purely Babylonian.

It is, however, possible to fix some few leading historical points. The Babylonian priestly caste did, to be sure, formulate the cult, arrange the calendar of festal days, and systematize the Pantheon; but we do not find in Babylon a creed-maker who, like Zarathustra and Moses, through conceptual simplification deepened and elaborated the popular notions and aspirations into a powerful and vitally fundamental thought. Only through the genius of strong personalities are religions organized and myths and cults deprived of their autonomy and yoked in the service of an idea, i.e. a definite outlook on the world, and a clear unified belief. The closer the relation of myths and cults to belief, the more viable the religion, the greater its capacity to absorb alien thoughts and to reject those which are too diverse. Such a power of assimilation was displayed, so far as we can see, by Judaism toward the Babylonian myths.

We find Babylonian legends in the earliest period, and perhaps again in Christian times; but nowhere in Judaism can we discover Babylonian beliefs. The Babylonian influence must accordingly have taken another direction than the Persian and the Greek. The dualism of these two succeeded in rending the strict monotheism of the Jewish faith, while the Babylonians furnished only colour and pictures, not thoughts or tendencies.

As Dante has inherited some of these pictures, we shall have to take note of them in connection with the subject of the artistic representations of the Hereafter. At present, however, we are less interested in the pictures than in the belief, less in the colours of the picture than in the outlines of the thought. So the most varied forces have united—philosophic ideas, symbolic customs, religious representations, and mythic figures, Persian, Greek, Babylonian, presumably also Egyptian and Syrian elements— to shape that late Jewish belief as to the Hereafter, which was destined to become the norm for Christianity.

3. The Christian Belief in the Hereafter

JESUS AND THE HEREAFTER [1]

The religious creation of Jesus embraces almost exclusively faith and morality. Hence to those investigators who fix their

---

[1] Cf. for this and the next section the work of Paul Wernle, *Die Anfänge unserer Religion*, 2d ed., Tübingen, 1904 (Engl. transl., London, 1903–04), the views of which I have largely incorporated, and the same author's *Jesus*, Tübingen, 1916, a book which has the advantage over others that the treatment is consciously subjective, as it should be to portray the Saviour.

eyes only on formal symbols, legends, and imaginative pictures, it appears insignificant; but to those who in religion place the emphasis upon the development of piety, it seems a thing of measureless value.

This much is certain, that the ethical demands of Jesus are founded upon the late Jewish belief as to the Hereafter. He neither invented nor created this belief, nor did he enrich it with more vivid illustrations, nor purify it by a conceptual revision; but he moulded into it a spiritual value, and thereby imposed on every human act, on every aim, on every form of thought, an immediate significance for our future life.

Yet it is not, as with Kant, the moral consciousness that strengthens the belief in the Hereafter; with Jesus it is rather the belief in the Hereafter that must be the foundation of morality. Only by the sharp emphasis upon future life, only through the firmest conviction that God's kingdom and the Last Judgment [1] are close at hand, does his ethics acquire its full force.

This drama is of frequent occurrence in the Middle Ages. Moral regeneration is always closely associated with the revival of eschatological interests. Most of the reformers are prophets of the Hereafter, heralds of the world's end, and preachers of repentance. They blow the flames of Hell to a brighter glow, and bring God's verdict closer to man's consciousness.

The firm intention to draw our strength for the contests of this world from our deep faith in a Hereafter is the chief religious motif of the *Divine Comedy*, and is also genuinely evangelical. For our poet bases his Heaven-seeking piety on Jesus himself. For him, too, the Last Judgment and final fulfillment of all things is a near and living hope, soon to be realized. The seats of the Blessed in the Empyrean appear to him so fully occupied that room remains for a few only.[2] What makes the *Comedy* truly divine in the proper sense of the word is the grounding of moral values on future existence, in conformity with Christ's teaching.

But the close connection of eschatology or apocalyptic literature with morality is observable both *before* and *after* the appearance of Christ. It had already been worked out in the Persian religion. What Jesus brought which was new could be, primarily,

---

[1] E.g. Matthew 24:33 and 10:23; Mark 9:1 and 13:30.
[2] *Paradiso*, XXX, 131–132, and *Convivio*, II, 15. "We are already in the last period of time, and truly await the completion of celestial motion."

only a keener sense of relations already established. Ever more strenuously, ever more vividly, ever more relentlessly, is each momentary action set face to face with its importance in eternity.

Herein at once appears something *qualitatively new:* the earthly and practical appraisal of life vanishes. The actual immediate consequences of our deeds lose their significance, for the eternal value of an act lies not in its results but in its intention. "But God beholdeth the heart." A sharp cut divides earthly efforts from the fulfillments of future life and separates usefulness from goodness. It may be that Jesus thought of God's kingdom as resting upon the soil of this earth. As to its actual location, he is not concerned, the boundaries of his divine kingdom being purely ethical, merely felt and believed.

Thus morality, even though it be conditioned by belief in the Hereafter, has become independent and absolute. God's judgment has become quite one with the conscience of the individual, no matter whether men hope to behold it in Palestine or above the clouds. Future retribution has become completely present in man's soul. Since every act is directed immediately toward its final goal, which is eternity, that final goal becomes the primary motive and mainspring of the act. With Kant the theoretical order alone, and not the actual state of moral consciousness, was reversed.

So the exclusively ethical valuation of the belief in a future life, wherein the true work of Jesus consists, leads to complete freedom of conscience.

This freedom was, in accordance with the conditions of the time, twofold. In the first place, the last remnants of national hopes were removed from the moral ideal and hence from the whole conception of the Hereafter; and secondly, the Church ceremonial as an end in itself, as well as the Church in general as the sole means of salvation, was set aside. At the same time the Hereafter, because of its universality, was withdrawn from the authority of the Church.

To be sure, even in Plato we find ultramundane purification. However, as he was moving in a quite different path, he reached quite different results. Plato's future world is a system of concepts or ideas which can either be grasped dialectically through the reason, or else can be contemplated directly in ecstasy; hence a Hereafter that reveals itself only to the studious toil of the philosopher or to the sensitive devotion of the mystic, a state of bliss which is attainable only by a contemplative being. Plato obtained the supersensuous purity and universality of the next world at the cost of excluding from it the majority of mankind and the impulse of active life. What a man could grasp neither through reason nor through intuition, that he should not have.

This pride of the philosophers Jesus did away with altogether. His Kingdom of Heaven belongs to the poor in spirit, and to all people. It lies on level ground, spiritually, temporally, and locally attainable by all. Men's images of it may be as primitive and as rough-hewn as they will. It demands no abstractions, no dialectic processes, no especial metaphysical organs of the soul, no fastidious abstinence or artificial rapture. The simple feelings of fear, of love, of trust in the personal God Who is our Father, the most childlike faith, suffice to uplift moral activity and make it a participant of future happiness.

The distinction between Christ's Hereafter and Plato's rests, in the last analysis, upon the fact that the one lives in the will, the other in the intellect. This contrast is not invalidated by the fact that neither Plato nor Jesus theoretically sundered the intellect from the will.

But what the Platonic Hereafter and the evangelical have in common is their supersensuous, universal, immaterial nature. Such a kingdom cannot be imaginatively depicted, and can only be defined negatively, as, for example, in the words of Jesus: "In the resurrection they neither marry nor are given in marriage." [1]

When, nevertheless, Jesus and Plato have recourse to vivid descriptions of the Hereafter, they make use of popular imagery so as to produce the desired effects. Here it may well be that Plato was more keenly aware than Jesus that he was expressing himself symbolically.

RETROSPECT AND PROSPECT

In the way of conclusion we may note that with Jesus the development of the belief in a future life is complete. The closest imaginable connection of morality with the Hereafter is attained. The belief in a higher world has become vital and active in the conscience to an extent that, to our knowledge, it had never

[1] Matthew 22:30.

before possessed. An advance in this direction is unthinkable—
nor has it in fact ever occurred.

Even so, in another direction the Platonic Hereafter marks
the highest point of development. A more supersensuous and
abstract Hereafter than Plato's cannot be conceived. Man cannot
more firmly detest the contamination of things material.

The Platonic conception of future life flows out of nature-
worship: out of the life of the senses and out of contemplation.
His predecessors were the Egyptians, the Dionysiacs and Orphics,
and the Greeks themselves. The sensuous element was eliminated
by the supersensuous ecstasy of the rapt Mystics. The contemplative gaze was won by the conceptual penetration of the philosophers. Plato perfected both.

The evangelical belief in a future life springs from a practical
and national belief in a personal God, a God that is not in nature
but above it, not for the land but for the people. Its forerunners
were migratory and conquering races: the Persians and the
Israelites, to a small extent probably the Babylonians also, and
perhaps the Phoenicians. The national and ecclesiastical foundations of this type of religion could not be removed either by
contemplative mysticism or by intellectual abstractions. They
must be pounded by the hammer of war, they must be overthrown
by a mighty moral will, through the faith of a "Son of God,"
valiant unto death, through the active mysticism of the one who
fought and was crucified.

The history of the soul in quest of the Platonic Hereafter is
through art, contemplation, idyllic repose, world-weariness, flight
from life, and rapture: that of the evangelical Hereafter is through
strife, conquest, defeat, enslavement, drama, tragedy, freedom,
and victorious confidence.

If these elementary differences are made clear, it will not be
difficult to surmise the direction that the pious faith in immortality will take. The oppositions must be fused together, the
Platonic and the evangelical Hereafter united in one.

This task is accomplished in the Catholic religion of the Middle
Ages—in Dante's religion.

CHRIST AND THE HEREAFTER (PAUL)

The point where the fusion takes place, the centre where the
evangelical and Platonic doctrines of future life unite, is Jesus's

person risen to divinity: Christ (the anointed one), the Messiah, the Deliverer, the Son of Man, the Son of God, the Lord. Each of these titles asserts a notable side of the remarkable apotheosis of Jesus. We do not know whether, or to what extent, He Himself claimed such titles. Yet He never would have won them but for the pre-eminent loftiness of His personality.

For the Jewish Christians it was easy to fit the superhuman form of the Master, whose return to earth they definitely expected, into their ancient apocalyptic prophecies, as was done in the Revelation of St. John.[1] Here Jesus appears as the judge of the world and the war-lord who gallops upon a white steed and destroys his foes—an ancient Jewish figure, but highly unevangelical.

It was no less natural to regard the crucifixion of Jesus as penance and legal atonement for the sins of others. To Jewish belief the thought of the vicarious sacrifice had long been familiar.[2] It is more or less common in all primitive religions.

So Christ was on the one hand avenger and judge, and on the other intercessor and atoner in the Hereafter—executioner and victim at once. Of this Jewish Christ, who is red with the blood of his foes and of his martyrs, we have a softened symbolic reflection in the Fifth Heaven of Dante's Paradise.[3] There the gleaming figure of the Crucified One stands out of the warlike Heaven of Mars.

It was Paul, a Jew of the Diaspora, who enlarged this narrow military and legal circle; but he did not, in truth, shatter it.

He elevated the conception of the vicarious effacement of guilt to the idea of redemption. An historical event, the crucifixion of Jesus, receives from Paul its deep religious significance. Christ's death wipes out our sins, Christ's resurrection opens Paradise to us.

The resurrection of Jesus, at first only hoped for by His friends, then asserted by His defenders, is elevated by Paul to a religious conviction and to a theological dogma. "If Christ be not raised, your faith is vain; ye are yet in your sins." [4] Thus, between our moral behaviour and its reward in the Hereafter—no matter how closely Jesus welded them together—there is intruded an alien magical factor: Jesus's act of redemption.

Doubtless the idea of redemption, of salvation through the

[1] 19:2 sqq.
[2] Cf. Volz, op. cit., p. 114; II Maccabees, 7:38; IV, 6:28 sqq., 17:21 sqq.
[3] Paradiso, XIV, 94 sqq.
[4] 1 Corinthians 15:17.

death and resurrection of a superhuman being, attached itself to ancient traditions which lived on in later Judaism and had been accumulated partly from Oriental and partly from Hellenic sources. Doubtless the figure of the Saviour had been outlined long before Jesus died upon the cross. But the personal inner experience and its active religious soul were first grafted upon this hitherto wavering and legendary figure by the teachings of Paul. Paul, a remarkable mixture of innocence and calculation, of inspiration and common sense, of trust in God and crafty shrewdness, this original type of the priestly soul, created the Christian Church and theology, and left to it, as a millennial heritage, the gift of his peculiar mentality.

In the centre of the new religion and midway in the history of earth and eternity, he sets the cross and the resurrection. From this point all relations are measured; it separates sharply the old from the new; it sets off the thought of Israel, of Greece, of the Gospels.

Adam's fall through sin becomes the first act in the drama of salvation. Through Adam, God's grace is forfeited; hereditary sin becomes dominant. Human nature must be degraded to the lowest depravity so that salvation through Christ may appear the more glorious. Here room is made for the late Greek pessimism, and here it entered in full force. By their own strength and their own faith in God, men are not able to uplift themselves. Only through the free initiative of the offended God, only through His infinite love, can the source of mercy be reopened. He sent His own son to a sacrificial death, so that under the sign of the cross, and under that alone, mankind might save itself. Baptism in Christ's name, and the confession of faith in Christ, are assurances of eternal life. The fall, the crucifixion, the resurrection, the last judgment, were all in God's plan from the beginning. Salvation and damnation are for each man determined beforehand. Nevertheless, the freedom of the will is not thereby impaired, for it is precisely faith and the spirit of God, or if you will of Christ, that sets us free. His ideas of revelation through the "Spirit" and of justification through faith enabled Paul to save the Fathers of Israel who preceded Christ and to find intimations of Christ in the Old Testament.

The character of Paul's dualism becomes perfectly clear in the doctrine of the Resurrection. Those who are justified and forgiven will receive their bodies again at the resurrection, not indeed the old earthly ones, but bodies of a new and heavenly matter. Earthly nature being sinful and perverse, it will, at the end of time, be destroyed and replaced by a heavenly one. It was easy for later theologians to identify this heavenly nature with that which surrounded the first human being in the Earthly Paradise. What is to become of the bodies of the damned, Paul does not further indicate, but from the spirit of his theology we may infer that he was disposed to take for granted their complete destruction. Paul's conception of a spiritualized body in contrast to the earthly flesh [1] is presumably a compromise between the Jewish idea of the resurrection of the old body and the more spiritual ideas of the Greek believers who must have taken offence at the crudeness of the Jewish resurrection.[2]

So Paul may well have been the first in whose writings the Jewish sense of justice, the doctrine of retribution and of sacrificial death, were combined with Hellenic pessimism and mysticism, and with the ideas of hereditary sin and of atonement. The point of contact is Christ's personality, and the means are the conceptions of the "spirit" and of "revelation."

PAUL AND DANTE

And now let us read Dante's doctrines of the Atonement and of the Resurrection, as they are outlined by Beatrice in the seventh canto of the *Paradiso*. If we put aside the scholastic form of expression, we shall not fail to recognize in every word Paul's mingling of legality and of love, of cleverness and of faith.

> By not enduring on the power that wills
> Curb for his good, that man who ne'er was born,
> Damning himself damned all his progeny;
> Whereby the human species down below
> Lay sick for many centuries in great error,
> Till to descend it pleased the Word of God
> To where the nature, which from its own Maker
> Estranged itself, he joined to him in person
> By the sole act of his eternal love.

---

[1] 1 Corinthians 15:35 sqq.
[2] Paul carried out several other such adjustments. Cf., e.g., E. Norden, *Agnostos Theos*, Berlin and Leipzig, 1913; and especially R. Reitzenstein, *Die hellenistische Mysterienreligionen*, Leipzig and Berlin, 1910, where the Hellenistic sources of Paul's doctrines of the God-Man, of the Resurrection, of visions of the psychic-spiritual double existence of the pious, are set forth.

Now unto what is said direct thy sight;
    This nature when united to its Maker,
    Such as created, was sincere and good;
But by itself alone was banished forth
    From Paradise, because it turned aside
    Out of the way of truth and of its life.
Therefore the penalty the cross held out,
    If measured by the nature thus assumed,
    None ever yet with so great justice stung,
And none was ever of so great injustice,
    Considering who the Person was that suffered,
    Within whom such a nature was contracted.
From one act therefore issued things diverse;
    To God and to the Jews one death was pleasing;
    Earth trembled at it and the Heaven was opened.
It should no longer now seem difficult
    To thee, when it is said that a just vengeance
    By a just court was afterward avenged. [1]

But why, asks Dante, just the Atonement through the death
of Christ on the Cross?

Buried remaineth, brother, this decree
    Unto the eyes of every one whose nature
    Is in the flame of love not yet adult.
Verily, inasmuch as at this mark
    One gazes long and little is discerned,
    Wherefore this mode was worthiest will I say.
Goodness Divine, which from itself doth spurn
    All envy, burning in itself so sparkles
    That the eternal beauties it unfolds.
Whate'er from this immediately distils
    Has afterwards no end, for ne'er removed
    Is its impression when it sets its seal.
Whate'er from this immediately rains down
    Is wholly free, because it is not subject
    Unto the influences of novel things.
The more conformed thereto, the more it pleases;
    For the blest ardour that irradiates all things
    In that most like itself is most vivacious.
With all of these things has advantaged been
    The human creature; and if one be wanting,
    From his nobility he needs must fall.
'Tis sin alone which doth disfranchise him,
    And render him unlike the Good Supreme,
    So that he little with its light is blanched,

[1] *Paradiso*, VII, 25-51. The deserved punishment which the Jews, without knowing it, inflicted on the mortal flesh of Christ was atoned for by them in the well-deserved destruction of Jerusalem.

And to his dignity no more returns,
   Unless he fill up where transgression empties
   With righteous pains from criminal delights.
Your nature when it sinned so utterly
   In its own seed, out of these dignities
   Even as out of Paradise was driven,
Nor could itself recover, if thou notest
   With nicest subtilty, by any way,
   Except by passing one of these two fords:
Either that God through clemency alone
   Had pardon granted, or that man himself
   Had satisfaction for his folly made.
Fix now thine eye deep into the abyss
   Of the eternal counsel, to my speech
   As far as may be fastened steadfastly!
Man in his limitations had not power
   To satisfy, not having power to sink
   In his humility obeying then,
Far as he disobeying thought to rise;
   And for this reason man has been from power
   Of satisfying by himself excluded.
Therefore it God behoved in his own ways
   Man to restore unto his perfect life,
   I say in one, or else in both of them.
But since the action of the doer is
   So much more grateful, as it more presents
   The goodness of the heart from which it issues,
Goodness Divine, that doth imprint the world,
   Has been contented to proceed by each
   And all its ways to lift you up again;
Nor 'twixt the first day and the final night
   Such high and such magnificent proceeding
   By one or by the other was or shall be;
For God more bounteous was himself to give
   To make man able to uplift himself,
   Than if he only of himself had pardoned;
And all the other modes were insufficient
   For justice, were it not the Son of God
   Himself had humbled to become incarnate.[1]

A new doubt arises in Dante's mind. If everything which springs directly from God is indestructible, how does it happen that material nature remains perishable? Beatrice instructs him that God created with His own hand only primal matter and the form-giving power, but not the individual living creatures.

[1] *Paradiso*, VII, 58-120.

>And thou from this mayst argue furthermore
>Your resurrection, if thou think again
>How human flesh was fashioned at that time
>When the first parents both of them were made.[1]

That is, an indestructible heavenly body, just as Paul taught.

Between the writings of the apostle and the lines of our poet, just cited, lie more than twelve hundred years. And yet the ideas of the first Christian theologian—for Paul is that—contain almost all the seeds of the later system.[2] But that which was uttered by St. Paul only incidentally, from personal conviction, and in the form of an admonishing and apologetic epistle, appears in Dante as the systematic exposition of a structural doctrine of the Church. Still lacking were the fundamental Catholic teachings: the doctrine of the Trinity, the sharp definitions of the Athanasian formula of God-Man, and the semi-Pelagian reconciliation of predestination with free will; but everywhere in Paul's mind there lay hid that mixture of reason and imagination which is the essence of ecclesiastical theology.

That which was Paul's own gradually became general property of the Church. Not from Paul but from the Church did Dante derive his belief in the Atonement; not from Paul the religious man, but from Paul as an ecclesiastical personality. For that very reason, because between Paul and Dante stands the entire Catholic Church, it is now almost impossible to determine exactly the direct influence of the apostle upon the poet, or to discover such an influence at all.

This same relation holds true as to all later teachers of religion and theology—and even as to Jesus himself. They were all transmitted to our poet through the Church, and appear in the *Comedy* consequently with an official and representative bearing. He who fails to understand this state of things merely studies one side of the question of religious sources.

It may be that Dante came into a more intimate relation with one or another of his authorities; in the main, however, he maintains toward them all a lofty objective independence, in that he stands firm by the Catholic point of view.[3]

---

[1] *Paradiso*, VII, 145–148.

[2] The first scholastic exposition of the doctrine of Atonement which was accepted by the Church is given by Anselm of Canterbury, *Cur Deus Homo?*

[3] That is what Goethe meant when he said: "Dante seems to us great, but he had the culture of centuries behind him." (*Conversations with Eckermann*, October 20, 1828.)

When a modern scholar with historical and psychological consciousness accustomed to receiving direct individual impressions approaches Dante, he will easily be inclined to regret as a serious failing the ecclesiastical and impersonal attitude of the poet toward the great creators of religion: Jesus, Paul, Augustine, Francis of Assisi. He feels that the failure to penetrate into the heart and soul of these men is too high a price to pay even for the most radiant crown of glory set upon their heads.[1] So far as this criticism is justified, however, it does not fall upon the poet but upon his ecclesiasticism, and ultimately upon the Church itself, whose task it was to transform the individual inspirations of its founders into the universally valid dogmas of an established institution.

DOGMA, CHURCH, AND THE HEREAFTER

It is immediately after Paul, and on his initiative, that the dogmatic formulation of the Christian creed begins. It is accomplished in the form of admission and exclusion, of assertion and negation. Believers feel themselves under obligation to draw a line between their own peculiar faith and all alien or kindred convictions. It is owing to the fact that syncretism has come to an end that the development of the Church begins.

The elasticity of Christian belief, its ability at once to yield and to resist, was decisively shown for the first time in its contest with Gnosticism.[2]

It was in a fight for unity of belief that the idea of one great church in contrast with that of the Gnostic sects took shape. We meet with the expression "Catholic Church" for the first time in Ignatius, Bishop of Antioch (*ob.* A.D. 115).

The Jewish religion rested on a foundation of ethical unity. The Catholic Church, on the other hand, grew out of a belief entertained in common. That is the reason why the constant policy of Catholicism has been for centuries unity of faith, unity of Church.

[1] Unless indeed he experience an edifying delight in this very dogmatic and ecclesiastical exclusiveness considered as a formal law and rule of life: as, for example, did Herman Hefele, whose *Dante* (Stuttgart, 1921) I criticized in the *Deutsche Literaturzeitung*, September 17, 1921.

[2] The details can be found in the standard histories of dogma and of the Church. For references to the literature, see, e.g. Karl Heussi, *Kompendium der Kirchengeschichte*, 5th ed., Tübingen, 1922.

However, before belief had become conscious of itself, it had absorbed the most diverse elements: ideas which could take harmonious shape and be reconciled with one another in no logical system, in no human intellect. How many elements that lay historically, psychologically, logically wide asunder did not Paul alone in his day bring together, or at least tolerate side by side!

The next age goes still further in this direction and accepts much more of the Gnostics' fusion of Oriental and Occidental religions. After the figure of Christ had been so enhanced by Paul, He could not but appear to those Christians who came over from heathenism as a hero and eventually as a god. Since myth-making was a tendency not only of the Greeks but in like degree of the Orientals, we are hardly in a position to decide whether the accepted doctrine of the Church is to be traced back to Persian, Babylonian, or Greek influences. Since, however, in the first century after Christ it was no longer Babylon or Susa, but Alexandria and Antioch that were the centres of intellectual life, the preference doubtless belongs to Hellenism. The ideas of Christ born of a god and a virgin, of Christ's descent into Hell, of his victory over the devils, of his pre-existence and ascent to Heaven, were already foreshadowed by countless journeys to Hell and Heaven by Babylonian, Phoenician, and Persian gods of light: Tammuz, Adonis, Mithras; and Greek heroes: Orpheus, Heracles, Pythagoras, Dionysus, and so forth.

Together with the myth of the atonement, its rites were also taken over: baptism and communion. Through their magical effect, eternal life was assured.

By all this the historical figure of Jesus is rendered dim, and the tone of His moral commandments is somewhat lowered. Nevertheless both are firmly maintained. In fact, the utterance of Paul, who was still inclined to promise future life unconditionally to every baptized Christian, is no longer accepted. Not only the sacraments and church membership, but also a pure and righteous course of life, come to be demanded as a prerequisite to heavenly happiness by people who were untroubled by the fact that the one requirement renders the other unnecessary. Men hesitate to deny Paul's doctrine of election and predestination; nevertheless they preach free will and responsibility for conduct. They accept from Gnosticism the idea of a divine revelation through the Spirit, and they break the force of it in that they assign divine illumination to the dignitaries of the Church alone; and they distort the division of esoterics from exoterics into a separation of clergy from laity.

Just as two forms of knowledge, one through instruction and reason and the other through revelation and mysticism, are allowed to stand side by side, so, too, we find diverse forms of morality, that of deeds and that of atoning renunciation; distinct types of love, goodwill to one's neighbour and devotion to God; two forms of faith, one painfully acquired, one bestowed by grace; even so, two types of hope, a consoling yet anxious prospect of recompense hereafter, and the yearning desire for escape from the world; the grim idea of the world's destruction, and the comforting thought of the blessed vision of the Divinity; and by the side of the Messianic Christ, who is to conquer the Antichrist, destroy the Roman empire, and establish His glory in Jerusalem, we find the transcendent Christ, who is to bestow upon believers His supernatural bliss—the human Christ and the God; and, finally, diverse ideals of future blessedness, the joyful possession of the resurrected flesh, and the beatitude of the released soul in its heavenly and immaterial form.

Again and ever again the discordant impulses and doctrines strove to diverge and threatened disruption. Over obvious details discord early showed itself. All sorts of dialectic art were tried in order to preserve unity; and when they failed, authority had to speak its word. So, for example, after it had been definitely established that salvation was completely dependent upon an historical event, Jesus's death on the cross, the question arose whether or not all who lived and died before Christ were doomed to damnation. The question is not answered absolutely in the affirmative only for the reason that when it was raised the person of Christ and His death had already been uplifted to universality through pagan and philosophical influences. Meantime the Spirit had taken its place beside the figure of Christ, and in it and through it salvation becomes retroactive. Accordingly, all men were to be saved who before the coming of Christ had lived and hoped in the Spirit. But as the apostles were Jews, and Paul, also, in many matters thought only in terms of the synagogue, the benefits of the Spirit were limited to the pious Fathers of the Old Testament. The patriarchs then have to thank the heathen philosophers and the Gnostics if they themselves are saved, and the heathen have the Jews to thank that they were not saved. The Christians of later times who could not be satisfied with this partial decision (which, as we see, was conditioned upon a single historical occurrence) are referred to the unfathomableness of the divine Will. If, however, they insist that this Will may well have been unfathomable even to Paul and his associates, then the authoritative voice of the Church commands silence, obedience, and unity.

By a more thorough fusion of Greek philosophy and Jewish belief, Clement and Origen, the Alexandrians, endeavoured to reconcile the contradictions in the creed of the Church.

They felt that an eternal Hell accorded ill with the goodness of a merciful God, Who had sent into the world His only Son and with Him His Spirit. They asked: Why does God punish? The usual answer of the Old Testament was: Partly for revenge, partly out of justice. "I am righteous," from Jahve's lips, often sounded the same as "I am avenged." [1] Against this, Clement and Origen turn back to the Platonic conception of a punishment that shall serve the purposes of education and purification. If then the sufferings in the Hereafter are purifying, they cannot be an end in themselves; they are and cannot but be steps that lead to perfection. Only the utterly depraved go down to eternal damnation. But they, too, are brought into relation with universal purification, for they are to serve as a deterrent example for the rest. Hell thus becomes a mere limit, a gloomy underworld, out of which rises the ladder to Heaven. The purification by fire ($\pi \tilde{v} \rho \ \kappa \alpha \theta \acute{\alpha} \rho \sigma \iota o \nu$) must be undergone by all, for no one is perfect. Paradise likewise shrinks to a mere limit-concept— the uppermost step in the ladder. Origen at times transfers this immense, all-embracing purgatorial fire to the end of time and connects it with the conflagration of the universe, and again he imagines it as an elaborate process of purification which is entered upon by each individual immediately after death, and which the Deity lengthens or shortens according to the sins of each. At times his fire is quite real; at others he spiritualizes it into an agony of conscience.

Had the Church accepted this profound doctrine in its full

[1] Cf. Max Pohlenz, *Von Zorne Gottes, Eine Studie über den Einfluss der griechischen Philosophie auf das alte Christentum*, Göttingen, 1909.

extent, the significance of the remission of sins through Christ's death would have been gravely weakened, if not quite done away with. For if the damned were made better, and the saved were also punished, for what purpose had the Saviour come down from Heaven? Origen's doctrine, therefore, must be rendered harmless by further theological elaboration. Augustine broke the force of it by again substituting for the Neo-Platonic doctrine of universal restoration Paul's long-forgotten doctrine of pre-destination. Not all are purified; some are destined to damnation, others to salvation. Hell thus wins back its terrors. But the ladder of sins and virtues cannot be given up; its usefulness is evident: it serves to soften the dualism of good and evil and to create a means of transition from a lower to a higher virtue. The purgatorial fire comes to be looked upon as a temporal middle realm, where the lesser venial sins are atoned for, where it is made possible for the forgiven and predestined Christians to pay their debt and make themselves worthy of Paradise. The two ideas of punishment, as atonement and as education, meet and soften each other in this Catholic Purgatory.[1] But to infuse real meaning and life into these makeshifts of the theologians, we need childlike faith and poetic genius. The ecclesiastical notion of Purgatory may be criticized ever so sharply, but Dante's Purgatory will always live as a profound and powerful creation of religious art. The pettiness which may be found in a pro-visional exaction of debts and dispensation of grace is destroyed in the fire of this poetry.

As the Church came to consider herself more and more the sole agent and purveyor of God's grace, it was natural that a practical head of the Church like Gregory the Great should extend the magic power of its sacraments and prayers to Purgatory. This last measure did not indeed remove the inherent contradictions, but it did complete the ecclesiastical assimilation of the doctrine of Purgatory. One need not concern himself about the theory of something that is controlled in practice.

Origen's doctrine of Purgatory stands in the closest connection with his doctrine of the soul's immortality. The human soul

---

[1] Even at the present day the Roman Church holds firmly to the double nature of Purgatory: "The purpose of the temporal punishment is twofold, first medicinal, to protect man from backsliding, and secondly punitive, so that atonement be paid to God for the insult offered to Him."—Joseph Bautz, *Das Fegfeuer*, Mainz, 1883, p. 28.

existed before birth. Its earthly existence is the result of previous guilt and slothfulness; its life after death will be purification and labour. The previous existence of the soul is logically demanded by its future immortality. For that reason the Church Fathers, Jerome [1] and Augustine,[2] do not venture to commit themselves definitely either for or against it. On the other hand, this doctrine threatens to place the moral responsibility of this life in an ultramundane remoteness. Augustine therefore commends an intermediate view, teaching that the soul of unborn man pre-exists latent in the mind (*in mente*) or in the works of God (*in operibus Dei*) but becomes actual only at the moment of generation. The Catholic doctrine of the soul's twofold creation was first stated clearly and definitely at the Lateran Council of the year 1179.

Not only those just discussed but all the other articles of the Church's faith have gone through essentially the same course of treatment. All the contradictory materials that had come together from all sides out of heathendom and Judaism, from history, myth, and philosophy, in the early days of Christianity, are worked over theologically, combined or fitted to each other, sometimes emptied of all force by an intellectualistic analysis, sometimes filled by an imaginative and mystical synthesis, but eventually linked together by practical exigencies. For it is the inward force of mighty, unruly ideas, threatening to tear themselves asunder, that has finally compelled the Church to establish its control over this world and the next by the actions and deeds of pious heroes and of clever priests. It sounds paradoxical, but it is a fact, that out of the many-sidedness and mutual antagonisms of the articles of Christian faith sprang the unity and compactness of the Catholic hierarchy. Simple and primitive religions have no need of an elaborate ecclesiastical organism.

Nowhere can this development be more clearly shown than in the history of the supreme and central idea, the doctrine of the Divinity.

The imperious god of the Jews became, in connection with Jesus, God the Father, whom sinful man approaches in trustful humility, without ceremonies, without intermediaries, in the language of familiar intimacy. The only human relation to be

---

[1] *Adversus Rufinum*, I, 5.
[2] Letters CXC and CLXVI (i.e. 127 and 128 of the old numbering).

compared with this reverent and loving attitude toward God is that of a son to his father. This is presently associated, chiefly through Babylonian and Persian influences, with the cosmic growth from the Jewish ruling god to a creating god. Since the concepts "Ruler," "Father," "Creator," are clearly personal, they can very well be applied together to one and the same person.

Since, however, Christ comes to the fore as the all-favoured sole Son of God, humanity is pushed from a direct into an indirect filial relationship to God. This is the first disturbance of the natural relation. At the same time the double nature of Christ—God and man—arouses theological speculation. The problem is to remove the incongruity between the concept of God the Father and of God the Redeemer, and again between the concept of a divine Christ and of a human Jesus.

In order to preserve monotheism, the divinity of the Father and that of the Son are united by the abstract concept of the Spirit. But in order that conceptual and personal divinities may not fall asunder, there are laid beneath them as a foundation the Platonic and Aristotelian concepts of divinity, which are nothing else than the ultimate, highest, and most universal Ideas—absolute Being, the True, the Good, the Beautiful; in short, the norm, extracted from and lifted above the multiplicity of appearances. The gap between this multiplicity and that absolute unity of being and values is filled by a rising pyramid, as it were, of intermediate and subordinate concepts. The relation of the philosophical God to the world may be represented as law or even as a mathematical rapport; intermediate powers are necessary, and are logically justified. The philosophical God can only work along normal lines; the personal God has reserved for Himself the miracle.

The whole labour of the theologians is an ingenious persistent effort to combine these two divine systems. Sometimes the subordinate concepts become angels and saints; sometimes the Saviour fades to a mere formal principle; sometimes miracle is identified with law; sometimes the opposite takes place. At one moment divine decisions are regarded as absolute, necessary, and irrevocable; at the next they become arbitrary, and alterable through sacraments and prayers.

The line of cleavage between the two conceptions lies just where the Person of the Hebraic Jesus Christ comes in contact

with the idea of the Greek Logos. It is here, therefore, that the
need is felt of a dogmatic soldering that shall preserve the unity
of the Christian Church.

Amid this theological give and take, final peace can be attained only if the Church itself takes full control over all paths
of knowledge and grace by which the individual approaches his
God and if it takes into its keeping man's most precious possession, his conscience; in short, if it identifies itself with the Truth,
the Will, the very kingdom of God. This done, there remains
between this world and the next but one single bridge: the Catholic
Church.

We have seen how the figure of Christ the Redeemer forms
the nucleus about which crystallize pagan and Jewish ideas, ancient culture and gospel. We saw at the same time how this
natural-supernatural, personal-impersonal God-man is also the
obstacle in the way of a logical union of these elements.

Only through the power of supreme mystical believers like
Paul and Athanasius, and by the Church's word of command,
could this union be brought about. Without a definite circum-
scription of creed and without a purposeful Church policy, this
mighty task in the field of Christianity could not have been
completed. In the face of this fact, any belittling of the mediæval
Church must appear petty and unintelligent.

After all that has been said, it might be supposed that the
union of antiquity and Christianity, of the Platonic and the
evangelical Hereafter, having been enforced by authority and
discipline, was regarded by the profounder spirits of the Middle
Ages as arbitrary and artificial. The very words *Divine Comedy*
suffice to destroy such a supposition.

DANTE AND THE DOGMA OF THE CHURCH

How is it possible that a work like the *Comedy*, the unity of
which is so absolutely personal, could arise upon the ground of
Catholic dogma, whose unity is so wholly impersonal? After
the Catholic Church had become the only bridge to the Hereafter,
how could one man venture to stride across in his own fashion?

Those who are hostile-minded toward the Catholic Church
have made the answer unduly easy by asserting that the *Comedy*
was not built on an ecclesiastical foundation, that Dante was
no orthodox Catholic. Only malice and ignorance can at this

day rest satisfied with such a delusion.[1] There is in fact not a single essential point in which Dante's faith diverges from that of the Church. It is true that a work of Dante's, the *De Monarchia*, was in 1329, after the poet's death, publicly burned by the Roman Curia. But the *De Monarchia* is a political, not a religious, work, and the attack upon it was a political, not a dogmatic, measure.

Other points wherein it might be surmised that Dante turns aside from Church orthodoxy will be disposed of in the detailed exposition of the *Comedy*. For the rest, fanatical foes of the Church may recall the clear and curt words with which Beatrice decides the question as to the extent to which an individual may unite himself with God by a special vow outside the Church:

> Ye have the Old and the New Testament,
> And the Pastor of the Church who guideth you;
> Let this suffice you unto your salvation.[2]

The statement could not be more Catholic, and yet Protestant Hotspurs will take pleasure in just these verses where the Bible is recommended beside the Pope, yes, before him, as a spiritual guide.

The most weighty fact which might indeed indicate an evangelical vein in Dante's piety is undoubtedly his unusual acquaintance and familiarity with and preference for the Bible. A statistical inquiry, for the accuracy of which I cannot vouch, indicates that in the complete works of Dante reference is made five hundred times to the Bible, five hundred times to the greatest Catholic philosopher—and that was then Aristotle—and only ten times to the greatest Father of the Catholic Church—who was and still is Augustine.[3] But of a contradiction, or even rivalry, between Bible and dogma, not a word is said anywhere. Only when such a thing enters consciousness does Protestantism begin.

It does indeed result from *De Monarchia*, III, 3, that the Bible does not derive its authority from the Church, but the Church

[1] This delusion has been most thoroughly and completely refuted by Edward Moore, "Dante as a Religious Teacher, especially in Relation to Catholic Doctrine," in *Studies in Dante*, Second Series, Oxford, 1899. Cf. also F. X. Kraus, *Dante, sein Leben und sein Werk*, Berlin, 1897, p. 701 sqq.

[2] *Paradiso*, V, 76-78.

[3] Edward Moore, *Studies in Dante*, First Series, Oxford, 1896, pp. 4-5. There are besides about two hundred allusions to Virgil, about one hundred to Ovid, fifty each to Cicero and Lucan, between thirty and forty to Statius and Boëthius, ten to twenty to Horace, Livy, and Orosius.

from the Bible. But even the austerest Catholic of Dante's day had no objection to that. It was the Council of Trent, awakened to the danger of this doctrine by the immediate effects of the Reformation, that first protected itself against it by suitable measures.[1] Not until then, i.e. in the year 1554, was the *De Monarchia* put upon the *Index Librorum Prohibitorum*, from which it has been, furthermore, very recently removed under Leo XIII.[2] Although the Catholic Church declared itself to be the same before and after the Council of Trent, those who think historically must emphasize the differences all the more distinctly and must state clearly that it is not Dante who clashed with the creed of the mediæval Church, but the modern Catholic Church that contradicts Dante.

Whether Dante, at the present day, after the discrepancies between Catholic dogma and Holy Writ, and no less clearly those between the Bible and the facts of religious history, have been revealed, would have remained a Catholic or become a Protestant, or even, as it has been thought, an Old Catholic— that is another question and an utterly idle one.

In *his* time he was a strict Catholic. He not only believed all the dogmas, but also treated all the important points of doctrine theologically in his poem. He has, in a certain sense, recapitulated the results of ten centuries of theological inquiry. His relation to his Church is not merely that of a devoted layman, but that of a competent theologian. Without being a professional cleric, he felt the need to give an account not only of the doctrines but of the organization of his Church. He felt impelled to convince himself how sound the cause was.

[1] Cf. A. V. Harnack, *Dogmengeschichte*, 4th ed., III, 697 sqq., 730 sqq. Only from the point of view of the Council of Trent is the dogmatic criticism justified which a Catholic scholar of our own day, so ardent an admirer of Dante as Hermann Grauert, could not refrain from uttering: "It must be conceded that on certain points Dante, measured by the test of strict Catholicism, is not quite correct in his ideas as to dogma. The book *De Monarchia* assumes such a sharp distinction between the body and the soul of man, separates so sharply his earthly from his future destiny, that it is not altogether consistent with the unity of human nature; and when Dante sets the beginning of the Church after the books of the New Testament (*De Monarchia*, III, 3), i.e. declares those books to have been written before the Church was founded, that also is open to criticism from the Catholic standpoint." H. Grauert, *Dante und Houston Stewart Chamberlain*, 2nd ed., Freiburg i. B., 1904, p. 15.

[2] As for the rest, only the oversensitive Spanish Inquisition has been able to scent out three passages in the *Comedy* which seem to them worthy to stand upon the *Index* (Madrid, 1612). They are *Inferno*, XI, 8–9; XIX, 106–117; and *Paradiso*, IX, 136–142—passages which have nothing whatever to do with dogmas.

In the course of this great reckoning, if I may call it so, a twofold result was revealed to him; in theory he found everything unified and correct, in practice he found numberless evil conditions and usages to record. That unity of the Church which, as we have seen, is the result of dogma and authority, appears to our poet as theoretically logical and necessary.

He distinguishes theory and practice from a point of view which is unlike ours. Dogma is to him, not indeed exclusively, but in great part, a scientific certainty; only the actual and contemporary policy of the Church is criticized by him as an arbitrary departure from its own doctrine. To us, on the other hand, the very conception of dogma excludes the possibility of logical demonstration. The diversity of these points of view—which is here merely recorded and not explained—is closely connected with the difference between the mediæval and the modern doctrines of revelation and knowledge.

All that is needed here is the demonstration that Dante's faith was not blind but well grounded and, as he firmly believed, provable and proved. Our task here is to view Dante's conviction and that of his generation as they saw it. We must imagine, assume, and concede that dogma has come into existence, not through mysticism and politics, but through revelation and investigation; and that it at once shows itself in its unified and necessary consequence, as an impersonal, universal human truth—as the truth itself. Every man, therefore, can perceive it, and if he is rational he must believe it.

At the present day dogma is indeed impersonal, but in quite a different sense—no longer because it excludes personal convictions, but because it claims the right to include and embrace all personal convictions. The Church did not break down all individual bridges between the Here and the Hereafter in order to set its own in their place;—no, there was from the beginning but a single one, and that constructed by God. This bridge the Church has completed, strengthened, watched over, and so broadened that all mankind can pass over it. When Dante goes in his own fashion to the Hereafter, the meaning is that he moves by his own strength, and with his own feet, but always and only upon this great Catholic bridge. The bridge is wider than he needed; dogma so completely includes his personal creed that the latter never rises above the former.

Therefore the *Divine Comedy*, despite its pre-eminent religious significance, can make no claim to have aided, or extended, or altered, the creed of the Church; and it makes no such claim. The extension of dogma can be accomplished only through the decision of a Council or of the "Holy Father," not through the poetry of the layman, be he ever so mighty.

And yet, according to our conviction and Dante's own, the *Divine Comedy* is much more than an unauthoritative, isolated, imaginative Hereafter, within the limits of dogma. Dante calls his work

<blockquote>
the Poem Sacred
To which both heaven and earth have set their hand.[1]
</blockquote>

He cannot sufficiently express to his readers and himself the importance and the significance of his undertaking. The expressions "sacred poem" and "consecrated poem" prove that he credits his work not only with poetic but also with religious value, that he is conscious of having accomplished an extraordinary feat of piety.

PIETY IN THE MIDDLE AGES

General Characteristics

Genuine piety can flourish in every church, in every creed and cult. Its value lies in the spontaneity and confidence, not in the dogmatic correctness, of the faith. It is no theological art, but a spiritual gift, possessed in various moods, tempers, crises, more by one man, less by another. It can indeed be formed, practised, and strengthened, or neglected and stifled; but it cannot be learned or acquired at will.

Nevertheless it would be unfair if we were to define piety merely as a gift of nature, as a sort of spiritual geniality; for it comes to us as a consequence of an historic gift to mankind. Without the occurrence of a great and a special event, which in pious speech is called "miracle," "gracious summons," piety is not wont to appear. A merely psychological inquiry into its nature, a study of it as a natural succession or mixture of so-called religious or mystical feelings, yields empty abstractions. It has its history, its crises, catastrophes, and revolutions, its rises, declines, and re-births, its creators, leaders, discoverers,

[1] *Paradiso*, XXV, 1-2.

and heroes, its camp-followers, traitors, and foes. In this chain of events, dogma plays the rôle of a bulwark or of a stronghold which is reared, built, fortified, and again undermined, captured, destroyed, and yet again created in new forms—by piety. There are times when piety forges more dogmatic weapons than it destroys; there are others when the reverse is true.

The great epoch in the creation of Christian dogma closed about the time of the Council of Nicaea (A.D. 325); and an essentially dogmatic condition of belief was meantime attained, in that "the doctrine of Christ, as the pre-existent and personal Logos of God, had come to be accepted in the confederated local churches everywhere as the revealed fundamental doctrine of the faith." [1]

What came afterward is, to be sure, religious life and highly significant theological labour, but it is conditioned in a remarkable fashion by the dogmatic foundation. After the fourth century the officially settled creed begins to be the model and universally required test of piety. In a similar manner the external forms of the poetry of a long and unbroken creative artistic period stiffen into a mechanical scheme within which the later poets were compelled to move. As the conventional, stereotyped laws of prosody weighed down on the poet, so dogma acted on the pious. Both were compelled to fill a dead and external form with the living and original utterance of their souls. Both have an obstacle to overcome: the arbitrary, abstract, and authoritative nature of the pattern forced upon them.

But for divinely inspired poets, as well as for the naturally pious, this obstacle serves in the long run as an incentive to increase and intensify their native force. They do not at first break through the form; they warm, stretch, and bend it until it suits their nature as if it had grown upon them. Only those who are lacking in force and originality are content with being conventional poets or conventional believers and to accept the traditional form as a prop for their weakness.

Just as the great artist must wrestle with the traditions of the poetic art, so must the pious with those of the dogma. To be sure, poetic and dogmatic barriers can be overcome by other means than poetic genius and mystical enthusiasm; namely, through criticism and intellectual enlightenment. Accordingly, every-

[1] Harnack, *op. cit.*, I, 4.

thing that is of lasting value in the religious life of the Middle Ages is divided into two great currents which it is customary to call mysticism and enlightenment. We shall trace first, in broad outlines, the course of mysticism, or, to choose the more inclusive term, piety. The character of Catholic piety in the Middle Ages is determined by its dogmatic foundation; on the one side lukewarm orthodoxy and mechanical lip-service, outwardly formal, stereotyped, wooden, and self-satisfied; on the other, the most ardent mysticism, the profoundest longing for the next world, which rises to the gloomiest self-contempt and self-destruction. These are the extreme forms of piety, which flourish best in the dry soil of dogmatic belief: the hardened, servile bigotry of the Philistine, and the ardent fervour of the virtuoso in fanaticism. The simple, silent, infinite trust in God which with childlike assurance finds its way amid the unutterable confusion of existence—that was, in the Middle Ages, the rarer type. I do not mean to say that it was then unknown. It may have been more common than the edifying writings of those centuries bid us surmise, but it was inconspicuous and escaped the eye of the observer. Certainly it was regarded in the Middle Ages not as the best, but as a fairly good, form of piety.

From Jesus and Plato two great currents proceed, which determine the mediæval belief as to the Hereafter. In these same men the powers of feeling and of will which give to mediæval piety its character are revealed with especial clearness.

The spirit of reverence, the realization of God's presence among the followers of Christ, are the effects of the heroism of His mission. The feelings which govern Him unburden themselves in the holy zeal of His deeds. With Plato it is different. His pious feelings give wings rather to his imagination and thought than to his will. In the former, we have the practical piety of the hero and of the saint; in the latter, the contemplative piety of the prophet and the philosopher.

But what saint, or what prophet, can ever attain the desired goal by the purity of his will and by the clearness of his thought? How can the secret all-pervading aspirations which possessed him gain complete actuality and secure perfect satisfaction? There remains always some longing which, in so far as it cannot become fresh action and new discovery, must express itself in unattainable, passionate, wearied desire. Under such circumstances a man convinces himself that good deeds can be replaced, yes, even excelled, by fanatical violence, and the process of clear thought by hazy dreams, and that the heights we wished to scale somehow sink down to the level of our exhausted soul, or that some other miracle helps us on the way.

Now only the indolent masses have in all times given way in their weakness to the temptation of mysticism, but even the most powerful and heroic leaders have in moments of desperate crisis yielded to it. Jesus and Plato resorted to miracle, one for moral salvation, the other for intellectual enlightenment. But from its contact both received new energy. For mysticism was not a downy couch for them, but rather a springboard.

We are interested only in that piety which has accomplished something. We do not wish to regard it as luxurious enjoyment, but as profounder knowledge and progress.

Men of Piety in the Middle Ages in their Relation to Dante

The apostle Paul contrasted so powerfully the profound consciousness of the sinfulness of our will with the firm confidence in redemption through grace that these two poles, the pessimistic sense of sin and the optimistic sense of forgiveness, and the passage from one to the other, have become essential to the entire religious life of Christendom. Plato's piety, also, starts from a pessimistic mood. Indeed we have seen that Paul is indebted to the spirit of late Hellenism for his generalization of the consciousness of original sin. But the pessimism of Plato has less reference to the will than to the Nature which environs us. It is more general, but less profound; it makes the pious man suspicious of the world, not of himself; it isolates him. Accordingly the Platonist seeks not a victory over the world, but a way of escape from it.

These moods, kindred in form but diverse in content, moods of acceptance and of denial, recur again, mingled in ever-varying proportions, in the Middle Ages. At the very beginning two men stand out in contrast: St. Augustine and Dionysius the Areopagite, the former inclining more to Paul, the latter to Platonism. Dante knew them both and revered both as high authorities. He has nowhere definitely contrasted nor even compared them.

St. Augustine

Like Paul, Augustine has an especially representative rôle to play in the *Divine Comedy*. Paul appears in the court of Heaven as an apostle; Augustine as a Church Father and nominal founder of an order.[1] Otherwise it is rather the political theory, the ethics, and especially the psychology of Augustine, and not so much his mysticism, that have influenced Dante. Still, our poet seems to have borrowed from Augustine one idea wholly mystical in character.

> "Were the world to Christianity converted,"
> I said, "withouten miracles, this one
> Is such, the rest are not its hundredth part." [2]

Through such ideas, as soon as they are carried further, the boundary-line is effaced between the direct will of God as He makes it known in miracles and the natural course of earthly events. The human will is paralyzed by God's, or at least made superfluous. Practical mysticism takes on the form of quietism. But neither Augustine nor Dante fell into the danger of that blessed roseate contentment with the world that leaves God to manage all things. The free confidence in the general excellence of the world is more like the modern than the mediæval mood and has found its typical representatives in the cheerful philosophers and poets of the Renaissance and the Age of Enlightenment. Recourse was taken to the drugging of the will after the complete significance of volition was discovered and realized. *But wherever this realization makes its way, mediævalism is in retreat.*

So then, Augustine immediately invalidated the idea that the progress of the world essentially coincides with God's will, and is therefore blameless, by painting the darkest pictures of the misery and sin of this life. And Dante has unmistakably accentuated the extraordinary and exceptional nature of the Augustinian idea, by assigning it to the passage where he recites his mystical creed, as the pious man is about to proceed to his

---

[1] For information concerning Dante's characters and their relation to him, I refer the reader to the practical and reliable work of Paget Toynbee, *A Dictionary of Proper Names and Notable Matters in the Works of Dante*, Oxford, 1898.

[2] *Paradiso*, XXIV, 106–108, and St. Augustine's *De Civitote Dei*, XXII, 5 *ad finem*. "But if they do not believe that these miracles were wrought by the apostles in order that they, the apostles, might gain credence when they preached the resurrection and the ascension of Christ, then this one great miracle suffices, namely, that the whole world did believe, without miracles."

home. Only beyond, not within, this world, do the natural events
and mishaps of our life reveal themselves as divinely destined
miracles.

Nevertheless it is significant that precisely the weightiest
thought which Dante appears to have borrowed from Augustine
has its source in practical, not in theoretical, mysticism.   According also to our present-day valuation, the chief merit of
Augustine's mysticism consists precisely in this: that it brought
about a higher appreciation of the significance of the will.

Whether Dante's piety received other direct impulses from
Augustine is difficult to decide; for an unbroken tradition ran
from the one to the other, uniting and dividing them, and did not
permit a more intimate contact.[1] As to the fact that the artistic
and educative elements of the *Confessions* influenced Dante
powerfully, there can be no doubt.   These matters lie, however,
outside our present range of vision.

Dionysius the Pseudo-Areopagite

Dionysius's mysticism bears the mark of enthusiastic exuberance. This mysterious man plunged the system of Neo-Platonic
natural philosophy into a glowing fire of religious enthusiasm,
so that the conceptual structure was melted into a hymn and is
recognizable only in its main outlines. The stony forms of ecclesiastical dogma, also, he vivifies into poetic pictures. Every
sort of conceptual expression is for him, in his divine intoxication, useless and petty. Words lose their value, and the most
diverse images must help each other out in order to express the
unutterable. Here science is vanquished, and even art is bewildered.

"God is invisible, from excess of light. He who perceives God
is himself in darkness. God's all-pervading darkness is hidden
from every light, and veils all recognition. And if any one who
sees God recognizes and understands what he sees, then he himself has not seen Him." [2]

One cannot call the mysticism of the Areopagite heretical, but,

---

[1] Edmund G. Gardner, *Dante and the Mystics*, London, 1913, has credited to
Augustine, in his chapter on "Dante and St. Augustine," all sorts of thoughts and
expressions for which Dante may quite as well be indebted to other authors, by
which the influence of the Church Father upon the poet is notably increased and
the specific dependence is obscured.

[2] Quoted by J. Huber, *Die Philosophie der Kirchenväter*, Munich, 1859, p. 330.

rather, indifferent to dogma. And so the sanest and most orthodox theologians of the Middle Ages have not disdained to warm
themselves at his fire. Johannes Scotus Erigena and Johannes
Sarracenus translated his writings from the Greek; Hugo of
St. Victor, Albertus Magnus, and Thomas Aquinas wrote com-
ments on him.

On the shining heights of the *Paradiso*, where Dante struggles
with the difficulties of human expression and must repeatedly
confess to us the insufficiency of mortal utterance, where his eye
is blinded by the radiance of the Divinity—he may often have
thought of the Greek mystic.[1] Indeed he credits him with superhuman knowledge of matters in Paradise, especially of the angelic
choirs, and in describing them follows his statements closely.[2]

The book of Acts (17: 34) relates that St. Paul converted
several Athenian citizens, among them one named Dionysius
of the Areopagus (i.e. a member of the court). He was identified
in the Middle Ages with our mystic. But Paul, who converted
and taught him, according to another mediæval belief—which is
founded on II Corinthians 12—is said while yet living to have
risen to Heaven and there to have beheld the divine mysteries,
which he afterward revealed to Dionysius. Dante, like his whole
generation, placed in this ingenious combination of biblical
passages an unquestioning trust, whereas according to present-
day investigations, the Dionysian writings are those of a Neo-
Platonist of the sixth century.

Considering this extraordinarily authoritative position of
Dionysius, it may be assumed that his influence upon the construction of Dante's *Paradiso* was quite wide and deep. Is it
not probable, for instance, that the circular movement as symbol
of the mystic recognition and longing, or the central sun which
illuminates the universe as symbol of the Godhead, or the triple
steps of the mystical ascent through purification, illumination,

[1] At the time when he wrote the *Convivio* he evidently did not yet know Dionysius (*Convivio*, II, 6), for there he makes the order of the Heavenly Choirs different
from that of the Celestial Hierarchy, depending, as it seems, upon Gregory the
Great, *Moralia*, XXXII, 23, § 48. Cf. Giovanni Busnelli's article on the order
of the Heavenly Choirs in the *Convivio* and in the *Paradiso*, in the *Bulletino della
Società dantesca*, New Series, XVIII, Florence, 1911. This view of Gregory he
expressly corrects, in *Paradiso*, XXVIII, 130 sqq., and accepts the view of Dionysius. Furthermore, Dante must have known also the *De divinis Nominibus* of the
Areopagite, probably through the commentary of Thomas Aquinas (or Albertus
Magnus?). Cf. E. Gardner, *op. cit.*, p. 86 sqq.
[2] *Paradiso*, XXVIII, 98 sqq.

and apotheosis, or the flowing and mirroring of the divine light throughout the creation, or the comparison of spirit with the seal and of matter with the wax, or other kindred emanational ideas, were taken from Dionysius's book? Here again certainty is hardly attainable, for once more the mysticism of the twelfth and thirteenth centuries intervenes, uniting and separating our poet from the Greek source.

This much, however, is sure, that Dante has purified the hazy exuberance of Dionysius, thanks to the dogmatic firmness of his own faith and the plastic clarity of his imagination; and that this Oriental ecstasy exerted its influence less on the form and trend of his piety than on the details of his description.

Gregory the Great

Dionysius's mysticism exerted for a time no decisive influence on Western thought. The great question which St. Augustine had again raised and which had found an anxious echo in all Christian hearts—"How am I to save my soul, how shall I be redeemed?"—this question interested the Areopagite but little.

The leading counsellor of the human conscience was Gregory the Great. He knew how to enter into this question and how to find a practical solution. Only a few extraordinary men like Augustine were able to draw consolation from their unalterable trust in God's mercy. Gregory, however, took it upon himself to look after weaker, humbler souls. He increased, improved, and multiplied the Church's means of grace. The intercession of saints and helpers, the magic effect of the sacraments, all kinds of ecclesiastical practices and indulgences, were put forth to aid the troubled soul. Never may man be sure of his salvation, for "certainty is the mother of indolence." Precautions for the future life are never too many. The highway to salvation is built by the Church somewhat as a military road is paved, and provided with milestones. But piety thereby sinks to superstition and lets itself be mastered and exploited by priestly shrewdness.

On the other hand, by this well-meant solicitude Gregory strengthened the confidence of his flock in the power of the Church.

Dante, too, as he strides with uplifted head through the other world, is upborne by this confidence in the magic power of his Church. In baptism he sees the indispensable condition of sal-

vation; moral purity alone sufficeth not.[1] The indulgences issued
by Pope Boniface VIII, on the occasion of the Jubilee in the
year 1300, hasten and facilitate the entrance of the poor souls
into Purgatory.[2] Whoso dies under the ban of the Church,
even if he has repented before death, must wait thirty times as
long outside of Purgatory as the ban lay upon him in life. In
this it is, to be sure, taken for granted that the excommunication
was imposed on just grounds, and that it was through default that
the guilty one did not undergo due penance.[3] On the other hand,
the prayers of the living expedite the purification of the departed.

Furthermore, it is noticeable that in Dante those who wish
to lessen their penalty through prayers and intercessions are the
ones who have not yet been allowed to begin their purification,[4]
and before they are admitted to Purgatory proper, must give
satisfaction for their delay. The purification in Dante is, however,
spontaneous, proceeds primarily from the holy desire of those
who are doing penance, and is made possible by, and recognized
by, God's grace. Ecclesiastical indulgences or vicarious atonement have no validity here. The prayer of the living does indeed
always serve to hasten and complete, but not to lessen, the task
of purification. They never pray that those in Purgatory be
spared, but always that they be purified.

It is evident that our poet has outwardly accepted, but has
not inwardly submitted to, the common Catholic view formulated
by Gregory the Great and strengthened by others. Everything
in it that is superficial he has made more profound. Precisely
because he is able to appreciate in their original purity the feelings which underlie the formulas and functions of the Church,
he has no need to fight against things which appear to those at
a distance as superstition.

Even the naïve legend of the magic power of prayer, which is
connected with Gregory the Great, he can accept in all seriousness, for he has an open heart for its religious meaning.[5] John

---

. . . . If they merit had
    'Tis not enough, because they had not baptism,
    Which is the portal of the Faith thou holdest.—*Inferno*, IV, 34–36.
The meaning of these verses cannot be doubtful, though there is doubt as to the
reading, between *parte*, *patre* (father), and *porta* (portal).
[2] *Purgatorio*, II, 98 sqq.
[3] *Ibid.*, III, 136 sqq.
[4] Cf. Edward Moore, "Dante as a Religious Teacher," *op. cit.*, p. 43 sqq.
[5] *Purgatorio*, X, 73 sqq., and *Paradiso*, XX, 106 sqq.

the Deacon, in his *Vita Sancti Gregorii*, relates that the fame of the righteousness of the Emperor Trajan had reached the ears of Pope Gregory; and that the latter had the tomb of the emperor opened, wept bitter tears over the wasted corpse, and by the power of his prayers brought it to pass that the noble soul of the heathen emperor was translated from Hell to Paradise.

Even more critical spirits than Dante, men like Thomas Aquinas, put faith in this legend. But Dante regards the result of the prayer not as a magical, but as a mystical, event. It is not a thing that can be explained through investigation, nor indeed one that can be mastered by art or practice; it must be felt and believed.

Our poet's rationalism is exaggerated, and at the same time, the sincerity and simplicity of his religious feelings are depreciated, when it is said to his praise that he transfers unbaptized heathens like Trajan and Ripheus to the kingdom of Heaven for the reason that he did not share in the prejudices of ecclesiastical dogma.[1] Dante has neither directly nor indirectly questioned dogma; he has, on the contrary, searched for its truth and validity in the vitality of religious feeling.

To be sure, from mysticism to magic is but a step, but the poet Dante never took that step.[2]

St. Bernard

Catholicism, meanwhile, in the centuries which followed Gregory, moved on toward disruption, under the banner of superstition and politics. Before the great movements of the Cluniacs and Victorines, no religious event of importance occurred.

But now a new piety arises to oppose the Church that had turned worldly. As the need of the time demanded, this took primarily a contemplative and unworldly direction, and attached itself accordingly to Neo-Platonism and to the writings of Dionysius, which had been made accessible for the Occident by Johannes Scotus Erigena (A.D. 810–880).

According as the religious struggle against superstition and the worldliness of the Church is now carried on with greater or

[1] So, for example, A. Bartoli, *Storia della letteratura italiana*, Florence, 1889, VI, ii, 158 sqq.

[2] The indebtedness of Dante to Gregory as to the doctrine of sin is discussed in the third part of this work.

less intensity, this mystical movement takes the form of an heretical revolution or of a Catholic reform. Side by side with the heterodox mysticism of the Catharists, there runs in the eleventh and twelfth centuries the orthodox mysticism of the Cluniacs and Victorines; and the voices of the preachers Arnold of Brescia and Petrus Waldus mingle with that of Bernard of Clairvaux.

Only through the pressure of events were these two movements brought into opposition.

They both have their origin in the same state of mind. Both are inspired by world-forsaking spirituality, both are aroused by disgust at the greed and selfishness of the Roman Church; both seek peace and purity in the renunciation of worldly goods and in contemplative communion with the Divinity.

What the Gnostics were in the early days of Christianity and the Manichaean sects in St. Augustine's time, much the same were the Catharists in the later Middle Ages. And as in those days, the elasticity of Christianity again showed itself, in that it accepted on the one hand the austere renunciation of bodily pleasures, forbearance toward one's enemies, and the superiority of contemplation, yet at the same time defended itself sturdily against the nihilistic spirit of the Catharists. The evangelical and Augustinian mysticism protected the Church against that of the Neo-Platonists and Dionysius, and the vigour of the will shielded it from excessive imaginativeness.

These contradictions, united in complete and harmonious development, constitute the passionate character of St. Bernard. Nowhere is the religious crisis of that time mirrored so clearly and so typically as in him. This powerful man himself, indeed, was at times terrified by the contrasting forces of his own nature. "I am the monster of the century," he said, "neither cleric nor layman. I will not write about myself what you have heard from others—what I do, what I am aiming at, with what contradictions I am struggling." The same Bernard who by his excited but well-designed agitation drives the soberest folk— even King Conrad III—to the Crusade, urges upon his monks that they must hold aloof from the tumult of the world, and forbids them even to preach. He is intoxicated by the splendour of the papal throne, and yet exalts the poverty of the monastic cell.

These contradictions, however, disappear at the central point of his piety. "Let no one believe that he has received the kiss divine if he knows the truth without loving it, or loves it without understanding it. But blessed is that kiss whereby not only is God recognized, but also the Father is loved; for there is never full knowledge without perfect love." [1] *Est ergo animae vita veritas, sensus charitas* [2]—which I venture to translate, in the sense of the original: "The form of the soul's life is truth, but its content, love." What logic clearly cuts and the necessities of life blindly tear asunder—understanding and will, renunciation and victory—all this is again made one and harmonized by devotion.

Bernard did not preach the mysticism of the Areopagite, not the dissolution of individuality, nor its union with God, [3] but essentially only the unification of man with himself. Not in God, but through God, is our highest understanding reconciled with our loftiest desire.

To be sure, the delight of self-effacement in divine rapture is not unfamiliar to him. He speaks with longing of this highest plane of mysticism, but can hardly believe that it is to fall to the lot of a mortal, certainly not without the miraculous grace of God—and then only for a brief instant can a human being be lifted so high, and with the sorrowful consequence of a return to earth. "Blessed and holy would I call him who had been granted such an experience in this mortal life even once, and only for a moment. For to lose thyself somehow, so that thou wouldst be nothing, no longer conscious of thyself, released from thyself and all but annihilated—that is heavenly life, no human condition. And even if one among mortals sometimes in ecstasy can attain thereunto for an instant, yet the wretched world begrudges it to him, and the malignant light of day disturbs him, his mortal body weighs upon him, the demands of the flesh oppress him, his enervated inadequacy bids him sink—and what is mightier yet, brotherly love summons him back." [4]

This man who knows the blessedness and the perils of ecstasy and does not seek it as a permanent condition, but awaits it as

---

[1] *Sermones in Cantica,* 8, 6.
[2] *Sermones de Diversis,* 10, 1.
[3] The expression "deification" (*deificatio*) can be found only once in his works.
[4] *Liber de Diligendo Deo,* X, 27.

the supreme grace from above, has become, in the *Divine Comedy*, Dante's advocate. Through his prayer, the poet receives the highest gift; namely, the direct vision of the Deity. The words of the Dantesque Bernard are spoken wholly in harmony with his historic character:

> Now doth this man, who from the lowest depth
>   Of the universe as far as here has seen
>   One after one the spiritual lives,
> Supplicate thee through grace for so much power
>   That with his eyes he may uplift himself
>   Higher towards the uttermost salvation.
> And I, who never burned for my own seeing
>   More than I do for his, all of my prayers
>   Proffer to thee, and pray they come not short,
> That thou wouldst scatter from him every cloud
>   Of his mortality so with thy prayers,
>   That the Chief Pleasure be to him displayed.
> Still farther do I pray thee, Queen, who canst
>   Whate'er thou wilt, that sound thou mayst preserve
>   After so great a vision his affections.
> Let thy protection conquer human movements;
>   See Beatrice and all the blessed ones
>   My prayers to second clasp their hands to thee! [1]

It was neither the fanatical and hieratic preacher of the Crusades nor the penitent monk, but that which unites and explains both— Bernard the devout mystic, "suffused with benign joy," "with pious mien" [2]—who exerted his influence upon Dante. [3] He fixed his attention not upon the saint's strange and contradictory exterior, but upon the spiritual centre of his nature, and assigned to him the last and decisive word that quiets the inquiring mind with loving faith.

A great theological question which had repeatedly troubled Dante and which runs through the entire *Paradiso*, the relation between moral freedom and divine election, is finally decided by St. Bernard in a wholly mystical sense; that is, the riddle is not solved, but reverently referred to the unfathomable Divinity: "And let the result suffice thee." "As it is, it is well." Instead

---

[1] *Paradiso*, XXXIII, 22 sqq.
[2] *Ibid.*, XXXI, 61–62.
[3] E. Gardner, *op. cit.*, p. 121, makes it appear probable that Dante was influenced by St. Bernard's interpretation of the Song of Solomon (*Canticum Canticorum*, V, 1) in the *De Diligendo Deo*, XI, 31–32, to put into Solomon's mouth the doctrine of the resurrection of the body, *Paradiso*, XIV, 34 sqq.

of any further pondering, a reference to the ninth chapter of the Epistle to the Romans.

In fact, Dante has seen aright in that he connects the practical piety of St. Bernard with that of the apostle Paul. The former appeals to the latter most urgently in his treatise *On Grace and Free Will*.[1] Not only grace, but merit also; not only predestination, but freedom of the will as well, is God's handiwork.

The most lovable, most merciful, intercessor for divine grace is, for Bernard, the Virgin Mary. His piety has a feminine and sensuous quality. With glowing fervour he fixes his eyes on the Mother of God and upon the wounds of the Son. In mingled humility and delight, he gazes longingly upon the loveliness, the birth, the poverty, and the sufferings of Mary and Jesus.

But the pictures of this popular and almost sensuous devotion do not fit into Dante's *Paradiso*. After Bernard, and influenced by him, the erotic note grows ever clearer in mediæval mysticism. Loverlike devotion commingles with worship of Mary. Out of the glowing language of the Song of Songs, out of the lighter tones of the popular love-ballads and the gallant forms of knightly madrigals, new forms of religious expression take shape, whose unmanly and frivolous sensuousness was less pleasing to the taste of our poet. He did not indeed disdain it, but, as we shall see, transferred it to other relations than those existing between humanity and Divinity. The prayer to the Virgin Mary already quoted, as uttered by St. Bernard,[2] sounds like solemn and biblical adoration. Here there is nothing dainty, no languors; I would almost say, nothing personal.

Dante finds himself in full accord with Bernard, and presumably is indebted to him for his conception of Mary as the intercessor who reconciles sinful man once more with his Creator; and the providential contrast of the Mother of God, as agent of reconciliation, with Mother Eve, agent of alienation, is equally characteristic of the historical and the Dantesque Bernard.[3]

All in all, Bernard, although he leads our poet to knowledge and vision, both in history and in the poem is the great representative of an essentially practical mysticism. It was therefore only natural that those theologians who elaborated systematically

---

[1] *De Gratia et libero Arbitrio*, XIV, 48.

[2] *Paradiso*, XXXIII, 1 sqq.

[3] *Ibid.*, XXXII, 4 sqq., and St. Bernard's sermon on the Nativity of Mary, 7, also in *Dominica infra Octavam Assumptionis Mariae*, 2.

the sentiments and mood of Bernard's piety—Hugo of St. Victor and St. Bonaventura—exerted an influence rather on Dante's moral creed than on his doctrine of knowledge.

On the other hand, it is the more surprising to see how a mediæval man, though he may have been the profoundest spirit of his age, comprehended just the side of Bernard which psychological inquiry has discovered and recognized again only in our time. Dante was not concerned with Bernard's religious psychology, nor did he look upon him historically, in our sense of the word. He thought in historical terms as little as all other mediæval men. How did it happen that he overlooked the contradiction between Bernard's acceptance and denial of the world, or at least passed over it in silence, and brought out only the question of the inward and hidden nature of his mysticism? Did he wish to idealize his Bernard poetically, and for the sake of the higher purposes of his *Commedia* to purify him from the accidents and contradictions of history? Or did he behold him with essentially other eyes than ours?

Probably both these possibilities were operative. This much is certain—that Dante did not intend any discrepancy between his poetical and our historical Bernard. He is too fully convinced of the greatness of all the leading characters whom he introduces, and too firmly persuaded of the existence of divine providence in all human affairs, to wish to correct and elevate reality by poetry.

If he does not mention the double nature of Bernard's life and work, we may be assured that he was not aware of it, or at least did not ascribe any importance to it.

And he could not feel it, for between him and Bernard stands a man who removed this dualism from mediæval piety: St. Francis of Assisi.

St. Francis

This man preached and lived that supremely ideal existence to which St. Bernard had looked forward. He lived as Bernard in his most pious hours could wish to live. He solved in his own fashion the great problem of Christian piety: to conquer the world without debasing it.

The fundamental strain of his soul is no longer violent eagerness for battle against the foe that besets us within and without, but rather a victorious confidence. However austere his asceticism may have been, it was essentially a cheerful renunciation. The saint tortured his body, but his soul remained secure against doubts and pessimism. Salvation, to him, was not so much a need as a certainty. His piety is like the wonderful self-comprehension of those sunny and blessed souls that are set before us not as struggling champions, but as consummate examples, "a blessing to mankind."

St. Bernard felt himself drawn to the apostle Paul; St. Francis spontaneously takes his place beside Jesus Himself. What the Middle Ages anxiously strove for—to follow, or more accurately, to imitate, Christ—St. Francis accomplished naturally. That is, it was no imitation or repetition, but a unique reincarnation of the evangelical ideal.

To be sure, Jesus dealt with the Church of His time in far more vigorous and decisive fashion than did Francis. But the Jewish clergy was also a good bit more stubborn and less disposed to compromise than the Catholic Church. Therefore, Jesus overthrew the Church of His people, while Francis was gradually disarmed and in the main won over by his.

That dogmatic pressure which, as we saw, controlled all mediæval piety, lay heavily also upon Francis's pure soul. He, too, was able to attain an intimate relation with his God only by shutting himself off from the natural relations of life. His piety, too, though it flows so simply and clearly from his heart, is still not free from that artificial exaltation which can see no other way of completely pleasing God than seclusion and monastic retirement from social life. For him, also, "worldliness" and "sin" are equivalent conceptions.

It is especially at the beginning of his religious transformation that the unnatural violence of this decision is seen. After a full discussion with his own father, he is said to have exclaimed: "Hereafter I shall never have to say Father Pier Bernardone, but only our Father in Heaven." And when the companions of his youthful excesses mockingly asked him whether he was intending to marry, seeing that he had grown so solemn and tiresome, he answered: "Yes, a nobler and more beautiful bride than you ever saw." The bride he meant was Poverty.

To be sure, there is no conversion without renunciation of worldly activity. But if the convert does not straightway find a new path back to this world, he will be of no use to it. Francis honestly sought this path of return, but was unable to follow it to the goal. He persists in renunciation even after his conversion. Poverty is not only his bride, but becomes permanently his wife. Toward the end of his life he seems to have buried himself in the aloofness of contemplation and in violent ecstasies.

However naïve his mysticism seems to us in comparison with that of his predecessors, it has, nevertheless, a trait of elegiac enthusiasm. Francis, true enough, no longer apprehends the gulf between God and the world with the penitent's shudder; but neither does he view it with the sober and fearless eyes of a Christian of the time of the Reformation. He gazes upon it with the sad smile of yearning—and what finally carries him over is not so much valorous action as the wings of poetry. It is no accident that the piety of the Franciscans has exerted so decisive an influence directly upon art.

The saint's imagination, intoxicated with love, sees only goodness, finds only brothers. It transfigures all Nature. The beasts, the plants, the sun, the stars, the four elements, and even Death, are God's creatures and therefore our dear brothers. Even out of the dust breathes the breath divine. In the famous *Cantico del Sole* the final secret of Francis's mysticism is revealed. All Nature is hallowed by a process which in its own way is artistic and poetic. It is not in a reflective or in an argumentative, but in an intuitive and temperamental pantheism, that his piety finds rest.

And therefore the practical influence of the saint can be understood only from this point of view. He fights sin, cares for the sick, converts the heathen, and chooses poverty—not because he scents danger everywhere, but because he everywhere sees hope. For this reason, again, he destroys nothing nor does he wish to save anything; what he wants is to make people happier, not by strife, but by peace.

If he, in his love of poverty, persists in forsaking human society, he nevertheless does not thereby desert the positive foundation of his nature. For to him poverty is a thing of the heart, not a means to an end; a comfort, not a medicine. He realized, not philosophically but instinctively, that intimate communion with God is not disturbed by the love of mankind and of Nature, but is rather aided by it. When he discovered the happiness and joy of renunciation, he took the sting out of asceticism, and by his poetic outlook on the world, quieted the great dissension between the practical and the metaphysical will, between politics and ethics. He, the artistic innovator, is the forerunner of Luther, the moral reformer. Of all pious men, he is the most human. Through him and his school the old idea gathered strength again, that the Church should not fight and rule, but persuade and reconcile.

Thus the dualism which had ruled the minds of men since Augustine's time, the contrast between an ideal, invisible, mystical Church and the actual, earthly, political one, was overcome, at least in theory. He begins the struggle to strip the Church of worldliness.

But for this task the mild disposition of Francis was not adequate, and he could exert an influence only as example and model, not as radical reformer.

Such too is Dante's opinion of him: an example and a model. He knows no better way to set forth the religious worth of this man than to tell the story of his life.[1] In fact, as with Jesus, so with Francis, life and doctrine are one and the same thing. And the central point of this life, which is emphasized by Dante as decisive, is the symbolic wedding of the saint and Poverty.

> Their concord and their joyous semblances,
> The love, the wonder, and the sweet regard,
> They made to be the cause of holy thoughts;
> So much so that the venerable Bernard
> First bared his feet. . . .[2]

Poverty, widowed and despised since Christ's death, has now again for the first time found a lover in Francis:

> Parted by death eleven hundred years
> From her first lord, maltreated and despised,
> By none except this man hath she been wooed.[3]

The whole blessedness of renunciation and the historical importance of this poetic and mystical glorification of asceticism become alive in these brief words of the poet. We shall see

[1] *Paradiso*, XI, 43 sqq. Dante follows, in the main, the account of Thomas of Celano and of St. Bonaventura.

[2] *Ibid.*, XI, 76 sqq. The construction of these verses is doubtful, but their meaning is clear. The "venerable Bernard" refers to Bernardo di Quintavalle, the first follower of Francis.

[3] *Ibid.*, XI, 64–66.

later that Dante did not fail to observe the significance of this new kind of piety for morals and church polity.

To be sure, the natural and innate temper of Dante's life is not that of cheerful renunciation, which indeed smiles from these verses, but which only seldom and for brief moments could bring solace to his unhappy life. We know how painfully Dante felt exile and poverty, how bitterly he complains and rages against both in his *Convivio* and in many passages of the *Commedia*. It would be a radical misunderstanding of Dante's art if Franciscan piety were to be declared, as it has been by some, the true soul of his poem. With the heart of a Francis, no man could write the *Inferno*.

Nowhere has Dante's moral austerity permitted itself to be enfeebled by the poetic pantheism of Franciscan mysticism. It even seems as if our poet at a certain moment wished to utter a reproach, veiled with masterly skill, against the saint: I am referring to the episode which tells how the soul of one of Francis's brethren, Guido da Montefeltro, was wrested out of his arms by the logic of the Devil.[1]

RETROSPECT

Of all the great saints of the Middle Ages so far described, not one exerted a decisive influence on Dante's piety. Yet from each one the poet took over something valuable. The highest religious function, however, he assigned to St. Bernard.

If we take these five eminent men for what they actually were, spokesmen and leaders of religious development, and if we trace the connection from one to another, we see that piety never forsakes its intellectual basis, but within this limitation gradually approaches the practical goal.

The piety of Dionysius still consists wholly in contemplation, and puts the Christian's will in a state of rapture incapable of any action. At the head of the Western movement we must place, therefore, not the Areopagite, but St. Augustine himself. It was he who closed the gap between fear of God and trust in Him by teaching that the human will is indeed powerfully aroused by accumulated sins and by the fear of God, but that it is again quieted by the assurance of forgiveness. The first impulse of the will comes from sin and is negative.

[1] *Inferno*, XXVII, 112 sqq.

Gregory continued the work of Augustine by further developing the fear of God into a veritable dread, and, on the other hand, lowered pious hope to shrewd calculation, and utilized it for ecclesiastical purposes. The will was thus indeed strengthened, but it was also diverted from its truly religious goal. The impulse then becomes positive, but is wrongly directed.

Hence the will must again be broken by a more complete renunciation of this world. This problem is solved by the heterodox mysticism of the Catharists and by a partial return to the point of view of Dionysius.

Then and only then could the will, purified by self-denial and trained by political experience, be set free by Bernard. He, however, impelled man's will toward two goals at once, so that the whole opposition between positive and negative powers, between acceptance and denial of the world, was transferred from the intellect to the will. Augustine was dualistic in thought, Bernard in life.

Francis offers the final mediæval solution in that he does not, indeed, do away with penitential renunciation of the world, but gives it a positive direction by renouncing not through fear, but for love. Thus the asceticism ceases to be barren, and becomes a blessing for mankind. Piety becomes democratic; and through the foundation of the Tertiary Orders, the pious monk brings "the cloister into the home." [1] With Francis the will does not, indeed, as yet take the lead, but it has become consistent with itself, being still impelled solely by positive impulses. Man acts morally because, and in so far as, he becomes aware of God's existence in the order of the universe.

After this only one more step: the deriving of our knowledge of God from our capacity for moral action. We owe this to Kant, the illustrious pupil of evangelical pietism.

4. DANTE'S PIETY [2]

How does the piety of our poet appear when placed in this series?

Not only his dogmatic orthodoxy, but, strangely enough, the inwardness of his religious feeling has been questioned. God

---

[1] J. Marx, *Lehrbuch der Kirchengeschicte*, Trier, 1903, p. 363.

[2] Cf. my booklet, *Dante als religiöser Dichter*, Berne and Zürich, 1921, and the chapter on Dante's type of mind and development in Karl Jakubczyk's *Dante*, Freiburg i. Br., 1921, which brings out very effectively the Catholic view.

the Father and Jesus, it has been said, are all but wholly banished from the *Commedia*. They do not appear, have no influence, do not act, do not speak. The poet traverses Their eternal realms without being able to acquire any personal relation with Them: perhaps, somewhat as a curious traveller examines a magnificent royal palace, coming in contact only with servants and court officials, while His Majesty may at most be admired through a half-open door and from afar.[1]

In order to refute this conception, we need not drop the simile, but merely ask: Is it necessary, in order to prove oneself a loyal subject, to shake the king's hand? And is not a sentiment something different from its object?

It is true the intensity of the feeling will vary according as its object, God, is felt to be present at a definite place, or everywhere, or nowhere.

In absolute pantheism both the conception of God and all intense religious feeling come to naught. But there is a pantheism in which the universal presence of God is blended with the utmost reverence for Him. This type of pantheism we have in the *Divine Comedy*. Dante has formulated the omnipresence of God in a single verse:

> He governs everywhere, and there he reigns.[2]

Everywhere He is the supreme head, but there in Paradise He reigns in person!

> There is his city and his lofty throne;
> O happy he whom thereto he elects!

One could hardly imagine a more intimate union of God's omnipresence and of human longing for Him. Just because He is everywhere our Lord, all creatures would fain be near Him; and because all things press toward Him, therefore is He our Lord. But nevermore to be permitted to approach Him is Hell. Hell thus takes its shape from God's presence: from the curse and agony of His absence. As we move away from God, our conscious awareness of Him diminishes, but our dread of His might immeasurably increases. Dante's Lucifer, in night and ice, is the negative symbol of God, the caricature of the Almighty.

---

[1] Such ideas will be found, for example, in Houston Stewart Chamberlain's *Foundations of the Nineteenth Century*.
[2] *Inferno*, I, 127.

From the point of greatest distance from God to that of utmost nearness to Him, Dante has drawn a great bow. And according to the point at which we touch it, the bow-string gives forth a duller or a clearer sound. Each of the three parts of the *Commedia* has its own religious mode that controls from within the structure and its ornaments.

The poem is so planned that it moves first away from God, and then toward Him. The direct vision of God, the complete repose in Him, is therefore not accomplished until the close. It marks the last and highest spiritual level of piety. Its intense fervour is not quieted by a material approach to God, but by an intellectual reunion through love.

The *Commedia* represents the whole course of a religious conversion. It begins with the terror of sin, with a cry for help. To be in anxiety over sin, and to cry for help, is the only thing that man, of himself, can do against the ravening beasts of evil— a negative impulse of the will, nothing more: all else comes through grace, without which man could not even be aware of his sin, of his lost state, and of his helplessness. All the horror, fear, and wrath that the wanderer feels in his journey through Hell is the result of divine illumination.

In Purgatory, grace brings both illumination and deliverance. Through it alone, self-imposed atonement and purification become possible—a severe, yet hopeful and joyous task, followed by a repentant and contrite survey of one's own past sins. For all good deeds done before were not our merit but a gift of grace. Every advance of knowledge from one sin down to another is revealed by the efficacy of divine power. Every upward step of purgation requires a new special miracle of grace. Only after explicit repentance and an abject confession does divine love seize upon the pilgrim, to uplift him toward light and blessedness.

But does he not thus become degraded to a mere puppet of the Divinity? Has not Dante made of himself a sort of Virgilian Pius Aeneas who lets himself be pushed down or dragged up at will? After refutation of the criticism that Dante had no religious feeling at all, the doubt arises whether he has that, indeed, but nothing more, and has sacrificed man's independence of action to his desire for future life.

But that is not his feeling, nor is it true of self-surrender and subjection to God.

For the Christian believer the combination of independent action with dependent feeling indicates not a contradiction, but the solution of one. And in the *Commedia*, a thoroughly Christian poem, religious bondage is united with moral freedom. The question is only whether the religious or the moral interest is predominant.

If the dedicatory Latin letter, with which the *Paradiso* was presented to Can Grande della Scala,[1] was actually written by Dante, we have in it an authentic statement of the poet as to the purpose of his work. The proper (or as Dante says allegorical) subject of the poem, says the letter, is Man, who, by merits or demerits in the exercise of his free will, subjects himself to justice for reward or punishment.[2] Here the necessity of divine justice is set over against moral freedom of human action. And later in the same letter it is said that the "branch of philosophy" to which the work belongs is moral and not speculative philosophy, the latter being applied only occasionally and for the purpose of the ethical inquiry, not for its own sake.[3]

No religious edification, therefore, but only moral instruction, is foreshadowed; and of piety not a word is said. Supposing, then, the letter to be genuine, and granting that it was no part of Dante's intention to express mystic aspirations, we are still not relieved of the duty of inquiring as to the extent to which piety is included in the *Commedia*. It is altogether probable that Dante wished his work to be regarded as a moral and didactic poem, but it is no less certain that moral instruction in the Middle

---

[1] On the question of genuineness, cf. N. Zingarelli, *Dante*, Milan, Vallardi, n.d., p. 308 sqq., 723–24, who denies Dante's authorship, and E. Moore, *Studies in Dante*, Third Series, Oxford, 1903, p. 284 sqq., who endeavours to defend it with a series of strong arguments. The question is not yet settled, but no decisive evidence against authenticity is produced. Francesco Novati (*Lectura Dantis, Le Opere minori di Dante Alighieri*, Florence, 1906, p. 285 sqq.) has presented effective points of view for the question of genuineness of the whole body of letters. Konrad Falke, in his extremely uncritical *Dante*, Munich, 1922, pp. 447–48, opposed their genuineness without offering new evidence. G. Boffito, *L'Epistola a Cangrande*, Clausano, 1907, gives a critical text and commentary. The study of Dante's letters has been brought to a certain conclusion in the affirmative sense by the excellent edition of Paget Toynbee, *Dante Alighieri's Epistolae*, Oxford, 1920.

[2] ". . . Totius operis allegorice sumpti subjectum est homo, prout merendo et demerendo per arbitrii libertatem est justitiae praemiandi et puniendi obnoxius."

[3] "Genus philosophiae, sub quo hic in toto et parte proceditur, est morale negotium, sive ethica; quia non ad speculandum, sed ad opus inventum est totum et pars. Nam si et in qliquo loco vel passu pertractatur ad modum speculativi negotii, hoc non est gratia speculativi negotii, sed gratia operis; quia, ut ait Philosophus in secundo Metaphysicorum, 'ad aliud et nunc speculantur practici aliquando.'" *Epistolae*, X, 16.

Ages was generally communicated by means of religious edification. In such works the moral goodness was usually the end, and religious investigation the means.

So the instructive passages in the *Commedia* as well as the explanations, the prayers, and the vision of God, are instrumental to the moral salvation of mankind. That which holds the work together, and is repeated a hundred times, is the fundamental admonition that merit without faith and morality without religion do not suffice for our salvation; that the road to virtue must pass through the realms of the Hereafter.

We have seen how the dogmatic coupling of the future life and morality came into being, and was without question accepted by Dante. The personal element in his religion is not to be sought in that direction; it can be found only in some ulterior development of the doctrine, or in the new life he breathed into this dogma.

We see a development, but not indeed a transgression, of the dogma, when the poet represents the irreligious—or, more correctly, unchristian—morality of illustrious heathens, not, to be sure, as pleasing to God, but neither as deserving damnation. To men like Plato, Aristotle, Virgil, and Saladin he assigns a sort of Elysium in the Limbo of Hell.[1] They suffer no pangs of conscience, yet they live without hope of ever satisfying their eternal longing for God, Whom they have never known. According to the Church's doctrine, this Limbo, after the Fathers of the Old Testament had been transferred to Paradise through Christ's intercession, became the exclusive abode of unbaptized children. Dante goes yet a step further when he places the representative of a purely philosophical morality, the Stoic Cato, at the entrance of Purgatory, or more accurately, of the ante-Purgatory.

But Dante did not go beyond these slight attempts to set morality on its own feet. How high religion, for him, rises above ethics, becomes clear in the third part of the poem. The moral purification and salvation is completed on the summit of Purgatory in the Earthly Paradise, so that, strictly speaking, Dante's rapt flight through the kingdom of Heaven overleaps all the ethical intentions of the poem. And yet in Paradise also the poet has managed, with scornful and vengeful retrospective

[1] *Inferno*, IV.

glances at sinful earth, to give full expression to his moral indignation. Moreover, since he speaks to mortal readers, and since
in God's loftiest realm goodness flows spontaneously from truth
and holiness, through a perfection which is prototypical for all
creation, it can never be asserted that morality has been excluded by religion. On the contrary, it has cast off its earthly
limitations in Paradise and become cosmic.

> But now was turning my desire and will,
> Even as a wheel that equally is moved,
> The Love which moves the sun and the other stars.[1]

God's grace, which becomes alive in man's affections, is piety;
divine justice, which is mirrored in man's soul, is morality.
By the side of the driving forces of grace and piety stand the
quiet and sustaining ones of justice and morality. Just and
moral is the order in the Hereafter; pardoned and pious is the
path of men through it. Every progress in this journey is a gift
of grace and a consequence of piety; every position won is a
decision of justice and an act of will. Morality opposes evil,
piety aids the good.

It is natural that in Paradise, opposition to evil being no longer
needed, the moral will should merge into piety. Quite the contrary are the conditions in the Inferno. There everything which
the wandering poet has to accomplish may be best summarized
as opposition to evil. There piety remains enfolded within
morality, with no positive, mystical appeal to God. The names
of the divine powers, Father, Christ, the Holy Spirit, and Mary,
may not be uttered there. Dante behaves therein essentially as
a moral personality. But at the central point of the poem, in
Purgatory, out of this moral soil we see blossoming the bright
flowers of piety. All resistance now becomes progress; and all
progress is resistance. Here for the first time the power of divine
grace, which in the Inferno was not indeed absent, but only
faintly felt by the wanderers, appears as a brilliant sun in the
sky. In the first part of Purgatory, justice still has its rights;
moral sins are still expiated. In the second part, purification
is consummated through merciful punishment.

In the *Commedia*, Love progressively grows out of justice.
Everywhere both forces are present, but their influence develops out

[1] *Paradiso*, XXXIII, 143-145.

of the moral into the mystic type; so that the *Inferno* may be
characterized as the stern song of righteous retribution, the
Purgatorio as the joyous and hopeful chant of merciful vindica-
tion, the *Paradiso* as the jubilant hymn of mystic Love. Accordingly, in the plan of the poem mystical aspirations and pious
edification have been theologically assigned to the *Purgatorio*,
and more especially to the *Paradiso*.

Fortunately in Dante the theologian has not stifled the man;
and as man, he remains open to the religious influence where
in the theological plan morality was considered, and vice versa.

This moral quality matches the sentiment of dignity in the
sense that Schiller used this word, and the religious element
responds to the feeling of devotion. From dignified consciousness
of one's own worth to humble devotion to the Divinity, the poet's
soul swings back and forth.

In his work, or more precisely, in his theory, the religious
element is predominant, although the work itself is prevailingly
moral in plan. But now the question arises whether in his life
also, and in his nature, pious devotion triumphs over the dignified
affirmation of his own self.

The quality in Alighieri that impressed his first biographer
was dignity; it was that noble pride which he preserved even
in misfortune. "Our poet," writes Boccaccio, "was of a lofty
and very scornful disposition." [1] As a proof of this, he relates
how the exiled poet indignantly refused to return home under
the humiliating conditions of a brief imprisonment and a public
penance (*offerta*). Boccaccio refers in this connection to a letter
of Alighieri's to a Florentine friend. Happily this precious testi-
monial of Dante's character is extant, and there is no reason
to doubt its genuineness. Nowhere does the disdainful soul,
the *alma sdegnosa* (so Dante characterizes himself, in contrast
with proud spirits) more nobly and powerfully express itself.
He says:

"From your letter, which I received with due respect and
affection, and have diligently studied, I learn with gratitude
how my recall to Florence has been the object of your care and
concern; and I am the more beholden to you therefor, inasmuch

---

[1] *La Vita di Dante scritta da Giovanni Boccaccio*, § 12. Giovanni Villani speaks
similarly in his *Cronica*, IX, 136: "This Dante because of his wisdom was somewhat arrogant, haughty, and disdainful, and as an overwhelming philosopher
he did not know how to talk with common men."

as it rarely happens that an exile finds friends. My reply to what you have written, although perchance it be not of such tenor as certain faint hearts would desire, I earnestly beg may be carefully examined and considered by you before judgment be passed upon it.

"I gather, then, from the letter of your nephew and mine, as well as from those of sundry other friends, that, by the terms of a decree lately promulgated in Florence touching the pardon of the exiles, I may receive pardon, and be permitted to return forthwith, on condition that I pay a certain sum of money, and submit to the stigma of the oblation—two propositions, my father, which in sooth are as ridiculous as they are ill advised— ill advised, that is to say, on the part of those who have communicated them, for in your letter, which was more discreetly and cautiously formulated, no hint of such conditions was conveyed.

"This, then, is the gracious recall of Dante Alighieri to his native city, after the miseries of well-nigh fifteen years of exile! This is the reward of innocence manifest to all the world, and of the sweat and toil of unremitting study! Far be from a familiar of philosophy such a senseless act of abasement as to submit himself to be presented at the oblation, like a felon in bonds, as one Ciolo and other infamous wretches have done! [1] Far be it from the preacher of justice, after suffering wrong, to pay of his money to those that wronged him, as though they had deserved well of him!

"No! my father, not by this path will I return to my native city. If some other can be found, in the first place by yourself and thereafter by others, which does not derogate from the fame and honour of Dante, that will I tread with no lagging steps. But if by no such path Florence may be entered, then will I enter Florence never. What! can I not anywhere gaze upon the face of the sun and the stars? can I not under any sky contemplate the most precious truths, without first returning to Florence, disgraced, nay dishonoured, in the eyes of my fellow citizens? Assuredly bread will not fail me!"

Not only the biographers, but legend as well, seized by preference upon the dignified, self-conscious, stern, and haughty side of Dante's character. He himself in his great poem has not

[1] Evidently a certain Ciolo, otherwise unknown, had already accepted the offer.

delineated himself otherwise.[1] It is wonderful and in the highest
degree surprising how extraordinarily and how finely, in this
mediæval man, the feeling for the dignity of personality is developed, how even the slightest abasement, the most innocent
false step, the most harmless impulse of curiosity or insistence, is
instantly felt as a diminution of his own dignity. The last, the
final, the most delicate fruit of moral consciousness, that is, the
inner sense of decorum, is so unerringly sane and alert in Dante
that it could only have thriven in the worldly and democratic
society and culture of an Italian city-state, hardly in a theocratic
and feudal régime.

We shall see later the relation of Dante's morality to his environment and to his own nature. Here it may suffice to have
shown that the sense of his own dignity accompanies him, constant and true, throughout his life and throughout his task.
Therefore he appears as no puppet but as a complete man. Even
in the supreme moments of mystical devotion, even in the vision
of Divinity, he remains the old vigorous Dante who does not
sink back but still yearns to know:

> As the geometrician, who endeavours
>   To square the circle, and discovers not,
>   By taking thought, the principle he wants,
> Even such was I at that new apparition;
>   I wished to see how the image to the circle
>   Conformed itself, and how it there finds place;
> But my own wings were not enough for this. . . .[2]

Only where his own strength fails does Dante's mystical devotion begin. Had he not been unfortunate, maligned, banished,
maltreated and despised, made desperate amid moral bewilder-
ments and physical hardships, had not his destiny forced him
to the very limit of his endurance—he would hardly have become a
truly pious man, never would he have completed the "holy poem."

"Need teaches how to pray." Great believers of earlier days,
Augustine and Francis, had learned this for themselves. But
with neither of them had conversion been brought about by such
bitter suffering, and neither had required such pressure from
without to make real to him the inadequacy of his own will.
In comparison with Dante, Augustine, Bernard, and Francis

---

[1] Cf. especially *Purgatorio*, XIII, 133–138.
[2] *Paradiso*, XXXIII, 133–139.

appear as natural, born, professional mystics, while from the stubborn material of the banished Florentine only unhappiness could rouse the holy flame.

There was nothing habitual or professional in Dante's piety. I am inclined to call it occasional mysticism, using the word "occasion" not in the sense of a chance occurrence, but of a concrete experience. What is true of occasional poetry applies also to occasional mysticism; they are both a direct, sincere outpouring of the soul, arising not out of chronic exuberance, but from the momentary need of the heart. So there is nothing priestly or ministerial in Dante's piety, nothing of the virtuoso or of the monk. A pious man, but no saint. The lay spontaneity of Dante's piety fundamentally and favourably distinguishes his utterances from the sweetness, sanctity, and fanaticism of all apostles, prophets, and men of God, of ancient or recent memory. It sets him apart especially from the artificially aroused mediæval mysticism. Herein Dante is modern, more modern than a modern preacher.

Since his piety is personal, it creates for itself a personal manner of expression. In its own fashion Dante's poetry covers the whole range of sentiments, from crushing anguish to triumphant exultation.

He even originates certain religious acts, rites, and symbols. Even the traditional usages and functions of the Catholic service, so far as they are retained, acquire a new turn and application. Ordinary Church usage is not disdained, but elaborated, by the personal mysticism of the poet. To name here only a most famous example, I call to mind the profound treatment of the Lord's Prayer.[1] Even the Latin psalms and hymns of which Dante, recalling what is familiar to all, quotes only the opening words, receive new significance and force from the context.

However deeply rooted in personal feeling his religion may be, it yet by preference attaches itself closely to the social usages of the Church. This or that symbol which wakens old and dear memories in a Catholic soul may seem to one further aloof strange or artificial, e.g. the allegorical garbing of Confession in the ninth canto of the *Purgatorio*. But it must be considered how completely the objectivity and the solemnity of his future world depend on its foundation of dogmatic and mystical religion.

[1] *Purgatorio*, XI, *ad init.*

Furthermore, collective and traditional expressions find their full justification, as well, in the very nature of Dante's piety, which is personal only in its origin, not in its effect. The higher it rises, the wider, the more comprehensive it becomes: at first personal, then social, finally universal. Like the stream of Goethe's Mahomet, so Dante's belief grows:

> So it bears along his brothers,
> Bears his treasure, and his children
> To their sire who waits expectant.

The higher we climb, the closer is the communion of the pious. The gradation and separation of the blessed in the *Paradiso* are not real and are introduced merely as a help to our imagination, for "everywhere in Heaven is Paradise." [1]   In this complete unity of sentiment even speech becomes superfluous.   In God's mirror the blessed souls read each other's thoughts.   This magnificent oneness of comprehension Dante has symbolized in the gigantic Heavenly Rose wherein all degrees of blessedness unite. Always more transparent and universal do the forms of expression become, from the hardened rebel Nimrod, who in his verbal confusion understands not a word and howls unintelligible sounds, up to God, Who in silence knows and moves all hearts.

We know how such a spiritual communion comes to be. Not through the power of love alone, for love may, even when strongest, seek blindly an individual goal.   It needs the light of reason, which alone rises from the particular to the universal. The progressive widening of personal piety comes to Dante, as to us all, through dialectical and speculative elaboration of the truth that slumbers in our sentiments. As religion becomes universal and cosmic, it grows conscious of itself. Only philosophy creates universal religions.

Side by side with the progress of religious conversion and moral purification, the *Divine Comedy* shows the growth of philosophic enlightenment.   The moral interest, as we have seen, in the course of the poem passes over more and more to religious devotion. It is otherwise with speculative interest. Its task is to lift the poet's religion from its personal and occasional origin up to an universal and catholic plane. Hence, in the theological plan of the poem, provision is made for a constant increase of

[1] *Paradiso*, III, 88–89.

philosophic investigation. In fact, learned and scholastic explanations take up the greatest space in the *Paradiso*. The scientific interest finally leads to a threefold examination which the pilgrim of the Hereafter must pass, on the fundamental Christian virtues, Faith, Hope, and Love. After that the two highest Heavens open before him and disclose the superhuman beings, the angelic choirs, and the Divine Trinity there enthroned. But not even here have speculation and instruction come to an end; they are not satisfied until the final secret is unveiled in a dazzling ray of divine grace.

Where philosophic inquiry is an end in itself, it appears as theory of knowledge, logic, and metaphysics; where it is a handmaid of religion it takes the form of apologetics or theology; in the service of morality, it becomes ethics. How does it appear in the *Divine Comedy?*

Dante assures us in the dedicatory letter previously mentioned that the dominant philosophic bias of his poem is toward ethics. Even if this testimony be not genuine, it still remains accurate. According to the general plan, philosophic instruction serves the purposes of moral education. Accordingly, the method of teaching is not the logical one of the theory of knowledge, nor is it dialectically apologetic, as in theology. There is not much deduction and discussion, but chiefly instruction, question and answer. This process is conducted in accordance with the varying needs and progress of the pupil. Furthermore, as in every good educational plan, room is allowed for the most complex digressions. Examinations are not omitted, and even prizes might be pointed out, if one had the courage to squeeze the great poem into the mould of a school, a thing which to us moderns seems distressing, but to mediæval men appeared as elevating and solemn.

The pedagogue in Dante did not, however, stifle the man. Although in his plan speculation as a whole was intended to serve educational ends, yet the poet's urge for truth shot far beyond the pedagogic goal.

As to the strength of his thirst for knowledge and the energy of his investigating spirit, the biographers have almost as much to tell us as of the haughtiness of his temper. In the perusal of a book, he could forget everything.[1] He himself states how the study of philosophy consoled him for the loss of his youthful

[1] Cf. Boccaccio, *Vita di Dante*, § 8.

love.[1] We are somewhat doubtful whether he loved to lose himself as often, and as gladly, in pious prayer as in toilsome philosophic thought. One need only read at random in his scientific prose works to convince himself that this fervid poet ran a serious risk of withering away in the most barren and forbidding scholasticism.

Above all, in the last division of his *Comedy*, where he might have been content to lull himself in pious musing—for the moral and therefore also the educational end had already been attained on the summit of the Purgatorial mountain—he plunges deeper than ever into speculative investigation. Doubtless it lay in some measure within the plan of the work that speculation, at first applied to ethics, should eventually become independent inquiry, just as ethics itself must finally be merged in religion; still, conditions here are quite different.

In that Dante set piety above morality, he obeyed the dogmatic tendency of his age and his own theoretical conviction. By nature, he would doubtless have been inclined to reverse this relation; for his character is stronger than his mysticism. But in so far as he accorded an ever greater autonomy and import to speculation, he was following not only the current of the age and of his own scientific convictions, but at the same time the innermost impulse of his nature. For he was much more a thinker than a dreamer or a penitent.

Certainly he himself felt that on the shining heights of Paradise, humble acquiescence became him better than questioning, lecturing, and discussion. How often Beatrice and the saints bid him rest, but he cannot relax, and finds ever new excuses to involve his authorities in scientific conversations. To be sure, that which urges him is no mere pretext, but Truth herself, as he has glorified her in wonderful verses:

> Well I perceive that never sated is
>   Our intellect unless the Truth illume it,
>   Beyond which nothing true expands itself.
> It rests therein, as wild beast in his lair,
>   When it attains it; and it can attain it;
>   If not, then each desire would frustrate be.
> Therefore springs up, in fashion of a shoot,
>   Doubt at the foot of truth; and this is nature,
>   Which to the top from height to height impels us.

[1] *Convivio*, II, 13.

This doth invite me, this assurance give me
With reverence, Lady, to inquire of you
Another truth, which is obscure to me.[1]

That is a courage for the truth as fine as Hegel could demand.

This unwearying zeal for knowledge chains the wanderer to his guides, Virgil and Beatrice. As soon as they have nothing more to tell him, they disappear from his sight. The higher Dante climbs in Purgatory, the more Virgil's wisdom wavers, the more the bond between the two poets is loosened; nor is the case different with Beatrice.

But while he outgrows his teachers, he is not ungrateful to them. Virgil and Beatrice are infinitely more to him than mere schoolmasters; they edify him, console him, and help him as well. In addition to the technicalities of their ethical teaching, he derives from them valuable and broadly human inspiration. The Godhead Itself descends to him through these two human beings.

The ordinary allegorical interpretation sees in Virgil only natural reason and in Beatrice only divine enlightenment, and puts the living creation of the poet on the level of a logical concept. A fine representative of rationalism, this Virgil, who is forever mindful of the inadequacy of his own powers, who constantly looks beyond himself, who longs with mournful melancholy for the supernatural, on whose mysticism a book could well be written! If Dante had really been desirous of a representative of rationalism or of moral philosophy in ancient times, he would have had a wide choice among the great Stoics. And if he had cared more for a great thinker or scholar than for a great character, then nothing would have been more natural than to let himself be guided through Hell and Purgatory by the *maestro di color che sanno*, Aristotle, rather than by Virgil, who was neither a great character nor a great philosopher.

And the same can be said of Beatrice. To embody the conception of divine revelation, there were Old Testament prophets; and if he must have a woman, the Sibyl, or Pistis or Fides in person, was available. If, again, it had to be a personage who had lived since Christ, then there were apostles and saints of either sex in abundance. Why a Beatrice, of whom no one knew anything, who interested nobody, and of whom, even today, despite all symbolic transfiguration, scholars whisper that she

[1] *Paradiso*, IV, 124-135.

was Dante's early love? Is it not a strange device to palm off a youthful sweetheart as the representative of divine wisdom?

Such are the conclusions we reach; such are the misrepresentations of Dante's affections and human interests we are driven to when we try to rebuild the *Divine Comedy* out of abstract concepts. If Dante decided on Virgil instead of Aristotle, on Beatrice and not on a Sibyl, there is but a single reason therefor: the choice of his heart—his affection for Virgil, his love for Beatrice.

The embodiments of those forces that extend beyond what is merely subjective and individual have been attached by Dante to his own cause by the most personal bond imaginable: the bond of reverence and of love. Virgil, his good friend, proclaims human reason and is intended to embody it; Beatrice, a beloved young woman of Florence, teaches the world's religion and is meant to represent it. By a wondrously simple and ingenious stroke, the poet—and only one poet is capable of it—has drawn the superpersonal, spiritual, and divine world into the most human and personal relations. What is loftiest and most universal he has made most intimately his own. And the higher the superhuman rises, the deeper it becomes rooted in humanity. Beatrice, higher than Virgil in the structure of the metaphysical pyramid, stands also nearer to the heart, and even to the sensuous feelings, of Dante.

In this so simple and profound representation, the mediæval artist has foreshadowed the critical discovery of modern philosophy:

> He is but a fool who would seek it outside.
> From within thee once brought, 'twill eternal abide.

Dante's piety moves again and again from emphatic assertion to passionate self-sacrifice. Seen from every side, it is the sharp limitation and seclusion of his own personality which so presses upon the soul that it can only save itself by a mystical regeneration in communion with God. Not like a gentle dawn does the consciousness of the Deity arise in Dante, but, as he relates at the close of the *Paradiso*, it pierces him like lightning. The intensity of the pressure and the force of the regeneration gave to his poetical expression a temper unheard of in the Middle Ages, a form of speech which is all bone, muscle, and motion. And only motion calls into being, as if by chance, the soft and rounded lines and the melting colour-effects. As little in his style as in his piety is there any thought of niceties, of unction, of polish. The religious as well as the artistic harmony is far too rich, and much too hard-won, to serve as a pleasing pastime.

If we once again recall the development of mediæval Christianity, it appears that the deepening of religious feeling, the sharpening of conscience, and the philosophic widening of the foundations of belief, lay more or less heavily on the hearts of Dante's great predecessors Augustine, Gregory, Dionysius, Bernard, and Francis. Each of them brought enrichment in one or another of these directions. Compared to them, Dante brought nothing fundamentally new, unless indeed one should characterize as new his many-sided accumulation and combination of inherited wealth.

As a work of piety, the *Divine Comedy* marks the close of a development that had extended over a thousand years. In a history of religion it can count only for what it is, not for what it brought. It is the conclusion, it is the personal application and utilization of the accumulated wealth of the Christian heart. The long labours of the great Church Fathers, apostles, and saints are here, for the first and last time, made wholly present and living by the fiery spirit of a layman. All that has come to pass within the Church and for the Church is taken possession of by this one man and shaped in conformity with his personal needs. Professional monastic aloofness vanishes as at a magic touch. The Catholic religion, in the *Commedia*, becomes personal. Herein lies Dante's religious originality and modernity. He has worked out, if one may so speak, his own salvation.

At the close of the last chapter, we raised the question: How was it possible that the *Commedia*, a work whose unity is so entirely personal, could have sprung from the soil of Catholic dogma, the unity of which is so impersonal? There we found a one-sided and tentative answer. Dogma, we said, is for Dante not defence, affirmation, or clericalism, but knowledge and revelation; in short, universal truth, within which all convictions find their place. Now for the first time we see the positive and complete answer to the above question: The poet's mighty personality, his will, his emotions, his inquiries, his piety and imagination, have so filled, warmed, and adorned dogma, that bald doctrine has become a fiery and holy confession. Piety and faith have thus come to life. It is their personal touch and quality that give to the *Commedia* its religious value and make of it the symbol of Dante's faith.

II: THE PHILOSOPHICAL BACKGROUND OF THE "DIVINE COMEDY"

I. SYMBOL AND PHILOSOPHY

Religious symbolism has its deadly enemy in rationalism, which ruins it and desecrates it by sundering the historical, temporal forms of the symbol from its eternal significance.

God, who is represented to the religious imagination as king, lord, father, etc., but always as an outward shape, is made over by rationalistic abstraction into a concept which can no longer be felt, believed in, or imagined, but only defined. The personal names, king, lord, father, appear then as arbitrary tags for the abstract concept of the Divinity, with which they no longer have anything to do. Arbitrary these names really are, in so far as other signs, such as sky, sun, stars, earth, bull, boar, etc., could be substituted for them and have actually been so used. In this manner the numberless symbols of all religions become all alike, for they are "arbitrary," each and all. And they also counterfeit reality, in that they set a host of wavering shapes in the place of one sole concept.

From only one point of view, namely, that they constantly guide to the concept of the Deity, they are neither false nor arbitrary. The sole common, accurate, and necessary content of all religious symbols is the assertion of the idea of God. The form in which they assert it (boar, bull, sun, father) is unimportant; the fact that they do assert it is what counts.

What remains, accordingly, of all religions is a direction, an orientation, of men's thoughts toward a most lofty universal concept. And this idea of God may also be called the idea of Being or Becoming, or yet more universally and accurately, the idea of Ideas; for as soon as it is carefully analyzed, it asserts nothing but the act of our conceptual thinking. At this final goal—whether it be called the concept of thinking, of consciousness, or of the absolute; of substance, of spirit, or of Divinity—philosophers have again and again hoped to set up a religion of reason which would be capable of including and replacing all historical religions. But the attempt has never been successful.

Lessing has said that in the religion of reason there is neither religion nor reason. And rightly; for religion without fear, hope, faith, and love for the Supreme Being, is impossible. A concept can arouse neither fear, hope, belief, nor love. Our ordinary usage allows such expressions as "love of beauty, fear of truth, faith in virtue," but by them we never understand the concept of beauty, truth, virtue, but only the representation of works of beauty, etc., whether it be that these works are already existent or yet to be produced, i.e. to be wished for and willed.

In order to love beauty, or the Divinity, we must feel their impress within ourselves and somehow represent them to our imagination. For what we love, in the last analysis, is not they, not the concept of them, for through it we experience nothing, but what they create through our agency, their action and their effect in us, about us, and upon us. But now the philosophic concept also, the idea of Ideas—that, too, reveals itself by its results, in the efficacy of truth, or what is the same thing, by the activity of reason. And this effect, this act, can inspire in us love, hate, fear, and hope. So then there is, after all, a religion of reason. It is not, to be sure, love of or faith in the final concept, but for and in the energy or activity which creates and develops that concept; that is, love of and confidence in the living, actual reason. That is philosophy, in the original etymological sense of the word, which is still valid at the present time! So understood, philosophy is, in fact, a religion, indeed at times the highest form of religion.

This type of philosophic religion is no longer the foe of religious symbols. It destroys, to be sure, the historically conditioned forms of Divinity and takes the life out of mythical representations, not, however, in the name of an antireligious principle, but rather in the name of that very spiritual power which created all existing religions. To this philosophy Schiller's words apply: "What religion do I profess? None, of all those you mention to me.—And why none? In the name of Religion."

Philosophy begins by questioning the validity of symbols. It next discovers their relative value, and finally their absolute foundation. In asserting this last with all the force of feeling, philosophy again becomes religion.

> Common to all is thy thought, thine own is only the feeling.
> Shall it be truly thine own? Feel thou the God of thy thought.

The struggle toward the unity of thought and feeling, of faith and science, of life and concept, is the innermost spring of philosophy. Its whole history is a great untiring quest for the religion of reason, a progressive task in which destructive knowledge and creative belief, doubt, criticism, and speculation, rationalism and mysticism, investigation and religion, vie with each other, overthrow, purify, and strengthen one another.

A philosopher who invents problems for himself, instead of discovering them in the life of his time and of his own inner self, is an idle brooder. Dante's philosophic problems were not scholastic technicalities, but vital questions of his faith and of his poetic creation. His concern was for the salvation of his soul and for the sincerity of his art. He wished to prove to himself that his faith was sufficiently strong, and his art genuine enough, to withstand serious criticism. For no other reason did he submit them to the fiery ordeal of philosophy.

2. Ancient Philosophy

The fundamental opposition between faith and knowledge, as we have outlined it, is most clearly mirrored in the stream of Greek philosophy.

The mythical and cosmic representations of Greek popular belief were, in the beginnings of Greek philosophy, reshaped into general concepts of Being and Becoming. The question then arose: how does Being pass into Becoming, or Becoming into Being? Here rationalism can offer no solution. It is only able to trace the one back to the other; that is, to deny the independence either of Being or of Becoming.

In order to advance further, there was need of a new effort of feeling and will, which could not be derived from cosmic mythology, nor from outward beliefs. It had to spring from within, from the moral and social side of life. The relation of man to man was logically investigated by the Sophists and by Socrates. The concepts of *natural impulse*, *law*, and *morality* come to the fore. But the connection of a natural and political world-order with a moral one could be discovered no more easily by rationalistic means than could that existing between Being and Becoming.

So the Orphics, the Pythagoreans, and Plato introduce into philosophy a new impulse, a kind of belief in redemption, Eros, which was clarified by the more sober Aristotle into the concept of development. Thus the riddle is solved. Through immanent entelechy, Becoming develops out of potential Being, and the moral order grows out of the natural. Aristotle's metaphysics is the most magnificent attempt in antiquity to turn upon the mysteries of belief the light of critical comprehension. "Not the accidents of tradition, but the fact that mediæval religious thinkers in Islam, among the Jews, and in the Christian world, shared his deep interest in this problem, made Aristotle the intellectual leader of the post-Augustinian centuries, and his inner world was widened far beyond the bounds of the Hellenic spirit through the strife between belief and knowledge. The history of his development shows that even behind his metaphysics stands the *credo ut intelligam* ('I believe, that I may understand')." [1]

At this point, the supply of practical impulses was for the time exhausted. The time had come when philosophy undertook to take the place of religion. It was Stoicism that became the loftiest philosophic religion of antiquity.

The moral value of Stoicism is prized even by Dante the Christian. He made Marcus Porcius Cato, the Stoic hero, the guardian of his Purgatory. Such a distinction for a heathen and a suicide has been criticized, and a quest has been made, not without success, for the sources of Dante's knowledge concerning Cato. The profounder and more obvious philosophic reason will reveal itself to us with increasing clearness in the course of the inquiry.

As Dante did not know all Greek thought and belief at first hand, but only in the Latin and Christian elaboration of scholasticism, it seemed to him something complete, valuable and permanent in itself, and not capable of further growth. For him it was settled that human power, of itself, could go no further in clearness of knowledge and in purity and strength of will than Aristotle, *maestro di color che sanno*,[2] and Cato, *il santo petto*.[3] They are for him models, not problems. What they lacked could never be attained by effort, but only accepted and experienced: the grace of divine revelation and salvation.

Therefore Plato, Aristotle, Cato, and the whole "philosophic

[1] Werner Jaeger, *Aristoteles, Grundlegung einer Geschichte seiner Entwicklung*, Berlin, 1923, p. 404.
[2] "Master of those who know," *Inferno*, IV, 131.
[3] "The saintly breast," *Purgatorio*, I, 80.

family"; of antiquity appear in the *Commedia* as eternal and honourable types of the quest for truth and freedom. In their silent dignity and sadness they exemplify the natural greatness as well as the limitations of humanity.

3. The Reaction in the Age of the Diadochi

The Stoic doctrine gave to cultured humanity its balance and support. Pure thought, which everywhere strives for unity, found satisfaction in the concept of a wholly material world, where everything moves in accordance with strict causality, wherein a single force, the vital breath ($\pi\nu\epsilon\hat{v}\mu a$), engenders the elements and life, and rules intelligently as soul, spirit, reason, Providence, and Fate. Pure Will, on the other hand, which craves freedom of action, obtained its satisfaction in the certainty of an absolute Reason, which is strong enough to rescue man from the impulses of his nature and the misfortunes of his life and to uplift him to virtue and thereby to happiness. Virtue, as active Reason, victorious in its strife with nature, is " sufficient unto happiness."

It would be a mistake to think that such a union of theoretical monism and ethical dualism (a union which will always remain the goal) is contradictory in and for itself. In details the Stoic doctrine may have contained ever so many contradictions and unexplained questions; yet it was not an inner contrast of scientific inconsistencies that destroyed and transformed this system, nor was it an immanent critique. The weak point which was eventually to show its inadequacy, namely, the equalization of reason as natural power ($\phi\acute{v}\sigma\iota s$) and as postulate ($\nu\acute{o}\mu os$), was attacked neither by the Stoics nor by their opponents, the Sceptics and Epicureans.

Further progress demanded, therefore, a fundamental change in all relations of life.

The Stoic philosophy was embodied in the self-reliant heroism of the Roman cosmopolite. What it could not explain theoretically, it brought out practically, namely, the power of personality. Not until this power began to exhaust itself and weariness and doubt assailed the Graeco-Roman world did men begin to seek after its roots and to find in it something superhuman and mysterious.

Until then, the universe or cosmos, and man only as a portion thereof (as the microcosm), had been the appropriate subject of philosophy. Thenceforth man and his own worth, not as a microcosm, but as an unique personality, becomes the centre of interest. The cosmos alienates itself from him and becomes, instead of an harmonious and intimate Nature, an uncanny and hostile one.

In this new condition of things, centuries before the Middle Ages we discover that perspective under which Dante philosophized.

Whence came to these forerunners their depth of knowledge and their force of conduct, its epigones asked of the ancient world. Their glance turned from the average and commonplace to the solitary, extraordinary, and individualistic activities of the human spirit. After Nature-worship came hero-worship, and in the place of natural philosophy arose the philosophy of history.

The old theory of knowledge was based on material perception and was itself sensuous; the new one tends to establish itself more and more upon supersensuous revelations and upon authority. It becomes spiritual, mystical, and scholastic. The transition from one to the other may be sought especially in the eclecticism of the last century B.C., of which Antiochus of Ascalon (ob. 68 B.C.) is considered the originator. He found the criterion of truth not in the old theory of knowledge, whether of Democritos or of Aristotle, nor yet in the new, but in an altogether conciliatory "consensus of mankind."

The most prominent and influential thinkers of the Hellenistic-Roman period are Philo, Plotinus, and Origen—a Jewish, a pagan, and a Christian Platonist; for Plato, the discoverer of the supersensible world, becomes again, and now decisively, the guiding mind.

He had realized that concepts are never wholly contained in perception, and therefore are never acquired from that alone. What perception offers us is only an opportunity to discover a concept—not the concept itself. The sight of a beautiful man, a beautiful horse, and the like, reminds us, to be sure, of the concept Beauty; but it does not produce it. Finally, concepts of value such as beautiful, true, useful, good, as well as mathematical concepts, such as equality, circle, sphere, right angle, are never to be found perfect in physical reality; they are, rather, beheld by our mental eye as invisible pictures.[1]

---

[1] An accurate critical and historical exposition of the Platonic doctrine of ideas, such as is attempted by Julius Stenzel in his *Studien zur Entwicklung der Platonischen Dialektik*, Breslau, 1917, lies outside my subject. I am conscious of the crudeness of my outline.

But since, according to the ancient view, the human mind creates and shapes nothing out of itself, but only reproduces that which already is, these concept-forms which arise within us as subjective memories must somewhere exist objectively. Their home cannot be in the physical world. Consequently there must be an incorporeal realm of concepts, the home of the original forms. There the soul had its abode before its entrance into the world of matter; it had beheld and received within itself everything which here below appears to its inward eye, as soon as the outer eye sees the evanescent and incomplete shapes of this earth.

What perception is to concept, material reality is to the realm of ideas. Through perception we acquire incomplete recollections and images of the ideas. Therefore all reality is a mere likeness, $\mu \iota \mu \eta \sigma \iota s$ of the ideas. Here, in this repetition or reflection of the real forms, is to be found the logical root of all mediæval symbolism.[1]

Motionless, eternally pure, absolute, ideas stand out against changing appearances. They must, therefore, if the universe is not to fall apart, operate in one of two ways: either attract the world of appearances upward to themselves, or else flow downward to infuse life into it. Plato considered both possibilities, for he speaks at times of ideas coming and going to and from the bodies, and at others of a yearning impulse that urges bodies upward to the ideas. As a consequence of this, two great systems proceed from his philosophy: the Neo-Platonic system of emanations, and the Aristotelian system of development.

In the development system the idea remains what it is, or should be, in accordance with its dialectic: a pure concept, a cognized immanent norm and form in conformity with which our reason comprehends and Nature works. The idea is the significance of that which occurs, but in and for itself is nothing. It suffices for it to exist subjectively in our minds and objectively

---

[1] Already in Plato the symbolism of numbers plays a decisive rôle. The ideas of empirical things could hardly be for him anything else than numbers, and the value of mathematics lay for him in the fact that it reveals to us a hint of a higher harmony and shows our spirit the way toward the intelligible world of ideas. How he was inspired with this thought by the so-called Pythagoreans, a school of mathematicians which flourished in lower Italy about 400 B.C., is shown by Erich Frank, *Plato und die sogenannte Pythagoreer*, Halle, 1923. Even the Stoics were able to justify their allegorical explanation of popular religions, as well as their experiments in prophecy, only by making a concession, not indeed clear, but still decisive, to Plato's dualistic theory of knowledge in that they placed beside the process of perception that of inward assent, the $\phi \alpha \nu \tau \alpha \sigma \iota \alpha \ \kappa \alpha \tau \alpha \lambda \eta \pi \tau \iota \kappa \eta$.

to actualize itself in Nature.   Aristotle, however, ultimately re-ascribes to pure form a separate existence in the other world, quite analogous to the Platonic ideas.   Only at this one final point does Aristotle's scientific system acquire theological colouring.

Quite otherwise is it with the emanation system.   If the objective world of appearances is to flow from the idea as a result proceeds from its cause, then surely the cause also must have some objective existence, apart and transcendent.   This system, therefore, is theological, not because of a single isolated metaphysical residuum like that of Aristotle, but because of its entire essence.   For it is based upon an ultramundane substance which wavers between concept and representation, appearing now as norm, now as symbol (Divinity).   This manner of thinking, by which philosophical concepts of value are transformed into more or less vague divinities, this hybrid conceptual imagination and mingling of logic and poetry, bears the name of theology.

While Aristotle, then, carried out by preference the philosophic side of the Platonic doctrine of ideas, the Neo-Platonists clung to his theology.   By their work, not through the authority of the Church, philosophy was lowered to the rank of handmaid of theology.   Philo, Plotinus, and Origen are all theologians, not genuine philosophers.   In place of a critique of knowledge, they have set its mythology.   They no longer ask, "What is knowledge?" but only, "Whence does it come?"   And all three are agreed that the power to know is imparted to man by the absolute Being, that is, by the Divinity.   "All knowledge," as Numenius said, "is the igniting of a little light from that great one which illumines the world."   So between divine and human knowledge there can be differences of degree but not of kind.   All science becomes supernatural revelation.   Between true and false there is no fixed border-line, until finally, as in Tertullian, we come to the point of valuing what is most improbable as the highest truth.

In this cloudy mysticism people who had nothing definite to do in the world could be at ease.   Neither the brooder nor the dreamer had reason to criticize this spiritualistic theory of knowledge.

But the Church Fathers, the organizers of Christian belief, must quickly raise a vigorous protest against it.   What would become of their congregation when the emanational fancies of any fool were put on a par with the golden words of Christ? In order to save the historical core of Christianity, a new criterion of divine truth must be discovered and accepted.

It was found in historical coherence, that is, in the correspondence between the divine word and the course of events. That alone is revelation and true knowledge which is borne out by history. This method was laid down for the exegesis of the Sacred Books, and in such a manner that the Old Testament was shown to be the preparation for the New, and the New the verification of the Old. Revelation was seen to be granted by the Divinity according to a progressive, purposeful plan of education, not completed, but still in progress—but exclusively, or at least chiefly, within the channels of the Church's writings and traditions. The Church was regarded as the only interpreter of truth and as the sole voice of the Divinity. Apart from the biblical and ecclesiastical authorities, there was neither assured truth nor knowledge. Fettered instruction, scholasticism, displaced free investigation.

While Neo-Platonism was the chief source of mediæval mysticism, scholasticism, on the other hand, was founded on the Church Fathers, chiefly Irenaeus. Mystical knowledge had its source directly in divine inspiration and ecstasy; scholastic information was received through the Church's authority. For both, however, the acquisition of truth lay through passive reception and acceptance. Therefore both were incapable of going to the root of the problem of knowing. While they both believe that they have discovered the source, they usually neglect to examine the water of that source.

4. MEDIÆVAL PHILOSOPHY

AUGUSTINE

Before the problem of knowledge can be solved, it must be perceived that it exists. Augustine discovered it anew. He is neither scholastic nor mystic, but both at once, and more. In religion he raised the great question: How am I saved? Hand in hand therewith went the philosophic inquiry: How do I attain unto truth?

As the need of salvation and the certainty of it were contained

for him in the consciousness of sin, so the need of truth and the
assurance of it were to be found in doubt. "Should you not understand what I am saying, and be in doubt whether it is true, then at
least consider whether you do not doubt that you are in doubt.
And if you are certain that you are in doubt, then consider how it
is that you are certain. Every man who knows that he is in doubt
knows something true, and concerning this thing which he understands (his doubt) he is certain. He is therefore certain of something true. So every man who doubts if there is 'truth' has
within himself one thing that is 'true' of which he is not in doubt,
and where there is anything true, the truth must be. So he must
not have any doubts concerning truth, who doubts concerning
anything whatever." "If you perceive that the fictions of your
thinking are false, then even if they are not true your realization of it is itself true."[1] Here the inner certainty of one's own
consciousness is expressed, which has sprung up neither from mysticism nor from scholasticism, but out of the thinker's own personality; we are again reminded of Dante's words:

> Therefore springs up, in fashion of a shoot,
>   Doubt at the foot of truth; and this is nature,
>   Which to the top from height to height impels us.[2]

Only that temperament is philosophical which is stirred by
doubt without yielding to it. So mediæval and modern philosophy begins with Augustine, the first to whom doubt was a conscientious necessity and a sacred thing.

In Augustine's conception of doubt, the antithesis of faith and
knowledge, intellect and will, is taken up in a new fashion. Doubting, for him, means to assert, to love, to will the truth. The
problem of knowledge is complicated, enriched, and made difficult
through the introduction of a new factor; namely, the will, with
all the religious and moral anxiety, passion, and trust that go with
it. Between Plato and Aristotle only the relation of ideas to
appearances, or of concepts to perceptions, was considered. But
from this time on, the discussion covers three questions: perception, concept, and will; or appearance, idea, and action; or, again,
sensuous experience, conceptual abstraction, and certainty of

[1] Augustine, De vera Religione, XXXIX, 73. Cf. Huber, Die Philosophie der
Kirchenväter, Munich, 1859, pp. 248–49, and Adolf von Harnack, Augustin, Reflex-
ionen und Maximen, Tübingen, 1922, p. 39 sqq., where the more important
passages are collected and translated.
[2] Paradiso, IV, 130–132.

belief. Behind every error hereafter sin and damnation lurk; and truth alone leads to eternal life.

A new consciousness has now awakened which proclaims that the problem of knowledge is not a separate theoretical concern but that in it the whole condition of spiritual man is bound up. A Faust-like craving for truth, which the Church can barely check, takes hold of the thinking mind, and Dante's whole *Commedia* is carried away by this Augustinian fervour which made him "long for the immortality of wisdom with an incredible surge of the heart." [1]

For the relation between appearance and idea, Augustine harks back to Plato and contrasts with appearances the Ideas, as changeless, general, and impersonal norms. To this he adds that the psychological process of conscious perceptions is completed only by an act of the will, and further, that the relating of perceptions to concepts, and therefore the scientific elaboration of the world of appearances, is made possible only by a teleological and volitional inquiry.

But this very man who, in the psychology of knowledge, emphasizes so strongly the rôle of the will, returns to Greek intellectualism and Neo-Platonic mysticism in the metaphysics of knowledge, when he proceeds to establish the validity of knowledge. We come to know adequately the intelligible world—he teaches—only through enlightenment, which comes from that world itself; that is, God. This statement is, however, in contradiction with the first concept of doubt. For if the intelligible world is opened up to us only through revelation, then surely doubt also should be aroused by an initial enlightenment from above, and not, therefore, through our personal will for truth.

Augustine did not, then, solve the problem of knowledge, but restated it in a new and more fruitful form. The question will not down, and the whole Middle Age will be occupied with it.

THE STRIFE OVER UNIVERSALS

At this juncture it became vital for the further development of the theory of knowledge that it should be again approached from the impersonal and rational side. People did not question the validity of belief, in order afterward to measure thereby the valid-

[1] *Confessions*, III, 7; cf. also Georg Misch, *Geschichte der Autobiographie*, Leipzig and Berlin, 1907, I, 402 sqq.

ity of knowledge, but vice versa. Since that age could not doubt the certainty of belief, it strove before all else to assure itself of the value of science. Only after doubt arose as to belief did the position of the problem of knowledge shift.

The first important philosopher of the Middle Ages, Johannes Scotus Erigena, endeavours to give their rights to knowledge and reason by making them appear identical with revelation and belief; and therein he is a Neo-Platonist and a mystic.

But when he teaches that the universal concepts of reason are antecedent to, purer and more actual than revealed belief, and that the more universal the more perfect and actual they are, he reverts to Plato's idealistic realism. All world-events and world-knowledge seem to him in the last analysis a reflection and revelation from the most universal and most actual of all concepts: God. Being and thinking are to him different sides of the same substance; becoming and believing, on the other hand, the incomplete expressions thereof. His equation—Concept = reality; most universal concept = most actual reality—was never again accepted in the Middle Ages.

The Church treated this bold champion of reason as a heretic. Dante does not seem to have known him at all.

The amiable and tactful Anselm of Canterbury, however, the "second founder of scholasticism,"[1] he did not hesitate to greet.[2]

Anselm clips the wings of reason after she had been strengthened again through realism, and puts her in the service of the Church's belief. The humble duty of philosophy henceforth is to explain proclaimed dogma. Reversing, so to speak, the famous formula *credo ut intelligam*, Anselm tried to help belief to a scientific elucidation of itself. As a matter of fact, two different conceptions of belief are by him constantly confused. That belief which, according to Anselm's *reasons* and *formula*, should be through reason elevated to science, is the truly philosophical one; it is "receptivity to superrational truths," the inner metaphysical experience; in short, the *fides quâ creditur*. That belief, on the other hand, which, according to Anselm's *feeling* and *will*, is in need of philosophic demonstration, is nothing but the authentic Catholic dogma, the *fides quae creditur*.

[1] So he is called by J. E. Erdmann, *Grundriss der Geschichte der Philosophie*, 4th ed., Halle, 1896, I, 274 (Engl. transl., *History of Philosophy*, 4th ed., London, 1910, I, 311).
[2] *Paradiso*, XII, 137.

All of orthodox scholasticism after Anselm suffers from this confusion of terms, which seems natural enough to us when we consider the use to which it was put by the religious communities. People thought they were making dogma into philosophic concepts while in reality they were subjecting the inner experience of a super-sensible world to the doctrinal concepts of the Church. They thought they were rationalizing the *fides quâ creditur*, whereas in truth they were dogmatizing the *fides quae creditur*. They assigned to reason the educational task of guiding the personal convictions of individuals by the path of dialectics into the special and never-to-be-questioned doctrine of the Church. The gap was catechistic and uncritical.

We must not suppose that our poet succeeded in freeing himself from this trend of his age. He had less occasion to do so in that his poem was not intended to convert heathen, to refute heretics, to convince doubters, to oppose scoffers, but only to gratify those who were of his own mind. When, in the realms of hope and bliss where all contests over creed have been triumphantly settled, he arrays the whole dogma of his Church, it is as when at a jubilee over victory the cannon, covered with garlands, are paraded in martial order. The theological examination which Dante submits to in the eighth heaven of his *Paradiso* is intended as a festal performance, not as a penal test of the ignorant or of heretics. In fact, St. Peter's pupil first defines, in clear language, the philosophic faith, and then that of the Church. The first definition he takes from the Epistle to the Hebrews 11:1: "Faith is the substance of things hoped for, the evidence of things not seen," [1] which he explains in detail somewhat as follows: "The profound things which I am permitted to behold here in Paradise are so hidden from mortals down yonder that their reality consists, for them, in mere belief. On this the highest hope is based, and, to that extent, it, the faith, can be called a substance. And from this belief we mortals must draw our conclusions, without having any proof in sight, and to that extent it may be considered an argument." St. Peter proceeds to examine his candidate more closely: " Whence

---

[1] In the text of the Vulgate this reads: "Est autem fides rerum sperandarum substantia, argumentum non apparentium." In Dante:
"Faith is the substance of the things we hope for,
And evidence of those that are not seen;
And this appears to me its quiddity."
Paradiso, XXIV, 64–66.

came to you so joyous a hope?" Whereupon the pupil seizes promptly upon the second, that is, the Church's conception of faith, instead of deepening the first, and continues: "The syllogism which has clearly revealed it to me is the abundant revelation of the Holy Spirit, in the Old and the New Testament, compared with which all other demonstration seems weak to me." But the apostle presses him closer: "How dost thou recognize in the Church's holy books the utterance of God?" "From the miracles," replies the candidate. "Who assures thee that they have actually occurred?" Now the poet brings forth, as his final support, that mystical pantheistical argument of Augustine's, which we have already discussed.[1]

> "Were the world to Christianity converted,"
>   I said, "withouten miracles, this one
>   Is such, the rest are not its hundredth part."

If Dante had been examined by a critical philosopher instead of an apostle, he would have failed at this point, and would have had to thank his Italian fellow countryman Anselm, in the last analysis, for his failure. But, as we are in the ecclesiastical Heaven, the general joy at this last happy turn of the student bursts forth in an unanimous "Lord God, we praise Thee!"

The possibility of integrating by rational evidence, personal belief into the Catholic faith, is what the opponents of Anselm, the Nominalists, disputed. Not that they doubted the soundness either of the personal belief or of that of the Church; presumably both Roscellinus and Gaunilo were men of profound and orthodox faith; at least we cannot assert the opposite with assurance. But they denied the validity of rational concepts. Universal concepts, they taught, are arbitrary abstractions, mere signs and names, to which nothing real either here or in the other world corresponds. It was not belief that they denied, but philosophy, and that too not in the name of faith, but in the name of natural science and of empiricism, in so far as there was any at that time.

The strife over universals never came to a final decision in the Middle Ages, and could not come to any; for just as they had done in ancient times, men continued to confuse the empirical generalizations and concepts of relativity, abstractly derived (especially in natural science), with the metaphysical concepts of form or of value—which are created by reason, and furnish the absolute

---

[1] From this point this whole doctrine of faith seems to be taken by Dante from Thomas Aquinas's *Summa contra Gentiles*, I, 6.

basis for thought. Since Plato had united in a single realm the mathematical concepts of the Pythagoreans with Socrates's conception of virtue, concept of relativity and concept of value lay heaped together. Down to the present day, this confusion has haunted the theory of knowledge, and nominalism, now called empiricism, now sensualism, now scepticism, now materialism, owes to it the ever-welcome opportunity to rob philosophy of its dignity.

As the dogmatic premises of the Middle Ages allowed of no conclusion, a compromise had to be reached. The more important thinkers agreed upon a doctrine of concepts which, as far as the West was concerned, was formulated by Anselm and a few others, who were chiefly dependent on Augustine and on the Graeco-Arabian philosophy of Avicenna. The concepts, it was assumed, are acquired primarily by abstraction from the perception of individual objects. They are themselves, therefore, not real things, but just concepts, i.e. they do not exist as *res*, but *post rem* or *post multiplicitatem*. But abstraction is no casual activity; there must be in things themselves something which necessarily points out to our knowledge the path to abstraction. So the concepts are actually immanent in the objects; they exist *in re* or *in multiplicitate*. Again, the agreement, the normality, the *consimilitudo* of appearances, i.e. that factor which guides us to the abstraction, cannot be casual, but must already from the very beginning have determined the Becoming and the Being of Nature, as something superior and antecedent to it. It must have existed, therefore, as *ante rem* or *ante multiplicitatem*.

This new doctrine of knowledge, which is known by the name of conceptualism, offered the most manifold advantages for philosophic enlightenment. Inasmuch as it allowed the thinker to grasp, for example, the concept "noble" or "speech" as a resultant abstraction, it gave him an opportunity to make himself acquainted, in convenient fashion, with the various types of "nobility" or of "speech." Inasmuch as it reminded him that in these forms there must be some common element, it urged him on to seek after a logical definition of what "nobility" or "speech" is. Inasmuch as it finally convinced him that the definition so found exists as an absolute ideal and pattern, *a priori, in mente Dei*, it gave him the right and the courage to deny and to reject as spurious everything in the historical forms of "nobility" or of "speech" that he had thrown aside as inessential and as not pertinent to the definition.

By such suppositions, and in such a fashion, Dante philosophized on nobility, state, Church, morality, art, speech, science,
and religion.

The next addition is a formal development, the dialectic nimbleness of argumentation "for" and "against," of *sic et non*, and the
pedantic joy in the stringing of authorities and data—a method of
procedure which was developed and made available for later scholasticism by the most ingenious, most belittled, and most dreaded
enlightener and controversialist of the Middle Ages, Peter Abelard
(1079–1142). Not a little of this French liveliness and wealth of
material was inherited by Dante without his having read, it appears, anything of this author. He nowhere mentions him. But
on the one hand the long lists of notable names in the *Commedia*
and the veneration for authors of compilations and of encyclo-
pædias (Hrabanus Maurus, Isidor, Peter Lombard, and Peter
Comestor), and on the other hand the liveliness of citation,
argumentation, deduction, and refutation, make our poet appear
a liberally dowered even if indirect heir of Abelard's spirit.

THE PROBLEM OF INDIVIDUATION

The most violent opponent of Abelard was Bernard of Clairvaux. Not in the name of experience, like the Nominalists, but
in the name of belief and religion, he denied the independence of
reason. The champions of theoretical mysticism, Hugo, Richard,
and Walter of St. Victor, rallied to the side of this advocate of
practical mysticism.

Hugo, without entirely rejecting dialectics, makes of it an instrument, but not the foundation, of religious knowledge. His
theology is based on psychology rather than on philosophy. "The
soul knows nothing rightly if it does not know itself aright. But if
it has learned accurately to observe itself and to know itself, then
no mere appearance, no false reflection of truth on other things,
deceives it."[1] Hugo seeks less after the norms than for the course
of development of the inner life. In that he proceeds from religious experience, he stands out as the most notable reviver of
Augustine's psychology.

This theologizing psychology of development hardly influenced
Dante directly at all. The man who carried it furthest, John of

[1] From the *Soliloquium de Arrha Animae*, cited from A. Liebner, *Hugo von St.
Victor*, Leipzig, 1832, p. 61. On Dante's relation to Hugo and Richard of St. Victor,
cf. Gardner, *Dante and the Mystics*, pp. 144–183.

Salisbury, seems to have been quite unknown to our poet. To be sure, the *Divine Comedy* offers the typical, indeed the most famous, example of the soul's mystical ascent to its Maker, and in as complete a fashion as the Victorines could wish. But the scientific psychology of Dante had little to do with it. What for Hugo was theological method became for Dante poetical reality. At most in the *Convivio*, where philosophic study is not merely represented as adoration and supersensuous love, but is also didactically allegorized, might the question perchance be raised of a direct influence of the Victorines. But after the religious ascent of the soul in the *Commedia* had developed into a fundamentally poetical motif, it could no longer remain the goal of a philosophic quest.

The more clearly the analyses of these mystics revealed the theological outlines of the concept of the soul, the more distinctly did the physiological and the metaphysical concepts of the soul stand out. Out of these conditions arose a new and mighty problem, the question: In what manner do the sensuous and supersensuous potencies and activities unite in the human soul? What is it that gives the soul its unity? Wherein is the *principium individuatonis?* [1] The cleft between the supersensuous and the sensuous which had been evaded in the doctrine of conceptualism now reappears more threateningly in the psychological inquiry.

About the time when the problem of the cause and origin of individuality came up, the influence of Arabian Peripateticism, especially that of Averroës, was making itself felt in Occidental scholasticism. This by no means accidental coincidence marks the beginning of a new epoch, which is for us also the most important in mediæval philosophy (about A.D. 1150-1250). At the same time the theologico-philosophic battle begins to shift more and more from English and French soil to the Italian arena, so that, in time and space, the great spiritual events draw nearer to our poet's range of vision. [2]

However clearly men like Abelard realized the spirit of Aristotelian philosophy in its opposition to Platonism, yet it was only at

[1] This problem is foreshadowed also in Plato's philosophy. Windelband in his monograph, *Platon* (Frommann's *Klassiker der Philosophie*, Vol. X), Stuttgart, 1900, p. 131 sqq., has made clear how the theological and the metaphysical conceptions of the soul are constantly intermingled in Plato's philosophy.

[2] Cf. for this last period G. Gentile, *La Filosofia* (in the series, *Storia dei generi letterarii italiani*), Milan, Vallardi, n.d., pp. 1-142, and Philip Wicksteed, *Dante and Aquinas*, London, 1913.

this time and through the work of the Arabians that a more comprehensive view over the whole system of the greatest Greek thinker was attained, though, to be sure, what the Arabians offered was not the genuine Aristotle but a thoroughly Platonized one.

Aristotle, by the eternal process of creation and development, had wedded Plato's kingdom of ideas to the kingdom of matter, so that there could be no longer immaterial forms, or formless matter. Only at one point had the philosopher pushed pure form as pure Intelligence and ultramundane Divinity over and beyond the successions of becoming.

The two opposed fundamental ideas of immanence and transcendence were carried on to their remotest consequences by Averroës, the last and most important Arabian thinker (A.D. 1126–98). Starting from the idea of immanent form, he arrived at the conception of eternally vitalized matter, and ended in atheistic naturalism. Starting from the thought of a pure and transcendent Intelligence, he reached the conception of an impersonal and immaterial Reason and ended in pantheistic, or panpsychic, supernaturalism. The personality of the human individual falls into the cleft between these two principles: under it, the ever-productive nature of sensuous existence; above, the ever-radiant clarity of pure knowledge; and man divided between the two worlds—one half a dull, irrational animal, the other an ever-thinking divinity.

Thus, then, the unity of the individual was seriously threatened from two sides. The mysticism of the Victorines drew the dividing-line between body and soul; the naturalism of the Averroists drew it between matter and spirit. Nothing less than the immortality of the individual soul and, what is yet more, the value of personality, was at stake. Had Dante's mind been reared on these two conceptions of life, had he been a contemplative mystic or an Averroist—by what right could he have taken with him, on the journey to the other world, his unsundered character, his passions and convictions? By what right could he have dared to say:

> . . . With that swathing band
> Which death unwindeth am I going upward . . .

> . . . God . . . wills that I behold his court
> By method wholly out of modern usage . . .[1]

[1] *Purgatorio* XVI, 37–38; 40–42.

Where would he have found the courage—to put it bluntly—to appear in God's presence in flesh and blood, with clothes and shoes, just as he had come from Italy? That, to be sure, is only semblance and poetry, but under it lies the most real and mighty conviction of the eternal value of individuality.

The scientific justification of this certainty is drawn from the sturdy scholasticism of Albertus Magnus and Thomas Aquinas. Our poet owes to them everything that his intellectual universe shows in the way of firmness, co-ordination, discipline and logical order; his system, in short.

By this I do not mean to say that all Dante's thinking coincides with Aquinas's. Dante was no professional scholastic thinker; less than that on one side, in that as philosophic layman and dilettante he allows himself in his Italian writings inaccuracies of terminology which will keep modern scholars occupied in settling the question, to what school of thought he really belonged; inaccuracies, however, which do not arise from any indecision or vagueness in his thinking, but from the fact that he—and that is the other side—was also more than a specialist in scholasticism and logic; he was a passionate man and a powerful poet.

Furthermore, in his day Albertus's and Thomas's contest against the Averroists was over, and although the fight against the scientific and mystical Nominalists still went on, he yet felt that as popularizer—which he was, and wished to be[1]—he was under no obligation to take an active share in it. This free and human attitude of the cultivated layman toward the specialists enables us to understand why Dante honoured Avicenna and Averroës in his *Commedia*,[2] and placed Siger de Brabant, a Christian Averroist, in Paradise.[3] It would be pedantic to conclude therefrom that he was inclined to Averroism, or was an uncertain follower of the orthodox philosophy. He doubtless appropriated all sorts of material, and by preference much that was picturesque and poetical, or even ethical and political, out of Averroist, Nominalist, Neo-Platonic, Augustinian, Victorine, and Franciscan writings, and in general from all the intellectualist and mystic trends of his age. Nevertheless, his logical basis and his intellectual training remain scholastic and Thomistic.

[1] *Convivio*, I, 1: "And I, therefore, who do not sit at the blessed table, but having fled from the repast of the common folk, at the feet of those who do sit thereat gather up of that which they let fall . . . "
[2] *Inferno* IV, 143 sqq.   [3] *Paradiso*, X, 133 sqq.

The Contest against Averroës

The backbone of the system which is called, after its organizer, the Thomistic, is to be sought where the systems of the mystics and Averroists stand apart: midway between nature and spirit, matter and form, body and soul, sensuousness and reason, reason and revelation. Since all these principles meet in the human being, the chief interest of Thomistic philosophy centres at this point. While the systems of the mystics are prevailingly theological and those of the Arabians naturalistic, it is the anthropological tendency that is peculiar to Thomism. The easiest view, therefore, of this speculative structure can be had by standing at its central point in the midst of its psychology. There is the battlefield where the unity and immortality of the individual are defended against the attacks, above all of Averroës and of Averroism.

If, as Averroës assumes, man is only a product of vitalized matter, and if beyond this exist only pure Intelligences, i.e. immaterial rational essences, then it follows that:

1. We are no more immortal than the other living creatures, since the principle of our individuality lies within mutable matter.
2. We cannot rise to purely rational comprehension, i.e. to philosophy, through our own efforts, since the principle of reason lies outside of matter.

Nevertheless, Averroës, who regarded himself as a philosopher, must after all have found a way to bring together individuality and rational comprehension. But since the individual could not rise to reason, reason must descend to him. Of himself man possesses, according to Averroës, only what other animals have, though in a higher degree: the power to form sensuous representations and to weigh one of them against the other, a *vis aestimativa*, or, if we will, a "material understanding." Whenever man, in his blind impulse, develops certain representations to some degree of clearness, pure reason from above is imparted to him, i.e. radiating downward from the sphere which lies nearest our earth, the Heaven of the moon. From the streaming of this lunar intelligence into the human brain, philosophy arises. Of course it is not the whole Intelligence that flows to us, not the entire *intellectus immaterialis* and *activus;* it illumines our representations only according to the special need and opportunity. This occasional union is called by Averroës *intellectus possibilis*, to distinguish it from the *intellectus activus*, which is the subsistent form itself. The result of this occasional union he calls the acquired intellect—the *intellectus adeptus*.

When the philosopher was challenged to explain how each single individual attained to a particular and different amount of knowledge, he answered with a figure of speech that has become famous, and which Dante also made his own: Just as the sun's light, common to all, falling upon different bodies creates various hues according to their diverse colour-receptivity, and yet preserves its separate oneness as an illuminating power, even so does the active intellect exert its influence differently upon different individuals. This Neo-Platonic figure of the effect of light, which pours from above over the world, precisely because it was a figure and not a logical concept could be utilized also by men of other minds, and was useful and popular for the entire cosmology and cosmogony of later antiquity and of the Middle Ages.[1]

Averroism gave it a special turn, making Truth, one and eternal, appear under a thousand varying shapes to the brains of men; and showing how pure philosophic knowledge, darkened and diversified by contradictions, shimmers varyingly in the popular religions. Compared with philosophy, no single religion possesses Truth; compared with one another, they possess each a separate fragment thereof. Yet every priest values his own creed as the fool his cap and bells. But the wise man keeps the genuine coin in his purse and smiles, letting believers quarrel over the value of their counterfeit money. There is a truth *secundum fidem*, and that is the false gold which men accept and will forever value, and another truth *secundum rationem*, and that is the good metal which only few possess. With their famous formula of twofold truth, the Averroists, who in the course of the thirteenth century became more and more numerous in France and Italy, protected themselves against the persecutions of the Church, and at the same time made merry over that Church's creed.

So this far-reaching system hides in its bosom truth and duplicity, daring enlightenment and hypocritical toughness. Therefore the struggle of the great scholastics against this dualistic school was not only over the value of personality but also on behalf of honesty.

[1] *Paradiso*, I, 1 sqq.; II, 112 sqq.; VII, 67 sqq.; and XIII, 52 sqq.

Among the keenest and most fruitful arguments advanced by Albertus and Thomas against the Averroist doctrine, we should note the following. If rational knowledge comes to us as enlightenment from without and from above, then the fact of self-consciousness cannot be explained. Self-consciousness comes neither from the sensuous perceptions and representations of the individual, nor from an impersonal World-Mind. The sensuous perception is never conscious of its act, for "no sense knows itself. The eye is not aware of itself, and does not see that it sees." This knowledge is therefore due to a higher but personal faculty, the intellect. Furthermore, the intellect itself does not know itself by its essence, but by its act. By its nature it is directed toward the sensuous perceptibility, and only through the outer world of appearances can it arrive at self-knowledge. Self-consciousness is the reflected action of the intellect. Thus, an intelligence which enlightens us from without can produce knowledge but no action, hence also no reflection, and therefore no self-consciousness. When a sunbeam strikes a wall, the latter becomes visible but sees not. So the wall cannot know the sunbeam, much less itself.[1]

In this argument St. Thomas takes up again Augustine's conception of doubt and gives it that positive turn which was to acquire complete distinctness in Descartes's *cogito, ergo sum*. In other respects he was able neither to utilize nor to hold fast to this fruitful thought. With him as with Augustine, the concept of act remains limited to the psychology of knowledge, and vanishes as soon as we pass over to the metaphysics of knowledge. In other words, Thomas distinguishes the essence of the soul from its effects—as though its essence could be anything else than its activity. Here in the separation of essence from its action, in this sundering of substance from act, in this assumption that substance is not act alone, but *potentia* plus *actus*—as if the concept of *actus* did not include within itself the concept of potency as *non-actus*—here lies the logical root of error.

The Thomistic Doctrine of the Soul

So in Thomas, too, the intellect which in the polemic against Averroës had been defined as act, again is petrified into a substance made up of action and non-action, of *actus* and *potentia*.

[1] Cf. Thomas, *Summa contra Gentiles*, II, 59 sqq.; *Summa Theologiae*, I, i, Qu. 87, Art. 1.

And now arises the perilous question: What is the relation of the immaterial soul-substance of conceptual thinking to man's material body? Whoever raises this question has in truth already completed and acknowledged the separation of soul and body, and will hardly again unite the two into a single individual.

Nevertheless, Thomas accomplished the best that was possible under these unfortunate conditions. Where lies—this was the question—the *principium individuationis?* Some placed it in the material body, and thereby fell into Averroism; others assigned it to the immaterial soul-substance, to the pure intelligence, and thereby were compelled to admit the existence of as many intelligences as there are individuals, of as many rational truths as there are heads, as many spirits as human noses; they fell into nominalism, scepticism, mysticism, and relativism.

These perils Thomas had seen and considered. Therefore, to state it briefly and clearly, he put the principle of individuality neither in matter nor in form, neither in the body nor in the soul, but in the occasional union[1] of the two. To be sure, Thomas could not but hesitate to think out and state this relation as clearly as we do. For if the principle of individuality lies in this occasional union, then after the dissolution of this union by death, the individual perishes, principle and all. Therefore he chose a more obscure expression, and taught that every soul is made commensurate with its body. This body, so fitted and disposed, he called *materia signata.*

Certainly a deep philosophic meaning, as Giovanni Gentile rightly says, lies hidden in this conception of *materia signata* and the *commensuratio,* that is the thought that the spirit does not tumble down blindly and headlong into matter, but that it progressively and gradually prepares and stamps the linked chain of organisms in which it proposes to unfold itself. What is philosophically valuable in the *materia signata* and *commensuratio* is the fundamental conception of a constantly acting teleological principle.

Viewed from this side, Thomas's doctrine saved the conceptual unity of the soul for his metaphysics also, albeit most narrowly. It is in the domain of theology that he finally loses it.

---

[1] I say occasional union, not union in and for itself; for as to this union it is yet to be determined whether it exists necessarily and permanently, i.e. formally, or contingently and temporarily, i.e. materially. The escape from this by putting the principle of individuality in the union as such was reserved later for St. Bonaventura. But he veiled the question instead of answering it.

For everything which in the concept of *materia signata* had not been fully elaborated with philosophic clarity takes on, in his theology, the shape of a mythical shadow. The dim remaining fragment of the *materia signata* becomes a supernatural product, and what remains of the *commensuratio* becomes an immaterial body.

The doctrine of the creation of the human soul most unmistakably forces Thomas back into dualism.[1] From organic generation only what is organic and perishable can arise, not that eternal substance which is the human soul. First the mere embryo is generated with a vegetative soul, which is able of itself to develop next into the animal stage. Here the power of Nature ends, and there is need of a divine miracle. God creates out of nothing an immaterial, rational soul, and forges it into an eternally indissoluble oneness with the natural soul of the embryo, as soon as the latter is sufficiently developed.

This doctrine of creation which stamps man as the product of two master workmen, Nature and God, and which appears to the modern eye a piece of physiologico-theological patchwork, is unconditionally accepted by Dante, and set forth as in the following verses:

> The perfect blood, which never is drunk up
> > Into the thirsty veins, and which remaineth
> > Like food that from the table thou removest,
> Takes in the heart for all the human members
> > Virtue informative, as being that
> > Which to be changed to them goes through the veins
> Again digest, descends it where 'tis better
> > Silent to be than say;[2] and then drops thence
> > Upon another's blood in natural vase.
> There one together with the other mingles,
> > One to be passive meant, the other active
> > By reason of the perfect place it springs from;
> And being conjoined, begins to operate,
> > Coagulating first, then vivifying
> > What for its matter it had made consistent.
> The active virtue, being made a soul
> > As of a plant (in so far different,
> > This on the way is, that arrived already,)

[1] He could not do otherwise, for from the Lateran Council of the year 1179, the doctrine of the creation of the human soul was canonically settled.

[2] This is founded on the ancient view that the seed is prepared out of the heart's blood.

Then works so much, that now it moves and feels
    Like a sea-fungus,[1] and then undertakes
    To organize the powers whose seed it is.
Now, Son, dilates and now distends itself
    The virtue from the generator's heart,
    Where nature is intent on all the members.
But how from animal it man becomes
    Thou dost not see as yet; this is a point
    Which made a wiser man than thou once err [2]
So far, that in his doctrine separate
    He made the soul from possible intellect,
    For he no organ saw by this assumed.
Open thy breast unto the truth that's coming,
    And know that, just as soon as in the fœtus
    The articulation of the brain is perfect,
The primal Motor turns to it well pleased
    At so great art of nature, and inspires
    A spirit new with virtue all replete,
Which what it finds there active doth attract
    Into its substance, and becomes one soul,
    Which lives, and feels, and on itself revolves.[3]
And that thou less may wonder at my word,
    Behold the sun's heat, which becometh wine,
    Joined to the juice that from the vine distils.[4]

All this, to be sure, is in itself neither science nor poetry, but yet a notable mingling of both; in which the spirit, half understanding and surmising, half guided by faith, uncertain and reverent, approaches the mysteries of Nature somewhat as in Goethe's poem on the metamorphosis of plants, but with more seriousness and less grace. It is the naïve expression of an unclarified, half-rational, half-mystic view of the world.

        So grasp thou unflinchingly
        The open, holy mystery!

With a similar mixture of criticism and sacred awe, Dante had related this same tale of creation in Italian prose before he moulded it into the concise verses of his *Commedia*.[5]

---

[1] The sea-fungus was looked upon in ancient biology as a zoophyte. Throughout this entire scientific explanation, Dante follows Aristotle quite closely. Cf. Edw. Moore, *Studies in Dante*, I, 136 sqq.

[2] The allusion is to Averroës.

[3] Dante here takes the reflective action of self-consciousness as the highest characteristic of the human soul.

[4] *Purgatorio*, XXV, 37–78.

[5] *Convivio*, IV, 21.

But what will happen after death to this naturally generated and yet divinely created human soul? The substance created by God and breathed into the embryo is invulnerable and imperishable. It must accordingly live on, after the death of the body, as pure divine breath without any individual limitations, somewhat as a fluid pours forth into space and is diffused—not indeed destroyed, but lost as soon as the vessel which held it goes to pieces.

But it is precisely with the individual permanence of the divine breath that the Church and its philosophers are concerned. By its entrance into the material body, this breath has, so to speak, become compact. The outlines which were given to it by this vessel it preserves eternally. Indeed it succeeds, by a wonderful feat, in communicating its own indestructibility to the individual outlines which it has itself assumed. The individuality is imparted by the body to the imperishable, rational soul, which in turn bestows its immortality upon the individuality—a process which may be compared with the casting of a bronze statue. The plastic individual form is transferred from the fragile clay to the enduring metal. The soul has, in the course of a lifetime, so felt itself as one with its natural shell that the feeling of it remains even when the husk falls off. It has appropriated the idea of the body, so that not even in the Hereafter can it escape from its longing for that body. Like an egg without its shell, it drifts through eternity.

Justice and logic demand that at the end of time this homesickness shall be allayed, and that the shell-less soul shall receive once more a material, but this time an imperishable, body.

A soul that thirsts for a body, which has won for itself the idea of its body, which retains its fitness for the body, which cannot lose its memory thereof, and yet has lost its actual body, finds itself in an unnaturally hybrid and transitional state that craves for a solution and arouses the speculative imagination of the theologian as well as that of the poet. This difficulty and its solution, the systematization of the realm of the dead and its graphic representation, have to our understanding the charm of a riddle, and for the imagination the lure of a mystery. The most important thinker, Thomas, and the most important poet, Dante, have therefore busied themselves with equal zeal on this problem, the philosopher striving to solve the riddle, the poet endeavouring to behold the mystery.

We today believe that we have come to realize the uselessness of the undertaking, and all these efforts over a question wrongly put must annoy and weary us as mere trifling; and they would, if a deep and profitable thought did not lie hidden behind them, i.e. the thought that spirit rules matter, and that the meaning of life—whether viewed from this world or the next—consists in ever and again mastering, shaping, and spiritualizing obdurate matter. This thought makes the modern mind sympathetic toward the mediæval preoccupation with the Hereafter.

After death, and until the Last Judgment—so Thomas teaches —the human soul has neither frame nor body. Nevertheless, it does not cease to exist and to know. Sensuous impressions, indeed, it cannot receive, having no longer material organs. All individual objects are shut off from it except that type of supersensuous individualities of which it is itself one. Therefore the dead man himself knows most clearly of all—more clearly and more directly than do the living. This utterly naked self-comprehension is joy for the good, torture for the sinful. With similar clarity the dead man beholds unveiled the departed sister soul.

Of his physical organism the spiritually conditioning principles remain, but no longer the capacity for bodily action. Likewise the sensuous perceptiveness remains, but as a closed memory, as a storehouse which can receive no more accumulations. His glance is turned backward and inward; he lives a retrospective and introspective life. He is absolutely and wholly absorbed in the joy or in the pain of his own worth or worthlessness. Furthermore, being a spiritual substance, he recognizes all the spiritual substances above him—the angels, i.e. the higher intelligences, and the Divinity. These, however, only according to the measure of his own being; not as they are in themselves, but as they are reflected immediately in the narrower frame of his individuality. Accordingly, the damned behold a terrible God, the saved a clement one, and in general each soul has an understanding of the higher intelligences that is proportionate to the magnitude and colouring of its own personality. Whether the soul is also able to perceive anything of the progress of life and activity on the surface of the earth depends on God's grace, for the soul can no longer immediately apprehend what is going on here among us; it can only know immediately through the mirror of the Divinity, since it is no longer held down by intuition to the accidents of reality, but is enabled now to grasp its abstract, universal essence. Of the particular it can seize only what hangs now and then in the wide meshes of its conceptual net. These will usually be events whose preparation and foreshadowing it had already observed with earthly eyes before death, or those to which it is bound through an inclination of its own will, or which God for any reason sees fit to make known to it. So a more or less fragmentary, dim, and inexact knowledge of the earthly present and future does indeed lie within its range of vision.

What is said of the intellect applies also to the will. It, too, after death is directed, above all else, inward and backward upon itself and its past. The departed soul strives upward and forward only in so far as God determines. Yet it is also able of its own free will to affect, by its joy, sympathy, or malice, the condition of kindred souls. The idea that the blessed rejoice in beholding the tortures of the damned[1] is a logical result of this profound speculation. Those who for this reason accuse the great Dominican of savagery of soul understand neither his philosophy nor his character. On the contrary, any one who interprets the problem of the condition in the Hereafter aright will be able to admire the ingenuity of this solution. A dreamlike community of irrevocably banished souls, ranging between darkness and light, bondage and freedom, stubbornness and self-surrender, independence and helplessness, the inner doom of a half-disembodied, half-senseless spirit, cut off from the natural world and yet wholly dependent upon it, has never again been shaped into psychological conceptions with such knowledge of mankind and such mental keenness.

Within this frame, the departed souls of the *Commedia* move. This remarkable next-world psychology is one of the most fruitful poetical motifs that Thomas's theology could present to our poet. This becomes more convincing if the state of things be reversed. Let us try, accordingly, to analyze the mental state of each soul portrayed by Dante, and to formulate in general terms the conditions to which all, damned and blest, are alike subjected. Immediately we are forced to recognize in our analysis the outlines of a psychology which coincides with that of Thomas. When, for example, Farinata degli Uberti explains that to the damned not present but only future events are visible,[2] we find the key to this strange condition in Thomas's psychology of the Hereafter.

[1] Thomas, *In Sententias*, IV, Dist. 46, Qu. I, Art. 3, *ad quart.*
[2] *Inferno*, X, 100 sqq.

Occurrences which are still in the lap of the future, that is, in the Spirit of God, can be unveiled only by an act of God's grace, and in universal terms, to the disembodied eye of the departed ones; but as soon as the event has passed out of the future into the present, and thereby out of God's spirit into the world of phenomena, it escapes the vision of the departed. Thomas has, so to speak, formulated the natural laws which encompass the life of Dantesque souls. To be sure, just as the infinite variety of natural phenomena is never completely covered by laws, so in the poetical world of the *Commedia* a multitude of incidents can be pointed out for which Thomas's constructive doctrine offers no formula.

This variance, which I might call inevitable, between natural law and actuality, is seen in the Dantesque souls which move and walk visibly before the wanderer's eyes, while Thomas expressly denies to the dead any sort of fleshlike raiment. This exception whereby things invisible are made visible is imposed by artistic consideration, and demands no special justification. Thomas himself used the simile, then so popular, of the seal that is stamped upon the wax, to illustrate his doctrine of the union of the pure soul-substance with the material body. Dante, however, tried to offer a scientific justification. And therein he did indeed actually depart from Thomas's doctrine, ascribing to the figments of his imagination the significance of an actual occurrence, and treating his own poetry as if it were external reality. We shall have to speak again later of this naïve and amusing belief in the objective validity of a subjective vision, but we must first see how Dante goes on to describe the dooms of human souls.

> Whenever Lachesis has no more thread,
> It separates from the flesh, and virtually
> Bears with itself the human and divine;
> The other faculties are voiceless all;
> The memory, the intelligence, and the will
> In action far more vigorous than before.
> Without a pause it falleth of itself
> In marvellous way on one shore or the other;
> There of its roads it first is cognizant.
> Soon as the place there circumscribeth it,
> The virtue informative rays round about,
> As, and as much as, in the living members.
> And even as the air, when full of rain,
> By alien rays that are therein reflected,
> With divers colours shows itself adorned,

So there the neighbouring air doth shape itself
   Into that form which doth impress upon it
   Virtually the soul that has stood still.
And then in manner of the little flame,
   Which followeth the fire where'er it shifts[1]
   After the spirit followeth its new form.
Since afterwards it takes from this its semblance,
   It is called shade; and thence it organizes
   Thereafter every sense, even to the sight.
Thence is it that we speak,[2] and thence we laugh;
   Thence is it that we form the tears and sighs,
   That on the mountain[3] thou mayhap hast heard.
According as impress us our desires
   And other affections, so the shade is shaped.[4]

According to Thomas, after the dissolution through death the material outline (*commensuratio*) has taken the place of matter; in Dante, air has taken the place of flesh. Thomas taught that not men, but certainly the higher beings, angels and devils, have the gift of endowing themselves with physical outlines and colours by thickening the air.[5] Dante, for the sake of his poetry, has bestowed the same gift on mankind. An essential deviation from Thomas's doctrine, or even as has been surmised a conscious adherence to the Neo-Platonists Clement and Origen, or to St. Bonaventura, I am unable to discover here.

Whether in the biology of this world or in that of the Hereafter, whether in the history of man's origin or in his doctrine of immortality, Thomas was unable to escape dualism. The idea of immortality is in fact, as we have seen above, the creation of dualism. It stands and falls with it. The supernatural side of Averroism, the doctrine of an impersonal and separate reason, offered a chance of escape. But the complete conquest over the contradiction between nature and spirit would have cost him Christian salvation and Paradise, together with his personal God.

"The Dominicans," says Gentile, "proud of the fame which their order won through St. Thomas's philosophy, were certainly not wrong when in the portraits of their great brother painted in their churches, Santa Caterina at Pisa and Santa Maria Novella

---

[1] The ancients distinguished the common element fire from the individual manifestations of its flames.
[2] Statius's ghost here speaks.
[3] We are on the Purgatorial mountain.
[4] *Purgatorio*, XXV, 79–107.
[5] *Summa Theologiae*, I, i, 76.

at Florence, they had him represented as vanquishing the Arabian
Averroës, who lies at his feet, overthrown by Dialectic. But Averroës, though vanquished in psychology and in his metaphysical
doctrine of the principle of individuation, had been able, without
laying down his arms, to take refuge in the last stronghold of his
philosophy; namely, in his doctrine of the eternal contrast between God and the world." [1]

The necessity, however, of separating the theological from the
purely physiological concept of the soul, and of accepting at this
point the inevitable split, made it all the more indispensable to
insist at least upon the specifically psychological unity. [2]

The three powers of the soul, rising from the *anima vegetalis* to
the *animalis* or *sensitiva*, and thence to the *rationalis* or *intel-
lectiva*, were arranged in such a manner that the higher was always
prepared by the one next below it. This view is in direct opposition
to the mechanistic solution offered by Platonism and further developed by Augustine and the Victorines, which arrayed the
soul in three distinct superposed strata. Thomas has the three
faculties rather growing, as it were, one out of the other. Indeed
he even goes so far as to assert that the *anima sensitiva* develops
out of the *anima vegetalis* in such a manner that the lower form
is destroyed by the higher and absorbed without a residuum. [3]
Dante has not, to be sure, literally made this doctrine his own.
In the *Convivio* he still calls the lower the basis (*fondamento*) of
the higher faculty. [4] He does not ascribe the entire generative
power to the human seed, and in order to explain the mystery of
growth he has recourse to the supposition of a magic influx of the
stars, ascribing to the heavens an importance that conforms more
with the doctrine of Albertus Magnus than with the teachings
of Thomas. [5] At a later period he presumably gave up again
this supernatural explanation, this fragment of a Neo-Platonic
emanation-theory. At any rate, in the *Purgatorio* [6] he is able to
corroborate effectively the closest possible dependence of the

[1] *Op. cit.*, p. 61.
[2] On the details of the Thomistic and Dantesque psychology, cf. the excellent
sketch by Philalethes in his German translation of the *Divine Comedy*, Part II,
Dresden and Leipzig, 1849, p. 182 sqq., as well as his commentary on *Purgatorio*,
XXV; also Wicksteed, *Dante and Aquinas*, London, 1913, Chapter VI.
[3] *Summa Theologiae*, I, i, Qu. 118, Art. 2.
[4] *Convivio*, III, 3.
[5] *Ibid.*, IV, 21: "And the formative power prepares the organs for the celestial
influx which, from the potency of its seed, brings the soul to life."
[6] *Purgatorio*, IV, *ad init.*

powers of the soul by means of the concept of psychological concentration:

> Whenever by delight or else by pain,
>   That seizes any faculty of ours,
>   Wholly to that the soul collects itself,
> It seemeth that no other power it heeds; [1]
>   And this against that error is which thinks
>   One soul above another kindles in us. [2]
> And hence, whenever aught is heard or seen
>   Which keeps the soul intently bent upon it,
>   Time passes on, and we perceive it not,
> Because one faculty is that which listens,
>   And other that which the soul keeps entire;
> This is as if in bonds, and that is free.

In other words, the meditative reason has, at the moment of listening, become all ear.[3] It is, accordingly, to use a modern expression, not the "parallelism" but the reciprocal influence of sensuousness and reason upon which the unity of the human soul establishes itself. Man is the central point of the universe, in which, actively and passively, the natural powers come in contact with the supernatural. At one time the spiritual wave overflows the sensuous earth within him; then again that which is material declares itself within him, and the spirit ebbs away. Scientifically the shore-line between them stands firm. But in the events of human life it depends on the behaviour of the individual whether he is to take his stand on fruitful soil, open to the divine sea, or upon a stony dike. The ethical shore-line is movable; the freedom of the will is saved.

The Ethical System of Thomas [4]

Averroës, by denying to man a personal reason, deprived him of the freedom of the will. For Socrates, Plato, Averroës, Thomas, and to a certain extent Aristotle, were agreed as to this: that they made the will dependent on the reason. They were one and all

[1] The reference is to the Platonic (perhaps also to the Manichaean) doctrine of the soul, which had already been refuted by Aristotle and Thomas. Gentile, *op. cit.*, p. 137 sqq., surmises that Dante was thinking of the doctrine of Pier Giovanni Olivi, which was condemned as heretical by the Council of Vienne, A.D. 1311.

[2] *Purgatorio*, IV, 1–12.

[3] Cf. *Convivio*, II, 14: "Music besides draws to itself the human spirits (which are like vapours of the heart) so that they become almost inactive. For the soul then becomes totally wrapt in it and the power of all the other sensitive spirits rushes, so to speak, towards that one which receives the sound."

[4] A fuller account of the ethical system is given in the third section of this work.

intellectualistic determinists. To them the will is free only in that it follows reason, and free only so far as it is able to follow it. The freedom of the will is its rationality. Only the rational man is virtuous; the virtuous alone is free. Neither virtue nor freedom of the will was given to us as a cradle gift. They must be won by effort; they are values and ideals, not accomplished facts.

These thinkers, however, did not completely understand by what efforts it is won. The state of things in which a man sees what is right, but has not the strength of will to attain it, was known to them; but they paid little attention to it and were inclined to evade the question. They clung firmly to the profound and, in the last analysis, accurate idea, that he who is completely and entirely possessed of the whole truth can no longer will evil, having already realized the good. From this profoundest insight they drew the hasty conclusion that the will has only a rational or irrational quality, but no foundation, no essence of its own, as if it were a bridal gift which the intellect regularly and transiently received at its ephemeral wedding with truth, an accident of the intellectual substance, not a substance in itself. So it came to pass that the contest between scholasticism and Averroës was fought and settled, not over the doctrine of the will, but over that of the intellect, and that Thomas, by assuring to man his individual reason, gave him at the same time his individual will.

Thomas's Dialectics

But this intellectual determinism has another result, decisive for the doctrine of the gradual progress of human knowledge. That is, if it is true that the will is an accident of reason and receives from it its content and its freedom in such a way that the purer the reason, the freer and fuller the will, then it must also be true that a certain stage in the development of reason must finally be attained in which the highest truth appears as an object not only of reason, but also, at the same time, of the will. It may therefore be said that the more indispensable and evident the participation of the will in the acquisition of knowledge becomes, the nearer we are to ultimate truth. From the more or less involuntary to the more or less voluntary knowledge, from science to faith, from philosophy to theology, we have an organic gradation and transition.

This chain of thought, contained and hidden in intellectual determinism, was accurately brought out by Albertus and Thomas.

With a simple and clever touch they set Aristotle on ecclesiastical ground. Nor did they drag him thither, but rather led him by the leading-strings of his own doctrine.

Now the problem is solved which Anselm of Canterbury stated: How can reason be put at the service of dogma, and philosophy be made the servant of theology? The answer is: Reason, in accordance with its nature, rises beyond itself and develops into the Catholic faith and dogma. Order is also brought into the relation between the two concepts of belief. Philosophic belief, or "receptivity for metaphysical truth," is nothing else than incipient Catholic belief, at first existing only potentially, which, however, strengthened by reason, develops into the pure dogma of the Church. The Averroist doctrine of the two truths is thus deprived of its force, for rational truth now appears as a lower, and, to be sure, diverse—not contradictory, but rather introductory—aspect of the truth of faith.

Philosophy thus takes on the rôle not so much of a handmaid as of the mother of theology. What harm if the daughter is nobler than the mother, the egg wiser than the hen? Reason and philosophy have once more regained their rights.

Heresy, thus driven from its position, is not downed, and soon reappears from another direction. If reason has within itself the power to rise to faith, what need then of revelation, what need of ecclesiastic authority?

The time has now come to set down accurately and unmistakably the boundaries between the philosophic and rational domain on one side and that of theology and religion on the other. Just as between beast and man, so between reason and revelation the continuity of development, already established, must be again interrupted. A separation as to materials and objects could not be seriously considered; for from the beginning philosophy had taken possession of the questions that concern religion and the future life. Accordingly, the distinction must be one of method. Such a one was elaborated in the traditions of the Dominican order. St. Dominic had set as the paramount task for himself and his followers the refutation of heretics by means of rational arguments. He was, to use Dante's words, the "saintly athlete":

> Then with the doctrine and the will together,
> With office apostolical he moved,
> Like torrent which some lofty vein out-presses;

And in among the shoots heretical
  His impetus with greater fury smote,
  Wherever the resistance was the greatest.[1]

So it was only natural that his best followers, Albertus and
Thomas, should in combating religious errors limit their task to a
sort of negative or defensive communication of the truth. What
revelation gave and theology positively construed, philosophy must
protect against the attacks of doubters. It is not, however, nor
could it be, its task to strive for new revelation; God alone can
create divine truth.

Philosophy, then, was looked upon as criticism, not of revelation,
but of men's opinions. While it refuted and corrected, it must not
appeal to revelation, which was the very thing unbelievers denied.
Not from the Church's armory, but from the common arsenal of
mankind, from reason, it must draw its weapons.

Since philosophy had fought with its own weapons it had become
independent. Since it had limited itself to criticism it had become
conscious of its own innermost nature, had renounced all enthusi-
asms, and had grown sober and serviceable.

Such a self-assured philosophy could be trusted and loved once
more by all who were tortured with doubt and by those who had
scientific interests. After swinging for centuries between rash
speculation and timorous retreat, philosophy found its equilibrium
and centre of gravity in criticism. As when Kant in his time set
critical reason firmly on its own feet, so in the very bloom of scholasticism a general almost irresistible passion for philosophy took
possession of men's minds. It was the beginning of one of those
rarest and best moments of humanity, in which philosophy is
honoured and universally beloved. One need only recall the enthusiasm with which Schiller studied Kant's works; then he will
understand the reason of that remarkable love-song in which
Dante woos scholastic philosophy. He has the great scholastics
to thank, not only for the scientific basis of his consistent personality, but also for his well-grounded reliance on criticism and
reason.

On these two pillars, completeness of the individual and independence of reason, on this double foundation of character and intelligence, raised by twelve centuries of philosophic labours, the
mighty personality of Alighieri rears itself. The background

[1] *Paradiso*, XII, 97-102.

against which his gigantic figure stands out, and which floods him with hellish fire and heavenly light, does indeed appear mediæval and theological. But not on air and light, not on mysticism and theology, but on solid earth rests the artistic and philosophic pedestal of this lofty monument to human greatness.

Before life in the Renaissance could noisily disclose the glory of the individual, the thought of the Middle Ages had quietly built up individual. To him who knows how to harken to the history of mankind, the whisper of men's thoughts announces the storm of deeds yet to come.

Since Thomas's philosophy fixes man's place between beast and angel, matter and God, as the most important middle link, and finds in the soul of the individual the iron ring that holds together the terraced structure of the universe, and since it assigns, furthermore, to critical reason a similarly central position between sensuous perception and divine revelation—and, in short, sets man and his reason in the centre of all things—it has found the fulcrum by which to draw to itself all knowledge, all culture, profane and sacred, Jewish, Greek, Roman, and Arabian, and to subordinate it all to the Christian-Catholic idea: the idea of divine and human unity.

The popular view is, to be sure, different. Symbolism, it is supposed, is a means by which the Middle Ages interpreted all alien forms of culture in terms of Christianity and so assimilated them. But in reality, symbolism was only the means, only a method, not the primary force behind this remarkable assimilation. Symbolism in and for itself furnishes no outlook on the world. On the contrary, it leads to the dissolution of any general view, since it regards all visible things, the entire experienced reality, as an unreal semblance, and cannot therefore regard as original or important anything that happens here below. In the hypocritical formula of twofold truth, bottomless symbolism found its expression, and at the same time its destruction. A supersensuous reason decomposes and devours all that is real, historical, individual, and visible, all *art*. Plato, himself the father of symbolism, banished from his ideal state the poets as makers of unreal pictures, as liars and exciters of unmanly feeling.[1] This condemnation has been repeated and emphasized every time that the invisible

[1] *Republic*, Book X.

Hereafter has come into man's consciousness as the true and higher reality in contrast with the visible present.[1]

The Thomistic Doctrine of Art

The two extremes between which artistic doctrine in the Middle Ages vibrated, and which were already visible at the close of classical antiquity, were repudiation of art and deification of art.[2] At one time art is rejected as an ignoble deception, at another honoured as the loftiest truth. In all cases it is measured by the standard of truth. How highly it is valued depends on how much it enables us to understand. Beneath the shell of this intellectualistic prepossession, the kernel of the ethical problem remained hidden until the time of modern philosophy.

The one work which seriously attacked the problem, the *Poetics* of Aristotle, did not become known again until the end of the fifteenth century, and so need not detain us.

To Plato, Nature is a copy of the Ideas, and art a copy of Nature; so the copy of a copy, the imitation of an imitation, the pretense of a pretense, not an approach to truth, but a double flight from it, and for that very reason to be rejected. But as Plato had not denied the existence of art, merely its justification, even his disciples had an excuse for bringing back, on whatever pretext, the muses he had frightened away. Sensuous pleasures and enjoyments, it might be said, also do not lead to truth; are they therefore necessarily to be condemned? While the artist was degraded to a jester, and the muses, as Croce says, to hussies, it was still possible to enjoy their society. Yes, from a properly managed association with them, some benefit might be derived. Even if art is condemned as a veiling of truth, and as a lie, there have yet been at all times useful and well-meant lies, lies which with sweet mien point to a bitter truth. And do we not endeavour to lead our children to the truth by the circuitous path of deceptive amusements and pleasing shams? All education

---

[1] The most popular authorities which were cited in the Middle Ages against the poetic art were, besides Plato, the *Disticha Catonis*, III, 18, Boëthius, *De Consolatione Philosophiae*, I, St. Jerome, *Opera*, I, 75 (*Epistola* XXI), and Gregory the Great, *Epistola* XI, 54. The fiercest enemy of art, however, was Tertullian.

[2] Cf. the historical sketch in Benedetto Croce's *Estetica come scienza dell' espressione e linguistica generale*, 3rd ed., Bari, 1908, pp. 175–211, and the bibliographical appendix, p. 560 sqq. (Engl. transl. by D. Ainslie, *Æsthetics as the Science of Expression and General Linguistics*); and Jul. von Schlosser, *Die Kunstliteratur*, Vienna, 1924, p. 59 sqq.

must follow some such course. So the hussy becomes the teacher. To the pleasurable is joined the useful, as Horace joins it in his *Ars Poetica:*

> Either to teach or to please is ever the wish of the poet . . .
> Wholly successful is he who mingles the sweet with the useful.[1]

These not very profound hedonistic and moral æsthetics continued to prevail throughout the Middle Ages. "The pleasing falsity of art was justified from the practical standpoint; somewhat as sexual union was justified by marriage, and love was hallowed thereby. This did not disprove, far from it, that beneath the mediæval view the conviction always lay that as the perfect condition is celibacy, so is pure science free from all art."[2] It is evident that this whole train of thought grew out of the Platonic rejection of art.

This same Platonic influence yielded different results in the philosophy of Plotinus. The novel and peculiar tendency of his æstheticism appears chiefly in the fact that he endeavours to determine the position of art by its relation, not to the concept of truth, but to that of beauty, thus in a certain sense abandoning the scientific intellectualism of the others. Beauty is form, and matter can share therein only in so far as it acquires form. But this form is not individual and visible, but supersensuous, divine, and invisible; it is the Idea. And when the Idea shines through and illumines matter, then visible beauty is created. The Ideas themselves are again in their turn visible; they are intuitions, yes, intuitions of the Absolute. The artist's task is to intuit Ideas. He strives to imitate not what he sees with his corporeal, but what he contemplates with his spiritual, eyes; he copies the Ideas.

Thus spiritual vision is recognized as the fundamental principle of art. But since this vision is elevated to the position of spiritual action in general, inasmuch as it is directed not merely toward intuitions, but essentially toward metaphysical concepts, truth and beauty again become identical. And so Plotinus, too, remained caught in an intellectualism which was not indeed scientific, but mystical. Plato's doctrine of knowledge resolves all spiritual activity into rational concepts; Plotinus resolves them into imaginative intuitions. With the one, art took refuge in science; with the other, science in art.

---

[1] *Ars Poetica*, verses 333 and 343.   [2] Croce, *op. cit.*, p. 183.

Consequently we have, after the times of Plato and Plotinus, two distinct types of symbolism, the rationalistic and the mystical. Rationalistic symbolism characterizes all individual things, all artistic creations, as shadowy distortions of truth, as forms which do not express what they should—as lies. This type of symbols we call *allegories*.[1] Mystical symbolism, on the other hand, sees in the world of appearances the necessary and truthful expression of the Divinity itself, and in the artist a sort of human god who in his own way sees absolute truth and beauty, and gives it shape. These symbols, in contrast with the allegorical ones, may be called *visions*.

But this apparently positive æsthetics of Plotinus also becomes, as soon as we see its ultimate consequences, a denial of art. For if God, the supreme Artist, necessarily and with perfect beauty expresses the absolute in this given world of appearances— what can the little artist, man, add to that? The best he can accomplish will be bungling and lies.

This train of thought makes it clear why the Christian mystics, who developed Plotinus's theory, found neither courage nor means for a serious definition and justification of art. Some of them, like Francis and Bonaventura, did, to be sure, enrich and refine the artistic sense; but they left the philosophy of art where they found it.

Thomistic philosophy, which confirmed the independence of conceptual and rational knowledge, could not but see in the imaginative creations of art a web of lies, to be allegorically interpreted. But since that philosophy recognized in the biblical writings and in the visions of the saints a direct revelation from God, it, too, made provision for a mystical opening heavenward through which the rays of invisible beauty and inspired poetry could come down. So the questions of a friendly or hostile attitude toward art, and as to whether the creations of the imagination should be broken up into allegories or accepted as inspired visions, were no longer determined by individual adherences to scholasticism or to mysticism, to Thomas or to Bonaventura, to Plato or to Plotinus, but rather by each man's state of mind, according as he felt himself under the control of reason or of revelation.

[1] The allegorical interpretation of poetry had been current even in antiquity. It was first systematized, as a definite method, by the Stoic grammarian Crates of Mallos, in Pergamos (about 150 B.C.). Cf. Christian Jensen, *Philodemos*, Berlin, 1923.

Naturally a man like Dante was capable of either mood, and so it comes to pass that his artistic creed hesitates between Plato and Plotinus, but does not forsake Thomas.

For Dante, as for Thomas, metaphysical beauty is essentially identical with goodness. That which our human understanding finds beautiful, our will strives to attain as good. God is both beauty and goodness. Revealed beauty is recognized—so Thomas teaches—by three integrating qualities: by its perfection (*integritas* or *perfectio*), its perspicuity (*claritas*), and its harmony (*consonantia*). The highest example of God's beauty that has been revealed to us is Jesus Christ, His son. But physical beauty, the further removed it is from God, the more imperfect, i.e. the more evanescent, it becomes; and also proportionately more obscure, and therefore more dependent on allegorical interpretation; and more discordant, that is, uglier. The beauty of human works of art was not expressly discussed by Thomas.

To fill this gap consistently with the system set forth might have been an easy task for our poet. He has done it only incidentally and, as it were, in passing. In his political essay, *De Monarchia* (II, 2), we find this passage: "It must be understood that in art three stages are to be distinguished; namely, first the work of art in the artist's mind; second, in the instruments, and third, in matter which has been formed by art. Even so it is with Nature. It exists first in the mind of its primal mover, who is God; next, in the heavenly spheres as in the instrument by means of which a likeness of the eternal goodness is moulded in changeable matter. And just as it happens with a fully competent artist working with a faultless instrument, that if a fault appears in his artistic form the blame rests wholly on the material, even so—since God is the highest perfection, and since His instruments, that is, the heavenly spheres, also suffer from no imperfection—everything that is deficient here below finds its reason solely in the material employed, and not in the creating God nor in His heavenly spheres. And everything that is good here below owes its goodness not to matter, which has only potential existence, but primarily to God its maker, and next to the heavenly spheres, the instrument of the divine art which is commonly called Nature."

We find the same comparison of the divine with the human artist in the words of the Dantesque Virgil:

"Philosophy," he said, "to him who heeds it,
Noteth, not only in one place alone,
After what manner Nature takes her course
From Intellect Divine, and from its art;
And if thy Physics carefully thou notest,[1]
After not many pages shalt thou find,
That this your art as far as possible,
Follows, as the disciple doth the master."[2]

In making such comparisons Dante may have been thinking rather of the mechanical arts and handicrafts than of poetry, though that, too, was regarded by him as an imitator and child of Nature.

The ancestors of art are also its inspirers. So we may assume that our poet differentiated the natural from the supernatural inspiration. Parnassus, he says, has two peaks,[3] the natural powers of the spirit, which he invoked at the beginning of the *Inferno* and of the *Purgatorio* under the name of muses, and the supernatural mystic vision for which he beseeches Apollo at the beginning of the *Paradiso*. Accordingly, there are also two ideal types of poet: the poet-philosopher and the poet-theologian. The first of these he sees realized in Virgil; the second he would at times fain hope to embody in his own person, but must have recognized in the biblical prophets, and especially in the psalmist David, the "minstrel of the Holy Spirit." How high Dante set the value of his *Commedia*, and whether he actually hoped to rival the prophets, are delicate questions, which can be determined primarily from his own philosophy and not solely from the doctrines of Thomas.

The haughty designation of the poet as the humanly and divinely inspired herald of beauty, truth, and goodness has, however, both with Thomas and with Dante, its reverse side. In his book, *De vulgari Eloquentia* (II, 4), the poetic art is defined as "nothing other than rhetorical and musical fiction," devoid of any real essence. And in the *Vita Nuova*,[4] after the poet has glorified his Beatrice in a delightful sonnet as a divinity of love, his conscience smites him, and he feels himself in duty bound to warn the reader against the tricks of his muse, and to justify as best he can the charming figures of his poem.

"It may be that some person, entitled to have every doubt cleared away, may here be perplexed at my speaking of Love as

---

[1] The allusion is to Aristotle's Physics, II, ii.   [3] *Paradiso*, I, 16–17.
[2] *Inferno*, XI, 97–104.   [4] § 25.

if it were a thing in itself, and indeed not simply an intellectual substance, but also a bodily one. This in truth is false, for Love exists not in itself as substance, but is an accident in a substance. And that I speak of it as if it were a body, and further as if it were a man, appears from three things which I say of it. I say that I saw it come from afar off . . . that it laughed, and also that it spoke."

What Dante says to remove his readers' doubts may be summed up under three heads:

1. The ancient authors, especially Virgil, Lucan, Horace, and Ovid, permitted themselves the same freedom. They also are guilty of untruths, in that they present what is lifeless as living; they make concepts into persons and turn accidents into substances.

2. The poets employ such fictions not without reason.

3. "It would be a great shame if one chose to write poetically under such figurative disguise, and afterward, when questioned, were unable to strip his words of this covering so that their true content might then clearly appear." In other words, poetical colouring and disguise are only justifiable where a rational content of truth can be extracted therefrom. In and for itself all imaginative invention is deception.

But why, then, poetry at all? Why not truth at once, naked and unadorned? To this also, Dante makes answer with the old familiar arguments, and reaches with the one hand for the hedonistic, with the other for the pedagogical and moral, doctrine of art. The first poem of his *Convivio* closes with the characteristic verses addressed to the poem itself:

> O song of mine, I think there are but few,
> Who thy significance will clearly grasp;
> So hidden and so laboured is thy speech.
> And if, by any chance, it should befall
> That thou before such people must appear,
> Who to thy deeper meaning shall be deaf,
> Then, my belovéd creature, I beseech,
> Calming thyself, do thou declare to them:
> "Then note, at least, how beautiful I am."

Those who cannot appreciate the muse as a teacher can at least find pleasure in the muse's meretricious charms. Not until Poesy has allured the dull-witted public with her outward adornment is it to be hoped that the finer spirits will seek to discover her inner worth.

By his acknowledgment that the beauty of a work of art can be enjoyed apart from the appreciation of its intellectual content, Dante takes the first questionable step in the direction of the formalistic taste of the Renaissance. In his commentary on the poem above quoted, he calls poetry "a lovely falsehood." We shall see that he is rather inclined to lay the emphasis on "lovely" than on "falsehood," thus turning quietly away from mediæval poetry. In his essay *De vulgari Eloquentia*, the most characteristic and independent creation of his artistic creed, he actually lays the foundation for Renaissance poetry.

As soon as he considers the outward side of poetry, our form-loving artist parts company with his master. But he clings to him all the more closely when the interpretation of its inward side comes to the fore. Bit for bit Dante took over his method of explanation from scholasticism and from the general practices of mediæval exegesis.

"The written words, it must be understood, may be intended in fourfold manner, and must be accordingly interpreted. The first is the literal sense, which extends no further than the letter declares. The next is the allegorical, which conceals itself beneath the cloak of the poetic fable and points to a truth hidden under a pleasing falsehood. . . . The theologians indeed view this allegorical meaning differently from the poets. . . . The third is the moral sense, which the readers should follow up zealously, to the benefit of themselves and of their pupils. . . . The fourth is the anagogical or supersensuous meaning. This appears when a composition which already—that is, according to the letter—refers to heavenly things and to eternal glory is interpreted in its spiritual sense."[1]

The importance of the three meanings other than the literal is illustrated by Dante. It is an allegory when Ovid relates of Orpheus that he by the power of his song tamed wild beasts and set plants and stones in motion; which means "that the wise power of his eloquence softened and humbled the hard-hearted, and drew to itself those who were deaf to art and science." A moral meaning is conveyed in the Gospel, for example, where it is

[1] *Convivio* II, i.

said of Christ that He took with Him to the Mount of Transfiguration only three of His twelve disciples, from which we should
infer that only a small and select company is fitted for the holiest
and most mysterious things. The song of the prophet is to be
interpreted anagogically when he sings: "When Israel went out of
Egypt, the house of Jacob from a people of strange language;
Judah became his sanctuary, Israel his dominion."[1] That is, this
historical truth also contains within itself the affirmation "that
the soul in escaping from sin is sanctified and freed."

The relations between these three methods of interpretation
have often been misunderstood by modern students of Dante.
Endless confusion arose, which finally led to the most serious
pedantic maltreatment of the *Divine Comedy*.

It is to be remembered first of all that the fourfold interpretation
developed in the course of the Middle Ages, or, more precisely,
after the time of Philo the Alexandrian, and that it dealt with
the book of books, the Bible, so that Dante presumably received
it from the biblical interpretations of the scholastics and mystics.
It should further be noted, what Dante expressly states, that the
progress from the first to the second, and doubtless also from the
second to the third and fourth interpretations, must always follow
progressively.   So it is a question whether in each case the lower
step warrants the passage to the next higher.

As to the Bible, there can be no doubt in this matter. But how
was it with profane writings? Dante utters a covert doubt. The
spiritual (anagogical) interpretation he appears to seek by preference only in those texts which even in their literal interpretation
have reference to religious subjects. Thus he does not leave the
decision of the question as to how far in each case the various
forms of interpretation may be carried to the caprice of the expositor, but to the nature of the text itself. He makes another
reservation concerning the allegorical sense; he distinguishes theological from poetical allegories. The latter, he states, are veiled
by a fable, i.e. an invented occurrence; the former by a fact, i.e.
a real occurrence. What follows from this? That the specifically
poetic texts can be carried only so far as the allegorical interpretation, not, like the religious ones, to the moral or even to the anagogical? And again that the truthful content of poetical fables
cannot be allowed without the addition of the practical applica-

[1] Psalm CXIV.

tion, and carries with it a moralizing obligation? Dante has not expressed himself clearly. But it is natural to draw these conclusions. Certainly the division of allegories into purely poetical and theological was familiar in Dante's time.[1]

If we cast a glance at the Thomistic philosophy of history, it becomes clear that those thinkers knew how to distinguish accurately, at least in principle, between poetry and fact, even though frequently, in details, they did accept a legend as truth, a miracle as a fact. Indeed they were at bottom far more realistic than we. For us there exists an æsthetic reality beside the empirical one. For Thomas and Dante only the empirical existed. A poem like Virgil's Aeneid was for them either history, or falsehood, or a mixture of the two. The fourth possibility—that the poet might combine things empirically unreal, quite as well as historical events, into an independent truth and reality possessing æsthetic validity—was not recognized in the Middle Ages. The pure creation of the imagination, so far as it did not rest on definite occurrences or depend on rational concepts, hung in air and was nothing. Every fully attested occurrence, on the other hand, was accepted as a fulfillment of God's will, as a sacred fragment of the history of humanity, or, which is the same thing, of the history of salvation that ran from Adam through Christ to the Day of Judgment.

Now the relation is clear. If the artist suspends his fictitious fable or his illusory picture from a rational concept, the allegory is specifically poetical. But if he rests his presentation on the historical ground of reality, then he is no poet, but more than a poet— a recorder of the history of salvation, and so in the last analysis a theologian, or if he limits himself to profane history, at least a philosopher. But even when he relates ancient historical events, Greek or Roman, even if he is himself a heathen, he is still working for the eventual understanding of the tale of salvation, and consciously or unconsciously, is in the service of theology. In this sense, that is, in so far as Dante regarded the events of the Aeneid as historical truths—and he did so for the most part—Virgil was to him a theologian, a poet-seer. Accordingly, theological allegory appears wherever the poet relates no fables, but human history. And since in human history a higher will is always and everywhere

---

[1] Cf. K. Vossler, *Poetische Theorien in der italienischen Frührenaissance*, Berlin, 1900, p. 6 sqq., p. 18.

revealed, the right interpretation must point, above all, to that loftier will, and so be prevailingly moral. History is mankind's moral picture-book.

So the method of Dantesque explanation may be reconstructed and systematized as follows. Religious texts contain and demand an anagogical interpretation, historical texts a moral one, and poetical texts an allegorical or conceptual one. Whether other combinations are possible, whether the poetic fable permits also a moral interpretation and the historical event an anagogical, Dante has not positively stated. He is evidently of the opinion that this does not depend on the text, but on the will, or on the tact and ability, of the expositor. There is certainly no lack of examples in mediæval literature of the moral as well as of the anagogical interpretation applied to any type of fable. A well-known example of it is the *Gesta Romanorum*. In spite of this, it must be conceded that Dante at least made an effort to limit the arbitrariness of manifold interpretation by insisting that due consideration be given to the varying nature of the several texts. The personal inclinations of arbitrary expositors were not done away with nor adequately regulated by him. I cannot, therefore, recognize any notable originality in his theory of interpretation.

Certainly Flamini's view,[1] that Dante wishes us to find a concealed allegory only in those parts of his poem where "poetic fiction" appears, is over-hasty. Who knows whether Dante the critic would not have hailed with delight a commentator who succeeded in discovering an allegory, an abstract conception, in his "historical" Francesca, in his Farinata and Ugolino? He might have welcomed a scholastic juggler who could defend him against the reproaches of a scientifically trained Cecco d'Ascoli by demonstrating that Francesca signifies adultery, Paolo seduction, Farinata blind partisan hatred, and so on for the other characters.

But this much I know, that Dante the poet would have found a place in his Hell for those modern commentators who even to this day break up his glorious poem according to antiquated Thomistic and Dantesque prescriptions, and for those school-

---

[1] Fr. Flamini, *I significanti reconditi della Commedia di Dante e il suo fine supremo,* Vol. I, Leghorn, 1903, and *Avviamento allo studio della Divina Commedia,* Leghorn, 1906, p. 25.

masters who in all seriousness, in the face of blooming youth in the schools of Italy, distort his beloved Virgil and his divine Beatrice into scientific types. He would have placed them, if I am not mistaken, among the *accidiosi*, the ill-tempered and spiritually indolent, who, plunged in the mud, can only gurgle:

> . . . We sullen were
> In the sweet air, which by the sun is gladdened,
> Bearing within ourselves the sluggish reek.[1]

It is high time that every one who devotes himself to Dante should come to realize that the mediæval theory of art does no justice to the essence of art, whether, starting from Plotinus, it makes the poet a prophet and theologian, or with Plato, stigmatizes him as a liar. A work of art is not created when an individual intuition is didactically superimposed on an universal concept (allegory), nor when the mind becomes absorbed in a mystical idea beyond the realm of intuition (vision and ecstacy), but when our individual spirit by its own effort sets clearly and intuitively before itself the particular impressions and experiences which move it from without and from within. Beauty is found neither in scientific concepts nor in mystical ideas, but in the spiritual originality of our own intuitions. A concept can only be adjudged true or false; a mystical idea only credible or incredible, sacred or profane. Values like beautiful and ugly, form and formlessness, shapely and shapeless, have reference solely to the moulding and forming power of our own spirit, and apply to the work of art. An æsthetic inquiry that measures art by the standards of truth and holiness, or by those of usefulness and morality, denies the validity of æsthetic values as such, itself becomes meaningless, and cannot serve as a foundation for art-criticism.

Dante poured out the imperishable and pure gold of his art on the table of all aftertime in great quantities. Beside it he placed the dusty ledger of his exegesis, and the schoolmasters do not know, even to this day, for which they should reach.

Applied Method and Cosmology of Thomas

Having investigated scholastic symbolism and found that its success lay on the one hand in rationalistic allegorizing and on the other in mystical, visionary, and trustful contemplation, it is

[1] *Inferno*, VII, 121–123.

easy to set forth clearly the rôle that this symbolism is going to play in explaining the universe. The mystical attitude of the seer represents the higher plane of comprehension of the universe; the rational and allegorical view, the lower one. Hence the rule: Everything in the world which is already rational, and therefore capable of being grasped by the human understanding, reveals to the delighted eye its profounder divine meaning; while what is irrational must first be explained allegorically and be cast in the form of concepts.

All civilization is in its very nature rational. Hence its development, considered in the light of universal history, leads up to the mystery of future salvation. Everything rational that comes to pass in our world is a step forward in the history of man's redemption. All irrational cultural efforts, however, such as falsehood and deceit, superstition, heathenism, sensuous enjoyment, and, as we have just seen, even profane art—in short, everything which irrationally happens here—must be rationalized by allegorical interpretation. Hence falsehood and deceit reveal themselves as the forces opposed to investigation and truth; superstition, as an alluring imitation of the Christian religion; sensuous pleasure, as a spur to morality; profane art, as a beautiful veil cast over rational truths, etc.

All natural events on the earth are essentially irrational. Therefore they are elaborated and elevated by allegorical analysis and abstraction into a basic concept of natural rationality (*status naturae integrae*), a basic concept which in Thomas and Dante spells natural innocence as opposed to sensuality; natural law in contrast with violence; the Earthly Paradise in its opposition to pain, illness, and death. This *natura integra*, idealized and rationalized out of the *natura depravata*, is next related and lifted to the mystical factor of divine grace through the doctrine that happiness in Eden and the virtue and wisdom of Adam and Eve were in their essence no natural attributes, but a gift bestowed and maintained by God's grace.

Thomism found the means to solve all the riddles of the world by this process of rationalizing the irrational allegorically and of elevating what had been so rationalized by means of mystical symbolism. Thomas can never be refuted by his own method. As the rational conceptions are uplifted to the realm of faith, his opponent has no time to assail them. So Thomism appeals against criticism to belief, and against unbelief to criticism; it overthrows erroneous opinions with the aid of philosophy, but escapes from philosophic criticism behind the mysticism of ecclesiastical dogma. Thomas moves within this circle with a nimbleness and agility unheard of before.

Dante was able to appreciate the advantages of this rationally mystic method. He could not, therefore, in his *Commedia* fail to give St. Thomas himself a memorable opportunity to show the resources of his argumentation.

Thomas, introducing his blessed companions to the poet, pointed to King Solomon, and declared that no one had been so wise as he.[1] Dante doubts whether Adam, the man created by God, and Christ, God and man, were not wiser. Thomas dispels this doubt in most remarkable language, at once scholastic and poetic, in a style which exactly befits the mystic rationality of his thought. He says to Dante:

Into that bosom, thou believest, whence
　　Was drawn the rib to form the beauteous cheek
　　Whose taste to all the world is costing dear,
And into that which, by the lance transfixed,
　　Before and since, such satisfaction made
　　That it weighs down the balance of all sin,
Whate'er of light it has to human nature
　　Been lawful to possess was all infused
　　By the same power that both of them created;
And hence at what I said above dost wonder,
　　When I narrated that no second had
　　The good which in the fifth light is enclosed.
Now ope thine eyes to what I answer thee,
　　And thou shalt see thy creed and my discourse
　　Fit in the truth as centre in a circle.
That which can die, and that which dieth not,
　　Are nothing but the splendour of the idea
　　Which by his love our Lord brings into being;
Because that living Light, which from its fount
　　Effulgent flows, so that it disunites not
　　From Him nor from the Love in them intrined,
Through its own goodness reunites its rays
　　In nine subsistences, as in a mirror,
　　Itself eternally remaining One.
Thence it descends to the last potencies,
　　Downward from act to act becoming such
　　That only brief contingencies it makes;

[1] *Paradiso*, X, 109 sqq.

> And these contingencies I hold to be
>   Things generated, which the heaven produces
>   By its own motion, with seed and without.
> Neither their wax, nor that which tempers it,
>   Remains immutable, and hence beneath
>   The ideal signet more and less shines through;
> Therefore it happens, that the self-same tree
>   After its kind bears worse and better fruit,
>   And ye are born with characters diverse.
> If in perfection tempered were the wax,
>   And were the heaven in its supremest virtue,
>   The brilliance of the seal would all appear;
> But nature gives it evermore deficient,
>   In the like manner working as the artist,
>   Who has the skill of art and hand that trembles.
> If then the fervent Love, the Vision clear,
>   Of primal Virtue do dispose and seal,
>   Perfection absolute is there acquired.
> Thus was of old the earth created worthy
>   Of all and every animal perfection;
>   And thus the Virgin was impregnate made;
> So that thine own opinion I commend,
>   That human nature never yet has been,
>   Nor will be, what it was in those two persons.[1]

Solomon, Thomas explains further, was the ideal type only of kingly wisdom. This distinction and the example here given shall be as lead to Dante's feet—

> To make thee, like a weary man, move slowly
>   Both to the Yes and No thou seest not;
> For very low among the fools is he
>   Who affirms without distinction, or denies,
>   As well in one as in the other case;
> Because it happens that full often bends
>   Current opinion in the false direction,
>   And then the feelings bind the intellect.
> Far more than uselessly he leaves the shore
>   (Since he returneth not the same he went,)
>   Who fishes for the truth, and has no skill;
> And in the world proofs manifest thereof
>   Parmenides, Melissus, Brissus are,
>   And many who went on and knew not whither;
> Thus did Sabellius, Arius, and those fools
>   Who have been even as swords unto the Scriptures
>   In rendering distorted their straight faces.[2]

[1] *Paradiso*, XIII, 37–87.   [2] *Ibid.*, 113–129.

It is significant that Thomas cites, as examples of men who pursued a faulty method, three Greek thinkers, all of whom had followed the monistic tendency: Parmenides, who declared physical nature to be an empty phantom, and only the conceptual possessed of being; Melissus, who carried this doctrine still further; and Brissus, who, belonging to the Megarian school of Euclid, espoused the doctrine of Illusionism. The latter is also said to have solved, by an unsound theorem, the problem of the squaring of the circle. Beside them stand Sabellius and Arius as the founders of rationalistic disbelief in the doctrine of the Trinity. Then Thomas turns against one-sided rationalism, whether it be found in philosophy, doing away with all sensuous experience by conceptual disintegration, or whether in theology it imperils faith by allegorical interpretation of mystical symbols. In contrast with this one-sided method, Thomas emphasizes his own distinction between reason and faith, which permits him—to revert to his own example—to separate complete from incomplete nature, and Christ's wisdom from Solomon's, and yet to unite them both in a higher connection.

But the historical Thomas would hardly have taken up this question and handled it in such a fashion as the Dantesque Thomas does in the *Paradiso*. Instead of making heavenly wisdom descend before our eyes to the human, he would probably have defined the nature, problems, and limitations of this human wisdom itself; and starting therefrom he would have revealed its origin from a higher wisdom, and then, finally, would have discussed the differences between the two types of wisdom. In short, the historical Thomas would have proceeded less theologically and less deductively than Dante makes him do, although he must have come essentially to the same conclusion. But it is quite evident that Dante's Thomas appears decidedly more mystical than the historical one, the primary cause doubtless being that a believer, in Paradise, is argued with in a different fashion from unbelievers, on earth. Thus the mystical colouring of the Dantesque Thomas·may be sufficiently explained by the poetical setting in which he appears. It may be that still another motive had its weight: that Dante was in general of a more mystical temper than Thomas. But more of this later.

As the Thomistic theory of knowledge rises from sensuous perception to the rational conception and from the latter to the mystical Idea, it is able to grasp the universe in its entire extent. Below, nature: rich in stones, plants, beasts, the earth with its vegetable and animal kingdoms. About the earth, which is thought of as a sphere, arches the sky with its stars, embracing nature, but itself no part of nature; it is the boundary in space between the earth and God, and also the medium through which God exerts influence on the earth. Since Pythagoras had contrasted the starry heaven, as the world of complete movement and eternal harmony, with the "world beneath the moon," with its incomplete and changing forms—astronomy and mathematics had, for thousands of years, preserved their metaphysical significance. The starry heaven had become an immaterial and yet material realm: a realm which Greek philosophy peopled with Intelligences, and the Christian religion with angels. The Intelligences are Ideas, the angels are symbols. Heaven is the realm wherein concept and symbol, reason and faith, embrace each other. The departed soul of man also becomes an Intelligence; therefore Heaven is not the dwelling-place of angels alone, but also of those men who parted at death from their bodies and from all sin.

As to the astronomical structure of the heavens, both Thomas and Dante held firm to the Ptolemaic system. Revolving about the earth as their centre, seven hollow transparent heavenly spheres move in varying speed with the planet which is encased in them. Nearest the earth is the heaven of the moon, for the moon as well as the sun was looked on as a planet; next follow the heavens of Mercury, Venus, the sun, Mars, Jupiter, and Saturn. Enclosing the heavens of the seven planets, the heaven of the fixed stars revolves, like them a transparent, spherical shell. Outside this, as a ninth, the crystalline or moving heaven revolves with utmost speed. This heaven is invisible; that is, it bears no star. It transmits its motion to the other spheres. The Intelligences, represented as eight of the nine angelic choirs, are the transmitting power. Here they have their seat, and each one of them bestows on one of the lesser spheres its proper speed. But the ninth and highest angelic choir, the Seraphim, draw from the direct vision of God and from their love of Him that original moving force of the ninth heaven, the *primum mobile*. Beyond the resonant crystalline sphere of the *primum mobile* lies, outside all the spheres, the Empyrean Heaven, the resplendent abode of God. Eternally motionless it rests in itself, beyond space and time. Time and space are conditioned and limited by the nine lower heavens and their harmonious musical revolutions.[1] With the planetary heavens, this rotatory movement is double: first the daily movement from east to west, and second the movement along the ecliptic from west to east. The general movement from east to west, it was assumed, was the cause of the stability and changelessness of natural events, while the movement along the ecliptic determined the interchange of birth and death, conception and creation. The ecliptic movement is imparted to the planetary heavens by the heaven of the fixed stars, the slowest of all the spheres, but their daily rotation is bestowed on them by the *primum mobile*, the swiftest of all; so that the *primum mobile* may be called the conserver, and the heaven of the fixed stars the transformer, of earthly events and of human destinies.

This magnificent, mysterious, and yet law-bound drama of the heavenly spheres and heavenly choirs that intervene between God and man had a mighty effect on our poet's fancy. How often is his imagination fired by the sight of the starry heaven, which fills him with a blissful and uplifting feeling of the familiar nearness and the remote glory of God! No other part of the universe was capable of engrossing and delighting to such a degree his tireless mind, as well as his wakeful imagination. Here the warring powers of his soul found peace and rest, for here scientific comprehension and accuracy grew into the enchantment of poetry. In the framing of his *Inferno* and *Purgatorio*, he had to do his own constructing; but here reality turns of itself into a religious symbol.

A certain influence of the stars on earthly life inevitably went along with this picture of the universe. But Dante limited it, in complete harmony with Thomas, to the natural, i.e. to the mechanical, climatic, vegetative, animal, and sensuous processes, and expressly excluded it from the spiritual field of reason and the will. In harmony with this, he derives the individual basis of man, and the very nature of his genius, from the constellation under which he came into life. He therefore greets on his heavenly journey the Twins (Gemini) as the constellation of his birth:

> O glorious stars, O light impregnated
> With mighty virtue, from which I acknowledge
> All of my genius, whatsoe'er it be,

[1] The Platonic music of the spheres, though denied by Aristotle, Albertus, and Thomas, is revived by Dante, *Paradiso*, I, 76 sqq., as a poetic motif.

With you was born, and hid himself with you,
He who is father of all mortal life,
When first I tasted of the Tuscan air.[1]

As soon as scholasticism began to view the universe from the astronomical and mathematical standpoint, the conviction of an eternal matter, filling all space, forced its way upon the minds of men. Averroës had been more determined and serious than others as to this. Beside the eternal, uncreated God, he set eternal uncreated matter. A temporarily limited matter was, for him, contrary to reason; but the idea of uncreated matter contradicted faith in the Bible. Thomas hoped to remove this contradiction also, and with ingenious devices he united the concept of creation with that of eternity.

He distinguishes a creation "out of nothing" (*ex nihilo*) from one "after nothing" (*post nihilum*); that is, translated into modern speech, a metaphysical and an empirical creation. The latter is, as Thomas keenly and accurately observed, an irrational conception. Motion and matter have been in existence as long as time and space, for time and space proceed solely from motion and matter, which are therefore as endless as they. But—as Thomas rightly saw—there is a beyond to time and space. The transition from that beyond into the here of time and space is metaphysical creation, or, as the unfortunate expression goes, creation *ex nihilo*. This is outside of time and of all sequences, or, speaking metaphysically, it goes on constantly; speaking empirically, it never occurs. It can only be thought, indeed it must be thought; but it cannot really be imagined. The distinction between metaphysical essence and empirical existence, between what is valid and what occurs, could hardly have been more clearly and exactly defined. To be sure, all mythical accounts of creation are thereby pushed aside; and no room is left for the book of Genesis.

From this conclusion the Catholic thinker could not but recoil. He escaped it by a clever dodge, but nothing more than a dodge. If the concept of a creation "after nothing" (*post nihilum*) is irrational, this can only mean that it cannot be proved philosophically, and is not logically necessary. Yet it is possible. An empirical creation of matter is to us unthinkable, and yet it may have occurred. But if it did occur, reason knows nothing of it. Only

[1] *Paradiso*, XXII, 112–117; on the influence of the stars, cf. *Inferno*, XV, 55 sqq.; XXVI, 23; *Purgatorio* XVI, 73, XXX, 109; *Paradiso*, I, 38 sqq., IV, 49 sqq., VII, 136 sqq., XIII, 64; and *Convivio*, IV, 21.

revelation can teach us, and has in fact taught us. So God made
the world, not only after nothing, but out of nothing. Therefore
there was time before time; and the birthday of "eternal" matter
can be reckoned from the Bible. This contradiction, which limits
the eternal drama of Nature to a petty millennium or two, for a
time amazed even our poet.[1]

At the close of this inquiry into the Thomistic system, the old
contradiction again stares us in the face: the clash between the
independence and dependence of reason. In psychology it appeared
as the opposition of body to soul, in the theory of art as the contrast between allegory and symbol, and in cosmogony as the
opposition between eternity and creation. Ever and evermore
that which we can know is crossed by that which we are required
to believe, so that finally nothing any longer seems certain, and
what is closest at hand, i.e. perceptible reality, comes to seem most
dubious. The world of appearances is indeed accepted by Thomism, but as something given, the intuitive perception of which we
are unable to explain. There is lacking an æsthetic foundation
upon which to build the conceptual structure, which seems to hang
in the air with its sole support in revelation.

Under these conditions it was only logical that supersensuous
revelation be made the foundation both of rational and of sensuous
knowledge. This step the Franciscan mystics took. Bonaventura,
Roger Bacon, and Duns Scotus carry on the movement of the
Victorines in direct opposition to Thomism. Dante knew the
writings only of the first of these three men, and seems to have
remained unaffected by the weighty ideas of the two northern
philosophers.

Doubtless it was rather the unhappy vicissitudes of his life than
a lack of interest in mystical speculation that prevented him from
becoming acquainted with these great thinkers. It is to be considered also that the strife between the disciples of Thomas and
the Scotists did not fully develop until the early part of the fourteenth century—at a time, that is, when Dante's views of life were
fully settled, after he had attained perhaps his fortieth year. His
essential adhesion to Thomism was by that time complete, and it
is not to be expected that at that age a man like Dante would
desert the systematic groundwork of his philosophy. The mysticism which arose at that time, and which was destined to bring

[1] *Convivio*, IV, 1.

about the victory of nominalism and of the natural sciences, affected only the feelings, not the intellect, of our poet. It rustles and murmurs like a warm breath through the waving tree tops of his song, whose philosophic roots reach back into the past. For the deepest and most fruitful ideas of Franciscan mysticism were those which Dante did not live to share. He could find them in Bonaventura only in the bud, not in the full maturity of consciousness.

If the final goal of reason is divine revelation, then its lowest foundation must also be in some sense revelation. This alone is for the mystic thinkers their final cause, i.e. source and object at once. There is no step in the gradual development of our knowledge which does not represent some form of revelation. Knowledge without revelation is error at every stage of our perception. Our whole spiritual life, so far as it aims at truth, is for Bonaventura a journey of the mind to God (*itinerarium mentis in Deum*).

While Thomas distinguishes three stages of knowledge, essentially diverse in quality, (1) sensuous perception, (2) understanding or reason, and (3) divine revelation, the mystics, on the other hand, have always striven to efface or bridge over these distinctions. With this intention Richard of St. Victor, in his time, had already inserted a middle term between each pair of traditional steps.[1] Bonaventura followed him in this. His whole theory of knowledge is summed up in the following sentence of the *Itinerarium Mentis in Deum:* "By the side of the six steps of the ascent to God, there are six stages or six psychological faculties whereby we progress from the lowest to the highest, from the outermost to the innermost, from the temporal to the eternal. They are called sense, imagination, reason, intellect, intelligence, and supreme comprehension (*sensus, imaginatio, ratio, intellectus, intelligentia, apex mentis* or *synderesis scintilla*). These steps are implanted in us by nature, distorted by guilt, restored by grace, cleansed by righteousness, and are to be used with understanding and perfected by wisdom." Even the lowest step, sensuous perception, reveals to us "the traces wherein as in a mirror we recognize our God." Even the immediate contemplation of daily reality has in it something mystical, as of a vision, transcendent; even the lowest stage of knowledge contains potentially the highest *apex mentis.*

[1] In his *Benjamin major.*

The *Divine Comedy* has not been unaffected by this unified upward progress. Just as Bonaventura by the insertion of intervening steps sought to give a closer unity to the gradual ascent toward knowledge, so Dante interposed several other persons between the chief representatives of supersensuous knowledge, Virgil and Beatrice. Above Virgil, the heathen poet-philosopher, he set Statius, the convert; above Beatrice, as speculative wisdom, he sets St. Bernard, as the intuitive wisdom of belief; and between Virgil and Beatrice the notable figure of Matelda intervenes. All these interposed persons mark a transition and represent relatively brief moments in the ascent of the soul to God. They all have a pronounced mystical character. Statius approaches more closely to contemplative, Matelda to active, mysticism; and Bernard unites both tendencies. It is clear that Dante intends to assign to these figures tasks similar to that which Richard and Bonaventura ascribed to their intermediaries between understanding, revelation and the highest stage, *apex mentis*.

This does not indeed prove that Richard and Bonaventura furnished the direct suggestion for increasing the number of spiritual guides in the *Commedia*. But we may assume with confidence that these figures owe their origin to a mystical intention of the poet. Besides, no more than Virgil and Beatrice can they be wholly transmuted into figurative conceptions of the processes of knowledge. Now and again mere allegory may be reduced to pure concept. But for the genuine creations of his poetical imagination, a rationalistic interpretation cannot satisfy; profounder purposes must be sought. Neither Statius nor Matelda nor Bernard is pure allegory. No one of them therefore can be interpreted as a designed mystical attack on or opposition to the scholastic doctrine of knowledge.

An express contradiction between the doctrine of Thomas and that of Bonaventura does not exist. For both, the goal of knowledge is in the Hereafter; to both, the path of knowledge is progressive; for both, the topmost step consists in speculative and contemplative comprehension of the Godhead; both concede a certain independence to natural reason. It will, therefore, always be easy for Catholic scholars to demonstrate an agreement between the systems of the two saints, even in their fundamentals. Dante regarded them as identical in their main features. He indeed appreciated both the Franciscan and the Dominican tendency, each in its peculiar features, and strikingly characterized the founders of the two orders:

> The one was all seraphical in ardour;
> The other by his wisdom upon earth
> A splendour was of light cherubical.[1]

But even if he saw the inherent opposition between the two tendencies, he certainly wished to see it softened and reconciled. He cannot be emphatic enough in the assurance that Dominicans and Franciscans are striving toward one and the same goal.

> One will I speak of, for of both is spoken
> In praising one, whichever may be taken,
> Because unto one end their labours were. [2]

And in the next canto we read:

> 'Tis right where one is, to bring in the other,
> That, as they were united in their warfare,
> Together, likewise may their glory shine.[3]

To bring before us more vividly the unity of the two, he puts the praise of St. Francis on the lips of the Dominican, and the eulogy of St. Dominic is uttered by the Franciscan Bonaventura.

It is true that as long as the general doctrinal aim of Christianity alone is considered, and only the external structures of the two systems are compared, a decided similarity may be noted. The mystic can set up his workshop in Thomas's edifice, the philosopher can toil under the roof of Bonaventura. But in Thomas's abode the mystic must be contented with the attic; in Bonaventura's the philosopher must be satisfied with the mezzanine.

For we must consider not what can be tolerated in a system, but rather what its whole aim and purpose is. Bonaventura's tendency is unfavourable to philosophy. Philosophical speculation is accepted by him as a necessary but dangerous evil. It cannot be dispensed with because it helps to the full understanding of the Church Fathers, especially of Augustine. But we should study it only to work our way out of it.

In his commentary on the *Sententiae* of Peter Lombard, Bonaventura discusses the question whether science or faith gives us the fuller assurance. He there distinguishes two forms of certainty:

---

[1] *Paradiso*, XI, 37–39.   [2] *Ibid.*, 40–42.   [3] *Ibid.*, XII, 34–36.

the *certitudo speculationis*, which belongs to the intellect, and the *certitudo adhaesionis*, which belongs to the affections. In the former, science overrides faith; in the latter, faith is superior to science. Bonaventura admits without question that there are self-evident and immediate scientific truths, but he invalidates this concession by the doctrine that the peculiar certainty of belief, the *certitudo adhaesionis*, is the higher and the stronger of the two. Neither promises nor the tortures of martyrdom can deprive true believers of their certainty, whereas a geometrician who died to defend a mathematical proposition would be accounted a fool. Bonaventura seems, however, to have had a suspicion that this illustration rather strengthens the superiority of mathematical certainty, since a truth for which there is no need of fighting or dying carries its own certainty with it, needs no martyr, and is thus, so to speak, more certain than the other. He therefore finally rejects all evaluation of the sciences according to their degree of certainty. It is not true, he says, that a science is the more valuable (*nobilior*), the greater its certainty. The certainty of mathematics is greater than that of theology; yet theology is more valuable than mathematics. It is better to know even a little of God than to know all about the starry heaven and the earth. So the true measure for the value of science is practical, not scientific. Theology is prized by Bonaventura as eminently practical wisdom, and the final union of the pious man with his God he regards as not primarily an act of the intellect, but one of the will, of the human as well as of the divine will. The very expression *synderesis scintilla* indicates this.

Accordingly it might be assumed that Bonaventura gives precedence to the will over the intellect. In fact, he does and does not. He agrees with Thomas that reason precedes revelation, and in his psychology and ethics he declares his allegiance to the old doctrine that love comes after the act of the intellect (*affectus sequitur intellectum*). But just because revelation and will are later in time, they are regarded by him as metaphysically higher, and as such they become the decisive forces.

It is quite proper that the will, which as a theoretical factor comes after the intellect, should yet precede it for its practical importance. But it is hazardous to draw from this practical primacy of the will theoretical conclusions that tend to weaken philosophy and belittle reason. Bonaventura played this double game single-heartedly and with sincere intention. He is like a child that mistakes the gaily decorated outriders of the king for the king himself, for in all spiritual activity which precedes revelation he sees something of revelation itself.

Dante, especially in the *Paradiso*, has more than one passage where profane science is judged, that is, condemned, on practical and mystical grounds. Even the Dantesque Thomas, the philosopher, must hail it as the highest peak of wisdom if he tells us that we, like King Solomon, must not concern ourselves with useless questions of angelic intelligence, dialectics, and physics, but only with what is needed for our purposes.[1] And when the poet asks how freedom of the will is consistent with predestination, Peter Damian makes the remarkable reply:

> But that soul in the heaven which is most pure,
> That seraph which his eye on God most fixes,
> Could this demand of thine not satisfy;
> Because so deeply sinks in the abyss
> Of the eternal statute what thou askest,
> From all created sight it is cut off.
> And to the mortal world, when thou returnest,
> This carry back, that it may not presume
> Longer tow'rd such a goal to move its feet.
> The mind, that shineth here, on earth doth smoke;
> From this observe how can it do below
> That which it cannot though the heaven assume it?[2]

And Dante himself declares to the apostle Peter that in comparison with the "syllogism" of the Holy Spirit all human logic seems to him pointless. Numerous other passages in the *Paradiso* emphasize, now warningly, now consolingly, the limitations and the insufficiencies of human reason, and stand in direct opposition to the poet's philosophical studies.

This opposition cannot be removed by logical means. It must be explained historically and psychologically. It is the same contradiction with which the scholastic systems tortured themselves and which forced the mystics to relinquish reason. The mystics did away with the contradiction by finally doing away with scholasticism and preparing the ground for a new philosophy. In this destructive work Dante no longer followed them. His philosophy does not begin, but ends, with doubt. Virgil is not dismissed until his service is completed. Attention is called with strong emphasis

[1] *Paradiso*, XIII, 94 sqq.   [2] *Ibid.*, XXI, 91–102.

to the limitations of reason only after they have been surpassed
in the *Paradiso*. Like the sphere of the earth, which bore him, so
does human reason appear as an insignificant point in space as
Dante beholds it from the contemplative heights of his pious pilgrimage through heaven.

> I with my sight returned through one and all
> The sevenfold spheres, and I beheld this globe
> Such that I smiled at its ignoble semblance;
> And that opinion I approve as best
> Which doth account it least; and he who thinks
> Of something else may truly be called just.[1]

Everything in the *Paradiso*, to some extent in the *Purgatorio* also,
that is brought out against the validity of rational conclusions, is
essentially the expression of pious impulses, but not of mystical
philosophy. How the divinely enlightened souls of Paradise
value human reason is for us mortals as important as their estimate
of the earth's size as viewed from their Heaven. A heavenly viewpoint is well adapted to elevate us above ourselves, to uplift us to a
freer mood, to bid us gaze with a smile on the limitations of our
own nature—but it does not increase our knowledge. So it is with
Dante. His mysticism is the irony of reason, turned against itself,
the elegiac and yearning humour of the philosopher, not his self-
destruction, not his renunciation.

We have seen how in Thomas reason, through the consciousness of its own limitations, became sane, competent, and
independent. Now we observe how this self-same awareness of
the limitations of reason gives rise to a mystical mood. What
happens here to Dante's philosophy every mature man has himself
experienced. The more accurately a man knows himself, the more
calmly he can rely on his own strength, and the more painfully he
must be conscious of his own weakness. The tree of self-knowledge
bears sweet and bitter fruit. Virgil, who represents Dante's philosophy, has eaten of both. In him Dante, by one of the simplest and
profoundest of poetical expedients, has removed the contradiction
which his logic could not efface.

The results of mysticism are, as the later history of mediæval
thought demonstrates, individualism, nominalism, voluntarism,
and scepticism. These Dante did not live to see. Therefore the
influence of mysticism on his philosophy remained secondary.

[1] *Paradiso*, XXII, 133–138.

We can indeed recognize in his system traces of mysticism, but no mystical foundation. Precisely because mysticism found no room in the system, it poured its mighty stream into his poetry.

Even Bonaventura, who is the chief source of Dante's mysticism, only partially and reluctantly drew the conclusions which we have just noted. The only philosophically important point in which Bonaventura diverges with full consciousness from Thomism seems to me to be his doctrine of matter. Like Thomas, he also distinguishes formed from unformed matter; or matter as substance (potency plus act) from matter as a logical concept (pure potency). The latter, which does not actually exist, cannot have been created by God. For creation is merely the union of potency and act. So all matter is formed, and all created form is material. Only God, the uncreated form and pure act, is immaterial. There are no other immaterial forms. Therefore also matter is not interpreted as a deficiency, but as something positive, which lies at the foundation of all formed beings, even the most spiritual. The creation *post nihilum*, which Thomas accepted only under the compulsion of dogma, thus leads Bonaventura, who takes dogma seriously, to the conception of a spiritual matter or of a material spirit.

What, then, is this abstract world-matter, this last principle of all reality, which embraces corporeal as well as spiritual beings? What is this predicate which, applied to all creatures, is able to bring them all into a common and unified relation to their creator? What is this last and palest accident which attaches to all substances? It is number: numerical unity, with its capacity to develop into plurality.

Antiquity and mediævalism delighted in the symbolism of numbers, but nowhere was it more at home than in the Franciscan Order.

Its wide dissemination and popularity are doubtless to be explained by the fact that it does not, of itself, commit us to any particular theory of the universe. It is, indeed, in the last analysis naturalistic in origin, and yet lends itself readily to quite opposite lines of thought. So from the earliest times we can distinguish a symbolism of numbers in natural philosophy and another in the philosophy of history. The former was cultivated by the Babylonians and the Pythagoreans; the latter was developed especially by the Persians and the Jews. By the former it is linked to astronomy, by the latter to eschatology.

The most remarkable eschatological structure, however, which was set up in mediæval Italy, is that of the Calabrian Abbot Joachim of Flora (ob. 1202), whom Dante in all seriousness regarded as a prophet.[1] In Joachim's writings the construction of the history of the world and of salvation in the form of numerical symbolism runs to the maddest extremes. The genuine and apocryphal treatises of Joachim have been zealously studied, developed, and interpreted by the most rigorous observants of the Franciscan rule. From that time the symbolism of numbers became a part of the special inheritance of Franciscan theology, and through its influence on the outer world a popular pastime. Bonaventura then found in the symbolism of numbers a fully developed method of the philosophy of history. His doctrine of spiritual matter subsequently built for it a "scientific" foundation.

It is not amiss, therefore, to assert that the symbolism of numbers that Dante valued as an indispensable means for artistic imagery is, in the main, a gift from Franciscan mysticism. Dante accepted it and used it freely both in the *Commedia* and in his youthful work, the *Vita Nuova*, but he probably never gave serious thought to the logical and metaphysical foundations of its procedure. The aerial bodies with which he provides his spirits are, as we have seen, chiefly for poetic effect, and have nothing to do with primal matter, for the very reason that an airy body is not a number.

We thus see once again that Franciscan mysticism furnished our poet with an abundance of motifs and much imagery, but with no ideas that were essential to his system. So far as mysticism was a part of that system, it had already been taken up and organized by Thomas. But since philosophy exists only as system, that is, as logical order, our poet's philosophy is no other than that of St. Thomas.

5. DANTE AS A PHILOSOPHER

MOTIVE AND OPPORTUNITY FOR STUDY

If Dante's philosophy is that of Thomas, why, then, a special study of Dante as a philosopher? Because the philosopher is something other than philosophy, the personal acceptance of a system something other than the system in and for itself. Why

---

[1] *Paradiso*, XII, 140. The Franciscans asserted that Joachim had prophesied the foundation and importance of their order.

did Dante decide for Thomism, not for Averroism or mysticism, or for some other school of thought of his time? What feature of Thomism was especially attractive to him? What rôle did it play in his spiritual life? These questions demand reply.

It was by painful, circuitous ways that Dante came to Thomas.

"After the joy of my soul (Beatrice) was lost to me, sorrow overcame me so that nothing could comfort me. Yet after some time my mind, which craved recovery, sought (since neither my own comforting nor that of others could avail) after a path which other disconsolate ones had trodden in quest of consolation. And I began to read Boëthius's book, unknown to many, with which he consoled himself in imprisonment and exile. And when I heard that Tullius also had written a similar book in which he, treating of friendship, recorded some consoling words of Lælius, a most excellent man, on the death of his friend Scipio, I began to read this also. And though it was difficult for me at first to comprehend their meaning, I did understand it at last in so far as my literary knowledge and a certain capacity of mine could help me, by the aid of which capacity I divined certain things as though in a dream, as may be learned from my *Vita Nuova*.

"And as it is wont to happen that one seeks for silver and un-expectedly finds gold, which some hidden cause reveals to him, perhaps not without divine command, so I also, who sought to console myself, found not only medicine for my tears, but also words and names of authors, of sciences, and of books. And as I considered these I judged that Philosophy, the mistress of these authors, sciences, and books, must be a mighty thing. And I thought of her as a noble lady and could not imagine her otherwise than as of a merciful nature. So my truth-seeking sense looked to her so gladly that I could hardly turn it from her. And after this imaginative apparition of her I began to seek her where she truly showed herself; that is, in the schools of the monks (*religiosi*) and at the discussions of the devotees of philosophy. Within the brief space of some thirty months, delight of her so seized upon me that this love banished and destroyed every other thought."[1]

Thus we know from Dante himself that the loss of his youthful love was the motive, and Boëthius's *De Consolatione Philosophiae* and the Ciceronian dialogue *Laelius* (*De Amicitia*) were the guides, that led him to philosophy.

[1] *Convivio*, II, 13.

Both Cicero and Boëthius were eclectics. Neither of the writings mentioned could provide the young poet with a philosophical system, but both were suited to give him a lively sense of the moral value of philosophy; for the fundamental idea of both is virtue, which uplifts man out of himself, liberates him, and assures him a higher happiness above the vicissitudes of life. This Stoic position acquires in the *Laelius* a significance that is mainly practical, in the *De Consolatione* an essentially religious one. In the former the Stoic idea of virtue is brought to bear on this moral and political question: What relation should the free activity of one man hold to that of another? In Boëthius, however, the following metaphysical problem is raised: How is man's free action related to the omnipotence, goodness, and omniscience of God? A wise destiny put into the hands of the youth who, despondent from sentimental love of woman, sought consolation in the ancient philosophers, first the pious considerations of Boëthius, and later the noble and manly counsels of the *Laelius*.

Whoever devotes himself with unprejudiced mind to the perusal of these books can still feel their effect, even at the present day. What comfort must they have brought to the wounded feelings of the young poet, whose powers were threatening to exhaust themselves in sentimentality, effeminacy, and self-indulgence! The tearful period of the *Vita Nuova* was followed by the dry and austere scholasticism of the *Convivio*. The transition was guided by the eclectic moral philosophy of Boëthius and Cicero.

So Dante became a philosopher, not out of thirst for knowledge, but from an inward craving for clarity and strength. To him who knocks at the philosopher's door in curiosity and with a mere fancy for culture, the temple will never be opened—only a card-index will be shown him. Philosophy gives itself to him who needs and loves, not to the sight-seer. Dante himself tells the tale of his philosophic studies under the poetic figure of love and the service of woman. "Be it known that by love in this allegory I mean study, which is nothing else than the inclination of the loving soul to the object of its love."[1] "And," he continues, "when this love found that my life was ready to receive its ardour, it blazed up as a fire from a small flicker to a large flame, so that not only when I was awake, but even while I slept, a light from this lady (Philosophy) entered into my head. How great a desire to behold her was awak-

[1] *Convivio*, II, 16.

ened in me by love can neither be told nor understood. And not only of her was I so desirous, but also of all people who stood in any way near to her, whether in friendship or kinship. How often in the night when all other men's eyes rested in slumber, have mine own gazed straight toward the abode of my love!"[1] He tosses "in burning heat on his couch."

His thirst for knowledge robs him of his sleep. "While my thoughts, reasoning about her, often wished to infer things concerning her which I could not understand, and I was bewildered so that I appeared as one mad: just as when one looks forward in a straight line, and clearly beholds the nearest objects; and then, gazing farther, sees dimly; and, farther still, is quite uncertain; and striving beyond this, the baffled eye sees nothing more."[2] A man who can utter such words knows what goes on in the brain of the brooding philosopher, because he himself has experienced it.

PHILOSOPHIC DILETTANTISM

But need, love, impatience, meditation, still make no philosopher. To be sure, one does not become master without having first been an impatient lover; but the art of investigation demands clarity, persistence, capacity, and calm. For a long time, something of the dilettante clung to our poet's philosophic efforts. He was too impatient, too restless, or rather too temperamental, to become a thorough philosopher. His more largely planned scientific works, the *Convivio* and the *De vulgari Eloquentia*, he left incomplete before they were half written.

The mood out of which the *Convivio* sprang was that of an overzealous layman. In the most personal manner imaginable, he woos and glorifies Philosophy as a dearly beloved woman.

> The love that in my soul is eloquent
> Doth speak to me with so much longing for my lady,
> Utters within me such strange thoughts of her,
> That over them my reason goes astray.
> So graciously her words of love resound,
> That hearing it and feeling it my soul
> Declares, "Alas, I am without the power
> To utter that which I have heard of her."[3]

What is in reality logical demonstration takes the form here, according to the poet's own declaration, of a lovely lady's glances;[4]

[1] *Convivio*, III, 1.   [2] *Ibid.*, 3.
[3] *Ibid.*, second canzone.   [4] *Ibid.*, II, 16.

and the convincing form in which philosophical truths are expressed appears as a smile upon the lips of Lady *Philosophia*.[1] Dante's personal conception of the matter possessed him so completely that at a distance it seems almost comical, and looks more like a mannerism than genuine artistic or scientific devotion. The yearning toward a peculiar scientific attitude has thrown the poet back into the hackneyed and pedantic oddities of his less original contemporaries.

He moves in the same circle of laboured and therefore tasteless originality in the passage where he believes that he has discovered a significant likeness between the heavens of the seven planets and the seven free arts, and, rising higher, between the three loftiest heavens on one side, and philosophy (physics and metaphysics), ethics, and theology on the other.[2]

Opposed to these efforts, which finally lead to caprice, stands an almost schoolboyish joy in dialectic performances. Dante is eager to show how much he has learned, heaps distinctions on distinctions, definitions on definitions, and one learned digression on another.

He cannot put the word "philosophy" on paper without adding to it an outline of its history. He cannot mention the sky without detailing its entire astronomy, nor the emperor without expatiating on his system of statesmanship.

So his poetic eulogies on science serve him as opportunity and pretext to pour out the abundance of his knowledge. On allegorical poems which in themselves are unintelligible he hangs scientific explanations in prose which are in themselves utterly disconnected. This contradiction between personal enthusiasm and bookish pedantry makes the *Convivio* a hybrid and unpleasing structure. In it is mirrored the transitional condition wherein the thinker has found his thoughts, but the poet has not yet devised the form. Dante seems to have felt the internal immaturity of this work, and perhaps for that reason let it drop.

REASON AND MORALITY

However, the tendency to clarity and unity begins to appear even in the *Convivio* itself. "Absorbed in the eyes of his mistress Philosophy," that is, occupied in rational demonstrations, the poet strikes a difficulty. "And as this my mistress changed some-

---

[1] *Convivio*, III, 15.   [2] *Ibid.*, II, 14–15.

what her gracious expression toward me (especially on those points where I considered and inquired whether the primal matter of the elements originated with God), I withdrew somewhat from her sight." [1] That is, having arrived at a difficult point in metaphysical speculation, Dante halted; and in order not to remain idle he turned to a matter of moral philosophy, namely, to the question of the essence of nobility. What puzzled him was nothing less than the doctrine of Creation; that is, as we have seen, the very point on which even Thomas Aquinas was no longer able to dispose of Averroistic dualism. When the young philosopher had run aground here, it was natural, perhaps inevitable, that he return to practical questions—in fact, to that point from which he had originally approached philosophy.

It is instructive to notice here how in the course of his inquiry into the nature of nobility, he comes after all on a theoretical problem, and what he had not been able to solve in metaphysics confronts him now once again, and most unexpectedly, from the side of the theory of knowledge. Toward the middle of the fourth discussion in the *Convivio*, he demonstrates that material riches cannot constitute the basis of nobility. Wealth is in its essence not noble but vulgar, and chiefly for the reason that instead of satisfying the possessor it always creates need and craving for more riches. Noble, he declares, are those goods alone that lead us to repose and happiness. But then—this doubt arises—science also would not be noble. For it, too, promises repose and happiness to the possessor of truth, but hardly is the truth attained when there arises fresh doubt, new unrest, and need of further investigation. Quite like the craving for riches, the thirst for knowledge also grows by an unceasing progression. So the one is as devoid of nobility as the other? No, Dante responds, for between the increase of greed for wealth and of greed for knowledge there is a difference. The one gains in strength, but always directs itself toward the same object, namely, riches; the other, on the contrary, gains in quality, that is, it expands and aims at ever new problems. When the greedy man has accumulated a hundred marks and now craves a thousand more, that is no new goal, for a hundred is a part of a thousand. But when he that thirsts after knowledge has come to know Nature in accordance with her laws, and now inquires further into the essence of these laws, the object and aim

[1] *Convivio*, IV, 1.

of the inquiry have changed and have become broader. To the knowledge of natural science, metaphysical knowledge is added as a new and nobler companion. The possession of a hundred marks derives from the addition of thousands more rather a decrease than an increase of value; while the worth of a lower knowledge is multiplied by the addition of a higher one.[1] The malevolent opponent retorts: After all, the thirst for knowledge is never sated, any more than the thirst for gold. Not so, replies Dante; knowledge has in itself a natural ground, a natural limit. And here he cites Aristotle: "The trained investigator seeks, in things, that certainty of which they are in their nature capable."[2] And: "Man should uplift himself to divine things so far as he can." "In short," our poet concludes, "however the desire for knowledge be regarded, whether in general or in particular, it attains its fulfillment; therefore perfect science has a noble perfection, and—in contrast with accursed riches—it does not, because of the existence of its desire, lose its perfection."[3]

Nowhere, to my knowledge, has Dante more clearly and positively proven the independence of reason than here. These two chapters contain the germ of a phenomenology of the spirit. Between the empirical incapacity ever to attain complete knowledge and the metaphysical possibility and necessity of a universally valid conclusion of knowledge, Dante has clearly seen the distinction, and outlined it by a topographical and mathematical figure. "In fact," he says, "the path to knowledge is lost through error, even as are the roads on this earth. For as there is from one city to another necessarily one best and straightest road, another which always diverges from it and so leads somewhere else, and many others which now diverge and now go directly, so there are also various paths in human life of which one is the truest, another the falsest, and certain others less false, and others again less true."[4] "The knowledge of reason," he continues, "is part of our natural desire, and just as every other natural desire attains its goal, so too does this." Thus the limits of reason are determined by its own force, and not narrowed unduly by supernatural interference.

Reverence for pure morality is most closely associated with reverence for pure reason. Dante believed that he saw them em-

---

[1] Dante has not expressed this thought, but did clearly enough foreshadow it, so that I feel justified in inserting it, for the sake of clearness.
[2] *Convivio*, IV, 13.   [3] *Ibid.*   [4] *Ibid.*, 12.

bodied with especial purity in the Stoa and in the character of
Cato. Perhaps his reverence for the Stoa was heightened by the
fact that he regarded it as the eldest among the schools of philosophy. "There were very ancient philosophers—and the first and
highest among them was Zeno—who recognized as the aim of
human life the most austere virtue; that is, to follow strictly and
exclusively truth and righteousness, without utterance of pain,
without utterance of joy, without a breath of passion. And this
virtue they defined as that which without profit and without
reward is in itself rationally praiseworthy. They and their
disciples were called Stoics, and one of them was the glorious
Cato." [1]

If Dante, nevertheless, set Aristotle high above the other philosophers, and characterized him simply as "*the* philosopher," he was
following the intellectualistic current of his time, especially the
usage of the Thomistic school. That Cato, however, was closer
to his heart he leaves us nowise in doubt. In the *Commedia* Aristotle must content himself with the ante-Inferno, the Limbo of
the noble heathen; while Cato rises at the foot of the Purgatorial
mountain to the rôle of a symbol of moral self-deliverance.

However numerous and clear the literary sources are which
might be cited for the honour bestowed by Dante on this hero, it
remains essentially an act prompted by the poet's fullest conviction, and a proof, indeed the strongest proof, of his mainly practical attitude toward philosophy. The same causes, and the same
manner, that brought Dante through philosophy to the recovery
of his spiritual health, brought his Cato up to Purgatory. *The
true source of this figure is that inward experience which lies at the
foundation of the entire* Convivio.

THE POPULAR PHILOSOPHER

The *Convivio* is, as we have seen, upheld by the conviction that
the craving for knowledge is natural, innate in every man, and
therefore wholly justified. It begins with a sentence from Aristotle:
"All men by their very nature yearn for knowledge." But since
only a few are in a position to satisfy this desire in suitable fashion,
Dante wishes to come to their aid. For those who have no mastery
over the Latin language, and therefore cannot read the books of
the philosophers, he proposes to set forth the most important doc-

[1] *Convivio*, IV, 6.

trines in Italian speech, and to prepare for them a public philosophic banquet (*convivio*).

After having experienced in his own case how much consolation, what benefit and profit, philosophy has the power to bestow, he exerts himself to share this same happiness with the lay world of Italy. The layman in philosophy becomes the first popular philosopher of the Middle Ages. The historic importance of the *Convivio* lies in this purpose of popular enlightenment. Beatrice's death became for Dante the occasion for his study of philosophy. The misfortune of his banishment from Florence became the occasion for his publishing these studies.

The malicious and unjust condemnation which thrust him out of the position of an honoured citizen into exile and poverty had been a heavy blow to his sentiments of justice, dignity, and honour. It must have been with sorrow that he declared that since his banishment, in his aimless wanderings, he had displayed against his will the wound that destiny had inflicted on him. He learned how the misfortune of an exiled man is accounted a disgrace, and how he had "to the eyes of many appeared ignoble." [1] Against all this his pride revolted. He wished to show that he was no worthless vagabond, that he had not, with home and prosperity, lost also character and self-respect. On the contrary, and according to the wont of noble natures, the injustice he had suffered only made him prouder, more sensitive, more suspicious and self-conscious. Even for the innocent love-songs which he had published he feared misinterpretation. Therefore he wished to set over against them this philosophic commentary. *Movemi timore d'infamia.* (" Fear of evil repute moves me to seize my pen.") In order to escape the chatter of the ignorant, he made himself their teacher and enlightener.

The rôle of popular instructor, educator, and expounder, which was assigned him by misfortune, he made in an ever profounder and more definite sense his life-work. Everything that he writes after his exile is more or less in the service of this lofty mission. He actually made it a habit to proclaim, at the very beginning of his writings, their practical utility. His next work after the *Convivio* was presumably the *De vulgari Eloquentia*. It begins: "Since we do not find that any one before us has discussed at all the doctrine of the vulgar speech, and since we see that such speech is absolutely

[1] *Convivio*, I, 2–3.

necessary to all, because not only men, but women and children also, strive to attain to it, so far as their nature permits, therefore we, desiring to illuminate somewhat the understanding of those who, as it were, wander blindly in the marketplace, usually placing after what should come before, will endeavour, with Heaven's favour, to be of service to the speech of ordinary people." In his political work, the *De Monarchia*, he is no longer content to instruct his contemporaries; he turns also toward the coming generations. Every generation, he begins, has handed on to the next a certain treasure of truths; hence our duty is to labour for the future. "Therefore, pondering often upon this matter, lest I should ever be accused of the sin of burying my talent, I desire not only to put forth blossoms for the public good, but also to bear fruit and to demonstrate truths attacked by others." Even the *Quaestio de Aqua et Terra*, the genuineness of which can hardly be doubted any longer, is no exception in this regard.

Like Lessing, Schiller, and Fichte, Dante became an educator of his people. He did not feel himself primarily, as Goethe did, the mouthpiece of his age, nor a model for humankind, nor did he pose as such, but rather as a fellow worker and champion. This lifelong devotion to practical rather than to artistic ends determines the character of Dante's future philosophic work.

THE PHILOSOPHY OF SPEECH

The most indispensable tool of the popular educator and enlightener is speech. Of which language shall I make use: Latin or Italian? This doubt harassed Dante throughout his entire artistic and scientific career.

Boccaccio relates that the poet had begun the *Divine Comedy* in Latin hexameters, but afterward gave preference to his mother tongue, first of all, because he wished to reach a wider circle, and secondly because he noted in his contemporaries a falling off in the understanding of Latin poetry.[1] Whether this statement is correct we do not know. But Dante's philosophy of speech reveals that he narrowly escaped presenting us with an artistic and scholastic epic in Latin instead of the *Divine Comedy*.

How strongly the prejudices of the educated classes even at the close of the Middle Ages, especially in Italy, favoured Latin and belittled their mother speech, which they stigmatized as vulgar,

[1] Boccaccio, *Vita di Dante*, § 15.

this is not the place to discuss. Dante himself, at the time when he wrote the *Vita Nuova,* was wholly possessed by such prejudices. Poetry in the vulgar tongue, he declares, must limit itself to the subject of love; for it has been called to life in the service of woman, since the singer wished to declare himself to his lady, who knew no Latin. To this original use, which had given birth to Italian song, must the language remain fettered. [1] But even as love grew to philosophic heights with the poet of the "new style," so did his language struggle out of its limitations and extend its peculiar rights into fresh fields.

After the death of his earthly Beatrice, Philosophy became Dante's second love. And her praises, also, he sings in Italian canzoni—but "because no vernacular was suited to speak openly of the lady I was falling in love with, and because my readers were not ready to understand my naked demonstrations," [2] therefore the poet employed the veil of allegory. However warmly and passionately in the *Convivio* he defends his mother tongue, its entrance into philosophical poetry was permitted only conditionally, and by the circuitous path of allegory. Yet as early as the third canzone of the *Convivio,* the allegorical veil is thrown aside, and while other contemporaries, e.g. Francesco da Barberino, composed their commentaries to allegorical poems in Latin prose, Dante determined to make use of the popular speech for three reasons, (1) because the poems which are to be explained, and to which the commentary is therefore subsidiary, are in Italian; (2) because the treasure of his knowledge is to be at the service of all his fellow countrymen; and (3) because he loves this wonderful speech of his homeland. As out of a burning house the flames break through the windows and plainly reveal the fire within, so he must proclaim his burning love for his native speech. [3] He had even already reached the determination to indicate in a separate work the value he set on the vulgar speech. This work was to be the *De vulgari Eloquentia,* the most characteristic of our poet's philosophic performances.

Even the Greek Sophists had debated whether human language came into being naturally or by convention. The same question came up in the Middle Ages, in connection with the strife over universals. The nominalists were inclined to see something arbitrary not only in concepts, but also in words, while the realists

---

[1] *Vita Nuova,* § 25.   [2] *Convivio,* II, 12.   [3] *Ibid.,* I, 12.

ascribed to language a sort of natural necessity and an imminent content of truth to be elaborated dialectically. Both these lines of thought are united in Dante's doctrine of language. For him there is a language which is the gift of Nature, and one fixed by convention. The former is the native mother tongue, or vulgar speech; the other is the literary language fixed by art and rules. In the Apennine peninsula we accordingly have a vulgar speech, Italian, and a literary language, Latin.

Their position side by side is not, however, the original, but a subsequent, condition. When God created the first man, he provided him with a fully developed language as a natural gift, which, in harmony with the whole character of the unspoiled creation, was complete, regular, unified, and changeless. The confusion and mutability of language were imposed on men, as the Bible testifies, by a divine curse, as a penalty for the building of the tower of Babel. It would have been more logical to connect the ruin of language with the deterioration of our nature; that is, with the sin and fall of the first pair. Dante saw this, and later made the correction, in the *Paradiso*. While he teaches, in the *De vulgari Eloquentia*, that the divinely created language was Hebrew, and that the first word spoken by Adam was the Hebrew name of God, *El*, he makes Adam himself announce in Canto XXVI of the *Paradiso* that the first human language was extinct long before the tower of Babel was built, and that the name for God was not originally *El* but *I*.[1]

No matter whether the divine curse was launched when the tower was built at Babel or at the original fall through sin, it continues in force, dispersing all living languages into a thousand branches and subjecting them to constant decay. Through time and space an eternal change goes on in human speech. If today the old inhabitants of Pavia should come again to their city, they would hardly be able to understand the speech of their latest descendants. In order to check this confusion, the learned, as "inventors of the grammatical faculty," artificially created something permanent: the indestructible grammar, the eternally unchanging Latin, a mediæval Esperanto. How they managed to build up this artificial continent in the billowy sea of human speech, the

---

[1] This subject is further discussed in two of my essays—*Sprache und Religion*, in my *Geist und Kultur in der Sprache*, Heidelberg, 1925, Chapter III, and *Dante und die Sprache*, in *Die Pyramide*, Karlsruhe, Sept. 14, 1921.

poet fails to tell us. He is aware, also, that apart from Latin there are, or were, other forms of grammar, e.g. an artistic and literary Greek language.

But he regards the vulgar speech as naturally better (*nobilior*) than grammar; first, because it is more original, and to be traced back to the first pair; second, because, though divided and sub-divided, it is spread over all the earth; and third, because we have received it from Nature, not from art. Grammatica (that is, Latin) has, to be sure, the advantage over the vulgar speech of being indestructible and indivisible.

Now, if I am not mistaken, the half-purpose, yes, perhaps the whole intent, of the *De vulgari Eloquentia* is to raise the vulgar Italian speech to a form of grammatica, and to create out of the changing dialects a unified literary Italian language. It is not possible, indeed, to speak positively as to the final purpose of this work, as it breaks off in the middle of the second book.

But in that portion with which we are acquainted, all the elements tend toward the idea of one united literary Italian language. All the dialects of the peninsula, of which Dante enumerates fourteen, are rejected as insufficient, alien, and of inferior value. That the rationalistic philosopher should find no justification for the popular idioms is only natural. But outside of and above the dialects there stands, for him, "a lofty, fundamental, courtly, glorified vulgar speech, which belongs to all the states, and seems to belong to none; and by which all the provincial dialects are measured, weighed, and compared." [1] Just as all numbers are measured by unity, all colours by white, all civic acts by law, all properties of Italians by the concept of the Italian, even so all Italian dialects are measured by comparison with a standard Italian language. This, however, is no *res*, but a *conceptus;* no reality, but an ideal. Especially eminent poets, like Cino da Pistoia and his friend—perhaps Dante means himself—come nearest to this ideal vulgar speech. They approach it through art, and Dante praises them therefor. Those linguistic imitations which proceed from it more directly, not through art but through Nature, the dialects of Florence and Rome, are much more definitely condemned than the remoter dialects of the South and North. The reason is clear; Dante has himself indicated it, but his commentators have not noticed it. From no other side could corruptions

[1] *De vulgari Eloquentia*, I, 16.

creep into the ideal normal speech as easily as from Rome and Florence.

Francesco d'Ovidio has attempted to show that in the *De vulgari Eloquentia* there is a constant confusion of language with style. If we are to understand by language etymology and accidence, and by style dictionary and syntax, D'Ovidio may be right. But if by language we understand the given medium of expression in use, and by style its artistic shaping, then Dante has accurately distinguished between language and style. The literary and stylistic improvement of a language with grammatical regularity, with choice vocabulary, with accurate and scholarly distinctions between the types of poetry, with strict division of styles into a tragic (lofty), a comic (mixed), and an elegiac (humble) style, and with fixed metrical units—this is, as it seems to me, the most important goal of the *De vulgari Eloquentia*.

It is a program which two centuries after Dante the classical school of the Cinquecento men like Bembo and Trissino strove to carry out. "We have given to those who write verse in the vulgar speech the name of poets, and undoubtedly with reason; for they truly are poets, provided one takes the right view of poetry, and defines it as a musically composed, rhetorical invention. Nevertheless these vulgar poets are to be distinguished from the great (ancient), that is, from the regular (classical), ones; because the latter composed their poems in a lofty and standard language and art, but the former in an irregular speech, as we have said. From this it follows that the more exactly we imitate the old masters, the more artistic is our poetry. And therefore, in our theory of art, too, we must strive to follow the poetical doctrines of those men (the ancients)." [1] Next comes a reference to the *Ars Poetica* of Horace. So far has Dante outrun his time! He composed, with mediæval profundity and mediæval heaviness, the first Renaissance "art of poetry."

By uplifting the natural language of the much-degraded vernacular tongues to the artistic speech of the unified *vulgare illustre*, he opened up to it the whole range of human expression. The purified poet of the vulgar tongue was thus enabled to sing whatsoever stirred his soul: that which the vegetative soul seeks; bodily strength and feats of arms; that which delights the sensitive soul, happy love; that for which the rational soul longs, morality and virtue.

[1] *De vulgari Eloquentia*, II, 4.

It is clear that, by this definition, theological and religious sub-jects still remain forbidden ground for the Italian muse. Dante's Parnassus, it is to be recalled, has two peaks, the first of which befits the natural, the second the mystical, powers of the soul. Of the ascent to the second peak there is no mention in the *De vulgari Eloquentia*. So it is more than probable that Dante, be-fore he began his *Divine Comedy*, seriously wavered between Latin and Italian. What led him to the latter decision, the boldness of which cannot be sufficiently emphasized?

It would be an excusable evasion to answer: the didactic in-tention, the desire to give moral instruction. Dante informs us, in his dedicatory letter to Can Grande, that the true subject of his poem is man, as he is rewarded or punished according to his merit or guilt; and quite superfluously he adds that the *genus philos-ophiae* under which the poem develops, both as a whole and in detail, is moral philosophy, ethics. He should accordingly have defined his own work as a poem on virtue and morality, and every-thing should have been in faultless harmony with the suppositions of the *De vulgari Eloquentia*.

Perhaps it was an afterthought of Dante's to give this turn to the matter and to defend his Italian flight to Heaven as a useful and moral undertaking. But we know that the *Divine Comedy* is infinitely more than a didactic poem; it is an act of the most personal piety. We know that the innermost impulse was mystical, not educational. The moralizing and popularizing philosopher becomes then, by his mighty flight, a divinely inspired seer. The champion of his age, whom we compared with Lessing, Schiller, and Fichte, yet feels and acts, like Goethe, as the voice of his century and as a symbolic image of mankind. The Dante of the *Divine Comedy* is no longer the Dante of the *Convivio* or of the *De vulgari Eloquentia*. If the *Commedia* were lost, I should like to see the scholar who, from the *Convivio*, the *De vulgari Eloquentia*, or, for all I care, from the entire prose works of the poet, could give us any approximate notion of what the *Commedia* is.

It is the peculiarity of artistic genius that it reaches, in happy moments, a height for which its own understanding has no measure or rule. To Goethe his best creations and the manner in which he attained to them remained a mystery. Even so it may well have been for Dante a marvel how he arrived at the divine Italian terzets for which his theory of art, progressive though it was, failed to account.

PHILOSOPHIC IMAGINATION AND IMAGINATIVE PHILOSOPHY

When a mighty poetic genius is associated with a vigorous reflective capacity, it may come to pass that the poet outwits the thinker, and the thinker the poet. Dante is an example of both.

But the more significant drama is not that in which the poet is interrupted and prejudiced by the thinker, but that wherein the thinker reflects on the creations of the poet, causes him to elaborate them in this or that direction, and finally accepts the gold of the imagination as real coin.

We have seen an example of this. As philosopher Dante, no less than Thomas, rejected the conception of spiritual matter. Intelligible substances, such as the angels or the departed souls of men, he thought of as immaterial. But as artist he shaped for them a shadow-body, and then himself believed, with the naïveté of genius, in the reality of this body of his own creation, and then made Statius explain to him in all seriousness the how and why of this phenomenon, as if it were a reality. Or again: he arrives in the course of his pilgrimage at the bank of the subterranean river Phlegethon, whose source is in the realm of the poet's fancy. Nevertheless, he inquires as to its geographic source and is told of the mysterious legend of the old man of Crete. He sees in the Inferno cleft walls of rock and broken bridges, and learns that this havoc was wrought by the earthquake on Golgotha. It happens that certain spirits prophesy future events, and others do not even know the present; and he learns the theory of the knowledge of the departed souls. There is hardly a poetic marvel for which this rationalist forgets to ask the cause.

Here lies, however, a great secret of his art. What his imagination has created, his intellect takes seriously. He dissects his dreams as if they were corporeal things. While his clear-eyed critical faculty surrenders to his own poetical deception, he takes his readers captive also. The boundary-line between empirical reality and poetry is effaced, and finally we are all much like the women of Verona of whom Boccaccio tells. When the great man passed their door, one said to the other: "Here comes the man who was in Hell; as often as he pleases he goes thither again and tells here on earth what is there below." "Yes," declared the other, "you can see from his crisp hair and the brown colour of his skin that he has been in fire and smoke."

It is quite as much the power of his imagination as the strong philosophic vein therein that makes the poetic world of the *Commedia* seem real. Ariosto and La Fontaine also have set before us with the most impressive picturesqueness a fabulous world of marvels. But we know exactly what to think of it. In Dante's case, on the contrary, the mediæval public could not but ask, in all seriousness, whether his Inferno was not the real Hell, and his mountain of hope the real Purgatory.

This much was certain, that his Paradise was the true Paradise. The ten heavens which arch above the earth were not in truth his invention; their existence, form, and order had previously been scientifically worked out. On this astronomical foundation the rest of the structure is raised. The astronomico-theological light of the heavens floods Dante's constructions of Purgatory and Hell with the deceptive semblance of reality.

A silly positivist criticism, incapable of comprehending the philosophic vein, the scientific re-enforcement, the critical and theological aspirations, and the religious foundation of Dante's imagination, strives to identify this or that Roman amphitheatre, this or that volcanic crater, as the model of the Dantesque Hell, and this or that cone-shaped mountain as the model for the Purgatory. This kind of inquiry after sources might be called picture-postcard scholarship.

The assumption of a Ptolemaic and Christian system of Heavens makes the construction of the other two realms intelligible as being derived from it. This is not meant to deny that the poet's imagination was nourished on earthly realities, and especially that he carried over the lines and colours of the Italian landscape into the other world. But in the main, this natural scenery serves rather as decoration than as framework. The constructive thought of the poem is essentially speculative and theological, imagination and poetry, piously working and scientifically planning. The frame was set up with the measuring-rods of symbolism and parallelism, so that we may venture to trace out the poet's lines of thought from his own spiritual tendencies, which may be called conceptually imaginative. Such a reconstruction will not be exact and faultless, but surely approximately probable and instructive.

Of the ten Heavens which arch about the earthly sphere, Dante must first set apart the uppermost, the Empyrean. It lies beyond time and space, is wholly invisible, and could not offer any helpful analogies for the construction of Hell and Purgatory; it crowns with its immaterial unity the divine number nine, and rounds it out to the perfect ten. This completion must be permanently denied to the two imperfect realms of the Hereafter. So they must consist of nine sections each. But the arrangement of these nine in the comparatively more perfect realm of Purgatory will follow the sacred number-units: 1 (Ante-Purgatory), 7 (the true Purgatory), and 1 (the Earthly Paradise), and so be a triple division; while in the Inferno the division into two less perfect units must prevail: 5 (upper sections of Hell), and 4 (Lower Hell). Paradise, however, cannot be subjected to any such dissection. Here the number ten of the circles may not be divided or interrupted.

As the numerical arrangement, so too the spatial arrangement of Hell and Purgatory may be derived from that of Paradise. Just as the heavenly spheres lie within and above one another, so the divisions of the other realms must stand in a similar stereometric relation to each other. It is well known that the sphere was from ancient times regarded as the most perfect form, and therefore could not be suitable for Hell and Purgatory.

Even in the *Convivio*,[1] Dante, employing a favourite philosophic figure, had represented the spiritual ascent of man from the sensuous life to God as a pyramid; that is, we start out from a single, definite object of our desires. This object is the apex of the pyramid. From this we uplift ourselves, step by step, to ever higher and larger things until we reach the highest and greatest: God Himself. He is the base of the pyramid. It was natural that this inverted pyramid that seeks after God should be once again inverted to represent progressive alienation from God. If one draws a straight line at a point anywhere outside the nine spheres from God to the earth, which is the common centre of all the spheres, then it appears that no matter where the divine centre outside the spheres may be set; the point of maximum distance from God always falls at the centre of our earthly sphere. There, then, we find the absolute denial of God; there Lucifer must have his abode. From this point one is to imagine a constantly enlarging hollow space which rises to the upper surface of the earth, inhabited by

[1] *Convivio*, IV, 12.

man. This hollow is the realm of Lucifer, the kingdom of estrangement from God—Hell. Since the spherical form was impossible, mathematically as well as symbolically, to the nine divisions of Hell, he chose conic sections parallel to the base—which is the surface of the earth—increasing in size in proportion to their distance from the centre. So, doubtless, the shape of an immense funnel, diminishing step by step, came to be imagined; a funnel at the tip of which is Lucifer, while its upper surface is vaulted over by the surface of our earth. Upon the middle of this surface stands the holy city Jerusalem.

The realm wherein release from sin is accomplished is, according to its theological significance, and therefore to its spatial form also, the positive antithesis of Hell; so it is no hole or funnel, but a cone-shaped mountain. This mount of purification rises heavenward, and has its basis not on the inhabited earth, as was the case with Hell, but on the uninhabited Southern Hemisphere.

A careful examination of these constructions at once gives rise to a series of new, half-scientific, half-mythical problems. For example: How and when did Lucifer come to be at the centre of the earth? God hurled him, the rebellious angel, toward the earth so that he crashed down, struck the ground at that point which is diametrically opposite to the present city of Jerusalem, ploughed into the earth from the force of his fall, and stopped at the centre. In so doing he pushed out an immense mass of earth, which shot up over him and formed the Purgatorial mountain. So the fall of the first angel provided for man the opportunity for purification even before he had fallen. But the land drew away with a shudder from the falling Devil, and the waters of the sea flooded the entire southern half of our globe.

These events are indicated by Dante in six brief and not overpicturesque verses,[1] just as one sets forth a scientific hypothesis. He does not need to relate it at length, because every one who knows the general hypothesis can fill in the details for himself; also because such serious matters forbid all imaginative elaboration.

The poet has defined, with a remarkable expenditure of theological astronomy and speculative mathematics, the exact time of his journey. It may be assumed, with approximate certainty, that he makes his entrance into Hell on the eve of Good Friday

[1] *Inferno*, XXXIV, 121–126.

in the year 1300, which was April eighth; that his ascent into Purgatory begins early on Easter Sunday, and his entrance into Paradise three days later, on the morning of the following Wednesday. The flight through the kingdom of Heaven, however, seems to be timeless. The Christian symbolism of this itinerary is quite transparent.

Such a speculative structure is poetry in the service of a systematic philosophy—a conscious, mythical invention, fundamentally analogous to the processes of mediæval theology. What does Hell look like? For Dante that is no idle romantic problem, but a theological one. He does not let his fancy play with the question how it might appear, but he deduces its appearance and constructs it in the manner in which it necessarily must be built if the laws of consistency are observed and errors are avoided. I regard it therefore as quite impossible to distinguish in detail the poetic invention from what Dante as a theologian regarded as fully ascertained. The moral subdivision of Purgatory in accord with the seven deadly sins he canonically regarded as at least probable. Could he have considered the invented moral divisions of Hell improbable? Was it with him a matter of conviction or of imagination that the souls destined for Purgatory assemble and await their destiny near papal Rome, at the Tiber's mouth? And is it to be believed that Dante put his enemies, ay, and many of his dearest friends, into Hell jestingly? Never was a poem fortified with more scientific accuracy, objectivity, and conscientiousness. We know of no other work of art in the world's literature that is so profoundly saturated with philosophy.

So at some point the critical consciousness must have made itself felt, and the realization must have awakened in Dante that he, like a landscape gardener, was planting colourful fables in the colourless unsubstantial soil of the other world. The passages of the *Commedia* where he points out the dreamlike, fictitious, or veiled nature of his creations, recalling himself and the reader to sober reality, are well known. That he was always and everywhere able to distinguish what was religiously believed and theologically assured from what he had personally invented, or what had been handed down in legend, will not be expected of him as a poet. What creative genius does not yield to the blessing of a certain self-deception? He thinks he is following the ocean highway to India, and he discovers a new world; he believes he is describing Paradise and Hell as they actually are, and he creates a mythical epic.

THE MYSTIC

If the pious poet had not believed in the Hereafter, how could he have put himself under the yoke of the Christian myth and meditated upon it philosophically?

When he composed his poem, the compelling force was a mighty longing for immortality, made keener by earthly sorrows; and out of that longing the Hereafter rose before him as a mighty imaginative vision of desire. All that is human and earthly he treats like the giant in the tale: he sweeps it as if it were a jerky toy into his great apron, carries it off, and sets it up again among the clefts, shelves, and arching rocks of his theological wonder-palace. That is a faith which removes not merely mountains, but things heavier still—the destinies of men. If it were mere art and not also genuine faith, then such a transfer of human beings and things to a supernatural world would have the effect of a jest or caprice, somewhat like Ariosto's voyage to the moon, or Baldus's journey to Hell in Folengo, or like a picturesque scene in the humanistic visions of Petrarch, Boccaccio, or Francesco Colonna. That the most serious belief is everywhere at work in Dante's poetry is realized from the fact that the poet submits himself completely to the laws of his other world, that he never trifles, not even in the jesting of his devils, but lets everything pass by like a vision of the Judgment Day. I find no passage where he drops the rôle of the true believer. His faith was no player's part. How completely possessed he was with his divine calling he makes Beatrice testify in the presence of the apostle James:

> No child whatever the Church Militant
> Of greater hope possesses, as is written
> In that Sun which irradiates all our band.[1]

By this "hope," Dante means not the ordinary human feeling, but, as he definitely explains, the divine gift of grace, which comes only to the deserving and the worthy. David, the singer of the highest God, had first made him, so he tells us, eager to receive this gift of grace.[2] At such an instant of intense mystical feeling, he best knows—or rather, betrays—himself. His own work, which

[1] *Paradiso*, XXV, 52–54.   [2] *Ibid.*, XXV, 71–72.

seemed to him in cold blood a moral and philosophic didactic poem, becomes a holy psalm.

So not merely the poet, but even the mystic has in Dante overcome the philosopher.

When we were discussing his piety, we came to the conclusion that the philosophic thinker was stronger in him than the mystical dreamer. Now we see almost the opposite: his faith was mightier than his science. But we must distinguish accurately between faith as an object in itself and as a motive of philosophy. By mystical dreamers we mean those with whom faith remains a motive without becoming an object of serious thought. But Dante put his faith, bit by bit, under the lamp of reason and so far as possible rationalized it. If he had completely rationalized it, it would have been exhausted as a motive, and all the riddles of the universe would have been solved. Dante did not consider himself so clever. As soon as his understanding had disposed of one question, his will to believe raised another. Sometimes the first solution did not suffice, and a second must be found. The phenomenon of the spots on the moon which he had explained physically in the *Convivio*,[1] in the *Paradiso* he treats by the speculative method,[2] and finally relegates the ultimate causes of natural science, as he had already done in the *Quaestio de Aqua et Terra*, to the inscrutable mysteries of God.[3] So it finally came to pass, especially in the *Paradiso*, that the will asked more questions than the intellect could answer, and that faith as a motive to philosophy remained infinitely more powerful than philosophy itself.

Dante had begun as a layman; he laboured on as a popular philosopher, became more and more deeply involved in speculation, learned by his own experience to observe the limitations of reason, and returned, a mystic at last, to a modest veneration of those inmost impulses which had made him a philosopher. Thereafter he set a mystical as well as a philosophical valuation on life and on his own accomplishment. Sometimes he regarded reason as man's noblest part, sometimes as the most regrettable hindrance to divine blessedness; poetry was to him at one time falsehood, at another revelation; he himself was now an educator and champion, now a symbol and type, of mankind; his *Commedia*

---

[1] *Convivio*, II, 14.   [2] *Paradiso*, II, 58-60.
[3] *Quaestio*, 22; cf. *Purgatorio*, III, 28-33.

he regarded at one time as a moral and didactic poem, at another as a pious and holy prophetic utterance.

He is rarely aware of these contradictions. It is only in unimportant matters that he tries to reconcile them scientifically, e.g. in the questions as to the origin of the spots on the moon, or as to the first cause for the confusion of human speech.

Usually the contradiction does not come to the surface, because between the philosopher and the mystic the poet intervenes, reconciling the other two. The *Divine Comedy* is the first and only poem where that reconciliation is accomplished.

Out of this unique poetic interweaving of practical, mystical, and philosophic threads comes forth the fabric of the *Divine Comedy*. The poetic motive is always foremost. The others serve it.

THE OUTLINES OF HIS PHILOSOPHIC DEVELOPMENT

Dante's philosophic development is so organic and sane that it would in his case be rash to speak of a period of exclusive rationalism or of exclusive mysticism. Karl Witte tried to show profound contradiction between the *Convivio* and the *Divina Commedia*. In the former he believed that he recognized the residuum of religious doubt; in the latter, the repentant return to the Catholic faith. This theory has been repeatedly refuted in excellent and thoroughgoing fashion. Dante's greatest feat of rationalism in the *Convivio* is, as we have seen, his doctrine of knowledge, and the glorification of heathen morality as embodied in Cato. Both these conquests the poet holds securely and fully in his *Commedia* and sets them side by side. At the very beginning of the *Purgatorio*, the second canzone of the *Convivio* resounds: "The love that in my soul doth speak." It is the glorification of philosophy. And Cato, representing free and rational will, stands, as the guardian of morality, at the foot of the mountain. Not one essential conviction of the *Convivio* is denied in the *Commedia*. The poet corrects only trifles and incidentals. Neither is the mystical limitation of the inquiring spirit missing in the *Convivio*,[1] nor is there any falling off of the philosophic impulse to be observed in the *Paradiso*.

But if Dante's mind had grown in such organic and healthy fashion, so that the earlier contained the later stage and the later the earlier, that does not indicate that the development was without inward struggles. At the close of the *Purgatorio*, the painful re-

[1] *Convivio*, II, 6 *ad init.*, and II, 9 *ad finem.*

membrance of such crises and struggles is especially vivid. There Beatrice sets forth in relentless words all the errors into which her friend had fallen in his quest for false happiness.[1] It would be idle and profitless to attempt to surmise in detail the nature of these errors. Presumably they were not only moral, but also scientific, transgressions of "natural" bounds. A temporary leaning to Averroism is an obvious conjecture. Clear indications of it are not to be found in Dante's writings, unless we strain their meaning.

The feeling for the eternal value of one's individuality is too vital in him to permit him to be contented with Averroism. And on the other hand, he felt too keenly the range of his own powers to be able to rest peacefully in mysticism. So he went over to the scholastics. Yet he was not sufficiently won over by the limitation of the understanding to feel permanently at home among them. To his restless effort, mysticism opened up remoter visions, a more congenial home. His passionate will found in it more steadfast goals of moral and political activity. Its beckoning hand he followed, and in his book on government (*De Monarchia*), he parted company, though with painful effort, with Thomas and his disciples.

[1] *Purgatorio*, XXX, 73 sqq., and XXXI, 1 sqq.

III: THE ETHICAL AND POLITICAL BACKGROUND
OF THE "DIVINE COMEDY"

1. RELATION OF ETHICS TO POLITICS

Ethics is the science of good action; politics is the science, or a science, of the ends of activity.

The moral end is ideally one: the Good. But the forms in which it actually appears are numberless. Numberless also are the directions in which all human action moves, rightly or perversely, in quest of this single goal. So with complete unity of final purpose, we have an inexhaustible number of means. The moralist seeks, among these many means, the end of all ends—the Good.

In order to act aright, one must act above all with a purpose and toward a goal, for only out of the conflict and rivalry of temporary, earthly, individualistic, passing interests, occupations, opportunities, goals, and purposes, arises the reconciling unity of the Good. But the Good is not conciliation, by compromise, of opposing individual aims, which still continue: it is not the Truce of God, but His Triumph. It is no adjustment and settlement of clashing interests, aims, and claims; it is nothing political, legal, or civic— no armistice, but the surrender of all arms, and the acceptance of new ones. Just as truth is pure thinking, the thinking of thought, so Good is pure willing, the willing of the will. Therefore out of all individual volitions, out of all efforts, the Good blossoms of itself as it can, and does not need to be constructed by political, legal, or other decrees or institutes.

When we define the Good as pure will, we do not mean that this will is to remain general, or that it must renounce all concern with particular, definite earthly and temporal action. On the contrary, we mean rather that worldly occupations become "good" precisely in that they are the goal of a will that wants them, wants them vigorously; not in a fretful, compulsory, reluctant, and half-hearted fashion, and not from mere wish or fancy. The Good, or pure will, could therefore also be defined as the unbroken unity of action and volition, of purpose and effort, of means and end, of mood and deed. For how should the Good be realized save through the whole-hearted activity of resolute men of character?

175

We must at this point consider the fact that neither ancient nor mediæval philosophy, with their fundamentally intellectualistic tendency, could attain to a clear understanding of this independent ethical value of the will, of this self-sufficing goodness of the strong, genuine, and pure will. As there was an inclination to subordinate the rôle of the will to that of the intellect, it was not possible to grasp the distinction between ethical and political, legal and economic, action, and to recognize in these distinctions the oneness of will and act. The ethical criteria were confused with the political, so that neither an ethics nor a political science was developed that could be accepted at the present day. The very fact of this confusion authorizes and compels us to discuss ethics and political science side by side, as if they were one; for they had not then yet been duly differentiated.

If we now at the very beginning deny the logical validity of the ethical and political science current before and in Dante's time, and if we proceed to show their defects, we are nevertheless far from wishing to disparage in any way their practical value. On the contrary, we mean rather to exalt it. But this can be done, properly, only if we survey them in their connection with practical life, and therefore not merely philosophically, but in their relation to the history of civilization.

It may well be that with this double purpose of evaluation and of exposition our treatment will be more complex and less smooth than is usual in historical books. But those who are determined not to lose their bearings in the winding corridors of history know that historical investigation cannot always glide smoothly and simply—and will excuse us.

2. CLASSICAL ETHICS AND POLITICAL SCIENCE

THE SOPHISTS AND SOCRATES

The first who gave serious thought to the relation of political and social conditions, to the ethical ordering of life, were the Greek Sophists. They lived in a time (fifth century B.C.) when the Athenian state had ceased to exert absolute and arbitrary control over the individual and was beginning to assure to each man ever-widening liberties and rights.

This transitional condition is reflected in both their political and their ethical doctrines.

The state, they declared, is the creation of individuals, and its problem is the protection of individual interests. Only in so far as the individual finds it to his own interest must he conform to the existing order of things. If the law of the state does not guarantee that happiness which is owed to us, it can be attacked, overthrown, or altered. For—and now we come to the ethics of the Sophists— the urge toward happiness is the first and sole natural mainspring of human action. Each man, however, they add, seeks his happiness in a different quarter. General institutions, therefore, and even the political organization itself, can come into existence only through mutual concessions and agreement.

Ethical good is wholly bound up in what is politically expedient. Here we have a reminiscence of the older state of things in which the individual was still wholly lost in the state. On the other hand, the relativity and mutability of political finalities is clearly perceived; and therein is reflected the gradual alienation of the individual from the community.

The more thoroughly this alienation was carried out, the more clearly the sphere of personal interests must have detached itself, in the thinker's mind, from the political world.

Socrates placed it in virtue; that is, according to his use of words, in the knowledge of that which is good. Happiness, which to the Sophists was a matter of taste and the momentary tendency of the will, was by him made steadfast and definite through conceptual elaboration. Thus, in the realization of what is good and leads to happiness, that is, in the insight of the virtuous man, the means were found for testing the justice of existing customs and laws. Here it is taken for granted that what is truly good for the individual must also be binding on the community and state; that the laws and purposes of the commonwealth normally coincide with the happiness of the individual; that the welfare of one is also the welfare of all. The individual again feels himself an essential part of the state, but he stands forth with fresh consciousness distinct from the state: as a critic, as a man, as a citizen of the world.

With Socrates, to be sure, the critical judgment of the moral citizen of the world was on the whole favourable to the Athenian commonwealth. Only certain demagogical practices, the choice of officials by lot and the selection of incompetents, met his stern disapproval.

And not only philosophically, but emotionally as well, he sees harmony between the moral decisions of the individual and the political activities of the community. For this very man who laid the foundations for a scientific criticism of the state, cheerfully submitted to the death sentence passed on him by his fellow citizens. To the conservatives, who were concerned with his critical attitude, he could not but appear in the guise of a Sophist and as an enemy of the state; whereas the Sophists, preoccupied with his conservative tendencies, accused him of being a crafty supporter of the reaction. He stands out alone, with his critical and idealistic conscience and consciousness of righteousness, and is crushed between the mob impulses of the one party and the relativism and individualism of the other.

PLATO

On the other hand, in his pupil Plato, the aristocratic child of a demagogic age, theory and actuality break apart. His seclusion from the outer world gave him a profounder moral insight at the cost of political comprehension.

Plato established the absolute validity, in fact the very nature, of the Good. Whatever criticism one may make of the construction of his supersensuous world, he is the true founder of philosophical ethics.

Socrates had taught that the Good could, in each particular case, be dialectically mediated. Plato was conscious of having discovered it once for all in the ultimate end of human and of cosmic life, in the urge of all beings toward God, in the progressive assimilation to the divine. It is the loftiest concept in his realm of Ideas, but it is for that very reason the most colourless of all Ideas, and can, properly speaking, be defined only negatively, and can be attained only through abnegation, through ascetic practices and subjection of our impulses and of our worldly interests.

Seen from this side, Plato's ethics is unpolitical, yes, even antipolitical and Utopian. It can only reject every political organization, and can justify none of those in existence.

Plato was nevertheless an ardent patriot. His anti-political vehemence made itself felt therefore in his attacks on the degenerate condition of his native city. He admires the simpler times of the aristocratic Tory city-state and turns reactionary. But in that he applies his mind to the possibility of reform, he must pass over from the negative to the positive side of his ethics.

The Good is not only the denial of sensuous nature, but at the same time its higher sense, the creative, harmonizing, and conserving principle of the universe. In the harmony and order of the world, the Idea of the Good reveals itself. This order must be recognized and then imitated by the political community. In human nature itself the two realms of the cosmos meet, the material and the immaterial. The soul of man is in part rational, in part irrational. If it is to be set in harmonious order, the rational power must rule over the irrational forces of the soul, that is, over its spirited ardour and over its sensuous desires. That man is one with himself, righteous and just, in whom the spirited will and the sensuous appetites are obedient to reason.

This psychological analysis of moral behaviour reveals the four cardinal virtues: temperance, as the due control of greed; courage, as that of wilfulness; prudence, as that of the soul's rational power; and righteousness, as the harmony of these three one with another.

So old are the four stars or nymphs, those natural and political virtues, which appear at the beginning and at the end of Dante's *Purgatorio*.[1]

The state, which is "a human being writ large," must imitate the pattern of the righteous man.[2]

The control, accordingly, must belong to the rational and wise; that is, to the philosophers. In his second (and second-best) outline of his ideal state (the *Laws*), Plato makes the theologians and priests rule, instead of the philosophers; for he considered it more probable and easier that the common people should render obedience to a priest than to a philosopher. For such reasons he has, on second thought, given a priestly colouring to his philosophic state. The defense of the sovereignty and the execution of its commands are intrusted to the second class of citizens, the soldiers and officials. They represent the spirited element in the state, while the third and lowest, the class actuated by sensuous appetites, must provide for the support of the entire commonwealth by agriculture, manufactures, and trade.

Now exactly as justice, in the individual, is founded on harmonious relations between the faculties of his soul, so the pros-

---

[1] *Purgatorio*, I, 22 sqq., and XXXI, 104 sqq.
[2] In the *Republic*, Plato follows the opposite course, and seeks to descry not the political order in the moral, but rather the moral in the political. But he does this merely for didactic reasons, because, as he thinks, the moral law looms up larger in the state than in the individual.

perity of this remarkable commonwealth can be secured only when no one of the three classes encroaches on the functions of the others, and none makes undue claims for itself. Political degeneration sets in only when either the spirited or the sensuously motivated class comes to dominate the representatives of reason.

Quite Platonically, then, Dante at the beginning of his poem embodies in his three beasts our proneness to ambition and covetousness as the fundamental obstacles to moral and potential action. It matters not whether they be identified with arrogance, rapacity, and lewdness, or with violence, greed, and sensuality, or with pride, envy, and avarice, these three beasts represent the impediments to Reason in its control of the individual and of the state. Quite in the manner of Plato, too, he traces civil wars and disorders in Florence to the mixing of classes, to the incoming of peasant folk, to growth of trade, of luxury, and of extravagance; and finds in the simpler conditions of the old aristocratic Florentine state the glories of the Golden Age.[1] And he likewise follows Plato when in his *De Monarchia* he regulates the political differences between Church and state in accordance with the relations existing between the human soul and the body.

Not merely in these details, but in their entire ethical and political range, Dante's state doctrines are in the last analysis a consequence of Plato's creation. The Platonic state may in fact be regarded as a prophetic picture, painted in Greek colours, of a mediæval theocracy. The state as a moral and educational community, with ultramundane finalities, with sharp separation of the educational, the military, and the economic classes, with censorship and control of conscience, and with celibacy for the highest class, which Plato desired—this state was realized, more or less successfully, in mediæval theocracy.

Not that the Church or Dante had studied Plato.[2] The fundamental thoughts of the great Athenian, free from the bonds of paper and ink, lived on all the more vigorously in the brains of later generations.

These fundamental thoughts are two in number; first, equalization of the political with the natural order of the universe, particularly of the human soul; and secondly, the ultramundane and

---

[1] Cf. *Paradiso*, XV, 97 sqq., and XVI, 49 sqq.
[2] Dante could at most have read one Platonic dialogue, the *Timaeus*, in the Latin translation of Chalcidius.

essentially moral tendency of political ideals. At the foundation of the first lies the naturalistic and optimistic, truly Hellenic, belief that the capacities of our nature are in perfect harmony with the political as well as the moral goals of our effort. The second thought, however, is based on the supernatural and pessimistic conviction that there can be no definite rational goal for economic, social, or political activity. This second thought annuls the state and puts its whole emphasis on the Hereafter, while the first accepts the state and sets it on the firm foundation of Nature. It is out of the pressure of these two opposite thoughts that the despotic organization of Plato's republic, as well as that of the mediæval theocracy, came into being.

ARISTOTLE

Politics

The unworldly idealism which set political science on ethical and idealistic foundations was not merely the expression of Plato's temperament, but was so largely in the spirit of the age that even a practical man like Xenophon let himself be drawn into the political fancies and fictions of his *Cyropaedia*.

But Hellenism was yet destined to undergo a great political revolution. After the fall of the Athenian state and the advent of Alexander the Great, the political horizon widened so vastly that political science had to come into closer touch with reality. It seems, indeed, that Aristotle's studies in political science had already begun before he was invited to the royal Macedonian court, but there can be no doubt that his adherence to monarchical institutions was determined by the commanding personality of Alexander. The marked empirical and historical tone of Aristotle's *Politics* is in strong contrast with Plato's ideals.

In fact, Plato's two fundamental thoughts are both combated by Aristotle. First, the state is no "man writ large," no individual, but a combination of the most diverse individuals; second, that which gives it its unity is no supramundane ethical principle, but the earthly and natural demand for social relationships. Within itself, not outside or in the Hereafter, the state finds its purpose. It may indeed be characterized as a natural creation, but only in the sense that inclination and need for organized social life are innate in mankind, not in the sense that any harmonious state organization pre-exists in human nature. The state does not grow with the inevitableness of a grain of corn or a rolling avalanche. Nature is its source; its development is reason. "It comes into being for the sake of mere existence, but it continues to exist for the sake of the highest, that is, rational life."

But what is this complete life? Has not each individual his own views and desires on that question? Or, to put the matter more accurately and clearly: Can the goal of a community be identical with that of a single person? Has man as a citizen the same aims that he has as a rational being? Aristotle does indeed recognize that man is not *ipso facto* a citizen of the state, but only in so far as he is politically active. The possibility that one may deliberately hold aloof from political action is not unknown to him. But such a person is, in his opinion, either a beast, born to be a slave, or a god—a creature of inferior or superior intelligence. So, after all, man as a rational being is regarded as identical with man the citizen of a state.

In fact, the whole ancient world could not imagine man apart from his civic environment. It lacked the concept of the transcendental personality. With Aristotle, then, despite a notable attempt to distinguish the two, the moral ideal of personality still remains inseparable from the political ideal of the general welfare. The question asked above he answers as follows: Yes, the purpose of the state is in the last analysis identical with that of the individual. The total well-being, the εὐδαιμονία of the single individuals, constitutes the purpose and the well-being of the state.

Ethics

Hence the happiness of each individual must be of such a nature that it does not become complete in itself, but only in conjunction with the happiness of the rest. This is taken for granted in the *Politics*, but is demonstrated in the *Ethics*.

In this work he endeavours by the most delicate analysis and induction to reach an ideal of happiness that shall be valid for all mankind, for the individual as well as for the state. So it cannot be limited to this or that internal or external good, such as health or wealth or sensuous pleasure—or even moral virtue; for the attainment of none of these things frees us from further yearning. Even for the most virtuous of men, something is still to be desired, were it only physical comfort or family prosperity or peace in the state. Though in his own soul and his own house all may be as it should be, yet he can only felicitate himself for his existence when a similar felicity beams on him from all the faces about him. Whether he is happy or not depends only in part on himself, and in part on the social group in which he lives. But since this general happiness coincides with none of all the particular ends we can conceive for our activity, and since it does not abide in our successes, we must look for it in our striving toward success—in our activity itself. The identification of activity with happiness is the most precious discovery of Aristotelian ethics.

The various types of activity may now be defined, with the aid of psychology. The gradation of man's psychological faculties has its counterpart in the scale of ethical values of human activities. In psychology Aristotle is an intellectualist. To him the highest power is reason. Reason and rational activity for its own sake, that is, an essentially ideal rather than a practical attitude and effort, he regards as ethically the loftiest level of human action. And thereby, after parting company with the prevailing school of intellectualism in that he identifies ultimate happiness with activity and effort, he falls back again on its position.

Reason is active in two ways, in thinking, and so theoretically, and in the control or guidance of irrational Nature, and so practically. Hence arise the two forms of human happiness, those ideals which in mediæval times were famous under the names of the contemplative and the active life. The Middle Ages, as we know, succeeded in reconciling the Aristotelian preference for a rationalistic interpretation of life with the teachings of Jesus, which were surely anything but intellectualistic. Mary, who sits at the Master's feet and "hath chosen the better part," is recognized as the type of the contemplative life; and her sister Martha, who is "careful and troubled about many things," is the accepted type of the active life. Dante does not make use of these, but of the corresponding Old Testament symbols, Rachel and Leah, as they were interpreted in mediæval theology from the time of Gregory the Great onward.

Pure activity of reason effects itself, according to Aristotle, through the " dianoetic " (intellectual) virtues, wisdom and prudence. Out of the practical activity of reason, the "ethical" virtues arise, temperance (moderation), courage, and justice. The dianoetic virtues are therefore determined as to both content and form by reason, but the "ethical" virtues only as to form. We call that man temperate, for instance, who, exercising his natural impulses within the limits set by reason, neither completely suppressing them nor completely yielding to them, guides them in a due middle course. The rational mean between two extremes is what makes the essence of the practical (ethical) virtues. Hence sin takes the form of excess or defect in the realm of human action.

The life of natural impulse, which was regarded by Plato as the most serious obstacle in the path of the Good, and as detestable in itself, is shown by Aristotle to be ethically neutral and morally unimportant. Our natural impulses may be the making of a virtuous or of a sinful man, according as practical reason proves itself active or deficient, authoritative or submissive to them. This ethical neutralization of Nature is the second precious discovery of Aristotle's *Ethics*. To be sure, through the Hellenic and Christian doctrine of original sin, especially as it developed under the disciples of Plato and of Paul, Aristotle's discovery was again challenged for centuries and centuries.

Precisely because Nature is in itself neither good nor evil, there is need of rational action, of conscious effort, of systematic training, and of careful supervision and instruction through punishment and reward, in order to extract moral values from this stubborn matter. It is not a single act that makes man virtuous, but a permanent capacity and the inclination of the will toward reason, painfully acquired in oft-repeated tests. So the doctrine that proclaims the indifference of Nature as an ethical factor is inseparably associated with the doctrine that makes of action the source of happiness, and the two great discoveries of Aristotle are fundamentally the same thing.

If Aristotle nevertheless hesitated to take the final step, and did not go so far as to declare whole-heartedly that practical virtue is the sole basis of happiness, the fault lies in the conditions of his time. Where the feeling for the peculiar value of the moral personality had not yet been awakened, the personal happiness of a good conscience and the torture of conscious guilt could not fully reveal their significance.

So Aristotle fuses the political and economic welfare of the citizen with the ethical joy of the spiritual personality into a single concept of happiness.

An effort to distinguish these two does indeed appear. The

virtuous man who is unfortunate in his outward circumstances, says Aristotle, is not, to be sure, to be called happy (μακάριος), but fortunate (εὐδαίμων).

This effort to distinguish between outward and inward good fortune corresponds to the effort, described above, to draw a line of demarcation between the man and the citizen, and like it, was to remain a mere attempt. The consequences were not adequately seized. Hence, like the man who withdraws from civic life, so too the moral hero who in illness, misery, and bondage, exulting in the freedom of his soul, declares himself happy, could not but seem to Aristotle either beast or God, never a normal human being.

Dante and Aristotle

This fundamental and simple theory of ethical polity, though zealously and lovingly studied by Dante, was not grasped by him in its deeper meaning. Plato, of whom he had only a second-hand knowledge, is much closer to him than Aristotle, whose *Nicomachean Ethics* he memorized almost as thoroughly as the *Æneid* of his beloved Virgil. From Aristotle he indeed took over the general plan, the terminology, the scholastic divisions, the concepts of virtue and sin, but hardly one vital and fundamental thought.

He never took seriously either the doctrine that makes of action the source of happines and the condition of virtue, or the doctrine of the moral neutrality of the sensuous nature. If it were otherwise, how could he ever have insisted that moral purification comes through vision instead of through experience, through instruction and not through toil, through penance and not through discipline? It is rather the intellectualistic and reactionary side, the remnant of Platonism in the Aristotelian ethics, that appeals to him. Hence he accepts without question the preference for the contemplative over the active life[1] and the formalistic concepts of the practical virtues as a middle road between two extremes.[2]

Dante's relation to Aristotle may be best understood from a brief survey of their juridical and political philosophies.

Aristotle teaches that every human act that, considered in itself and purely in reference to our soul, appears as virtue or vice, when directed beyond ourselves and regarded as a social factor

---

[1] Cf. *De Monarchia*, I, 3, and the position given in the *Paradiso* to the purely contemplative hermits.

[2] Cf. *Convivio*, IV, 17, and *Purgatorio*, XVII, 125 sqq.

reveals itself objectively as justice or injustice. Virtue which pro-
duces its effects within the community takes the name of justice;
vice directed against fellow citizens is injustice. It follows—and
Aristotle asserts it expressly—that injustice cannot be committed
against oneself. At most, as he declares, it might be said in a
psychological sense of an intemperate man that he acts unjustly
against himself; that is, against his better reason. This "domestic" and not public injustice, as Aristotle puts it, this reflex iniquity, this offense against one's own reason, which in Christian
speech is called sin, is only hinted at but not discussed by Aristotle.[1] If he had grasped it, the distinction between virtue and
right, sin and wrong, would have been clearly brought out.

Not merely from the side of injustice, but also from that of
justice, Aristotle approaches this distinction. But here, too, he
fails to grasp its entire significance. He recognizes not only two
types of injustice, but two of justice, one general and one particular. By general he means every sort of practically effective and
active virtue, whether it be courage, temperance, liberality, or
wisdom and prudence in the service of fellow citizens; by particular virtue he means merely that sort of behaviour which
accords to every man his due and renders like for like, that virtue
the reverse of which is greed. Greed would thus become the particular political form of injustice. This it is that confuses and
destroys all legal equality among citizens. We recognize at once,
in this sin, the "ancient she-wolf" of the *Divine Comedy*. The
nature of general justice, together with its opposite, immorality,
is left decidedly in the shadow. If it had been clearly brought out
in its relation to virtue on the one hand and to the particular type
of justice on the other, then here too the inner forum would have
been distinguished from the outer. But Aristotle remains confined
within his political range of thought, and emphasizes on one side
civic equality and justice, and on the other only that phase of injustice which relates to other men, but not to ourselves.

Just because, and in so far as, man is master of his own actions
and the active cause thereof, he cannot possibly be at the same
time a passive object to them. No man can willingly harm himself or voluntarily subject himself to injustice. Suicide is a crime
not against the person, but against the state.

In Dante's Hell, on the other hand, not only suicides but even

[1] Cf. *Nicomachean Ethics*, V, 15.

gamblers and spendthrifts are punished for committing violence, that is, injustice, against themselves. We also find, beneath rather than beside these culprits, those who were unjust toward God and Nature. Among them are the blasphemers, the sodomites, and, curiously enough, the usurers. Here canonical and biblical ideas, and even in the last analysis the Christian conception of sin, come to the fore. The *Ethics* of Aristotle hardly offers room for such divisions.

Nevertheless, it would be an error to suppose that the idea of sin and what goes with it—the concept of righteous feeling and righteous will; in short, subjective justice—was unknown to Aristotle. On the contrary, he distinguishes very clearly between the subjective and the objective. And within the subjective he distinguishes, again, those acts of injustice which are prompted by passion from those inspired by malice;[1] in other words what the Roman jurist calls *culpa* from what he characterizes as *dolus*.

What kind of sins, one must ask—as Dante also did—lie at the root of passionate wrongdoing, and what sort of immorality is the basis of malicious evildoing? According to Aristotle, as we have already seen, virtue reveals itself as justice to our neighbour, and its opposite as injustice to him. We also saw that greed is the motive of political injustice in particular. The logical and necessary consequence of this is that the subdivision of subjective injustice into passionate and malicious acts should be accompanied by an analogous subdivision of immorality. We accordingly find at the beginning of the seventh book of the *Nicomachean Ethics* that on moral grounds we must avoid three things (not two!): baseness (κακία), intemperance (ἀκρασία), and bestiality (θηριότης). But savagery, or bestiality, is presently dropped; for, as Aristotle demonstrates,[2] it is an extraordinary sin, devoid of all human attributes. It is the gigantic distortion of intemperance, as well as of baseness, something animal and morbid, a pathological excess which lies outside of ordinary human intemperance and baseness and therefore beyond ethical appraisal. Thus only intemperance and baseness remain, and it is clear that the former bursts out in passionate, the latter in malicious, acts of injustice. Thus the ethico-political parallelism between immoral and unjust acts, which we surmised, is fully set forth.

Dante read his Aristotle better than many modern expositors.

[1] Cf. *Nicomachean Ethics*, V, especially 10.   [2] *Ibid.*, VII, 6.

He mentions bestiality or savagery (θηριότης = *matta bestialitade*) only in passing, and as an extreme conception. Otherwise he bases his whole plan of the *Inferno*[1] on Aristotle's twofold ethico-political division, so that in the upper Hell those sins are punished which are prompted by passion or incontinence, by *culpa*, to use the legal expression; and in the lower Hell, those which spring from malice or baseness (κακία = *malizia*), or, legally, from *dolus*. We shall seek in vain, however, either in Aristotle or Dante, any especial provision for bestiality—unless we wish to include under it the extremest cases and examples either of intemperance or malice. But in that case this savagery would be dispersed through all the circles of Hell, and would still have no class of its own.

As a matter of fact, the bestial aspects of sin seem to be sketched rather in the various monsters who are the guardians of Hell. The pathological element is admitted only under the symbolic forms of the misshapen and monstrous, almost as grotesque caricature. Except for this poetic and imaginative recognition, it finds no place in Dante's moral system. The sinner is regarded not as diseased, but as wicked; not as blind or lame, but as self-blinded or self-crippled.

What is most remarkable in Dante's divisions of Hell is, after all, the free and unhesitating manner in which he puts Aristotle's conception of subjective injustice on a level with the Christian conception of sin. In this way he arrives at the twofold criterion of violence and injustice against oneself, against Nature, and against God, and treats God, Nature, and Reason as, so to speak, juridical personalities. The questionable consequences of such a treatment were never consciously realized by Dante. If we human beings can commit a wrong against our own reason, against our nature, or against our God, then all these three must also be capable of wronging us; for justice, at least according to Aristotle, properly rests on civic equality and reciprocity. Therefore the clever Greek philosopher excluded from his political ethics gods, slaves, and beasts.

But because Dante takes from Aristotle only the letter, but not the spirit, the fundamental achievements of that thinker do not, except in mere matters of form and arrangement, add to his doctrine of future justice or to his metaphysical ethics in general; they do, however, give it a dogmatic tone.

[1] *Inferno*, XI, 16 sqq.

That they could not be fundamentally significant for his political theories is clear from our comparison with Plato. If we take out the Platonic threads from Dante's political doctrine, very little of Aristotle remains. He is, to be sure, responsible for Dante's doctrine of the social, gregarious nature of man, and also for the fundamental conception of greed as the peculiarly political sin. Aristotelian, too, is the principle that peace and the perfection of life are the ends of the state. But these ideas were already more or less definitely included in Plato's theory, and Dante took them over with more of a Platonic than an Aristotelian colouring. The anti-Platonic Aristotle, who denies eschatological finalities to the state, whose conceptions of morality and society are wholly founded on earthly experience and limited to the present life—our poet never knew. And that Plato whom Aristotle had hoped to refute was actually handed down by his quotations, untouched by his attacks, to the Arabs, to the mediæval world, and to Dante.

Furthermore there intervenes between Aristotle and Dante, at once parting and uniting them, the latest great political theory of antiquity, constructed by the Stoics and by Cicero, which opened the way for a revival of peripatetic influences.

THE STOA

The State and the Law of Nature

The political theory of the Stoics was the first to grow on international ground. Socrates, Plato, and Aristotle philosophized within narrow national and civic frontiers. When the frontiers receded with the founding of the world-empires of Alexander and of the Romans, political science also had to be established on a broader foundation.

First of all, it demolished the walls of the Greek city-state, so that its first phase was destructive. Under such circumstances it was inevitable that the new theory should accept the anti-national, more or less anarchistic, ideas of earlier days and to a certain extent make common cause with the Sophists, the Cynics, and the Epicureans.

These sects, by their extolling of the autonomy and self-sufficiency of the individual, had gradually undermined civic and patriotic loyalty, and with it the internal structure of the state, effacing all class distinctions. Human happiness, according to the teaching of these schools and sects, should not be striven for, as Plato and Aristotle taught, in and through the state, but outside of it and in spite of it.   It may be that the state has need of the wise man, but by no means has the wise man any need of the state.   This philosophic and theosophic rejection of one's own country spreads wider and wider and prepares the ground for a spiritual fatherland and a state outside all states: the Church.

The Cynic and Epicurean finds his country in the cozy nook of his own comfort.   *Ubi bene, ibi patria!*   But the Stoics transformed this selfish and complacent sentiment into a serious moral commandment and a world-wide law.   Socrates had already, in doubtful cases, appealed to the unwritten against the written law. Stoicism now fundamentally and definitely raises the natural, simple, universal, and eternal law of reason high above the conventional, manifold, particular, and changeable ordinances of the nations.   Long before St. Augustine wrote his *Civitas Dei*, the contrast between the heavenly and the earthly state was familiar to the Stoics.   "Our life is spent in two states," says Seneca in his essay *De Otio aut Secessu Sapientis*.   "The one is the great and truly public state, which includes gods and men.   It is in no remote nook; the sun alone measures its expanse.   The other is the little state, to which we belong because of the particular conditions of our birth." [1]   The realm of Nature, with its eternal laws and its harmony, includes and sustains all human realms and states.   Its mighty frame serves as a model and also as a foundation for every individual state.

What relation does the unity of natural law bear to the diversity of political laws?   The Stoics gave two answers, which can hardly be reconciled with each other.   Sometimes they asserted that natural law is the universal moral law, and therefore the absolute test by which to judge, approve, or condemn all political laws. At other times they pointed out that the whole course of the world, all plant and animal life, the starry sky, together with all the political institutions of men, are made and determined by Nature in accordance with her eternal laws.   Sometimes they regarded it as the law of human, sometimes as that of cosmic, reason.   Now they saw in it a moral demand, an ideal to be reached, and the complete freedom of our will, or again an inevitable fate, a reality conditioned on every side, the absolute compulsion of our whole

[1] Cf. also Seneca's *Epistolae*, LXVIII.

existence—in short, either the world as it should be or the world as it is.

So it comes to pass that the Stoic, without belying his doctrine, can act at one moment as the obedient son of his country's law, and at the next as its most irreconcilable foe. Cato, who commits suicide in order to escape the law of tyranny, and Brutus, who slays the tyrant to save the law, were both convinced and persistent Stoics. But the one saw in Julius Cæsar the embodied natural law, the other, that law defiled. The first, Dante exalted as the guardian of the Purgatorial mount, the highest position which he could assign to a heathen; the second he put in the jaws of Lucifer and condemned to the most terrific punishment of Hell. These two unflinching representatives of one and the same creed mark for him the opposite bounds of ancient morality. This exemplary treatment indicates a solution of the ambiguity of the Stoic position as rigorous and complete as could be desired.

And yet, as we shall see, the significance of the concept of natural law was not, even in Dante's mind, made entirely clear. The ambiguity inherent in the Stoics' law of nature was not removed, but merely pushed aside by the practical philosophy of the Middle Ages. Indeed it is older than the concept itself. We discovered it, long before the time of the Stoics, in the dualism of the natural and supernatural, optimistic and pessimistic, position of the Platonic ethics and politics.

But while the Platonic state-theory shows that it is conscious of the necessity of removing this contradiction, and strives to transform this aspiration into a reality, the ethics of the Stoics increasingly emphasizes the contrast until finally the moral character of man is sundered from his political conduct, and the inner unity of our life is destroyed.

The Strict and the Lax Ethics

For a moral man everything depends on intention; for the political man, on the outcome; therefore in this system of ethics, purely political and economic concerns or acts are neither moral nor immoral. The wise Stoic may very well, as a shrewd and sharp business man, secure and enjoy the goods of this world. His character suffers no harm therefrom; the two spheres can well be kept apart. He will not forget that neither the most splendid and luxurious possessions nor the direst oppression and peril of his sensuous life have anything whatever to do with his inward happiness, which abides wholly and solely in the peaceful consciousness of virtue. The true Stoic may soil his hands, nay, even his whole body; but his soul need not be aware of it, and may still delight in its purity. The firmer and higher virtue is enthroned in his soul, the more inaccessible it becomes, and therefore all the less exposed to earthly contamination, and as such deserving of the utmost license and dispensation. One might almost say that the loftier the intention, the more ignoble the behaviour. Precisely because moral goodness is metaphysical, independent, and sovereign, it cannot meddle with daily life. "One gets here the impression that, as again later in the ecclesiastical ethics of the Middle Ages, on one side the ideal of perfection was carried almost to superhuman heights, while on the other hand an ethical code was announced for the ordinary man which, to be sure, ever and again gives indication that what is expressed in it cannot possibly be called morality in the higher sense, but has at least this in its favour, that it abides in a region which is accessible without the complete surrender of natural feelings, and without a complete departure from the natural course of life." [1]

With this second division of morality, which does not attempt to be ethics, and in fact is not, with the doctrine of the morally indifferent, the Stoics opened the little postern gate through which the worldly ethics of Aristotle could slip in again and carry on its fruitful work. It thus came to pass that this weaker and less characteristic side of its teachings proved the more significant in after times, especially when the political wisdom of Aristotle was reinforced by Roman jurisprudence.

The earlier and purer doctrine, the heroic morality of genuine Stoicism, in its austere seclusion from life could not offer any support for any kind of practical polity. For this very reason, however, it was able within any political community, even the most debased, to produce solitary examples of noble deeds and genuine humanity. It did not turn to the state, but to man's character, and even in the degenerate Roman empire quietly fulfilled a lofty mission of justice and benevolence, and left also a public imprint of its efficacy in legal and social reforms.

[1] F. Jodl, *Geschichte der Ethik als philosophischer Wissenschaft*, 2nd ed., Stuttgart and Berlin, 1906, p. 90.

Dante and Stoicism

Dante felt the force of this personal and private trend of the Stoics. Especially in those crises of his unhappy life where he felt he could rely only on his own moral dignity he drew courage and strength from the heroism of the Stoa. Nowhere does its spirit breathe more proudly or more powerfully than in those writings of Dante which took shape under the immediate pressure of his exile, the *Convivio* and the *canzone*, "Three ladies close unto my heart have come."

Not I alone, says the banished poet, am cast forth; with me Justice and her followers are exiled. Within my soul doth persecuted virtue find abode.

> I hear how in their heavenly utterance
> The homeless powers
> Console themselves and make lament:
> And I account my exile as my pride!
> And if by force of fate, or by Decree
> It is ordained
> That the white lily shall be coloured red,
> Then am I ready fearlessly to fall [1]

In such mood Dante understood and honoured, if he did not approve, the suicide of Stoics. In his *Convivio* he sets the voluntary death of the Stoics Zeno and Seneca on the same plane as the sacrificial death of Socrates. What drew him to the consolatory writings of Cicero and Boëthius, as we have seen, was above all the Stoic resistance and steadfastness in misfortune.

How deep these principles had grown into the soul of this mediæval Christian could be accurately judged only if we were in the position to realize all the occasions on which moral pride and defiance expressed themselves freely in his actions and words. In that case it would doubtless be revealed that the better part of Dante's Stoicism was not learned, but inborn.

How little actual information he had concerning the Stoa may be seen from the fact that he believed the idea of immortality to be a cornerstone of its creed, and that he did not even mention the names of its foremost thinkers, Cleanthes and Chrysippus. The only genuine Stoic with whom he seems to have become at all familiar is Seneca. In the main, however, the eclectics Cicero and Boëthius were his authorities.

[1] *Rime*, CIV, in *Opere di Dante*, Florence, 1921, p. III.

THE ROMAN SPIRIT

The Stoa is therefore of essential importance for Dante only so far as it was Roman, not Greek.

Hellenic influences had to be stressed in theoretical and particularly in religious questions, but here, in the field of political action, the Roman element must be emphasized.

For the national, or rather the international, and the legal, and to some extent the ecclesiastical, foundation on which the *Divine Comedy* rests, is Roman.

The national consciousness of the Romans expressed itself martially in successful wars of conquest and of defense, and constructively in art, in poetry, and in history. Dante drew inspiration from the military leaders and statesmen of ancient Rome as well as from her patriotic poets and historians. It is true that, for him, the real Rome begins when the national characteristics are disappearing in the changed conditions of a universal empire. To the race or nation of the Latins he concedes political importance only in so far as it becomes the support of a world-wide power. What the Israelites were in religion, the Latins were in statesmanship: the chosen people. Not by Nature, but by God's choice and will, did the Latin people overcome all others. Only in the direction of religious and legal ideas is our poet in a position to sympathize with the national pride of the ancient Romans.

How could it be otherwise? The Roman national consciousness existed from the beginning only in a religious and legal form; the people were united not by blood-ties, but by common forms of worship and government. The father of its family (*paterfamilias*) had in ancient Rome an authority not merely natural, but legal, comparable to that of a magistrate. Virgil, the truest poet of the Roman spirit, was born near Mantua, had perhaps rather Celtic than Latin blood in his veins, was regarded by Dante as a Lombard;[1] yet neither we nor Dante could find a more authoritative spokesman of Rome. By "Roman spirit," therefore, in ancient days and in Dante's times, we must understand not a national sentiment, in the present sense of the phrase, but above all else a feeling of religious and legal communion.

For Dante, "right" and "Roman" are so synonymous that he traces all that is good in his native city back to Rome; and what is

---

[1] *Inferno*, I, 68.

ignoble he ascribes to the barbarous Longobardic Fiesolan stock. In the veins of his Florentine enemies, the enemies of law, he sees not a drop of Roman blood. Peasants and rascals from Fiesole were disastrously mingled with the Romans when the city was founded.

> Their litter let the beasts of Fiesole
>   Make of themselves, nor let them touch the plant,
>   If any still upon their dunghill rise,
> In which may yet revive the consecrated
>   Seed of those Romans, who remained there when
>   The nest of such great malice it became.[1]

As soon as the consciousness of justice becomes emotional, it takes on the colour of religious feeling and becomes what the Romans call *pietas* (loyalty to superiors—parents, rulers, or gods).

Although Roman religion, for the most part, always remains natural religion, yet it is distinguished from the Greek religion by a far more simple and ethical conception of the Divinity. Jupiter and Mars in particular are stripped of their nature-attributes and elevated to the plane of real persons—not, however, as with the Greeks, as a result of artistic creation, but through moral and legal personification. Indeed the Romans distinguished the personal god (*deus certus*) with considerable care from gods who were mere qualities (*numina, dei incerti*). This distinction, as we now know, was established in the Roman pontifical law. The *deus certus* granted a patronage (*tutelas, licentias, potestates*) which could be demanded of him but not of any other god. Hence he exacted his due festal rites.

This essentially juridical development of the concept of personality is a Roman contribution. It is to be distinguished on the one hand from the concept of moral personality as it was developed in the Jewish religion, and on the other hand from the æsthetic concept of individuality that is peculiarly Greek. The Jewish god has character; the Roman, authority; the Greek, traits and temperament. The political attitude of the Greeks, and with it their ethical and political ideas, waver between clannish feeling and individualism. It was the Romans who first worked out the juridical adjustment of the individual to the community in a practical and logical fashion. They were the ones who inserted Law between ethics and politics.

[1] *Inferno*, XV, 73-78; cf. also *Epistolae* V, 4.

Indeed, the structure of positive jurisprudence was erected and completed in Rome long before any Roman had given a thought to political or ethical speculation. The juridical habit of thought had grown strong and dominant, unaided by foreign influences. So the first man who transplanted Greek philosophy into Roman soil, Marcus Tullius Cicero, saw before himself the unique problem of laying a philosophic foundation under the already existing structure of traditional jurisprudence.

In all the domains of practical science—in political science, legal science, ethics—he had to struggle with the difficulty of fitting what was historically given and real into conceptions and norms developed by speculation. He lacked the power to shape a new national philosophy out of the living achievements of the Romans, and especially out of their consciousness of the law. So he contented himself with compromises and eclecticism; and instead of removing the difficulties, he created a host of complications, in the solution of which many a century since has been kept busy. They were not foolish or idle, but extremely fruitful and significant, complications.

CICERO

Cicero is the first who attempted to construct a political science of his own on a foundation essentially Stoical. But precisely his most important works on the subject, the *De Republica*, which did not come to light again until 1822, and the *De Legibus*, which in the fourteenth century was one of the greatest rarities, remained unknown to our poet. So they did not directly influence Dante's political theories, though they doubtless did have some indirect effect on their development.

Cicero looks back from the height of Roman power on the mighty past of his people. His historical outlook is enlightened and bounded by Rome. But his philosophic scope includes the great cosmic ideal state of the Stoics, that invisible world-empire which embraces gods and men and which is upheld by the *lex naturalis*. He remarked, for the first time so far as we know—and it was an important and fruitful remark—that the colonial empire of Rome and the world-realm of the Stoics interpenetrated. To be sure, the historical conception of the Roman empire could not be identified exactly with the philosophic and cosmic realm, but at many points their frontier lines coincided.

They were brought together first of all in the domain of the philosophy of law. Here Cicero, if he has not identified them with each other, still has confused the conception of the natural law (*jus naturale*) partly with that of the law of nations (*jus gentium*), partly with that of the civil law (*jus civile*). His general view may be summed up to the effect that the *jus gentium* in an international frame, and the *jus civile* in a Roman one, present a positive copy of the *jus naturale*. As to their content and validity, positive law is identical with natural law, though they are different in their application and form. What is true of one is true of the others, but natural law is valid in all cases, while international and civil law are applicable only to particular matters. The possibility that the sanctions of positive law contradict the ethical requirements of natural law, or even must inevitably do so, did not occur to Cicero.

After the Stoics had forced ethics and politics so far apart that a false mixture or even a proper synthesis of the two became impossible, Cicero, not in the least disturbed, tossed law and morality together.

And not only morality and law, but even religion and law. For the Roman, in a far more literal sense than for the Greek, the relation of the citizen to the gods was just as much legal as that of one citizen to another. Religion was a special principle of law, and in Rome the *jus sacrum* constituted an independent element of public law. Cicero puts the legal principle of religion on an even footing with the other juridical principle, equity. Aristotle had dismissed the gods from the state, but the Romans crowded them so closely into the legal community that it was very easy for Cicero to connect Jupiter as godhead of polity and the substance of law with the universal moral legality of the Stoics and with its norm, the law of Nature.[1] In his enthusiasm for such unity, Cicero, the republican, goes so far as to praise monarchy as the original and natural form of government.

Since the gods had been drawn into the legal community and thrown into the political affairs of the Roman empire, the question could not but arise in Cicero's mind: What is the relation of the divine to the human law?

The concept of the *lex naturalis* was invoked here to serve as a connecting link. Just as, in the downward direction, international

[1] *De Republica*, I, XXXV-XXXVIII.

and civil law sprang from the natural law, so, upward, the natural law rose to the divine. It is true that Cicero generally uses the expressions *lex naturalis* and *lex divina* without distinction of meaning. Indeed he asserts that gods and men are likewise subject to one and the same law of Nature.[1] On the other hand, traces are to be discovered of Neo-Platonic and even theistic influences, and there is no lack in Cicero of expressions that reveal that he sometimes thought of the *lex naturalis* as an emanation, and at others as an utterance, of the will of the gods.[2] A theistic and personal tendency must, sooner or later, spring out of the character of Roman religion, as we have seen it. This tendency is felt more strongly in Seneca and Epictetus than in Cicero. The source of their pantheism and naturalism is obviously Neo-Platonism. According to the various naturalistic or theistic versions of the concept of divinity and of the *lex naturalis*, Cicero at one time defines virtue as the perfect nature of man, at one with itself, and at another as the divine likeness imprinted by God in man. Two conceptions of virtue, destined to struggle with each other for many a century, here lie peacefully side by side.

Now if, to return to Cicero's state doctrines, the whole cosmos is held together by the *lex naturalis*, interpreted as an objective order, and if according to the Stoics the state is a little cosmos within the great one, then the essence of this state must likewise be an objective order, an harmonious division of political powers or of sovereignties which, at least for the model state, must be derived from the universal laws of Nature. This derivation Cicero promised to trace, though he never completed it, and in his book *De Legibus* he proceeds without delay, in regular Roman fashion, to define legal authority dogmatically.

A new conception of the state now comes more or less consciously to the fore. Cicero no longer inquires critically into the division of state powers regarded as ultimate ends, but dogmatically investigates the lawful handling of that power. Thus he comes to a conclusion of great juridical insight—that the whole power in the city rests with the people, and that the organs of the state, i.e. the senate and the magistrates, have no power of their own (*potestas*), but only *consilium, auctoritas, auspicium, imperium.*[3] While then, he at first regarded the state as a political unit,

---

[1] *De Natura Deorum*, II, 31.   [2] *Ibid.* Cf. also *De Legibus*, II, 4.
[3] *De Legibus*, III, 12, 27.

he now came to see it as a juridical personality, or corporation. The logical relation of these two views he never clearly grasped. They stand isolated side by side; they traverse and confuse each other, so that thereafter—and this is the third and last complication of the problem for which Cicero is responsible—the juridical doctrine of government becomes a rival to the political theory of the state.

To sum up, the ethico-political writings of Cicero occupy a central position in the history of these sciences. In them Greek and Roman ethics and politics become intertwined in such a fashion that, first, in legal philosophy natural law is confused with the positive codes; second, in ethics natural and divine law become intermingled; and lastly, in the theory of government politics and law are confounded.

This threefold complication, as we saw at the beginning, arose because the Stoics' universe had to be brought into relation and harmony with the Roman world-state. When, immediately after Cicero's death, the Roman republic actually became an empire, the similarity between the universal monarchy of Rome and the monistic world-empire of the Stoics became more and more striking. The mighty rule of Rome gradually acquired a highly significant, natural and spiritual, physical and metaphysical background. The historical and philosophic vision whose outline had been sketched by Cicero's uncertain hand became more and more definite and clear, until it charmed and captured the imagination of the whole Middle Ages, and especially our poet's.

DANTE, CICERO AND THE ECLECTICS

Seneca and Boëthius

In the midst of all these complications, at least one border-line was left undisturbed. The high level of Stoic spiritual morality is maintained in Cicero without the interference of practical considerations.

Cicero teaches that the profitable, when it is opposed to the Good, brings only an apparent and transitory gain, never a genuine and permanent one. A rule of conduct or an action that realizes no ethical value may, perhaps, at times be morally unimportant, but is usually absolutely reprehensible. Neither Cicero [1] nor in-

---

[1] Cf. especially Cicero, *De Officiis*, III.

deed any pre-Christian teachers of ethics ventured to deny the
existence of actions which are neither good nor bad. They were
able to ignore and veil them, but they could not do away with this
neutral ground, nor transfer it to an independent sovereign—the
homo politicus.

The pathos of world-renunciation was not forgotten by these
later and milder Stoics, Cicero, Seneca, and Boëthius. On the
contrary, they heightened it. It is precisely from them that Dante
borrows the weapons with which to oppose the human, all too
human, value set on riches, noble birth, and good fortune.

From Cicero's *Paradoxa* he translates the following passage of
his *Convivio*: [1] "Never truly have I counted as good things nor as
things worth striving for the money, the palaces, the wealth, the
political power, nor the pleasures to which certain people are most
devoted. For I saw that those who swam in the greatest abundance
were craving most violently the very thing which they already had
in excess. For at no time does covetousness become sated. And
they are tortured not only by the craving to increase their possessions, but by the fear of losing them." And in the same passage,
next to quotations from the Bible, Horace, and Juvenal, he invokes
the authority of Seneca, and cites from Boëthius the impressive
lines:

> If plenty from her copious horns should pour
> Wealth as innumerable as the sands,
> That Pontus driven by the gusts upheaves,
> Or stars that glitter in the cloudless sky,
> Nor ever stay her hand, the human race
> Would still not cease its pitiful complaints. [2]

—lines which were still in Dante's heart when in the dark abyss
of Hell he drew the glowing picture of Fortune, and in the presence
of unresting, stone-rolling greed, composed the lines:

> For all the gold that is beneath the moon,
> Or ever has been, of these weary souls
> Could never make a single one repose. [3]

The independence and inward freedom with which the ethics of
the Stoa, and of later Rome generally, regarded earthly goods, were
considered by our poet one of the most beautiful and precious
features of pagan antiquity. He seems actually to have formed the

---

[1] *Paradoxa,* I, 6, in *Convivio,* IV, 12.
[2] *De Consolatione Philosophiae,* Book II, Metr. II.   [3] *Inferno,* VII, 64–66.

conviction that a natural bridge united this antique virtue with Christian morality: "Be not a miser nor a spendthrift; be the master of gold, and let not thyself be mastered by it"—these, he believes, are principles on which the best men of antiquity nourished a Christian life. This, if I am not mistaken, is the definite moral teaching and purpose underlying the Statius episode in the *Purgatorio.*

The Dantesque Statius confesses that he has lived a heathen and a spendthrift, and was led to a moral conversion by two verses of Virgil:

> To what dost thou not drive the hearts of men,
> Accursed greed for gold!

the meaning of which is distorted violently, but perhaps not erroneously,[1] by Dante's Statius:

> O sacred hunger, why dost thou not curb
> Mortals' desire for gold?[2]

Thanks to such a warning and with such understanding and encouragement, Statius escaped not Purgatorial pains, indeed, but eternal punishment, and discovering a Christian meaning in other verses, likewise of his predecessor Virgil, he became a convert to Christianity. Here we have, as I believe, under a veil of symbolism the broadest recognition of ancient morality.

He who does not let himself be dazzled by riches will preserve his independence in the face of other external inducements, particularly noble birth. Nobility is either founded on possessions, and we have just seen how they are to be regarded, or else on birth, and in that case, too, Stoic ideas come to our poet's aid.

In the world-realm of the Stoics, caste distinctions vanish before the judgment-seat of Nature's eternal law. Only inner worth, nobility of soul, abides. Epictetus, the slave, becomes the master of the emperor Marcus Aurelius. This democratic and universal trait of Stoicism, if it may be so called, Dante had come to know especially from Boëthius's *Consolatio,* but it must be recalled that the criticism of the privileges of feudal nobility and the stern antithesis between aristocracy of birth and nobleness of soul were among the moral commonplaces of the later Middle Ages. It was in the spirit and inclination of the ambitious bourgeoisie of medi-

[1] *Aeneid,* III, 56–57. [2] *Purgatorio,* XXII, 40–41.

æval cities, and need not necessarily have been derived from ancient philosophy. What Dante borrowed was not the thought itself, but its authoritative form. When with the fullest use of his many-sided knowledge he wrote his canzone on the nature of nobility, and a commentary on it, he certainly remembered Boëthius's verses:

> All the race of men on earth
> From like origin arise:
> One is father of all things,
> One is governor of all.
> He to Phœbus gave his rays,
> Unto Luna gave her horns.
> Men he gave unto the earth,
> And unto the sky its stars.
> Souls within our frames he set,
> Summoned from his lofty home.
> So all mortal men
> A noble seed produced.
> Why boast your birth and ancestors?
> Seeing your origin
> And author still is God,
> Ignoble is no man,
> Unless, by faults debased,
> He may his birthright lose.[1]

He likewise refers, while scourging the foolish presumption of the man who looks down on his neighbour, to a passage in Cicero's *De Officiis*.[2]

The wise man who calmly ignores social distinctions and all vicissitudes of fortune must be absolutely convinced of the freedom of the human will. But we have seen how ambiguous Stoic philosophy is on this very point, and how on the one hand the identification of moral with natural law led to a belief in destiny, and how on the other hand the idealization of Nature's law became an assurance of human freedom.

The Stoics, aroused by these contradictions, gave special attention to the problem of the freedom of the will, and solved it in their fashion. Under the conditions of scholarship in his day, however, Dante could hardly have known anything of these efforts, whereas the Christian solution given by Boëthius was familiar to him. To be sure, as far as I know he never refers directly to it, but that he did know and use it can hardly be doubted.

[1] *De Consolatione Philosophiae*, Book III, Metr. VI; cf. *Convivio*, third canzone, fourth strophe, and the corresponding prose section.
[2] Evidently *De Officiis*, I, XXVI, 91.

It is the loftiest and purest side of Roman and eclectic Stoicism that always and everywhere directly attracts our poet and whose utterances he utilizes to give force, emphasis, and classic colouring to his own convictions. The lower, lax, and complacent doctrine of ancient worldly wisdom, however, remained always repugnant to him.

Practical Wisdom in Cicero's Philosophy of Law

It must therefore be surmised that Dante's morality, wholly subjective and inward, would find no outlet to public everyday life. Or if it did, it surely could not be among the Stoics of ancient Rome.

In fact, he was indebted for it to Cicero, whether he accounted him a Stoic or not. It is Cicero's merit to have distinguished what is ethically *good* from the politically *profitable* by inserting between them legal right as the *political good*.

We saw above how Cicero threw law and morality together; here we must emphasize the fact that he grasped the nature of legal righteousness better than his predecessors when he defined it as the social realization of the metaphysical moral law. According to Plato, he is righteous who keeps the powers of his soul in the right order. With Aristotle, as with Cicero, it is he who acts socially, yet—and here he differs from Cicero—not with reference to an absolute law of morality, but to the temporal welfare of the community. It was Cicero who gave to the political and social ideal of righteousness of Aristotle a personal, metaphysical, and essentially Stoical foundation. This is, as it seems to me, the most valuable contribution made by Cicero, and is contained in his concept of duty (*officium*).

It is among the duties of a righteous citizen—and here Cicero is still somewhat under the influence of Aristotle's teachings—not merely to return like for like, but also to aid his neighbour by forbearance, kindness, and love. According to present-day ideas, kindness and love for our neighbour are something different from justice; to Aristotle and Cicero they mean merely a special case or a minor aspect of justice. So Cicero's conception of justice includes more than the modern one, but it also embraces more than Aristotle's definition. The latter insists on justice only within the political community. Toward those who stand outside it, gods and slaves, there can, strictly speaking, be no injustice. Cicero, on the other hand, expressly demands justice not only for his enemies, and, in a certain sense, for the gods, but even for the slaves. "Let us not forget that even toward the humblest members of human society, justice must be observed. It is a sound principle that they are to be regarded as hirelings; that is, we are to require their service, and must also give them due recompense. But injustice is shown in two ways: either by violence or by deception. Deceit is the way of the fox, violence that of the lion, both altogether unworthy of man. But the more hateful is deceit. The greatest injustice, however, is committed by those who, while guilty of the most shameful deceit, pose as honourable men."[1]

These noble words made a deep impression on Dante, and determined his divisions of his Lower Hell. Dante completed, with the aid of Cicero, the Aristotelian conception of justice. From Aristotle he accepts the division of all acts of injustice into two classes: those which are committed in passion (*incontinenza*) and those inspired by malice (*malizia*). The latter acts of injustice, prompted by malice, which are punished in Lower Hell, he further divides, on the authority of the passage above quoted, into acts of violence and deceit, and yet again divides the acts of deceitful injustice according as they are committed with or without betrayal of a special confidential trust; that is, into simple fraud or treachery.[2] Even Cicero's symbol of the lion as the violent beast and the fox as the deceitful one, Dante makes his own.[3] When he further assumes, as we recalled above, that human violence and even to some extent human deceit, may offend not only our fellow men but also God, Nature, and our own reason—he then comes much closer to Cicero's conception of justice than to Aristotle's.

Thanks to his broad, too broad, extension of the idea of justice, Cicero succeeds in bringing within its range even the so-called æsthetic virtues, thus placing a cheerful smile on the stern and imperious visage of the Stoa, and approaching once more the worldly path of Aristotle's citizen.

Liberality appears to be closely akin to justice. Compared indeed with the generosity of knightly Christendom, ready to give away its last garment, the Ciceronian virtue bears itself like a very prudent and thrifty dame. "For one must above all see to it that benefactions do not prove harmful to the recipients and to others, and that they be not shown to the unworthy. For this is demanded by justice, according to which all such action is to be regulated.

---

[1] *De Officiis,* I, XIII, 41.   [2] *Inferno,* XI.   [3] *Ibid.,* XXVII, 74 sqq.

. . . But there are many who, evidently in greed for glory or fame, rob one man of what they wish to present to another. In so doing, they believe that they appear as benefactors to their friends in so far as they in any way enrich them. But this is as far as possible from one's duty; even utterly contrary to duty." [1]

How remarkable, how Italian, that Dante, the mediæval and Christian nobleman, fully accepted as his model this genuinely bourgeois, democratic, economic ideal of liberality! Here [2] he literally follows Cicero and Aristotle,[3] whom Cicero copies.

Yet not only Aristotle and Cicero, but the entire ideal of ancient life with its morality softened by art and social refinement, the whole Hellenic καλοκαγαδία and σωφροσύνη, became alive in the soul of the mediæval poet as soon as he undertook to portray the ideal nobleman, the intellectual aristocrat. His canzone on the nature of nobility, which we are inclined in agreement with the poet to call "against prejudice," [4] contains in its last strophe (verses 121–140), and in the corresponding passages of the commentary, the precious nucleus of a "nobleman's book" in the spirit of the Renaissance. Among the most important qualities which Castiglione, two hundred years later, insists on for his *Cortegiano*, hardly one is missing here. The elaborate commentary on this stanza of the poem is enriched with examples and citations from all antiquity, so far as it was known to the poet: Aristotle, Cicero, Virgil, Ovid, Lucan, and Statius—they all offer confirmatory evidence. The only biblical writer who is at all freely quoted is worldly-wise King Solomon. Much in the same vein is another poem of Dante, his canzone on attractiveness, beginning "After my love has quite deserted me." [5] But it may suffice for the present to have noted and emphasized the fact that the gate through which these worldly thoughts and humanistic views make their entrance into the mediæval ethics was built by Cicero. At first, however, Christianity barred this gate with iron bolts.

3. CHRISTIAN ETHICS

THE JEWISH SPIRIT

While with the Romans belief and conscience became political, almost the opposite process went on among the Israelites.

---

[1] *De Officiis*, I, XIV, 42–43.
[2] *Convivio*, IV, 27, and nineteenth canzone, strophe 2.   [4] *Convivio*, IV, 30.
[3] *Nicomachean Ethics*, IV, 1.   [5] *Poscia ch'Amor del tutto m'ha lasciato.*

Jehovah made his definite compact of solidarity with the chosen people. In their simple, sober and austere ethics there could be no prevarication, evasion, exception, or favour for the individual. The exclusive and jealous God required from all men the strictest obedience. The moral behaviour of individuals became of utmost importance to the whole people, for on it the national welfare depended. The Levites as teachers and guardians of the divine commands, and the prophets as the proclaimers and interpreters of them, led the people, while the kings, with their realistic policy, could not permanently hold their ground.

As a consequence of this victory by the servants of God and their disciples, a victory of Utopian and theocratic hopes over the shrewdness of the children of the world, the nation indeed was broken into fragments; but its law, its prophets, its God, and its synagogue remained alive; and the idea of the moral will as the general will, inseparably bound to the one and only God, lived on and became permeated, more and more as the God of the Jews became the god of the world, with the Greek and Roman ideas of personal freedom. The theocratic spirit, which made the books of the Old Testament so attractive to Dante, became, through contact with the Hellenistic and Roman world, an universal instead of a national leaven.

EVANGELICAL ETHICS

Christianity, risen out of the most national of all religions, the Jewish, became the most international of all. International, to be sure, were also the doctrines of the Cynics, Epicureans, and Stoics; but they became so on essentially different grounds. The Greek or Roman sage lived in the midst of a social life from whose political thrall he gradually escaped, thanks to his self-created strength of mind. As he painfully acquired inward vigour and discipline, he raised himself above the ordinary run of practical desires and popular tendencies. What there is of internationalism among the Stoics and the Epicureans and in kindred movements rests mainly on spiritual aristocracy, in the good and bad meanings of the word. Even their gentle, benevolent feeling toward the poor and the oppressed has in it something superior, aristocratic, patronizing.

It is from utterly different sources that the international spirit of the later Judaism arises. While with the pagan sages moral feeling alienated itself from the national sentiment, with the Jewish people the two converged. The Jew lived in a divinely ordained community, wherein the law of the state and the moral law were alike sacred. To withdraw from the one in the name of the other would have been an absurdity. Both had the same divine origin. Only two possibilities were open: either that the moral law and religion go to destruction with the Jewish state, or else that the political and legal conditions of life take refuge, under external pressure, in the sanctuary of religion and morality and become spiritual.

Both events actually occurred. Some lost their nationality, their God, and their conscience with their fatherland, and wholly ceased to be Jews.

The larger and better portion of the people, however, under the pressure of foreign rule, gave their national and legal aspirations a moral and religious significance. This recasting of values was begun by the prophets and completed by Jesus. Through an unparalleled series of spiritual acts, the older Jewish law acquired an ever deeper and more universal pertinence, until even its last letter was turned to spirit and its last statute became devotion and love.

To be sure, those who were able to keep pace intelligently with this progress and transformation became fewer and fewer. A new division of the people followed hard on each new interpretation of the Law. The older conception lived on, asserting itself by the side of the new. When the prophets set up a heavenly kingdom in place of the promised world-hegemony, the people divided into the Sadducean and Pharisaic sects, and the Samaritans fell off. Other matters of dispute remained limited to theological circles. The most serious schism, however, was caused by Jesus.

How He came to be in such sharp opposition to His people and what brought Him to the death upon the cross can hardly be indicated in a word. In the last analysis, however, and looked at practically, it was doubtless the national question. At least no pronounced religious or moral dissension between the evangelical and the late Judaic spirit can be definitely pointed out. But there is a very tangible and irreconcilable national contradiction in the fact that Jesus rejects all the old and popular conceptions of the Law in order to enforce exclusively a new and purely ethical interpretation.

Thereby He struck at the very heart of the most powerful feeling of a people: the instinct of national preservation. For evidently as soon as the golden promises and protection of Jahve are no longer bound up with racial descent and nationality, the chosen people, the people of God, have nothing more to do. Jesus wrests from them the best that they have, the monopoly of their God, and proffers it to all mankind. That purity and spontaneity of a child's love for a personal Father Who is in Heaven, the directness and warmth of their brotherly love, all this was the choicest fruit of an exclusive race-religion. That feeling of intimate connection between man and God, and between man and man, could develop so strongly only where the bond of blood-kinship and the jealousy of the national God encircled the people as in a wall and isolated it. To have broken through this wall is Jesus's ethical achievement.

When He transforms all political and ethico-political values into purely ethical and purely religious ones, He gives them the most universal and international significance imaginable. Paul, the apostle to the Gentiles, seems to have realized only in details and only in part what was already implicit in the teaching of Jesus: the supernationalism of the metaphysical.

Thus, for example, Jesus transforms the economic concepts of poor and rich into the moral concepts of independence of or dependence on earthly possessions. He changes the social classes of publicans and Pharisees into the moral division between the humble and the self-righteous; legal punishment and reward become the ethical concepts of justice and grace. The Jewish kingdom of God He interprets as the timeless and spaceless realm of the Holy Spirit. The ritual usages of worship, the temple tribute, the observance of the Sabbath, the form of oath, in short, all external functions, He empties of their value. The entire legal formalism of social order melts before the fire of this love.

Only those institutions which proceed not from legal formulæ, but from the life of the spirit, are left intact: marriage, the family, the state, and the congregation. Yet even these are threatened, for wherever they oppose conscience, their power is broken. The inward resistance of the sense of duty is the unsurmountable and natural barrier to all external compulsions, political or otherwise. He who is moved by compulsion from within, that is, by the Holy Spirit, deserts his wife, his children, his parents, his city, or his church. He is not to be turned back by statutes or penalties. To suffer violence, even to die, for his convictions, is no evil, but a privilege; not a defeat, but a victory. Humiliation, the contempt of man, and agony have been glorified to Heaven by the example of Jesus's Passion.

To be sure, He who uttered to Peter the remarkable words, "Put up again thy sword into its place: for all they that take the sword shall perish with the sword," is the one who drove violently out of the temple peaceful and busy traders and money-changers. It is inevitable that even the most patient spirit should act vigorously under certain conditions. There is here no inner contradiction, for passive resistance carried on inwardly takes on in turn the form of vigorous practical action. In fact, a stubborn inward struggle requires a much higher degree of capacity for action than does the most vigorous aggressiveness. It is a greater deed to suffer oneself to be nailed to the cross for conscience' sake than to seek a hero's death on the battlefield.

Precisely because the Christian spirit made its sons capable of martyrdom, it also made them the most venturesome of conquerors. The reproach of cowardice, weakness, and slavish spirit which has been cast, especially in the most recent times, at Christianity, rests on a grave psychological misunderstanding. The impatience and nervousness of an excitable and unsteady will are taken as indications of a powerful character.

As soon as over-excited and impatient impulses gain the mastery of a people, its soul becomes possessed with Utopian hopes. Then it dreams of a superman, of a Messiah, of an Emperor Barbarossa, who by an ideal policy, which here means an impractical one, is to set right all disturbed conditions. Even so did the Jews at the time of the Maccabees, so did the Christians at the close of antiquity, and again at the end of the Middle Ages, and especially Dante, expect a political idealist to be their deliverer. But instead of the deliverer and restorer, great destroyers and innovators came: Jesus, Luther, Calvin. And their work took wholly different shape from that which the dreamers of the earlier day had craved and imagined.

And so Dante's time was as ill fitted as the age of the Maccabees to understand aright the ethical and political rôle of Jesus.

DANTE AND JESUS

Dante appreciated only the metaphysical, that is, the ethical and religious, significance of Jesus's work; its political and historical side he interpreted most arbitrarily and in accordance with the feelings of his own age, if not of his own party.

Our present understanding of Jesus's political position may be defined somewhat as follows: "Jesus did not share the political hopes and the revolutionary efforts of his people. All the attempts which for him were no temptations, to set on his head the earthly crown of David, he eluded. He knew that his Heavenly Father had bestowed on him the rule of the kingdom of God, which has no mortal nature, but which is altogether spiritual and ethical. In the sovereignty of Rome, Jesus recognized a state of fact which the children of Israel must accept. Israel is under moral obligation to pay tribute unto Caesar. It had put itself under the sway of the Roman emperor by the acceptance, for use and trade, of the emperor's coin; so it may not refuse the payment of his tax. It must render unto Caesar what belongs to Caesar. Jesus did not thereby decree that it was the Christian's duty to obey every usurper who for the time being happens to exercise power; but that he was to render obedience where he accepted the power, and enjoyed the protection, of a state. And, as Jesus did this in his own case, he was assured that the providential power of God had accorded to the Romans their rule over Israel; and in Pilate's authority over himself he recognized a power granted by God 'from above' (John 19:11)."[1]

Dante, however, from the fact that Jesus bowed before the authority of Rome, draws a more extended, indeed an eternal, consequence. According to him Jesus recognized, not merely for his own person, not only for Israel, not alone for His own day, but for all mankind and for all time, the right of Rome to rule. He even morally justified and sanctified it. Jesus, by coming into the world under the rule of the first Roman emperor, bore witness to the fact that this empire was the only righteous rule on earth.[2] "And if the Roman empire did not righteously exist, then Adam's sin was not atoned for through Christ."—"If Christ had not suffered by command of the proper judge, then the punishment of crucifixion would have been no atoning one. But He alone could be the proper judge who had jurisdiction over all humanity; for the whole of mankind was punished in the person of Christ, who, as the prophet says, took all our sufferings upon Himself. And the

[1] H. Jacoby, *Neutestamentliche Ethik*, Königsberg, 1899, pp. 129–130.
[2] *Convivio*, IV, 5, and *De Monarchia*, II, 12.

Emperor Tiberius, whose representative Pilate was, could not have had right of judgment upon all mankind if the Roman empire had not existed rightfully. And precisely for that reason did Herod, though he knew not what he did, and likewise Caiaphas, when he spoke the truth concerning the judgment of Heaven, leave to Pilate the decision as to Christ . . . for Herod was not the representative of Tiberius, under the emblem of the Roman eagle, or of the senate, but was a subordinate king, who ruled only under the mandate of royal power conferred upon him." [1]

The same line of thought underlies the mysterious words which the Emperor Justinian speaks, in the *Paradiso*, in praise of Rome and the eagle upon her standard.

> But what the standard that has made me speak
>   Achieved before, and after should achieve
>   Throughout the mortal realm that lies beneath it,
> Becometh in appearance mean and dim,
>   If in the hand of the third Caesar seen
>   With eye unclouded and affection pure,
> Because the living Justice that inspires me
>   Granted it, in the hand of him I speak of,
>   The glory of doing vengeance for its wrath. [2]

The vengeance is Jesus's death upon the cross, ordained by imperial decree and recognized by Jesus as legal.

Thus the eternal value of Jesus's personality and of His moral work appears to the Ghibelline dreamer as the consecration of a world-empire. In taking this view, Dante puts himself in much the same position as the Jews in the time of the Maccabees. They expected from their Messiah that he would use his divine power to overthrow an alien rule, and if possible to create a world-empire for the Jews. Dante assigns to the same Messiah the task and intention of sanctifying the Roman rule over the world, a rule already established.

Regarded from this side, our poet's Christ acquires rather an apocalyptic than an evangelical character, if by apocalyptic we understand the combination of ethical and political hopes, and by evangelical the purification of moral action from all temporal considerations.

Therefore Christ appears on the summit of the Purgatorial mountain as an apocalyptical animal. He is the griffin who leans

[1] *De Monarchia*, II, 12.   [2] *Paradiso*, VI, 82–90.

the chariot of the Church against the tree of the Roman world-empire, whereupon the dead tree is filled with fresh life and puts forth blossoms.[1]

But not merely with the backward gaze of a philosopher of history, but as a prophet as well, Dante must envisage the moral regeneration of human society in the form of a political restoration; and conversely, the reconstitution of the collapsed Holy Roman Empire can only appear to him in the light of a moral rebirth. The deliverer whom he announces prophetically is an ethico-political apocalyptic being; symbolized sometimes as a beast, *Veltro* (hound), sometimes in the form of a number, "DXV." [2]   Wherever Dante gives expression to his political hopes and to his future dreams, he harks back to the apocalyptic books of the Bible; for it is a Maccabean or theocratic affinity that inspired him and created those figures and signs that best correspond to the trend of his thought.

Did then the Christ of Revelation quite hide from Dante the figure Jesus of the Gospels?

Christ appears three times in the *Divine Comedy*, each time under symbolic form; first, at the summit of the Purgatorial mountain, in the apocalyptic form of the Griffin—here He draws the Church and sanctifies the state; again in Heaven, as God's champion and martyr, a victor upon the cross—something apocalyptic still clings to Him in this form, as I have already shown; and lastly, in the Heaven of the fixed stars, as the triumphant guide of souls.

He is treated each time as a principle; first, of spiritual order; next, of spiritual victory; and finally, of universal spiritual redemption.   But never and nowhere does He appear as an historical personage.

If we understand then by "evangelical Jesus" the historical person, then the Christianity of the *Commedia* is not evangelical. But if we understand thereby a power of the next world and a principle and cause of moral salvation, then it must be conceded that the whole *Commedia* is upheld and permeated by Him, and to that extent reveals its evangelical character.

Taken in order, these three symbols of Christ, the griffin, the martyr, the victor, indicate that the purely mystical and religious nature of the Saviour gradually emerges more and more clearly

---

[1] *Purgatorio*, XXXII, 25 sqq.
[2] *Inferno*, I, 101 sqq., and *Purgatorio*, XXXIII, 43.

from the ecclesiastical, political, and apocalyptic figure, until finally in the Empyrean it is wholly merged once more in the Trinity.

Everywhere the divine and symbolic element remains so exalted that every comparison of Jesus with mortal men would appear a desecration. Therefore the earthly life and work of the Redeemer cannot even be regarded as an example for us. The favourite idea of mystical ethics in the Middle Ages was the imitation of Jesus Christ. To live, to suffer, and to die as Jesus did, yes, even perhaps to endure a greater passion than His, or at least to put ourselves, with the full force of our imagination, in His place, and to follow inwardly and outwardly on His path of suffering, was the aspiration of many a professional mystic. Dante knows nothing of such distortions.

In his *Purgatorio* he had abundant opportunity to bring out all the moral attractiveness of Jesus's life on earth. He entirely refrained from doing so. Of all the evangelical models and examples used in this world to clarify, purify, strengthen, and uplift our deeds, not one is recorded. The poet nowhere says directly, but must have felt, that the ethical greatness of the Son of God was too high for even the mightiest of men. The graceful adjectives and circumlocutions with which Christ is surrounded serve almost always to veil the human body in a symbolic garment of light: Word, Wisdom, Light, Source, Lamb of God, Love, Desire (*Verbo, Sapienza, Luce, Semenza, Agnel di Dio, Diletto, Disiro*), etc. Even among the concepts of personal relationships the poet chooses always the most official and the most general, the titles lord, master, emperor, husband (*signore, maestro, imperadore, sposo*), etc. The most intimate and most individual designation which he allows himself is "Son of the Virgin Mary." Those homely pictures of Jesus's childhood and poverty in which the Franciscan poets, notably Jacopone da Todi, took delight, did not allure him. The very name *Cristo* is for him something so unique and lofty that he does not venture to rhyme it, in the verses of the *Commedia*, with any word save itself.

Such elevation and remoteness accorded to Jesus's humanity take from His moral commands much of their naturalness, clarity, gentleness, and cheerfulness, and emphasize all the more their categorical austerity and their deep earnestness. It may fairly be asserted that Dante has revealed the spirit of Christ more in the depth of His heart and in the heights of Heaven than in the outward side of His daily existence and in the humbler walks of life. His Christ is not the gentle comforter, but the heroic pioneer who forced the gate of Hell, opened Heaven, and pointed out the moral path. He is, essentially, religious dogma and moral principle.[1]

THE DOUBLE NATURE OF CHRISTIAN ETHICS

The essential reason for this preference of Dante's is to be sought in the double nature of Christian ethics, which constantly sways between a religious centre that is love of God and a centre of practical gravity that is love of our neighbour. Its strength arises from this twofold attraction of God and of man.

No one has been more clearly conscious of this than Jesus himself: "Thou shalt love the Lord thy God with all thy heart and with all thy soul and with all thy mind. This is the first and great commandment. And the second is like unto it, Thou shalt love thy neighbour as thyself. On these two commandments hang all the law and the prophets." [2]

The history of the religious development of Christianity has shown us that the loftiness of its moral requirements was primarily attained only because Jesus and the first Christians were vitally convinced of the proximity of God, of the existence of a heavenly kingdom, and of the approaching destruction of the world. To them, who were waiting thus eagerly for the imminent end, all political and economic activities were but a temporary and minor matter, hardly deserving of the slightest consideration. Hence they faced with indifference, if not with hostility, the objective values of a worldly civilization. To be sure, they busied themselves in acts of neighbourly love, but they did not contribute to the cultural life of the political and economic community.

After Jesus's crucifixion, when the increasing contempt, scorn, and persecution heaped on the first Christian churches had strengthened the religious yearning for the Hereafter, their disenchanted brotherly love took refuge sorrowfully in its original source, the love of God. The desire to escape the social and political life grew into a misanthropic aversion for everything that was not immediately religious. The cheerful ethics of the Gospel took on the gloom of the cloister.

[1] Even so in the Middle Ages the arts of design treated not the purely human scenes in Jesus's life, but by preference those which have dogmatic and liturgical significance.

[2] Matthew 22:37–40.

Hence Christian morality could be put at the service of a national culture only if its practical aims were strengthened at the cost of its religious issue, or at least if those practical aims were brought out into public life, and the final goal was relegated to the conscience of the individual.

But for the time—and this period includes not only early Christianity, but the entire Middle Ages—the religious need was so great and so prevalent that the simple and natural path of practical Christianity could not be eagerly followed.

The Christian spirit then had to be made available for political life and civilization without sacrificing in the least its religious intensity. It was therefore necessary to combine the greatest possible growth and extension of religious belief in the Hereafter with the development of moral exigencies in this world.

This problem was solved at the close of the Middle Ages, and about the time of our poet. In his *Commedia* the practical moral values of the state, of the family, of civilization, the subjective value of the individual conscience, the social value of the general welfare, and the individual ethical value of separate persons—all these are united under the strictly religious and Christian viewpoint of salvation in the other world, and are as far as possible reconciled with it and with each other.

Compared therewith, our modern convictions appear at first glance somewhat disconnected. If we wish to unite in the service of moral culture, we are compelled to set aside each man's religion as a purely personal affair. If we on the other hand endeavour to build up a social community on the basis of religious or philosophical convictions, then men from the most opposite ethical and political camps, anarchists and reactionaries, band together metaphysically.

The harmonizing of ethics with religion is yet a distant aspiration; the specifically mediæval, that is, dogmatic, reconciliation of the two is antiquated and surpassed.

PAUL

The same man who, out of evangelical religion and Greek philosophy, moulded Christian theology, was also the first to take in hand the solution of this ethical problem.

The ethical side of Paul's work stands in the closest relation to its religious side. That can be most clearly seen, doubtless, in the two aspects of his belief—two aspects that occasionally become three, according as the apostle's eye rests on the Christian community or on the non-Christians, and according as he distinguishes, among the latter, the Jews from the Greeks, or again from the Romans.   Each of these three groups is met by Paul with particular and distinct religious weapons, which are, however, wielded all for one and the same cause.

Faith, in the last analysis, is for Paul a subjective ethical capacity, not very different from the modern explanation of belief; it is the personal assurance of conscience, weaker in some, stronger in others, and individually directed thus or so according to numberless conditioning causes.   The prescription for this ethical faith runs thus: "Let every man be fully persuaded in his own mind" [1]— nothing more.   One considers fasting a matter of conscience and fasts, another considers eating a duty and eats.   In their own eyes and therefore in the sight of God, both are justified by the convictions of their conscience which prompted them to fast or eat. It would follow from this that there is no reason why the heathen, as well as the Jew, as well as the Christian, may not act morally, justify himself by the assurance of his own conscience, and thus win salvation.   There shall be "tribulation and anguish, upon every soul of man that doeth evil, of the Jew first, and also of the Gentile.   But glory, honour, and peace, to every man that worketh good, to the Jew first, and also to the Gentile.   For there is no respect of persons with God." [2]   On the supposition that faith be present, any form whatsoever of religious belief suffices to bring about moral action and inward freedom.   Indeed, the moral loftiness and purity of our actions can be properly valued only according to the ethical force, not according to the theoretical content, of the motives of our faith.   Since morality is something under control of the will, it must be measured wholly on the volitional side of our faith.

But Paul did not draw these conclusions.

Although he bases the essence of morality, in entire harmony with Jesus, on practical faith, he nevertheless measures the height of morality by theoretical standards.   Here the contradictions begin.   Paul sets Christian morality, in and for itself, higher than that of the Jews, and the latter higher than that of the Gentiles.   For the heathen, he says, are cramped in their obscure and bewildered

---

[1] Romans 14:5.   [2] Romans 2:9-11.

views as to the nature of God; their faith, however, is both belief
and unbelief. The Jews have, to be sure, received the law in plain
words from God Himself; but they do not understand it, and
cling to the letter. (As if Judaism had never known the love
and mercy of God!) Through Christianity the law has been
spiritually superseded, interpreted, and revealed in its true nature.
Only the Christians possess the true faith in God's love and
grace.

This threefold illumination of faith is not won by human thought
and effort; it is a divine gift, a mystical communication of the spirit.
According to Paul, there are three aspects of the spirit corresponding to the three forms of faith; first, spirit as the principle of all
natural knowledge that can be acquired by man in general; second,
as the principle of the natural will and of moral effort, in the way
that the heathen and in a greater measure the Jews possess it;
and third, as the principle of moral power, as it was first communicated by Christ to those who believe in Him. Along with
the three forms of faith and of spirit we have also three kinds
of moral law: the natural, which is written in all men's hearts,
something like the Stoic and Ciceronian *lex naturalis*,[1] a conception which Paul might have borrowed from Greek philosophy;
next, the law of the Decalogue, given to the Jews by God under
the old covenant; and finally, the new Christian law of grace and
love.

Each of these three moral and religious steps presupposes the
previous one and includes it in itself. Regarded theoretically,
it is a peaceful ascent from man's natural morality to the ideal of
justice in the Jewish law and finally to victorious salvation from all
sin and to loving communion with Christ. But considered practically, this historical and philosophic outlook is of no avail for him
who is in the midst of life's turmoil; for him the three progressive
stages of faith and morality do not appear in an organic and graded
succession, but as a chaotic confusion of three elements; not as
the inclusion of one within another, but as a reciprocal repulsion.
Here the three ethical ways of life are at war with each other;
each would fain rule mankind without limitation and have complete control for itself. For Paul, however, only the third possesses unquestioned validity, for it alone has overthrown the other
two and absorbed them into itself. As an historical and spiritual

[1] Romans 2:14-15.

preparation for Christianity, Paganism and Judaism can justify themselves; but as its opponents, and so far as they adduce independent ideals of life, they are a vain delusion, sin and damnation. Only in the spirit of Christ, only through the miraculous transmission of this spirit by baptism, is future salvation from sin to be assured.

If we observe that Paul and all the later teachers of ethics who have in some degree accepted his view—Dante among them—stand in opposition, sometimes patiently and respectfully, sometimes in sullen hostility, to heathendom and Judaism, then it must be remembered that they speak in the first case as historical philosophers and theorists, in the second as preachers and proselytizers. Even within the bosom of Christianity itself, these two points of view have to be distinguished. If men had at all times acted intelligently and sanely, doubtless in modern Protestant theology strife would never have arisen over the question whether, according to the ideas of Paul, the baptized Christian is to be regarded as immune from sin or threatened by it, as unconquerable or vulnerable, as definitely saved or always in peril. The answer is clear: theoretically and fundamentally, Christ's work of salvation is accomplished and can nowise be further questioned; divine grace, wheresoever it casts its Christlike rays, destroys every trace of sin. Practically, however, in the lives of individuals, every man must be on his guard so that he may move safely and firmly in the light of this grace and not wander into darkness.

This much, to be sure, is certain: that Paul was wont to hold up before his Christian brethren and himself the joy of salvation oftener and more willingly than the danger of damnation; for of course the blacker he, the apostle to the Gentiles, depicted the prospects of the unbaptized, the more brightly and confidently must he let the hopes of Christendom shine forth.

This state of mind changes in the next age; as the dark area of heathenism dwindles and the bright surface of Christianity is extended, black shadows appear in Christendom, as the evangelical begin to turn away from the nominal Christians. Surely the hopeful apostle would hardly have dreamed that at a later day so many baptized brethren would be discovered in the Hell of a Christian poet. The feeling of Paul concerning Christianity differs from Dante's convictions somewhat as the mood of a buoyant youth from that of a disillusioned *laudator temporis acti.*

Paul is the Tyrtaeus, Dante the Juvenal, of the Christian community.

The more sternly Dante scourges Christendom, the more patiently can he deal with a heathenism that is now overthrown and no longer dangerous. But in the days of Paul, a Christian poet would hardly have dared to produce a series of heathens as models to the souls in Purgatory.

DANTE AND PAUL

However much the contradictions between heathen and Christian had softened in the meantime, they had not altogether vanished. Dante still arranges the successive grades of morality on the same principles as Paul. For him, too, the Christian virtues are the highest: faith, love, hope; that is, Christian faith, Christian love, and Christian hope. Only through mystical communication and operation of the specifically Christian spirit, only through the magic power of baptism, are true faith, true love, and true hope created. Not only the Church's catechism, but also its ethical doctrine is forced to admit—for the first time in Paul—a magical Christ who disturbs the self-reliance of conscience.

Our rapid survey of the history of religion has shown how the theological blending of law and grace, of retribution and redemption, which is chiefly Paul's work, was taken over by Dante, and with it the linking of morality and religion, of the freedom and the dependence of the will, of human responsibility and divine predestination, of justification by works and justification by faith. The contradictions present in religious theory, and which we met especially in Paul's doctrine of the resurrection of the body, have as far as possible been removed in ethics.

For here it is the concept of faith which, as a moral fact on the one hand, and as a religious fact on the other, bridges and unites the contradictions. For that very reason, the apologetic and dogmatic side is the weaker, the mystical and ethical side the more vital, part of Paul's work. The will, which feels itself bound and, in all its victories and merits, dependent on the divinity, in its actions is responsible, free, wholly self-determined: this is no theological subtilty. It is the profoundest and most real of all experiences, a psychological truth which can be analyzed and explained in detail, but by no means overthrown by the fact that the one-sided conclusions which Paul and all the theologians of the Church drew from it are seriously controverted.

We recall that the psychological fact of religious bondage and moral freedom of the will had been discovered and explained, independently of Paul, by the Stoics. Our poet, however, does not appeal to them, but to Paul, and so must accept the doctrine with all the Church's limitations.

The place in the *Divine Comedy* where the problem of the freedom of the will is specially discussed is the Heaven of the great men of action, of wise and religious princes, the Heaven of Jupiter. Nowhere does Dante show himself so fully conscious of the inconsistency of the Church's accepted version of Paul's doctrine of predestination. He says to himself:

> . . . Born a man is on the shore
> Of Indus, and is none who there can speak
> Of Christ, nor who can read, nor who can write;
> And all his inclinations and his actions
> Are good, so far as human reason sees,
> Without a sin in life or in discourse:
> He dieth unbaptized and without faith;
> Where is this justice that condemneth him?
> Where is his fault, if he do not believe? [1]

It is the same question which Paul had previously put to himself: "How shall they believe in him of whom they have not heard?" [2]

And the answer is in accordance with the teachings of Paul: the Church's wall suffers no critical breach, but is religiously strengthened. "Nay but, O man, who art thou that repliest against God? Shall the thing formed say to him that formed it, Why hast thou made me thus?" [3]

> Now who art thou, that on the bench wouldst sit
> In judgment at a thousand miles away,
> With the short vision of a single span?
> Truly to him who with me subtilizes,
> If so the Scripture were not over you,
> For doubting there were marvellous occasion.
> O animals terrene, O stolid minds,
> The primal will, that in itself is good,
> Ne'er from itself, the Good Supreme, has moved.
> So much is just as is accordant with it;
> No good created draws it to itself,
> But it, by raying forth, occasions that. [4]

[1] *Paradiso*, XIX, 70–78.
[2] Romans 10 : 14.
[3] Romans 9 : 20.
[4] *Paradiso*, XIX, 79–90.

Meantime a quiet deviation from Paul is revealed in these verses. It becomes more evident in other passages.

That union of freedom and bondage—for us a psychological fact with which we start, for Paul a matter of purely personal belief, which comes to him only from Christ—becomes for Dante a divine mystery, the inaccessibility of which is thereupon proved. And the proof is as follows:

> . . . He who a compass turned
>   On the world's outer verge, and who within it
>   Devised so much occult and manifest,
> Could not the impress of his power so make
>   On all the universe, as that his Word
>   Should not remain in infinite excess.
> And this makes certain that the first proud being,
>   Who was the paragon of every creature,
>   By not awaiting light fell immature.
> And hence appears it, that each minor nature
>   Is scant receptacle unto that good
>   Which has no end, and by itself is measured.
> In consequence our vision, which perforce
>   Must be some ray of that intelligence
>   With which all things whatever are replete,
> Cannot in its own nature be so potent,
>   That it shall not its origin discern
>   Far beyond that which is apparent to it.
> Therefore into the justice sempiternal
>   The power of vision that your world receives,
>   As eye into the ocean, penetrates;
> Which, though it see the bottom near the shore,
>   Upon the deep perceives it not, and yet
>   'Tis there, but it is hidden by the depth.
> There is no light but comes from the serene
>   That never is o'ercast, nay, it is darkness
>   Or shadow of the flesh, or else its poison.
> Amply to thee is opened now the cavern
>   Which has concealed from thee the living justice
>   Of which thou mad'st such frequent questioning.[1]

So the mystery is approached not, as with Paul, through the experience of faith, but through metaphysical considerations.

And now we recall that Dante did not take his definition of faith from Paul, but from an Alexandrian composition, namely, the Epistle to the Hebrews. Faith is to him not an ethical but a theoretical position, an argument for studious theologians, and

[1] *Paradiso*, XIX, 40-69.

for the laity a substance—that is, a concrete inward foundation. The Pauline conception of faith as a moral state and as the fundamental principle of virtue cannot be found explicitly in Dante. When he speaks of faith he thinks of it preferably as something objective, or which has been or should be made objective.[1] That subjective activity, however, which makes faith objective, is to him not practical but intellectual, partly philosophic study, which is actually represented by Dante as aiding at the birth of faith,[2] partly divine revelation. In short, not Paul's conception of faith, but the scholastic one derived from Anselm of Canterbury, dominates the *Divine Comedy*.

It might therefore be inferred that Paul's justification by faith also remained alien to our poet. As a matter of fact, it is not until long after his entrance into Paradise, long after his moral purification and liberation have been accomplished, that the pilgrim to the other world is questioned as to the content of his creed. In this respect Dante is much more theoretical and therefore also more tolerant than Paul. Faith, the acceptance and understanding of the principle of Christ's victory over sin, is for the poet the final reward, but for the apostle the first prerequisite of a truly moral life. What a man believes is to Dante far less important than to Paul, for to the former it is almost self-evident. But even the explanation of belief itself is to Dante less important, for he has in mind only the material content and the fixed dogma of faith, which therefore appears to him not as a principle but as the condition, the concomitant, the lure, and the beatific reward of moral conduct.

But where then, if not in faith, is this essential principle to be found? In love. In this view, however, Dante does not forsake Paul; he is merely leaning toward the narrower side of the apostle's ethics.

He follows here not so much the Epistle to the Romans as that to the Corinthians. In the latter, addressed to the intellectual Greeks of Corinth, the apostle did not preach the twofold power, practical and theoretical, of faith, but the purely active virtue of love.

"Though I speak with the tongues of men and of angels, and

[1] Where Dante uses the word *fede* of a subjunctive condition, it is in the popular sense, "good faith, loyalty." The only possible exception is *Paradiso*, XXIV, 38–39, which is an evangelical reminiscence of Matthew 14:29 sqq.

[2] *Convivio*, second canzone.

have not love, I am become as sounding brass or a tinkling cymbal. And though I have the gift of prophecy, and understand all mysteries, and all knowledge; and though I have all faith, so that I could remove mountains, and have not love, I am nothing. And though I bestow all my goods to feed the poor, and though I give my body to be burned, and have not love, it profiteth me nothing."[1]

Love, "the love that moves the sun and the other stars," is then also Dante's final word, and the nature of love is the last question of his theological examination.[2]

The task of uniting religion and morality, which Paul in the main assigns to faith, Dante endeavours to transfer to love. It is from this side that he answers once more, at the close of his poem, the question as to election through grace. Starting with faith, Paul had shown his fellow Roman Christians that God's judgment was righteous when he elected Jacob and rejected Esau, "before the children were born, when they had done neither good nor evil." Starting with love, Dante shows the same. The souls of the little children, who had done nothing moral or immoral, enjoy—according to the love that is innate in them, according to the grace that is accorded them—different degrees of heavenly bliss.

> The King, by means of whom this realm reposes
>   In so great love and in so great delight
>   That no will ventureth to ask for more,
> In his own joyous aspect every mind
>   Creating, at his pleasure dowers with grace
>   Diversely; and let here the effect suffice.
> And this is clearly and expressly noted
>   For you in Holy Scripture, in those twins
>   Who in their mother had their anger roused.
> According to the colour of the hair,
>   Therefore, with such a grace the light supreme
>   Consenteth that they worthily be crowned.
> Without, then, any merit of their deeds,
>   Stationed are they in different gradations,
>   Differing only in their first acuteness.[3]

This "first acuteness" (*primiero acume*), however, is the inborn inclination, the first and truest impulse of the heart. Dante never, so far as we know, used the word *acume* in the intellectual sense of insight or even acuteness. All doubt, however, is removed as

---

[1] I Corinthians 13: 1-3.   [2] *Paradiso*, XXVI.   [3] *Paradiso*, XXXII, 61-75.

soon as we recall the examination that Dante passed on the three theological virtues. Here, in place of Paul's sequence of faith, love, hope,[1] a different series appears: faith, hope, love. Here election by grace appears not as a fact, a point of departure, not as a postulate of faith, but as the mysterious manifestation of divine love. Men, too, on their side, can understand this divine love only through love and in love. And here[2] Dante quotes his second fundamental passage of the Old Testament, of which Paul had made use in the ninth chapter of his Epistle to the Romans: "I will make all my goodness pass before thee, and I will proclaim the name of the Lord before thee; and will be gracious to whom I will be gracious, and will show mercy on whom I will show mercy."[3]

If now, in fact, the concept of love serves the same ethical purpose for our poet[4] that the concept of faith did for Paul, then the distinctions which we have worked out seem to become a mere contention over words, the actual results remaining the same. The one says "faith," and yet ascribes only to Christian faith man's release from sin. The other says "love," and yet admits into Heaven only those who have experienced Christian baptism. However, if we look more closely we shall discover most vital differences under such similarities.

A morality whose principle is the inner certitude of belief can have, strictly speaking, no other goal than the actualization of this faith. The values it yields can likewise be measured only in terms of faith. But faith, man's most personal possession, is hidden from his neighbour. "Why dost thou judge thy brother? Or why dost thou set at nought thy brother?"[5]

Paul, on the basis of his ethics of faith, could then censure our poet thus: How darest thou sit in the judgment-seat of the Almighty? How canst thou undertake to send thy brother to Hell or even into the Paradise of God? Is it not madness and self-glorification to play the part of our Lord God and to anticipate the Day of Judgment? If only it were in jest or comedy! But thy "comedy" is terribly in earnest.

[1] I Thessalonians 5:8.
[2] *Paradiso*, XXVI, 42 sqq.
[3] Exodus 33:19.
[4] Compare especially *Purgatorio*, XVII, 91 sqq., where the moral gradations of the mountain of Purgatory are derived from love.
[5] Romans 14:10.

If Dante treats the non-Christians somewhat more gently than Paul, on the other hand he has cast a stone with a thousandfold less forbearance, and in a most unchristian spirit, at his fellow Christians. Modern Christianity which takes the evangelical ethics of faith earnestly and admits no other principle of morality save personal faith must detest this *Divine Comedy* as the most "devilish" of all works. But a single glance at the deep convictions, at the simple assurance of the poet's heart; and the devilish work is justified, by his faith, as a highly moral achievement.

Furthermore, Paul, as we saw, broke down his own system and set love beside faith. This love acts, however, at times, as we know, in a most unethical fashion. Mere love does not suffice as the source of morality. In its lowest forms of expression it is blind and animal. It is only available for morality when human reason or divine enlightenment undertakes the guidance of its impulses. Therefore Paul found himself compelled to introduce into his ethics an intellectual factor and standard—the spirit. Not through the idea of faith, but through the concept of the spirit, can he confirm the moral superiority of Christianity. In order to set the Christian law above all others, he requires the philosophical foundation of a universal and natural law. It is the necessity for apologetics in the early days of Christianity that forced on Paul, and even more strenuously on the later Fathers of the Church, an intellectualistic justification of their ethics. In order to convince their opponents, they needed an objective, scientific, graduated scale of moral values. They found it in the philosophy of Plato.

And not contented with constructing a progressive ascent from pagan and Jewish to Christian virtue, Paul undertakes to introduce distinctions within the limits of Christian ethics as well. He sets the Christian who works exclusively in the religious service of his congregation above the one who devotes himself faithfully to his secular employment; he rates celibacy higher than marriage, and in general places activity and thought directed to the Hereafter on a higher plane than worldly occupations. To be sure, these principles are rather hinted at than stated with precision, and they are, moreover, constantly limited and modified by emphatic references to faith.

Dante, then, is fully justified in appealing to Paul against monastic exclusiveness. Just as he refutes the claims of the nobility with the vigorous utterances of the Stoics, so against the claims of the monks, even against the great founders of the orders, Benedict, Dominic, and Francis, he arrays the personal character and the moral faith of the apostle. What the *Commedia* preaches, with a hundred examples, was already clearly and simply stated in the *Convivio:* "Not only he who in his dress and in his life imitates Benedict and Augustine, Francis and Dominic, uplifts himself to religion (that is, to spiritual worth), for in marriage, too, one may rise to good and true religion; since God wishes only that our hearts shall be religious.[1] Therefore St. Paul says to the Romans: 'For he is not a Jew who is one outwardly; neither is that circumcision which is outward in the flesh: but he is a Jew who is one inwardly; and circumcision is that of the heart, in the spirit, not in the letter; whose praise is not of men but of God.'"[2] As for the rest, Dante made use of Paul's ethics of faith always and only in this negative, defensive, and incidental fashion. A comprehensive regeneration of the idea of justification by faith, such as came with Protestantism, is quite foreign to him.

Paul refrained from constructing a strict system of virtues and sins on an intellectual plan. Political and civic virtues interest him but little, for even where he builds up ethical grades, he is chiefly interested in the higher steps that are close to God, rather than in the lower ones that have to do with human relations.

His attitude toward the state and its rulers is essentially that of Jesus. So our poet applies and interprets the political teachings and political attitude of the apostle in quite the same independent fashion as we have noted in the case of Jesus. We spare the reader, then, the task of following out a path which could not, for the present, lead to anything essentially novel.[3]

RETROSPECT AND PROSPECT

In Paul's teachings, then, two types of ethics run together. First, the evangelical ethics of faith. In it moral values can be defined only individually, and case by case. A universally valid test of morality cannot and must not be established. The free conscience of our own individuality, and nothing else, decides in each case

[1] *Convivio*, IV, 28.
[2] *Ibid.*, and Romans 2:28.
[3] For the student especially interested, the chief passages are noted here: Romans 13:2, utilized by Dante in *Epistolae*, V, 4 and VII, 7; Ephesians 1:5-8, in *De Monarchia*, II, 13; Acts 25:10 and 27:24 as well as 28:19, in *De Monarchia*, III, 13.

our own action. This ethics maintains an absolutely tolerant attitude toward those about us. Its danger is that it may grow all too gentle and may degenerate into moral naturalism, relativism, and scepticism—as often happens at the present day.

The second type, the ethics of love, requires for its orientation and stability a universally valid criterion. For not all love is moral. Love cannot be turned into its proper channel by man's personal impulse, but only through guidance or enlightenment from on high. Therefore this ethics endeavours to set up an objective system of moral values. As soon as it has elaborated one, it grows dictatorial and rigid in its doctrines. Its danger lies in hypocrisy, scheming, and sanctimoniousness.

With Paul the first type prevails, with Dante the second. The goal which we pointed out—utmost intensity of piety for our future life, combined with the utmost purity of our social existence—was not reached by Paul, though the road thither was by him distinctly indicated. The second type must prevail over the first; evangelical ethics must be modified in Platonic fashion. This is the road at the end of which the *Divine Comedy* stands.

4. The Church and the Middle Ages

ethos and ethics in the early catholic church

The strongest attack on evangelical ethics, in the post-apostolic age, was made by the Gnostic sects. Indeed they denied its foundation when they set knowledge (γνῶσις) high above faith (πίστις).

But knowledge is not a positive ethical principle at all, for it fetters the will instead of setting it in action. Such fettering and crippling is the highest moral idea of the Gnostics. They train their will through renunciation (asceticism), not in order to strengthen it for combat, but in order to withdraw it painlessly from all conflicts. Those who so radically renounce all positive and practical activity may end not in a renunciation of sensuous life but in complete subjection to it. As a matter of fact, Gnostic libertinism stands very close to Gnostic asceticism. Nor are the Manichaeans very different from the Gnostics in the matter of moral behaviour.

That they did not gain the upper hand in Christendom is due to the persecutions to which the churches were exposed. By them the chaff was separated from the wheat. At first, persecution had much the same effect as Gnosticism. Both forced the conscience away from action into religious meditation. Both strengthened the inclination to forsake the world, confirmed the hopes of the Millennium, and nourished the feeling that all earthly existence is extremely brief, evanescent, and worthless. They made a virtue of necessity; martyrdom was prized as the noblest Christian deed, and baptism in blood counted more than baptism in water.[1] About this same time, fasting and penance made their way into Christian communities. And the Neo-Platonic doctrine, with its intellectualistic and mystical ethics of salvation, did its part to shatter confidence in a worldly efficacy of the moral will.[2] Next to the martyrs, therefore, penitents, celibates, and fasting hermits and anchorites were regarded as the most perfect exemplars of morality.

But the persecutions of the Christians also developed among them natural leaders, able and valiant shepherds of souls, watchful lest their lambs be destroyed by the ravening wolf. The same pressure which drove a portion of the Christians to death or solitude urged others to forceful assertion and practice of the historical mission of Christianity. The early Church had followed the procedure not only of the Gnostics and the Greeks, but also of the Jews and the Romans. Men like Irenaeus and Tertullian fought by word and deed against the nihilistic doctrines of the will taught by Gnostics and Platonists. Against pessimistic and renunciatory asceticism they set up an optimistic and active one. They did not accept intellect and knowledge as the pillars of morality, but rather as the gate through which sin creeps in. They despised science and art, craved to see deeds and works, no speculation, no dreaming. In contrast to the evangelical and Hellenic ideals of justification through faith, of election by grace, and of salvation through the spirit, they restored to life Jewish and Roman hopes for retribution and justice. Irenaeus taught that even in the glory of Heaven there were distinctions in merit: one portion of the blessed will reach the earthly Jerusalem, another, Paradise, and yet a third will enter into the Heaven of contempla-

[1] The earliest evidences of this cult of martyrdom are found in Tertullian and Cyprian.
[2] The pagan Neo-Platonists, at least, sought escape from sin not through action and effort of will, but through meditation and renunciation. This does not apply however, to the later Christianized Neo-Platonists, e.g. Iamblichus and Origen.

tion before the face of God.[1] These sturdy men, with their feeling of moral responsibility, could have no joy in the idea of a levelling of sins through effacing Grace.

They agreed with their opponents only in the belief that the end of the world was imminent. For that reason, despite their, at times, excessive regard for merit and for laborious activity they could not duly appreciate the moral value of classical culture; so heavily did the true value of culture outside this life weigh on them.

Nevertheless they, the zealous opponents of culture and science, became the founders of the new civilization of the Church. The true foe of all culture is hidden in the ethics of the Gnostic and Neo-Platonic intellectual aristocrats, not in the teaching of the unlettered Tertullian, however loudly he may have thundered against art and science. Tertullian and his successor Gregory the Great attacked not culture in general, but only that of the heathen; not every form of government, but only a worldly one; not all science, only non-biblical science. In place of that which they destroyed, they set up something new: the Church. The ethics of the Gnostics and Neo-Platonists is like the wingèd horse, which because of its nature cannot possibly be of use, either for flying or for ploughing. Tertullian's ethics, on the other hand, is only apparently a Pegasus; if you take from it the impracticable wings of millennial hopes, it can be yoked as a sturdy draught-horse for any service, even for the unattractive task of Church politics.

At first, however, the useful animal behaved even worse than the genuine Pegasus, took to his heels, and fled to the mountains. "Montanism" is the extreme form of sanctimoniousness. The Gnostics prided themselves on being the penitential guardians of the spirit, but the Montanists demanded recognition as the guardians of the law.

Between these two heroic extremes of spiritual ethics and of sanctimoniousness the mass of ordinary Christians lived on. The idea of the approaching end of the world and the second coming of Christ was, to normal, everyday people, rather a disquieting and improbable matter than a living motive for moral actions. So they passed from compromise to compromise and pushed their Church, through the force of inertia, into ever deeper worldliness. "From all too different sides, with all too diverse degrees of in-

[1] Irenaeus, *Contra Haereses*, V, 36, and IV, 20, 5 and 6.

telligence, and with all too varied motives, converts entered the old Church, so that no complete identification of doctrine with life could exist. The ideal men, immersed in spiritual depths and fired by practical devotion, were surely a small minority, as in all earthly matters. The great mass had been attracted by the prominence accorded the forgiveness of sins, by the promise of a blissful immortality, by the mystery which overhung the sacraments, which, for many, were doubtless all but a repetition of the heathen mysteries. Slaves were allured by Christian freedom and brotherly love, and many unworthy persons were drawn in by the liberal alms that the Church in Rome, in particular, distributed to all." [1]

So the practices and the teachings of the early Catholics wavered in perplexity between martyrdom and self-indulgence, contempt of and fear of the world, meditation and active work, the penance of renunciation and the penance of toil. The Pauline justification by faith was quite forgotten. Gradually order came to take the place of this confusion. Practically and theoretically, the domains of the Church and of the world, of the clergy and of the laity, of the monks and of the priests, of heavenly and earthly morality, came to be separated one from the other, and a certain division of labour was introduced in human activities. Here we find the beginnings of that plurality of moral criteria, of those twofold and threefold ethical canons, according to which the monk's life and the deeds of the citizen were measured by different sets of standards. This institutional organization for the control of conscience, which is so characteristic of mediævalism and Catholicism, was the only practicable path between worldliness and future aspirations for a Christian Church living in a heathenish environment.

But Dante, both in sentiment and in historical knowledge, is as remote as possible from that age. The names Irenaeus, Tertullian, and Origen do not appear in his writings. He knows nothing of the growing worldliness of the Church, which was an accomplished fact a century or so before Constantine ascended the throne (A.D. 306); nothing of the barbaric greatness of the Church's martyrs. The principles of the Christian division of labour and class ethics, in accordance with which he was doubtless

[1] Jakob Burckhardt, *Die Zeit Konstantins des Grossen*, 2nd ed., Leipzig, 1880, pp. 138–39.

educated, he does not indeed reject; but his entire poem is as it were a gigantic effort to point out the dangers of manifold standards of morality, to assert the unity and independence of the individual conscience, and to advocate the acceptance of an universal standard, over and above the canons of class or guild.

The passive morality of sacrifice is as alien to him as self-indulgence. There is, indeed, in his *Paradiso* a special Heaven for the martyrs, but it is the sphere of Mars, and we meet there not the victims of persecutions but the heroes of religious wars, such men as Joshua, Judas Maccabaeus, Charlemagne, Roland, William of Orange, Renouard, Godfrey of Bouillon, Robert Guiscard, and Cacciaguida, the warlike ancestor of the poet. Stephen, the first martyr, regarded as the model of gentleness, is praised not for his steadfastness, but because he forgives his slayers.[1] Statius, who in the time of persecutions concealed his conversion and in a certain sense denied it, must atone for this lukewarmness with four hundred years in Purgatory; but that contempt with which the early heroes repelled their weaker brethren is spared him. In short, Dante, with his sane and enlightened nature, has no sympathy for the fanatacism of the confessors of the faith, for the frenzied imitators of Christ who hasten joyously to the cross and to the stake.

He knows that the courage to die for an ethical belief is among the rarest of gifts. So he allots to those souls who had good but not strong wills the lowest Heaven of his *Paradiso*. "Frailty, thy name is woman." The souls of Piccarda and Costanza have let themselves be prevented by violence from fulfilling their monastic vows. Their intentions were good; therefore they are mercifully treated by him. He is more humane, but not laxer, than the Montanists of the elder church.

> If it be violence when he who suffers
>   Co-operates not with him who uses force,
>   These souls were not on that account excused;
> For will is never quenched unless it will,
>   But operates as nature doth in fire,
>   If violence a thousand times distort it.
> Hence, if it yielded more or less, it seconds
>   The force; and these have done so, having power
>   Of turning back unto the holy place.
>   [1] *Purgatorio*, XV, 106 sqq.

> If their will had been perfect, like to that
> Which Lawrence fast upon his gridiron held,
> And Mutius made severe to his own hand,
> It would have urged them back along the road
> Whence they were dragged, as soon as they were free;
> But such a solid will is all too rare.[1]

Here the heroic fierceness of early Christian ethics is abandoned without in any way sacrificing power.

Dante has no sympathy with the monastic contempt for art and science, repeatedly echoed in the utterances of fanatical preachers; but instead of contending against it he prefers to ignore it.

In one respect only does he stand close to the early Church; namely, in his attitude toward almsgiving, benefactions, and economic life in general. His estimate of these matters has, however, a political rather than a religious background. The early Church favoured liberality because it thought the end of the world was imminent; the new Church should give because it has, in Dante's judgment, no right to possessions.

ST. AUGUSTINE

His Political Creed

Dante ascribes the secularization of the Church to the confusion of the lawful relations existing between state and Church, especially in consequence of the so-called Donation of Constantine, which he accepted as an historical fact indeed, without recognizing its legal validity.

This Church interference in worldly affairs was in truth a political and, if one will, an immoral action, but not illegal. If the Church had not already been organized into a stable and worldly political structure, if it had not controlled instruments of power and legal institutes, a statesman like Constantine would hardly have thought it worth while to recognize, to strengthen, and to utilize it.

According to our view, the secularization of the Church consists in the nature of its organization, not in its relations to the state or to property. The moment the priest ceases to exert his authority exclusively on the ground of morality, usage, and right, and bases it instead on religious faith, secularization begins. The moment he

[1] *Paradiso*, IV, 73–87.

lays commands on his flock, no longer in the name of the community and their common interests, but in the name of religion, of the
faith, or even in God's name, he becomes a hierarch. For then he
assumes superhuman authority, and, no longer content to exercise
his power on the outward behaviour and actions of those in his
charge, he lays his hand on the inmost springs of such behaviour
and action: on religion, thought, and faith. So it is not the state
of things in itself, not the measure of worldly goods or of worldly
power, but the tyranny over conscience exercised by political
means, that is the root and essence of all secularizing of the Church.
The greater the control over conscience, the more complete is
secularization.

The oftener the sword of the state was used to hew off the heads
of heretics, the more freely must orthodox folk be permitted to go
their own way, whether it were moral or immoral, provided they
showed outward conformity. The Greek church has trodden this
desolate path of secularization to its very end. It revered the
throne of the despot, actually made it a priestly see. It effaced
conscience, and with equal indifference tolerated the hypocritical
rascal and the monastic penitent, undisturbed by the fact that the
one tortured his neighbour, and the other his own soul. "It had
developed," as Burckhardt says, "an unique spirit of ecclesiastical
politics, a peculiar type of culture, Byzantinism, which one may
love or hate, but certainly must recognize as a world-power. At
the top, despotism infinitely strengthened by the union of Church
and state; in place of morality, orthodoxy; in the place of the
utterly degenerate natural life, hypocrisy and pretence; and, face
to face with that despotism, greed under the mask of poverty, and
the basest cunning; in religious art and literature, an incredible
persistence in the constant repetition of the obsolete—on the
whole, a trait which in many ways recalls the Egyptian, and shares
one of the latter's chief attributes, its tenacity."[1]

If the West did not fall into this condition, it owes it to a native African, Aurelius Augustinus. He, more powerfully than
others, aroused again the waning distrust of the Christian for
secular government. In order to awaken suspicion of the state
in the heart of his fellow believers, he revived the bitter memories
of the persecutions of the Christians and recalled the miseries
of heathen rule. He represented the state as an unchristian and

[1] Op. cit., p. 412.

immoral power, and in order to guarantee for the imperilled conscience at least that measure of freedom which was still possible
outside the state and within the Church, he returned to Paul's
doctrine of justification. He came just in time to save Christendom's most precious treasure, its morality, from the grip of the
state and from the morass of ecclesiasticism.

His chief work, the *De Civitate Dei*, by all imaginable means,
through criticism and sophistry, strips of any moral greatness the
entire heathen past, the whole Graeco-Roman world of culture, its
religion, its science, its art, its political life. It is incomparable
as a work of destruction. The memories and traditions, more than
a thousand years old, of civilized mankind, are laid in ruins—and
more than another thousand years had to elapse before they could
be laboriously built up again in a new spirit.

Augustine includes the entire heathen world in the expression
"earthly state" (*civitas terrena*), and condemns it *en bloc*, as a
work of the Devil, as a measureless structure of sin. However,
even the most immoral heathenism deserves the name of a state
only in so far as it is organized politically. So the question arises
whether immorality and sin exist in political groups as such, or
only in pagan political organisms.

Augustine lived under a Christian emperor and in a state which
was prevailingly Christian. Accordingly, it is to be expected
that he would condemn as sinful, not the state in general, but only
the avowedly heathen state. Here, however, the past of Rome had
more weight than the present. The Christianity of the Roman
state of his day was too young, too superficial, too worldly, and too
corrupt; its paganism was too deeply rooted in the empire to
permit the Church Father to extol that state as a model of Christian society.

Since he nowhere finds realized the ideal of a Christian state,
he goes on to teach that every political organism which had thus
far existed springs from sin. It is a degeneration of a natural and
perfect condition, a violation of Nature's law,[1] for according to
Nature, man should rule only over the beasts, not over his fellows.
Only when he yielded to sin did he become subject to an earthly
ruler.

The state, then, appears as organized sin. And yet, as doubt
leads us to truth, so sin drives us to virtue. And the very state,

[1] *De Civitate Dei*, Book XIX, 15.

which, in its origin, is an organization of sin, becomes presently in its purpose an organization against sin. Thus the state goes beyond itself, its mainspring comes to be a moral one, a virtue: justice. To be sure, that state which has only itself for its end and aim revolves in the same spot, like a ruler who merely wishes to rule, and it remains wholly imprisoned in sin.

The empire of his day was in that condition. It had nothing to do but serve itself; it represented the original type of the *civitas terrena* in a much profounder sense than did the ancient Roman state of heathen times. The other state, however, which develops out of it, moves, by the force of justice, away from its dark source, sin, and upward toward the superhuman goal of grace. The same poles, sin and grace, between which the pious Christian moves, are also the opposing forces of the pious state, the *civitas Dei*.

Thus Plato's doctrine of the state as a man writ large is utilized once more. Plato had justified it by naturalistic and psychological considerations; Augustine reaffirms and strengthens it from an ethico-religious point of view. With Plato the motive was theoretical and optimistic; with Augustine it was practical and pessimistic. For Plato, the state reflected the natural disposition of man; for Augustine, it was an imitation of supernatural salvation through grace. Plato thought of his state as localized in Greece; Augustine finds his *civitas Dei* everywhere and nowhere. It is at the antipodes of his *civitas terrena*, and hence undergoes the same transformations and modifications.

Just as the *civitas terrena* includes the entire historical mass of heathendom, so the *civitas Dei* embraces historical Christendom. To that extent both conceptions are empirical. The *civitas terrena* is organization through sin; the *civitas Dei* is organization through grace. Cain is the founder of the former; Christ is the founder of the latter. The two conceptions thus become ethical and religious. As the *civitas terrena* develops from sin to justice, so does the *civitas Dei* from justice to grace. Here the two meet and complete each other. While the one lies motionless, wholly immersed in sin, the other, upborne by grace, rises to a mystical Hereafter and leaves the earth behind it; here the two conceptions part company and diverge. Finally—and something new and contradictory now enters into the whole doctrine—since individual man cannot be at the same time a part of both realms, since the dividing-line cuts off not only the empirical from the intellectual and the political from the ethical character of men, but also man himself from other men, the sinner from the virtuous, the believer from the unbeliever, the damned from the elect—to that extent the two conceptions exclude each other, becoming not merely contrary but contradictory.

Whence does this new alien idea force itself into Augustine's political doctrine? It is Paul's doctrine of election by grace, heightened to relentless severity and transferred from internal conscience to outward social life. So all relation ceases to exist between the two realms; there is no friendship and no hostility. The icy rift of indifference parts the elect Christian from the state, and the divine city from the earthly. This is the dead-line of Augustine's political doctrine. It is the last desperate "Halt!" that the passionate Church Father can shout to his followers on the downward path of secularization.

St. Augustine's Ethics

This cry of warning died away. Our poet was too late to hear it. Even Augustine's contemporaries strove to deaden it.

For everything depends on whether, and to what extent, one may realize the Pauline doctrine of election by grace within himself and in his relations to his neighbour. On this question, more or less consciously, the Pelagian controversy turns.

If the idea remains restricted within its original limits, that is, the personal certainty of the individual and a purely internal valuation, it leads, as we have seen, to a tolerant ethics of faith. But if it is brought out of its inwardness and subjectivity and acquires a general validity, then it petrifies into dogmatic ethics of faith. Salvation and justification are then assured, not to all the faithful, but only to the "orthodox believer." If the decision as to orthodoxy or false belief be referred to the judgment of the priest, then the Church becomes the only source of grace and salvation. If, on the other hand, that decision be left to the almighty power of God, then all humanity breaks up into the two fixed groups of elect and damned, and we arrive at Augustine's doctrine of strict predestination. According to that doctrine, the children of grace, as well as the children of the Devil, are to be found both within and without the Church. God has chosen them and man knows nothing of it. We may be damned despite all the Church's means of grace, and saved without them, as God's inscrutable judgment decides. Above the historical and visible Church stands the mystical and invisible one, the true *civitas Dei*.

Accordingly, Paul's doctrine of justification through faith branches off into three distinct systems. First, the submissive and undogmatic ethics of faith, which has only in our time become dominant, though as evangelical leaven it was occasionally active even in the period of dogmatic ecclesiasticism, i.e. the Middle Ages. Second, the hard and fast ethics of ecclesiastical orthodoxy as it petrified in the Greek Church. Third, Augustine's ethics of predestination, as recognized by the Roman Church—only in part, to be sure, and with important limitations.

The limiting force or antidote of predestination comes from the ethics of love and was prepared especially by Pelagius. He taught that there abides in man a natural inclination to morality, an original and unperverted love of goodness. He that avails himself of this love acquires merit, and attains, by vigorous effort, to divine grace. There is no necessary proclivity to guilt, no original sin.

In this doctrine the optimism of the heathen world is revived, and the Christian idea of salvation is imperilled. It was therefore necessary that Pelagianism should be officially condemned. Its influence, however, continued to be felt, and crept unnoticed into the ethics of Catholicism.

For had Augustine derived morality from personal faith, had he firmly insisted that ethical conduct springs only from inward certainty, there would have been no room left for the assertion of Pelagius that virtue springs from the natural inclinations of man. Then it would have been shown that man signifies moral greatness, not as a natural being, but only as a personality. Now Augustine does indeed recognize faith, not merely as an intellectual but as an ethical condition. On faith, he declares, rests the morality of all human society. "Friendship rests upon it, for the friend's sentiment cannot be seen and therefore must be taken on faith. Without faith all bonds of marriage, or kinship, or other union would be loosed; for we put our faith in a requital which from its very nature can never be seen."[1] "The beginning of a noble life . . . is true faith. But," he continues, "faith is belief in what you do not yet see."[2] If man's heart were pure, he would need no faith; he would behold divine truth directly.

[1] *De Fide Rerum Quae non Videntur*, 1–2.　　　　[2] Sermon 43, *ad. init.*

So it is sin and the struggle against it that make faith necessary, and faith in its turn leads to knowledge, but not to moral action. Its reward is truth, not virtue; for the secure possession of truth seems to the anxious soul of the Church Father more precious than the quest for it. The final great principle, however, which leads alike to knowledge and to virtue, Augustine discovers, not in any spiritual power of man, but solely in divine grace. The will, guided by grace, attains to virtue; and faith, aided by grace, attains to knowledge.

Furthermore, Augustine has knowledge of a faith which brings us salvation and bliss. This is, however, nothing but the gracious gift of specifically Christian faith. So with Augustine we have a faith enlightened by grace; that is, the Christian faith, which makes us not merely moral but blest and immortal—and again a natural faith, which qualifies us for knowledge rather than for conduct.

In this doctrinal structure there is no universal human predisposition or inclination to moral action. Augustine even denied any such inclination. He insists that all human morality is created wholly and alone by the efficacy of divine grace. He declares that evil outlaws and cripples us, that it destroys the very force of our will, leaving no trace of it, exactly as the grace of the Lord effaces all sinfulness. By overvaluing grace, he came to exaggerate sin. Just as his theory of knowledge insists that our reason is held in check between human error and divine revelation, so too his ethics would fain leave our moral will to struggle vainly between all-powerful sin and omnipotent grace. But in both cases the over-straining proved indefensible.

Augustine had learned from the Neo-Platonists that there is no absolute evil; that evil, regarded metaphysically, is merely a lack, but nothing positive; no impelling force, but a mere hindrance to our action. He had further conceded that, even if not the full truth, certainly a considerable degree of natural knowledge and wisdom was to be found among the heathen. Side by side with the conception of natural knowledge he had tolerated, as had also Paul, the idea of a natural moral law. Finally, like Cicero, he had united the natural with the divine law. How was it possible, then, seriously to deny that there was laid in every man's cradle an independent moral inclination and power, placed there by Nature, that is, by God? So we have once more the Hellenistic equalization or parallelism of Nature and God.

And straightway, almost against Augustine's will, there arise out of his own doctrine the hybrid conceptions of a natural revelation, a natural miracle, a natural grace. The ethical consequences of this natural grace actually become, for good or ill, much the same as what Pelagius taught.

So it is Augustine's own conception of grace that in its broader optimism, and understood as natural inclination, creates a river bed into which the naturalistic and optimistic moral theories of antiquity again and again pour their stream—whether St. Paul's ethics of love, or Pelagianism; whether Aristotle's doctrines or Plato's political ethics. In its narrower and pessimistic form, however, and interpreted not as a natural gift but as divine election, Augustine's conception of grace became the source of dogmatic predestination on the one hand and of the evangelical ethics of faith on the other.

For those who have become familiar with these divisions and movements of Augustine's ethical conceptions, the philosophical and theological constellations and combinations in the ecclesiastical ethics of the Middle Ages will no longer offer any important surprise.

Thus our fundamental interest in the mediæval development becomes exhausted at its very beginning. We win space and strength to fix our attention on cultural conditions and on details as they successively present themselves.

Dante and Augustine

As to the position of St. Augustine in the history of culture, it must first be observed that he did not develop out of his time, but rather grew into it. The course of his development brings him from Africa to Rome and Milan; that is, from the older to the newer centres of culture. From the Manichaeans' Oriental mingling of religions he passes on to Greek philosophy, and thence to Christianity. At the beginning he is a free individualist. In denial and doubt he stands out against the most diverse currents of his age. He advances through search and doubt. Finally, by free choice and decision he takes his place in the disciplined service of what was to be the greatest of all institutions, and becomes a Christian bishop. The course of his progress has even been compared to that of Goethe's Faust. Both of them do in fact pass to social collaboration from doubting individualism and weariness of culture.

Dante was forced to follow almost the opposite path. His destiny cast him out of the young democratic community of his native city back into the dying universalism of Ghibelline theocracy. His convictions and feelings were rather reactionary than progressive. His whole heart was with the ideals of the past. The beginnings of a transformation in political, social, religious, and literary life, in the form that they assumed in his time, appear to him for the most part decay and corruption. His path leads from Florence, the cradle of the Renaissance, to Ravenna, the grave of Byzantine theocracy. Augustine grows more and more social, and even when a monk is the Church's toiler. Dante grows even lonelier and more self-contained. The Church as he would have it lies behind him like an irresistibly alluring past.

Augustine, therefore, the Father of this Church, is not to him a growing thinker and teacher, always pressing onward, but one mature and complete. He sees in him only the first and last premises and results, only his theoretical principles, not his practical efforts. The will, the personality, and the destiny of the man are foreign to him. He himself was, by choice and fate, far too different. He received from him only what was least personal and least flexible, the logic of his method.

For example, Dante, the champion of a free world-empire, could neither approve nor even understand Augustine's disposition to do away with, or at least distrust, the political state as a work of the Devil. So he ignores the negative definition of the *civitas terrena*, but makes his own its counterpart and logical basis, the positive definition. He regards the state, then, as an organization not of sin, but against sin; not as absolutely bad, but as relatively good, as a remedy "against the malady of sin."[1]

To this relatively good *civitas terrena*, capable of development, Augustine had almost against his will conceded justice as its motive, and peace as its object. Dante seizes on this idea. All that Augustine had brought forward to the discredit of Roman rule counts with Dante in its favour. Out of a long survey of Roman history, Augustine makes an indictment, Dante a defense. They have in common only historical material as evidence, and the philosophic presupposition that the history of the world sig-

[1] *De Monarchia*, III, 4.

nifies God's judgment on the world.   This fundamental idea
holds together all the two and twenty books of the *De Civitate Dei*.
Nowhere could Dante find it expressed more vividly and completely
than in this book.   It almost seems as if Augustine's historical argument would not let him sleep.   Three times successively, in the
Convivio (IV, 5), in the *De Monarchia* (II, 5), and in the *Paradiso*,
he undertakes to refute it.   He avoids, however, any direct attack
on the Church Father.   Instead of taking issue with him overtly,
he plunders him, distorts his meaning, and ignores what he cannot utilize.   By this shrewd and able method it was customary
in the Middle Ages to dispose quite peacefully and lovingly of
the most unwelcome authorities, notably the books of the Bible
and St. Augustine.

In the eighteenth chapter of the fifth book of the *De Civitate
Dei* Augustine admonishes the children of his Church not to be
elated over their Christian exploits.   For who has a right, he asks,
to boast of his efforts, his sufferings and sacrifices endured for so
great, so true, so inspiring, and so gracious a cause as that of the
City of God?   He reminds them of the ancient Romans, who per-
formed the most arduous exploits for so petty, false, unblest, and
thankless a cause as their *civitas terrena*, and for the sake of their
worldly glory!   And he gives the examples of Brutus, Torquatus,
Camillus, Mucius Scaevola, Regulus, Fabricius, Cincinnatus, etc.
These very illustrations, and others, were borrowed by the poet
from Augustine, but how differently used!   "Not only in its origin
but in its progress Roman rule comes from God.   For from Romu-
lus to its consummation under the first emperor, it prospered,
not only through human acts, but also through divine help. . . .
We shall learn how it was uplifted not only by human but by
divine citizens, in whom there dwelt a godlike, rather than a human, love for their city.   And this could not and should not
come to pass save for a special purpose aimed at by God through
these many celestial bestowals.   Who will venture to assert that
Fabricius acted without divine inspiration when in order not
to forsake his fatherland he rejected an immense amount of
gold?" [1]

And the same examples, sometimes cited in the very words of
Augustine, reappear in the *De Monarchia*.   In short, they are
the same fables, with morals reversed.   In Augustine the moral

[1] *Convivio*, IV, 5.

is: "These are the two motives, liberty and mortal desire for glory, that urged the Romans on to marvelous deeds." In Dante it runs: "The Roman empire sprang from the fountain of piety."

Other ideas, however, and precisely those wherein Dante agrees with Augustine, are not emphasized in the works of the Church Father as definite and clear conclusions, but appear as refluent and almost fortuitous side-currents, or eddies, in the stream of his doctrine.

The ideal of a cultural Christian state that stands in peaceful relations with the Church, constitutes the foundation of all law and all property, secures for all citizens normal conditions of outward life, has a benevolent unpropertied Church beside it, and at its head an emperor, glorified with ecclesiastical power, who rules in justice, freedom, and love, not in his own interest, but in that of all, in God's name, not in his own—in short, Dante's entire political theory could be put together, like a mosaic, from detached and widely separated suggestions in the mass of Augustine's writings. But what does that prove? The actual Church and the invisible one, the hierarch and the Franciscan, the Jesuit and the Protestant, the conservative and the anarchist, all of them could with equal justice make their final appeal to Augustine.

For one assumption they all have in common with him—the parity of the *lex divina* and the *lex naturalis;* that is, the conviction that all truly moral and righteous values, whether in thought or in reality, derive from God. The later Stoics and Cicero perfected the doctrine of this parity; Augustine strengthened it with all his might, and gave it an unforeseen scope. To Cicero it was only a panetheistic or theistic, certainly a philosophic and enlightened god, who worked in, or with, or in accordance with "natural law." But in Augustine the mighty Jewish God, with all his personal force and power, comes to the aid of this "natural law," and endows it with a direct and tangible validity, such as no heathen ever dreamed. This provided a means for the relentless overthrow of all existing law, and for its re-moulding into an adamantine structure of canonical law. The individual, for his part, could release himself from all human statutes, and obey in his own fashion the divine commands of natural law. State and Church, for their part, could elevate themselves to unlimited power over the individual, as the guardians of divine law, and take to themselves all control, even over conscience.[1]

With the battle-cry, "God, the Lord, hath commanded it!" social and individual, ethical and political, ecclesiastical and secular powers fight and slay each other from this time on. On all battlefields waves the banner of the divine law of Nature, lending to the struggles of mediæval humanity a fanatical, yet magnificent and passionate quality, a spiritualism and idealism that contrast uniquely with the character of the present-day contest.

As Augustine expressed, but did not invent, the equalization of God's will with natural law, he cannot be regarded as the creator of this ethico-political spiritualism. These contrasting aspirations are never created or discovered by individuals. They are like a doom that seizes and bears along whole centuries and a long line of human generations and hurls them against each other. So we should not characterize Augustine as the father, but as one of the first and greatest children, of the theocratic faith in natural law. And herein Dante is certainly his peer and brother.

Nowhere else, to my knowledge, is so far-reaching and unwavering a judgment of God and Nature pronounced on the historical and cultural condition of human life as in the *De Civitate Dei* and in the *Divina Commedia*. But, as we have said, not a personal bond, but the fateful force of the Idea, unites the first to the last gigantic work of the Middle Ages. That is why they are so diverse, despite their similar assumptions.

The greatest difference between them is best seen in the scope assigned by the one and by the other to the idea of predestination. Augustine extends election by grace from the religious to the moral and finally to political life. Accordingly, state and Church, in his eyes, stand in the same relation to each other as evil to good, as damned to elect, or as Hell to Heaven. Dante, on the other hand, exerts himself to make the state as independent, as valuable, and as moral as the Church. His ethics emphasize the power

---

[1] Cf., for example, in this connection, the following sentences of Augustine: "If the proconsul orders one thing and the emperor another, can it be doubted that the meaner will obey the other? If, then, the emperor orders one thing and God another, which shall you respect?" (Sermon 62, 13.) On the other hand: "Sin, then, is the mother of hopeless servitude, and first cause of man's subjection to man; which notwithstanding does not happen save by the judgment of God, in Whom there is no wrong. . . . Penal servitude is ordained by that law which commands us to preserve the order of Nature and forbids us to upset it." (*De Civitate Dei*, XIX, 15.)

and merit of the natural will, and his theology enshrouds in inviolable mystery the doctrine of election by grace, as a secret of unquestioning love. In short, everywhere we see him at work breaking down the bridges which lead from grace to moral and political radicalism or nihilism.

The trend of anarchism, quietism, Orientalism, and decadence in Augustine, the very thing which allured and held fast the gentle soul of Petrarch, had no appeal for Dante even if he scrutinized profoundly the soul of the Church Father.

Petrarch's favourite work was St. Augustine's *Confessions*. With this book he lived as with a friend. Dante regarded it simply as a moral work from which something could be learned. In fact, he intimates that if humanity were not benefited by it, the author would have had no right to come before the public with his subjective impressions, with such reflections on his inner self, and with the drama of his personal experiences.[1] To him the *Confessions* is an instructive example, useful to the many—and little more.

In studying closely the influence of Augustine on our poet, there is danger of overvaluing rather than of underestimating it.

GREGORY THE GREAT AND HIS THEORY OF SIN

No new moral principles or ethical systems appear in the age that follows. The doctrine of justice taught by Cicero and the Stoics received a Christian colouring, especially at the hands of Lactantius and Ambrose, and Augustine's theory of grace was adapted to the daily needs of souls and the Church's requirements.

This practical work was chiefly done by Gregory the Great. We saw how strong was the organizing ability of this Roman, and how completely he was guided by the immediate needs of the Church. On behalf of the Church and of its policy, he linked the doctrine of grace with that of justice, worldly virtues with the ethics of the Hereafter.

Meantime he took care not to conceal or question the differences between these two ideals of life. He felt, with good reason, that it was better to acknowledge such diversity and to define it in such a fashion that the difference between the two forces might not lead to hostility.

[1] *Convivio*, I, 2.

His solicitude for the souls under his care caused him to arrange the various virtues and sins in a progressive order of importance. Though he did not absolutely invent it, he is treated in the Catholic tradition, and rightly so, as the authoritative founder of the doctrine of the seven cardinal or deadly sins.

The distinction between venial and deadly sins had long been familiar; it had grown out of a division of moral requirements into advice (consilia) and commands (praecepta or mandata), and a division of the faithful into clergy, that is, folk who furnished a maximum of morality and merit, and laity, that is, such as might content themselves with a required minimum. It did not escape this shrewd man that the surplus of merit of worthy performances could be reckoned as offsetting a moral debit within the Church.[1] His doctrine of intercession and Purgatory is most closely connected therewith.[2] It is in his works that it can first be definitely established how moral demands are harmed by ecclesiastical influences, and conscience falsified by dogma.

While in this manner room was made for a morality which was both fanatically religious and enfeebled by worldliness, monastic asceticism was placing itself at the service of the Church. After Gregory and through Gregory, Western European monasticism took a share "in the solution of the Church's problem; but since it was not willing to sacrifice its original ideal of the contemplative life, its ideals also became problems, and, since it shared the aims of the Church, but could not always follow in the same path, it has a singular history."[3]

So it may be said that the great practical complications of the Church chiefly date back to Gregory. He did for ecclesiastical praxis very much the same thing that Cicero did for the development of systematic ethics.

In Cicero's time the question was: What relation does natural law bear to divine and historical law, and what in general is the relation of might to right? In Gregory's time no scientific questions arise, but tangible conflicts. The layman should build on his good works and have, in a certain sense, a personal moral consciousness, but even so he must leave to the Church the fate of his soul. The monk, through renunciation and meditation, can accumulate merit

[1] Moralia, XVI, Chapters 51 and 64.
[2] Gregory, Dialogi, IV, 39 and 55.
[3] A. Harnack, Das Mönchtum, seine Ideale und seine Geschichte, 2nd ed., Giessen, 1882, p. 37 (Eng. transl., London, 1901).

for the next world, but in this world he shall let himself be exploited and utilized by the cleverness of the priest.[1]

That it was primarily Gregory who drew the people of Western Europe into these conflicts is neither asserted nor perceived by Dante.   He knew the writings of this prince of the Church better than his acts, and was more seriously interested in Gregory's angelology than in his Church policy.[2]   He sees and judges the teacher, not the statesman.   That he read Gregory's chief works, the *Dialogi*, the *Moralia* and the *Epistolae*, is more than probable.   The arrangement of the seven deadly sins, as it underlies the divisions of Purgatory—*superbia, invidia, ira, tristitia (sive acedia), avaritia, gula, luxuria*—is exactly Gregory's,[3] though this by no means proves that the poet actually took the list from Gregory.   It can hardly be the creation of a single man, but rests on a long tradition. According to Cassianus there are properly eight deadly sins.   Pride is accounted a fundamental sin and vainglory as an offshoot of it. Gregory also distinguishes vainglory from pride.   When, however, evidently under St. Augustine's influence, he sets a sevenfold gift of grace over against the deadly sins, he opens the way to fix the number of deadly sins at seven instead of eight, to correspond with the seven virtues: love, hope, faith, prudence, fortitude, justice, and temperance.   Of these seven, the first three as religious virtues go back, it will be remembered, essentially to Paul; the last four, as worldly virtues, originate, in the main, with Plato.

Of the seven deadly sins, Gregory characterizes the first five as *vitia spiritualia*, the last two as *vitia carnalia*.   Dante, however, doubtless for the sake of the parallelism, divides the seven sins into groups of four and three.[4]   Furthermore, Gregory, even if the first, is by no means the only one in whose works the Dantesque number of seven chief sins may be found.   It occurs, for example, in Alcuin and in Peter Lombard, and, what is of especial importance, it was accepted into the ethics of the mystics Hugo of St. Victor and Bonaventura of Bagnarea.   Dante might have met with it also in the *Tesoretto* of Brunetto Latini.   Finally, it should be seriously weighed whether the poet was not forced of himself, for structural reasons, to make the arrangement of the *Purgatorio* correspond somehow to the order of his *Inferno* and *Paradiso*.

[1] *Moralia*, XXXI, Chapter 45 sqq.
[2] *Paradiso*, XXVIII, 133 sqq.
[3] *Moralia*, XXXI, Chapter 45.
[4] *Purgatorio*, XVII, 112 sqq.

A single and fixed order could not win the mastery in the mediæval Church. For the several mortal sins were derived from one
another not according to their degree of importance but according
to their psychological origin. It was customary to regard them
not as a flight of steps, but as a genealogical tree. Or, to go to the
root of the matter, they were regarded as a closed circle of immoral
states which mutually condition one another. What Gregory says
of the virtues, namely, that they support each other, and that
none of them can exist without all the rest,[1] he applies to the sins
as well. Accordingly, the sins might be arranged, strictly speaking,
one upon another, no matter in what order, and each of them resting on the fundamental sin. Where there is a circle, it does not
matter at what point one enters it.

If Gregory, nevertheless, puts pride unquestionably to the fore
as the fundamental sin and derives the rest wholly from it, he is
here also guided, consciously or unconsciously, by practical motives
of Church politics. The Greek Church, less judiciously, put lust
first, instead of pride. Regarded theoretically, the arrangement
was better to this extent, that lust is not a spiritual but a physical
sin, and that all evildoing is ascribed, in the last analysis, to the
flesh and to Nature. But for Gregory the question was to save
divine and ecclesiastical authority, and to that end he had good
reason to brand the spiritual rebellion of the individual as the
most abominable of all transgressions. Since that time, pride
has continued to be, for the Western Church, the source of all
sinfulness. Cyprian had indeed anticipated Gregory in this
respect, and in the story of Adam's fall and of Lucifer's rebellion a
welcome foundation for this arrangement was to be found.

Entirely in harmony with this, Gregory glorifies humility as the
most desirable of the virtues, and lays notable emphasis on obedience.

This authoritative and truly mediæval conception is not set
aside by Dante, but is decidedly weakened. Of the three beasts
that meet him in the forest, pride, though represented by the lion,
may well be the least dangerous. The poet knows too well the
prominence of pride in his own character to regard it as so utterly
detestable. The words for humility and obedience (*umiltà* and
ubbidire) are not exactly among those most frequently used in the
Commedia.

[1] *Moralia*, XXI, Chapter 3. Cf. also Chapter 32.

The reason for this is that Gregory laboured and wrote for the Church, and Dante for himself. This vital difference set the two men apart and permitted only superficial and fortuitous relations between them.

DANTE AND MONASTICISM

Hence it comes about that Dante does not regard with especial favour the age of the Church's political extension and worldly aggrandizement, i.e. the entire period from Gregory I to the great reform movement under Gregory VII.

The founding of the Benedictine order (A.D. 529) is the last ecclesiastical event over which he lingers with satisfaction. He elevated St. Benedict as the loftiest representative of monasticism. It is he who is made to relate its history and to pass judgment on it. He surrounded him with appropriate and carefully selected representatives of monastic life in earlier and later times.

The highest of the planetary heavens, that of Saturn, is assigned to the monks. For it was under the sign of Saturn that the earth had enjoyed its Golden Age. In those days the needs of men were satisfied directly by unspoiled nature. There was nothing artificial to keep us employed; hence man's leisurely spirit could be lulled and calmed in purest meditation. In some such fashion mediæval men thought of the Golden Age. It was a meditative ideal, and meditation as an act of the soul belongs to the Heaven of Saturn. Its symbol is the heavenly ladder of gold that leads directly upward from the spatially limited seventh sphere, through the crystalline Heaven, into the spaceless Empyrean. And St. Benedict explains:

> There perfect is, and ripened, and complete,
>> Every desire; within that one alone
>> Is every part where it has always been;
> For it is not in space, nor turns on poles,
>> And unto it our stairway reaches up,
>> Whence thus from out thy sight it steals away.
> Up to that height the Patriarch Jacob saw it
>> Extending its supernal part, what time
>> So thronged with angels it appeared to him.
> But to ascend it now no one uplifts
>> His feet from off the earth, and now my Rule
>> Below remaineth for mere waste of paper.
> The walls that used of old to be an Abbey
>> Are changed to dens of robbers, and the cowls
>> Are sacks filled full of miserable flour.

But heavy usury is not taken up
  So much against God's pleasure as that fruit
  Which maketh so insane the heart of monks;
For whatsoever hath the Church in keeping
  Is for the folk that ask it in God's name,
  Not for one's kindred or for something worse.
The flesh of mortals is so very soft,
  That good beginnings down below suffice not
  From springing of the oak to bearing acorns.
Peter began with neither gold nor silver,
  And I with orison and abstinence,
  And Francis with humility his convent.
And if thou lookest at each one's beginning,
  And then regardest whither he has run,
  Thou shalt behold the white changed into brown.
In verity the Jordan backward turned,
  And the sea's fleeing, when God willed were more
  A wonder to behold, than succour here.[1]

The idea that the loftiest duty of a monk's life is pious contemplation underlies not only this speech, but the two entire cantos
which are devoted to the orders. As modern followers of St. Benedict, Dante names the hermit of Fonte Avellana, Peter Damian,
and his predecessor, the founder of the Camaldulensians, Romualdus; as an ancient follower he introduces the Alexandrian saint,
Macarius.

The founders of the active mendicant orders, St. Dominic and
St. Francis, find their place three grades farther down in the fourth
Heaven as champions and teachers of the Church, perhaps as an
intimation that mendicant monasticism is of secondary importance
and, so to speak, not yet perfect.

The idea that the purely meditative soul mounts by Jacob's
golden ladder from earth to Heaven is one of the commonplaces
of the Middle Ages and is found especially in Gregory the
Great's life of St. Benedict (*Dialogi*, II, 37) and also in Peter
Damian and St. Bernard. It is natural therefore that Dante,
who shared the fundamental idea, should use the familiar
picture.

The second fundamental thought, however, expressed by Dante's
Benedict, pertains to the philosophy of history. I am referring to
his statement that all communities which rest on a religious and
therefore supernatural idea—such as the Church, contemplative

[1] *Paradiso*, XXII, 64–96.

monasticism, and the mendicant orders—degenerate and become worldly with persistent regularity.

DANTE AND THE MEDIÆVAL PHILOSOPHY OF HISTORY

How is the unhappy and unquestionable fact of such degeneration to be explained?

We moderns have two methods of going to the root of such questions. First, we study the historical conditions. We explain a given case of degeneration as a phenomenon that is due to general conditions and in a sense inevitable. Or we go back to the fundamental side of the matter and point out a conflict of cultural values. In the case before us we recognize an example of the conflict between the good and the useful, which has already been noted. Now the degeneracy reveals itself to us not as something unavoidable, but as something that should not be: as an interference with conscience more or less peculiar to the entire mediæval period.

The Middle Ages, however, did not distinguish between these two points of view, and hence the two became confused. If the mediæval historian is of a speculative turn, he studies all events in their relation to supernatural values, and neglects their earthly significance. All history, then, seems to him divine action, miracle. If he is unphilosophical, everything seems to him to happen as in a casual succession of events, and a ruler's death, an eclipse of the sun, a flood, a battle, are all thrown together in time and space as mere chronicle. Miraculous history and chronicle, legend and dates, are the extremes between which mediæval historical writing swings. "The relation of things to the ultimate divine end of salvation was so dominant in historical composition that their relation to earthly causes was only very inadequately taken into consideration. History fixed its eye not so much on efficient as on final causes. For the sake of the latter, it sacrificed the connection of this life with this world. The inner connection of events consisted, for these writers, merely in their relation to the final purpose of all things, in the remote future. Mediæval historians accordingly understood by the expression 'development of human history' an approach of events to the final goal of divine salvation, an approach nowise subject to the law of cause and effect. Hence it would hardly be possible to acquire a clear conception of the meaning which historical writers really ascribed to the profane and especially to the ancient records in relation to Christian salvation, if the solution of this question, which is missing from history, were not to be found elsewhere: namely, in theological literature."[1]

This gave to all political events partly a mysterious and divine significance and partly a figurative meaning, according as it derived political power and its effects from God or from sin. Hence, chronicle and legend, that is to say, all historical composition of the Middle Ages, is alternately intended to be edifying or moral, and cannot rise to critical investigation. We may, therefore, regard it as ethics so far as it is not pure theology.

Dante, likewise, treated all the notable events of Roman history as evident miracles of God. His words already quoted should be remembered: "Not only in its origin but in its progress Roman rule comes from God." Not merely at the beginning and end of Roman history, but also in the middle of its course, miracles appear. The causal chain of development is not indeed held together, but repeatedly broken by the unfathomable judgment of God, so that the rationalistic and moralizing tendency of Thomism unites with the ethical mysticism of Augustine.

But we must clearly understand that it is no theoretical incapacity on his part that prevented our poet and thinker from working out a logical method of historical criticism. Thomism could have furnished him with a philosophic foundation (as it has done for Thomas's present-day disciples) in its distinction between Nature and God. It was not a lack of keenness which dimmed Dante's historical insight, nor indifference to practical motives, nor defective logical conceptions, but his moral will and pious faith.

He cannot explain to himself historically the ever-recurring degeneration of the Church and of the monastic orders, because he does not wish it to be explained historically at all. He does not raise the question as to how it was historically conditioned. He strives to brand it only as misuse and crime and succeeds— or else he accepts it as a miracle willed of God, as a trial to be endured; but he consoles himself with the hope that the rescue will come in good time, and again through miracle.

> The sword above here smiteth not in haste
> Nor tardily, howe'er it seem to him
> Who fearing or desiring waits for it.[2]

[1] H. von Eicken, *Geschichte und System der mittelalterlichen Weltanschauung*, Stuttgart, 1887, pp. 647–648.

[2] *Paradiso*, XXII, 16–18.

It can be observed from case to case that the more strongly the poet's ethical passion soars with him, the more defective his historical criticism becomes. Throughout the Middle Ages world-history was treated arbitrarily, though definite conventions limited and guided such treatment. With Dante this conventional arbitrariness becomes markedly personal. He does not search for actual history, but creates what he desires. Of Ulysses he makes a sort of Columbus; of Statius, a Christian; of Cato Uticensis, an aged sage; of Minos, a monster; and of the prophetess Manto, the foundress of a city. Meantime, he gives himself the air of an historical student or seer, and doubtless believes himself one. As a matter of fact, he moralizes history. Even when he declares that his statement concerning the city of Mantua is the only credible one, he stands not on scientific but on moral ground. Evidently this history, which finds its place, not in vain, in the circle of the seers and magicians, is not so much a truthful statement as a warning to be truthful: "No falsehood may the verity defraud." [1]

Still, however personal such figures and interpretations may be, they need explanation. Dante did not invent the moralizing of world-history. It is one of the mightiest and most irresistible tendencies of mediæval thought.

THE MORALIZING OF NATURE AND OF THE SPIRITUAL WORLD IN THE MIDDLE AGES

Such a sentence as "Jesus Christ the Son of God founded the Catholic Church and appointed the disciple Peter as his representative to be its head" is one which I can turn to account in several ways.

If I utilize it for studying Church history, it is an hypothesis. If I use it didactically, as to explain to a child the miraculous power of the Church's sacraments, it is an axiom. If I employ it for political propaganda, as to win proselytes for the Church or to strengthen the faith of the believers, it is a dogma.

The validity of a dogma, according to its logical nature, is altogether different from that of an hypothesis or an axiom. The latter is conditioned by the aims of investigation and explanation, and so loses its meaning as soon as its theoretical purpose is attained. The validity of dogma, on the other hand, is conditioned by practical ends. It is in the very nature of dogma that, without regard to

[1] *Inferno*, XX, 99.

theoretical considerations, it be accepted, and recognized as true. In order that a sentence like the one just quoted may become a dogma, there is need of every kind of persuasion, from sophistry to bodily chastisement, from honest proof to compulsion.

Now if, by all sorts of methods, the statement as to the Son of God's being the founder of the Church is made a dogma, then a whole series of commands, counsels, requirements, political, legal, and moral in character, can be based on it.   The validity of the claim of the Roman bishop to supremacy over the others, the two programs of a Church released from the world and of a world annexed to the Church, in short, the most diverse intentions and measures, base their claims on such a construing of history—but only *quâ* dogma, and no longer *quâ* hypothesis or axiom.   Unless it be a dogma, no historical or naturalistic construction, interpretation, or explanation can ever become an axiom.   Dogma is belief; it is volition that sooner or later becomes obligation.   An historical or naturalistic truth or hypothesis is neither the one nor the other, and therefore never has the power to control man's action.   If, nevertheless, one speaks of "historical" rights, of "natural" duties, and of "natural " rights, the idea of obligation is forced into history and into Nature and not deduced from them.

This important distinction was ignored by mediæval men.   They confused that which is with that which should be, the real with the ideal.   They derived obligations not only from dogmas, but from every sort of interpretation, construction, and understanding of historical and natural reality, and even from the most irrational freaks of the imagination.   It was possible, for instance, to regard the relation between sun and moon, or the biblical passage as to the two swords, as a proof that certain rapports should obtain between pope and emperor.

All natural and spiritual events became moral fables.   The Lord revealed His commands by the motions of the universe.   The one valid, and therefore real, element in world-occurrences was the moral.   All else which appeals, not to moral man, but only to the artist or to the man of science, was fable.   Moral interpretation uplifted being to action, while scientific explanation degraded it to fable and dissolved it into appearance.   So in mediæval thought moral illusionism came into being as the complement of theoretical intellectualism.

The clash between these thoughts is beautifully illustrated in the twofold conception of the Church. Moral illusionism taught that because the Son of God was the *visible* founder of the Church, therefore the Church is the visible assemblage of the elect, and must be honoured as the highest realization of the divine will; it must rule all things, possess all things, take all things to itself. Theoretical intellectualism taught that the Church, like everything earthly and visible, is no reality, but a divine sign, the visible semblance of the invisible communion of the elect. The true Church is the invisible one, the *corpus mysticum*. Therefore the temporal Church must purge itself of all worldliness, withdraw into the conscience, vanish from publicity, renounce its possessions, abolish the clergy, etc.

This moral illusionism, like theoretical intellectualism, was a very gradual growth. We remember how even in antiquity, thanks to the conception of the *lex naturalis*, natural being and becoming were transformed into human obligation and volition.

But moral illusionism could not become a general habit of thought until in ecclesiastical dogma an apparently unchangeable truth was attained, out of which moral requirements could be derived unhesitatingly and imperatively. Only through the existence of a valid doctrine of faith did the remarkable illusion arise that every fact and truth leads to moral obligations. The sentence that Jesus Christ founded the Church, taken in and by itself, was put on a par with all other statements of the New and Old Testaments, with the result that every one of them had to yield some kind of moral commandment.

But the biblical word of God contained not only accounts and reports, but also parables; and especially such as had been uttered by Jesus as moral warnings. The Son of God himself, then, had opened and trodden the path of moral poetry. Starting with the Bible, moral instruction floods all life.

Three chief sources may be distinguished out of which the streams of moral instruction flow convergingly.

First, in Genesis men read of the creation of Nature by God's will. Therefore, since historically Nature had sprung from a will, logically it must contain a duty for mankind. To that extent, we must characterize Genesis as the foremost source for the moralizing of Nature.

Second, the biblical accounts of Adam's fall through sin and of Christ's atoning death and resurrection brought together the beginning and the final goal of human history. Never were God's intentions with regard to man, and with them the ethical bearing of our conduct, more clearly set forth than in these passages. To that extent we may characterize them as the foremost source for the moralizing of history.

Third, in the parables of Jesus, and in the figurative language of the prophets, imaginary occurrences and descriptions had also acquired a strictly ethical application, and to that extent we may characterize these as the foremost source for the moralizing of art.

Only a single aspect of human thinking now rises, like a lonely island, out of this threefold moralization: logic. Not even the Middle Ages succeeded in ethicizing logic. From this point, therefore, all serious attempts to unmoralize the universe will start. Logic will, therefore, be denounced by ethical mystics again and again as the sinful principle, as the child of Satan. Logic and the Devil fraternize. The most important logician of the Middle Ages, Abelard, was also one of the first to take up again the fight against the moralizing of what is neither moral nor immoral—and especially of Nature.

The first thing which, even as far back as the beginning of the Middle Ages, was moralized by symbolic interpretation in a Christian sense, was Graeco-Roman mythology. Next came the poems of Virgil, Ovid, Lucan, Statius, etc. Our study of the literary and artistic evolution of the *Commedia* will bring us closer to these, its forerunners.

For the present we are only concerned with those forms which became important in political and juridical doctrines. These are, particularly, certain efforts to moralize Nature and history.

DANTE AND THE PRINCIPLES OF CANON LAW

We recall that in the last periods of ancient philosophy, the naturalistic way of thinking came to be more and more superseded by the historical. We know, further, that the Catholic Church ascribed its origin to an *historical* event, and to the *personality* of Jesus Christ. Through this coincidence the moralizing of history, as it was carried on in the service of the Church, acquired from the beginning an advantage over the naturalistic political theories of the Platonists and the Stoics. Historical ideas, and not naturalistic ones, aided Augustine to demonstrate the superiority of the *civitas Dei* over the *civitas terrena*. After Christ was recognized as the founder of the Church, only the fratricide Cain presented himself within the historical range of vision as the founder of the state. For centuries thereafter the theory of the state is determined by the theory of the Church. Politics becomes ecclesiastical.

"The Church idea, in the form which it took through the speculations of the Church fathers, was potentially, and in its tendency, already a new and specific legal concept, which quite escaped from the limitations of the ancient legal system."[1] The line of thought in this speculation ran somewhat as follows: The Christian Church received from the Son of God (1) its existence, and therefore (2) its task, and with it (3) the ways and means to fulfill it. He is not only its past founder, but also its future leader, and the eternal principle of its ethical and political life.

Just as in the person of Christ we see the mystic union of God and man, even so His Church reveals the union of the present and the future life, or, as the famous formula has it, the Church is the "mystical body of Christ."[2] This doctrine, which makes of the Church a supernatural organism, contains and at the same time surpasses the naturalistic and Platonic doctrine of the state considered as a natural organism.

As soon as the theological concept of the Church had become dogma and had obtained general recognition as such, it was possible, thanks to its mystical double nature, to derive from it the most sweeping ordinances and claims. This was done by the mediæval canonists with the aid of both Roman and Germanic law. Their supreme maxim, however, was: "The Divine Founder Himself has bestowed upon His Church, together with the full power of salvation, the juridical independence requisite thereto. Only God and His vicar can bestow on the Church the privileges and rights which are accorded to it on account of its holy calling, while not even the loftiest earthly power can diminish these rights, though it may add thereto purely worldly privileges. But even so, the unified personality of the Church does not find its supreme pillar and representative in the entire body, but in God Himself, and mediately in His earthly vicar; so that, as subject of those rights which are claimed for and by the Church universal, God or

[1] Gierke, *Genossenschaftsrecht*, III, 107.
[2] This doctrine bases its claims on the familiar passages: I Corinthians 12:4–12; Ephesians 1:22–23; 4:10–13; 5:23–30; Romans 12:4–6; and Colossians 1:24.

Christ Himself, and vicariously the pope, can be designated." [1]
This is, to be sure, only an ideal condition which was worked out
comparatively late and as an afterthought; that is, after the Roman
Church had already attained to its lofty station in the world. It
must not be supposed that such speculations decided the struggle
for power and rights. But for the comprehension of Dante's state
of mind they are decisive. For it was not historical investigation,
but the prevalent conception of the true faith, that taught him
what was lawful.

According to this doctrine, the Catholic Church in its entirety,
and regarded as a dogmatic concept, exercises a multitude of
powers, which pertain to it by nature, so to speak, and which it
has received from the Godhead itself. The Church is called on to
execute here on earth the *lex divina et naturalis*. In its temporal
form, however, and regarded as a political concept, it can acquire,
actively or passively, a host of additional rights and privileges.
These positive rights, in sharp contrast with the natural ones, may
be alienated. They can be taken by stealth and seized by force,
but they may also be contested and lost.

So the Church stands midway between the natural norms given
by God and the positive laws made by man. From the former it
receives authority, which it bestows on the latter. The Church as
a source of power—whether it be the pope, the council, or the whole
body of the faithful: for this was a disputed question—creates
positive *jura*. It represents a *lex animata*, and from the very fact
that it directly submits to and obeys the *lex divina*, it is the living
principle of all human law. The Church creates human law as the
working tool of God-given natural law.

Therefore in Dante's allegory it moves on the natural soil of the
Earthly Paradise. In each particular case it decides and determines
what, according to God and Nature, is good and just or evil and
unjust. Accordingly in Dante's allegory the heavenly tree of
knowledge puts forth its leaves the moment the steering-shaft of
the Church's chariot touches it. [2]

---

[1] Gierke, *op. cit.*, pp. 249–50.
[2] *Purgatorio*, XXXII, 49 sqq. The word *temo, timone*, has the double meaning of
rudder and shaft. When the commentators take this steering-shaft as a symbol
of the Christian cross, or even of the Roman pontifical throne, instead of a conceptual meaning, they give us over again a symbolic one. Since, however, the shaft
serves to direct the chariot, it would seem that *temo* could hardly mean anything
else than the ethico-political and by nature lawful direction and conduct of Christendom, i.e. the papacy itself.

Dante's conception of the Church's task, and of its position midway between divine guidance of the world (*lex divina et naturalis*, especially canonical law) and human guidance of life (positive law, especially civil and international), is identical in its main outlines with that of the mediæval canonists. His endeavours to separate the *lex naturalis*, as an independent principle, from the *lex divina*, were not successful, and he remains pent within the circle of the canonical way of thinking. So he even elevated the author of the *Concordia discordantium Canonum* (Franciscus Gratian) to the level of his philosophic guides, Albertus and Thomas.

> That next effulgence issues from the smile
> Of Gratian, who asserted both the courts
> In such wise that it pleased in Paradise.[1]

Dante knows he agrees with the great canonist. His followers, however, the decretalists, are not of his people.

> For this the Evangel and the mighty Doctors
> Are derelict, and only the Decretals
> So studied that it shows upon their margins.
> On this are Pope and Cardinals intent.[2]

In an open letter to the cardinals he complains that the writings of Gregory, Ambrose, Augustine, Dionysius, Damascenus, and Bede are covered with cobwebs, while the clergy fish for legal claims to properties and benefices in the *Speculum Juris* of Gulielmus Durandus (circa 1270), in the commentary on the decretals of Pope Innocent IV, and in the *Summa aurea super Titulis Decretalium* of the Bishop of Ostia, Henry of Segusia (ob. 1272).

He criticizes not the foundations but the interpretation and application of the decretals. "There are decretalists," he writes in his *De Monarchia* (III, 3), "who, utterly ignorant and inexperienced in theology and philosophy, constantly refer to their decretals (which I certainly consider worthy of respect) and decry the empire, regarding these decretals alone as decisive." One of them had actually declared that this collection of Church traditions is the very foundation of faith, whereas the priority in time and therefore in dogmatic authority belongs to the books of the Bible. "But if," says Dante, "the traditions of the Church are later than the Church itself, then the Church cannot receive authority from tradition, but rather tradition from the Church."

[1] *Paradiso*, X, 103–105.　　　　　　　　　[2] *Ibid.*, IX, 133–136.

And now we have come to the very midst of the great strife between Church and state, pope and emperor.

DANTE AND THE MEDIÆVAL POLITICAL WRITINGS

After Constantine the Great had given the Christian Church a legal status, it became subject to those ordinances which, according to Roman law, applied to recognized corporations. In accordance with the old Roman principle that the *jus sacrum* is a part of the *jus publicum*, the emperor possessed the power to determine the relation between Church and state. Therewith he assumed the duty of watching over the internal unity of the Church and the observance of its commands.

But during the lawless age of barbarian invasions both political and ecclesiastical unity were destroyed. The Bishop of Rome was left to his own resources and acquired, through all sorts of gifts and legacies, immense territorial possessions. When he saw them threatened by the Longobards, he subjected himself as vassal and suppliant to the Frankish monarch, Charlemagne. The German suzerain took him under his protection, made him secure in his possessions, and accepted in return the crown of Roman emperor.

Thus the peculiar condition was brought about that he who was by canon law the head of the Church was according to German feudal law subject to a "Roman emperor," while the latter, according to Roman law, assumed the duty of watching over the unity of the Church. He was, however, not only a protector or feudal representative, but, so the canon law declared, an obedient son of the Church.

There must inevitably be friction on every occasion. The legal status became so complicated that it could only be set right through strife and force.

Down to the death of Henry III (1056) the German emperor had the advantage. Thanks to the efforts of Gregory VII, the advantage swung to the side of the Church.

Not until after this date do the events come within Dante's range of vision. But the remark which we made in connection with the history of monasticism applies here also. Dante does not treat the vicissitudes of the strife between emperor and pope with regard to chronology, but, as was the tendency of his time, with regard to their ethical significance.

This ethical evaluation of the political struggle, however, proceeded at first in the apodictic form of conceptual jurisprudence. The public contest between state and Church was not lawfully decided but legally passed upon.

Dante endeavours to place himself above the two parties as an ideal judge. The advocates, that is, the ecclesiastical and imperial publicists, he studied conscientiously. And we, too, must familiarize ourselves with the sophistries and scholastic arguments of these men, if we wish to understand the poet's judicial decision.

If we look on the whole affair as a lawsuit, Dante, as an ideal judge, must first of all state the controverted question. As a matter of fact, the question at issue between Gregory VII and Henry IV concerned feudal investiture; between Innocent IV and Frederick II, it was the control of Italy; between Boniface VIII and Philip the Fair, it came to be the taxation of the French clergy. These and similar circumstances, however, are ignored by Dante. He traces the three actual crises back to the fundamental question: Which is the suzerain and which the vassal: the emperor or king, or the pope? He ignores the personality of the litigants, and only asks: What is the relation of empire or kingdom to Church? The question is for him purely one of principle. We should thoroughly misunderstand Dante if we imagined him a prejudiced partisan of the emperor against the pope. He is concerned in a peaceful division of power and an harmonious co-operation of Church and state, in which the emperor should care for the earthly and bodily part of man, the pope for the eternal interests of the soul. St. Gelasius had already, as pope (492–496), proposed this solution, and it continued to be, for the political life and thought of the Middle Ages, the ideal whose realization and the problem whose solution were earnestly sought by both sides. However keen the contest over the execution of details, the wished-for ideal of an harmonious dual rule and of reciprocal furtherance of spiritual and temporal authority hovered above the battlefield. Dante, in fact, assumed this ideal rôle of mediator between the two sides in order once again to demonstrate the necessity of this dual solution to his contemporaries, who had nearly forgotten it.

And now let us hear the arguments of the contestants.

Gregory VII, and after him, with especial emphasis, Innocent III, used as evidence the illustration of the sun and moon. On account of the moralizing of Nature, which has just been described, this had a certain force. It ran thus: "Just as God, the creator of the universe, has set two great lights in the firmament of Heaven, the greater light to rule the day, and the lesser the night, so in the firmament of the Church universal also He has instituted two great offices, the greater to rule over souls, the lesser over bodies: they are the papal dignity and the kingly power. As the moon, furthermore, which is inferior in size and structure, in position and force, receives its light from the sun, so the royal power receives the splendour of its office from the papal dignity."

Against this, Dante, the judge, rises and says: The analogy is unsound. For these functions are but an accident of man, not the substance. As the argument would have it, God created first the accidents, that is, the sun and moon (with a logical jump Dante identifies them with the functions themselves) and thereafter their subject, man. "For, as it is recorded, these lights were created on the fourth day, and man not until the sixth." [1] Furthermore, the moon has surely an existence and effective force of its own. It has its own heavenly sphere, and even though it does receive the greater portion of its illuminating power from the sun, as the secular prince receives the blessing from the pope, yet, as can be observed, when the moon is in eclipse it is not wholly without light of its own. Furthermore, the syllogistic form of the proof from the two lights is vulnerable in that from the origin of the lights a conclusion is drawn as to the origin of the functions, whereas light and function are two diverse things.[2] But Dante seems to give the least weight to this logical criticism, which strikes hardest at the root of the proof, seeing herein merely a mistake in form, of minor importance.

However, he did not wholly escape the suggestive force of the argument from the two lights. The notion of the beneficent illumination of the emperor through the pope made a lasting impression on his mind, and it glimmers in the final words of the *De Monarchia*, not merely as a figure of speech, but as an idea. So again at the close of his fifth letter. But in the *Commedia* he has transformed the two different lights into

> Two suns . . . which one road and the other
> Of God and of the world made manifest.[3]

Beside the naturalistic proof, the papal advocates array a series of historical evidences.

[1] *De Monarchia*, III, 4.   [2] *Ibid.*   [3] *Purgatorio*, XVI, 107–108.

The spiritual power, they say, was instituted earlier than the secular.[1] Of Jacob's sons, Levi is the elder, Judah the younger. In opposition to this argument, our judge employs logic with increased emphasis. Here, armed with logic, he makes a sally which, in accordance with what has been said above, we may describe as an isolated attempt to unmoralize biblical history. Temporal distinctions, he says, are different from those of the hierarchy: Why should not the younger brother enjoy higher honours than the elder?[2]

Another piece of evidence: Samuel the prophet deposed Saul the king. This fact might, to be sure, says Dante, decide the question of the subjection of the emperor to the pope, provided Samuel had occupied the position of God's representative which the pope has. As a matter of fact, however, he did not act as God's representative, but only as his messenger.[3]

Further: Christ received from the Magi incense and gold as a sign that to Him belongs the temporal as well as the spiritual power. Very well, says Dante, but Christ is neither actually nor awfully identical with His vicar the pope.[4]

Our logician even manages to dispose of the most important biblical passage to which the advocates of the pope were wont to make their appeal. "Whatsoever thou shalt bind on earth shall be bound in Heaven: and whatsoever thou shalt loose on earth shall be loosed in Heaven."[5] In the first place Dante assumes that these words were not addressed to Peter alone, but to all the disciples.[6]

Next he states that the "whatsoever" is not an absolute but a relative concept. For example, a sinner who feels no repentance cannot be saved even by God. This "whatsoever" is intended to include only the particular field of spiritual power.[7]

The most disputed argument, however, was the statement: "Lord, behold, here are two swords. And he said unto them: It

---

[1] This idea is one of the most familiar, appearing in the writings of Hugo of St. Victor, Alexander of Hales, Aegidius Romanus, Boniface, and others.
[2] De Monarchia, III, 5.
[3] Ibid., 6.
[4] Ibid., 7.
[5] Matthew 16:19.
[6] Dante, by this argument, includes himself among those writers who consider the pope as the first bishop, as first among equals. His interpretation of the passage is like the one advanced by the advocate of Gallicanism, Gulielmus Durandus, in his De Modo Concilii generalis Celebrandi.
[7] De Monarchia, III, 8.

is enough." [1] The papal party, especially Boniface VIII, in his famous bull of November 18, 1302, drew from this the conclusion that both swords belonged to the Church. "That is to say the spiritual and the temporal sword. The one is to be carried for the Church, the other by the Church; that one in the priest's hand, this in the king's or the soldier's, but only at the bidding or with the permission of the priest." [2]

Dante contests the possibility of either an ecclesiastical or a political interpretation. He believes that the two swords stand for the instructive word and the effective deed. [3] Just as he put two suns in the place of sun and moon, so in the same lines of the *Commedia*, instead of the sword he gives the pope the crosier to bear.

> One has the other quenched, and to the crosier
> The sword is joined, and ill beseemeth it
> That by main force one with the other go,
> Because, being joined, one feareth not the other. [4]

The biblical, the naturalistic, and the pseudo-juridical proofs are followed by genuine arguments; and here the tactics of both parties change. For now it is no longer a question of the accuracy of this or that interpretation, but of the validity of this or that right; or, better still, of the ethical foundation of Church and state in general.

We have seen how the theological foundation of the Church's right was built up by the canonists and recognized by Dante. After it was settled that the Church had received its legal status from God and Christ Himself—whence did the state obtain its power? Either likewise from God—or from the Devil.

In fact, Gregory VII reverted to Augustine, and taught that the secular state is the work of the Devil and of sin, and hence no up-holder of right, but of unrighteousness. [5] The logical result was war against the state till it be conquered and absorbed into the Church. All the distrust which Augustine had heaped against the heathen state is transferred by Gregory VII and his successors to the Christian empire, and at this point the fraternal co-operation of the two powers, the long-desired ideal of the Middle Ages and of our poet, was threatened with destruction. This supreme peril

[1] Luke 22:38.
[2] Mirbt, *Quellen zur Geschichte des Papsttums.*
[3] *De Monarchia,* III, 9.
[4] *Purgatorio,* XVI, 109-112.
[5] Gregory, Letter to Bishop Hermann of Metz, March 15, 1081.

was realized by Dante. In order to remain the ideal judge, he must now side with the world-power whose right to exist had been questioned. The whole of the *De Monarchia*, and especially the first two books, are devoted to the demonstration of the political, ethical, and theological necessity of an universal Christian, Roman Catholic empire. Dante gathers for this all the available arguments in literature.

But the most that he could thereby accomplish was a transfer, or a transplanting, of the canonical conception into the domain of the state. For these arguments showed that exactly like the Church, and just as directly, the state too receives its legal status from God. No less than the *sacerdotium* is the *imperium* a divine institution. It, too, contains an independent ethical principle.

But when we seek out the peculiar character of this principle, we find that it is an inferior one. In the last analysis, the aim of the state also can only be to fight against sin and to prepare men for future salvation. The weakness of the imperial theory lies in the fact that it is a copy of the Church's canonical claim; that it propounds as the aim of the state a worldly and natural code of ethics, whose autonomy and distinction from the supernatural and spiritual ethics it cannot itself accept. A state of this kind "can only make itself superfluous by bidding all its subjects enter into the loving community of the spirit." [1]

No wonder that the ideal empire which Dante, by speculation, by faith, and by hope, shaped in the *Convivio*, in the *Commedia*, and in the *De Monarchia*, resembles remarkably the papacy of his day. The emperor derives his rights from the same original source as the pope, and in like manner. They both wield universal power. Though separate, they are parallel not only in their functions, but in their substances as well. In Heaven they are one; here below they become two.

The very last words of the *De Monarchia* show most clearly that a distinct worldly political principle cannot be derived from the premises of the transcendental, theological, and ecclesiastical view of life taken by the Middle Ages. Dante flatters himself, to be sure, that he has completely proved the utter independence of the *imperium* from the *sacerdotium;* but he ends his investigation with a sentence which once more leaves everything that seemed

[1] Fritz Kern, *Humana Civilitas, eine Dante-Untersuchung*, Leipzig, 1913, p. 25 sqq.

juridically determined to the good pleasure of the parties concerned; as though conscience was appealed to against the verdict
of the law. "This independence," he says, "is not to be taken so
literally that the Roman prince is in no respect subordinated to the
Roman pontiff. For earthly happiness (that is, the aim of the
state) surely is subordinate in a certain degree to future bliss (that
is, to the aim of the Church). Therefore Caesar (the emperor)
must have the same feeling of reverence for Peter (the pope) that
the first-born child cherishes toward his father, so that illuminated
by the light of paternal grace, he may shine so much the more
mightily upon the earth. . . ." [1]

Surprise has been expressed that Dante did not perceive the
vicious circle of this argument. But as a mediæval thinker, he
could not recognize it as such. For neither the secular nor the
ecclesiastical power was regarded in the Middle Ages as absolute
or sovereign, in the modern sense of the word. Above all authorities
and rulers of mankind stood the divine, or if you will the natural,
law; they were all limited, relative, and subject to the living
God; so that a collision between them could occur only in so far
as the worldly rulers usurped the authority of the Church, or vice
versa. A fight to the finish, carried on by the emperor against the
pope, or the reverse, was like a rebellion against God and the natural order of the world.

Since, therefore, the imperial party could at best accomplish
nothing with their borrowed religious and ethical premises, and at
the worst would cut into their own flesh, it was wholly to their
interest to shift the battle to positive and legal grounds. In the
course of the twelfth century, the emperor had secured the services
of the best specialists in Roman law, above all of Irnerius. Every
opportunity had been grasped to call attention to the early state
of things and to remind people of the old empire, and of the subordinate position of the Church in ancient Rome, in the Carolin-
gian times, under the Ottos, and in the days of Henry III. Dante
did not fail to make these arguments his own.

The Church also had its own historico-legal arguments. First
among them was the Donation of Constantine. Roman priests,
probably as early as the eighth or ninth century—for what purpose we know not—had forged this deed of donation. It was incorporated into a supplement to the *Decretum* of Gratian (*circa*

[1] *De Monarchia*, III, 16.

1150), and found credence even among those of the opposite party.[1] In this gross forgery Constantine the Great sets forth his belief in Catholicism, relates how he was baptized by Pope Sylvester and healed by him of leprosy, presents to him his crown, his palace, the city of Rome, Italy, and all the western provinces. He himself transfers his capital to Byzantium and is content with the Eastern Empire. "For it would be wrong if, where the head of the Christian religion had been established by the heavenly King, an earthly emperor should hold sway."

The validity of this gift was questioned by Dante, and on grounds for which he is indebted to the canonists. The imperial power is exactly as inalienable, he declares, as the divine right of the Church. "It would be contrary to human law if the *imperium* destroyed itself. But the *imperium* is that jurisdiction which includes all temporal jurisdiction, and is itself antecedent to its executor the emperor; for the emperor is ordained to the jurisdiction, and not vice versa. Hence it follows that he, in so far as he is emperor, cannot alter it; for it is through it that he becomes that which he is."[2]

As the canonists had derived the rights of the Church from the theological concepts of the Church, just so does Dante proceed with the concept of the imperial power (*imperium*). As a true conceptualist he ascribes the higher reality to the concepts. To be sure, there were among the canonists some who, after the manner of the Nominalists, broke up the concept of the corporate Church and saw in it merely a multitude of believers without will and without rights. But it is precisely the Nominalists among the canonists of whom our poet disapproves. As we have seen, he regarded Gulielmus Durandus, who took this theory seriously, as a fatally misleading authority. In fact, the breaking up of the corporative concept by the Nominalists led finally to absolutism,[3] and Dante's deadly enemy, Boniface VIII, took advantage of it. It may be said that as fast as Nominalism gains ground in philosophy, absolutism affirms itself in political life.

Against the second and last historical argument of the papal

---

[1] The suspicion of forgery is only occasionally heard, e.g. under Otto III and from a partisan of Barbarossa.

[2] *De Monarchia*, III, 10.

[3] Not indeed merely to absolutism of the pope, or of princes, but also to that of individual personalities in general. The Nominalistic habit of thought is the chief foundation e.g. of the religious communities of extreme Calvinists (Puritans, the Quaker sects, etc.).

publicists, Dante proceeds very much along this same conceptual-istic line. Charlemagne, they declared, received the imperial crown from Pope Hadrian I. (Dante confuses him with Leo.) In other words, in their plenary power the popes transferred the *imperium* from the Greeks to the Germans. "No," replies Dante; "usurpa-tion of right confers no right." In the same fashion, the sub-ordination of the pope to the emperor might be demonstrated. Remember the Emperor Otto, who set up Pope Leo VIII and de-posed Benedict V, and even drove him into exile.[1]

Here again the political action is put to the test of ethical right, and is condemned as null and void. Even when this wrong is done to the most lawless and detested head of the Church, who on his part is steeped in injustice, it violates Dante's sense of justice. When Philip the Fair replied to the Pope's excommunication and interdict with an act of violence and caused Boniface VIII to be attacked and maltreated at Anagni (September, 1303), and forced Clement V to abolish the order of Templars (1312), Dante, the idealistic believer in natural law, wrote the fierce words:

> I see him yet another time derided;
> I see renewed the vinegar and gall,
> And between living thieves I see him slain.
> I see the modern Pilate so relentless,
> This does not sate him, but without decretal
> He to the temple bears his sordid sails![2]

Thus Dante stands partly above, partly in the midst of, the political battles of the Middle Ages, judge and imperial advocate at once. He has his own imperialistic, or if one likes, Ghibelline, position. And to that extent he is a partisan.

But he no less firmly holds to his sense of right and to his philo-sophically grounded conviction of its certitude, and to that extent he is judge. Hence the twofold character, polemic and speculative, of his political doctrines; hence their inward intensity.

Probably Dante was acquainted with at least the most important political works that grew out of the three great phases of the struggle. He passes over Gregory VII, perhaps intentionally, in absolute silence. He was too great to be blamed, too imperious to be praised. That is why Dante proclaims so loudly his allegiance to the doctrine of Peter Damian.

[1] *De Monarchia*, III, 11.
[2] *Purgatorio*, XX, 88–93. These words are put into the mouth of Hugh Capet, ancestor of the French royal line.

RETROSPECT AND PROSPECT

Gregory VII and Peter Damian stand upon the summit of the Middle Ages. It is fitting to survey from here the road we have travelled and that which lies before us.

Down to the end of antiquity, the ethico-political questions interested us more on their theoretical than on their practical side. We saw how a clear distinction between ethical and political values was unattainable, even by Aristotle. Finally, the two domains were rent asunder by the Stoa in such a manner that between them there appeared the empty space of the morally indifferent. Into this gap Cicero thrust Roman legalism. The richest and most fruitful linking-up of the problem was thus accomplished. What relation, the question now is, have the good, the just, and the useful to one another?

Christianity emphasized the superiority of religious and metaphysical ethics, in life as well as in doctrine, over the empirical (especially Aristotelian) morality. So it came about that Cicero's problem was attacked not from the social and political but only from the religious and ethical side.

In the semi-Pelagian compromise, the solution was nearly reached, but only, as the name implies, by the path of compromise, concession, and adjustment. The good, the just, and the useful were set seriatim, one above the other. The slightest displacement to one side or the other could not but threaten the whole dogmatic structure.

At the very central point, in the inquiry into the nature of law, a rift opened. Practical needs required that the lay authority be differentiated from the ecclesiastical. The strife between pope and emperor arose. Under Gregory VII divine and papal rights gained the ascendancy over natural and imperial law. Augustine's *civitas Dei* was, as far as possible, realized in human society. Men were ordered and subordinated hierarchically in castes, one above the other, very much in the same manner that concepts were arranged.

All further movement in the ethico-political thought and life of man in Western Europe signifies disintegration of Catholic mediævalism.

In ethics the liberation of natural from Christian morality begins with Abelard. Thomas Aquinas, while attempting to reunite the contending forces by the logical structure of his distinctions, falls into contradictions. From this philosophically unsound position, ethics is driven to eclecticism and to mysticism, and political theory to a division and to an at least threefold partition.

At the same time a most bitter strife between emperor and pope is carried on. It ends with the complete exhaustion of the two mediæval champions, much to the advantage of the modern powers, the city-states and the country lords.

From the confusion and uproar, out of the ruins of the *civitas Dei*, the *Divine Comedy* arises, a tragic song of that glory which at that very moment was passing away under the poet's eyes.

Now, in the company of Gregory and his friend Damian, we must busy ourselves both with logical hair-splitting and with mystical syncretism, until, drawing closer and closer to practical life, we are rejoiced and rewarded by the personality of Alighieri, as it springs out of the soil of his native land.

5. The Dissolution of the Mediæval World in Dante's Time

DANTE AND PETER DAMIAN

Peter Damian (*circa* 990–1072), the Pier Damiano of the *Paradiso*, stands closer to Dante than any other of the mediæval publicists either before or after him. And yet between the writings of the two men more than two centuries lie, centuries filled with events. How could thinkers so far removed in time come so close to each other in their ideals of ethics and politics?

When in the year 1041 Peter Damian was appointed abbot of the Benedictine monastery at Fonte Avellana, the moral as well as the political life of the Church was again, after a long and grievous degradation, on the road to recovery.

It was primarily hermits and monks who simultaneously, about the middle of the tenth century, at various points in Western Europe, set about labouring for an internal reform of the Church: in England, St. Dunstan; in Lorraine, the monks of Gorze; in Burgundy, the Cluniacs; in Lower Italy, St. Nilus, a Greek monk; in Ravenna, St. Romualdus, founder of the Camaldulensian order, and immediate predecessor to Gualberto of Vallombrosa, to the Abbot Hugo of Farfa, and to our Damian.

The honourable efforts of these monks tended to the intensification of monastic and ecclesiastical discipline, strict adherence to celibacy, and abolition of simony. It was primarily a moral, and therefore a popular, movement. It arose out of the Church itself, from within and from below. The higher clergy, chiefly the bishops of Lombardy, took no pleasure in such innovations. But the popes, even with the best will, did not at first have the means for carrying out such reforms.

So much the more zealously did the German emperors, especially Otto I, Henry II, Conrad II, and Henry III, place themselves at the service of this holy cause. What urged them thereto was not merely their conscience and not only public sentiment, but especially the religious character of their sway; it was the force of Charlemagne's ideal of the emperor, who as overlord and protector of the Church, as "God's representative on earth," should watch over the internal and external welfare of the community of Christ. Hence it was precisely the best, the wisest, and the mightiest of the German emperors who strove for a new order of things in the Church and for a strengthening of the pope's authority that could not but be fatal to the monarchs themselves. They acted in harmonious understanding with the monastic party of reform, filled the highest offices of the Church with faultless, zealous, and austere men—preferably Germans.

But the Church endured this violent treatment only as long as it had need of it. No sooner had the bishops and popes, thanks to the emperors' interference, been won over to the cause of reform, than they demanded the right to direct with their own hands the transformation already begun, and insisted upon completing their ecclesiastical work without the emperor—even in spite of the emperor.

This reversal from a Church reform favourable to the emperor to a hostile one was accomplished immediately after the accession of Henry IV. It is most clearly illustrated by the changes in the significance of "simony."

Originally the name was applied to the sale of spiritual offices. The prototype of simony was supposed to be he who gave his name to the offence, Simon the Magician.[1] The conception was at first ethical. But, in the course of the political contest against simony it became necessary to find a legal definition also; and here the confusion began. The legal and the ethical conceptions clash. Sometimes both the buyer and the seller were characterized as

[1] Acts 8:18 sqq.

simoniacs,[1] and simony came to include not only actual purchase, the definition of which was very dubious, but any bestowal of a spiritual office upon the unworthy, or by the unworthy, or even by lay persons—and so, lay investiture. "The control of Church property as such by laymen (even by the emperor) was stigmatized as simony. That is to say, the accusation of simony became a label for entirely different acts of a purely hierarchical nature."[2] Thus the opposition to an abuse developed into a violent war for the political independence of the Church.

It is obvious that in Dante's *Inferno* simony always signifies an offence against ethics and religion. The punishment that the poet assigns to his simoniacs seems to me to diverge widely from the ordinary appraisal of this sin. Simony was regarded in the Middle Ages as a sin against the Holy Spirit, and even as the worst form of heresy. Dante treats it as fraud, a view which is by no means usual in mediæval literature. Furthermore, it may be conjectured that the stone pockets in which the simoniacs are set, head downward, and the fire which blazes over the soles of their feet, may be delicate allusions to the fiery graves of heretics. It is, at any rate, notable that the solemn ecclesiastical definition of simony as heresy is not expressly mentioned by Dante. Peter Damian had already protested against it. Some years after his death, the question of lay investiture was settled by Gregory VII in favour of the Church. Thereby its separation from the state was completed,[3] and much to its advantage.

Henceforth the strife between emperor and pope was not to be over this or that right, nor even concerning lay investiture, but for the mastery of the world. "The more the separation of Church and state was completed, the more did the empire lose its original religious character and appear as a purely worldly sovereignty; while on the other hand, the Church stood out no less emphatically as the embodiment of the religious idea, as the realization on earth of the supersensuous divine state. Together with this religious foundation, the empire lost all right to independent authority over the Church. Hence, in the sunderance

---

[1] E.g. by the Synods of Rheims (1049), Rouen (1050), and Toulouse (1056), and by Gregory VII.

[2] Mirbt, *Die Publizistik*, p. 371.

[3] That is, for the time being. The contest was never wholly closed, and no definite legal settlement of the question was ever reached, not even at the Diet of Worms.

which established the Church as a divine authority, infinitely superior to the state, her legal claim to unquestioned superiority over the state was included. The separation of Church from state carried with itself as a logical necessity the affirmation of superior authority on the part of the Church. The spiritual character of the Church must lead to world-control."[1]

This control, to be sure, the popes were wont to demand in theory only. Their first concern was for Italy, and chiefly for the sake of feudal supremacy over the kingdom of Sicily and the mastery of the central part of the peninsula.

The nearer they came to this goal, the deeper they plunged from ecclesiastical into civil politics, the more strenuous the resistance of the monks became. They saw themselves dragged again into secularism, and with renewed asceticism they braced themselves against it. This time it was the reaction of ethical renunciation against the political and world-seeking tendencies of the princes of the Church. What the monks of Cluny and Camaldoli and the followers of Bernard were in the days of Damian, the Franciscans were in Dante's time. These latter, like the former, constituted a popular, somewhat pro-imperial reform party.

As the former had fought against simony, so the Franciscans contended against all Church interference in worldly affairs. It was the same ideal, but in a larger and austerer form. Purification of the Church from all worldliness, its release from material bonds, its peaceful separation from the state, mutual good will and respect between them, development of imperial and papal powers—all this was, once more, the pious desire of the monks. These similar conditions were to give rise to similar thoughts and aims.

In all these matters Dante shares the ethico-political creed of the Franciscans. So it comes to pass that he finds, in the preceding centuries, no publicist whose writings appeal to his heart like those of Peter Damian, the former spokesman of the monks—like himself, favourable to the emperor.

Dante probably knew his writings. The final words of his *De Monarchia* remind one forcibly of the close of Damian's *Disceptatio synodalis*. "The pope, as a father, should always have the precedence by paternal right, and the emperor, as his only son, should repose in his loving arms."

Like Dante, he lashes—one would almost say with the same

[1] H. von Eicken, *op. cit.*, pp. 217–18.

whip—the greed of the clergy. Like Dante, he assigns to the emperor the right and the duty to interfere in Church affairs as a moral reformer. The nomination of austere and competent bishops by the emperor seems to him fitting and right. In short, he regards the emperor as the divinely appointed guide and physician of the whole world and therefore also of the Church. He extols Henry III as the victor who saved Christendom from the monster of simony.

Is it not to be supposed that the prophecies, the wishes, the hopes of our poet for a reforming world-emperor were inspired, at least in part, by the writings of this monk, and by the memories of the much-lauded measures of the emperors of those days?

The belief in the religious mission of the empire was seriously shaken, even in Dante's time. This was especially true in Italy, where for two generations no German emperor had been seen. The recent past, a dramatic demonstration of imperial helplessness, refuted the imperial claim. The belief, therefore, had its roots only in the past. The eulogies and pious epithets which Peter Damian, a saint, had bestowed upon the empire, must have proved valuable testimony.

To be sure, they were antiquated testimonies and hopes; their time was past; and despite the similarity of political conditions, it was an anachronism for Dante to revert to the ideas of Peter Damian. After cities and princes had grown over the heads of their suzerains, after men like Otto IV and Frederick II had been compelled to call themselves emperors "by the grace of the pope," after even Henry IV had gone to Canossa—after all this, only romantic dreamers could expect of the vanished imperial power the moralization of the world, the humbling of tyrants, and the spiritualization of the Church.

There were in those days three such dreamers. The first was the ignorant mass of monks and poor people, the second was Dante, and the third, the Emperor Henry VII. The common people invented their own legend of a great and good emperor, harbinger of peace, who must some day appear. Henry VII undertook a pilgrimage to Rome which cost him his life. But Dante had set together the credulous expectation of the people and the deeds of the emperor in a magic mirror—a mirror wherein the past appeared as future, and hope as memory, in a glow of reflected light.

With this we are approaching the dimmest and most enigmatical side—the romantic side—of the *Divine Comedy*. That is to say, at one point Dante turns aside from the path of the sober moral and political thinker, and joins the dreamers, the little, hopeful folk, the common people. The very persons to whom he owes, directly or indirectly, his entire scientific equipment—Aristotle, Cicero, and Thomas Aquinas—were at one definite point forgotten.

But before we reach that point, we must still follow our poet for a while in his relations to scholastic philosophers and political teachers.

THE ETHICS OF THOMAS AQUINAS

When the Roman pope had secured his independence and therewith his supremacy over the German emperor, i.e. after the separation of the ecclesiastical from the lay state—or rather, after the subordination of the lay to the ecclesiastical sway—Augustine's idea of a divine state was realized, at least to a large extent. The Church, as the supermundane principle of good, had overthrown the evil principle, worldliness, and the state. Now that this far-off goal was nearer, what had been accomplished?

"Are worldliness and sin, then, one and the same?" Peter Abelard, the most enlightened man of the day, asked himself. Must all that is good pour down upon the world from outside and from above, by divine grace? The Pelagian doubt as to the sinfulness of the world, the sane old pagan belief in the good origin of Nature, again came to the fore, bolder than ever. It could now gather courage from an abundance of historical comparisons. In the eleventh and twelfth centuries, human experience had greatly increased. The most pious crusaders had been forced to convince themselves that even among the Mohammedans there were excellent men. And a learned man like Abelard found noble characters in ancient heathendom. The doubt could no longer be suppressed: Were not the ancient philosophers just as virtuous, yes, even more virtuous than the Christians? Did they not all live in accordance with the same moral law as we? What advantage should a Christian have over them? Everywhere a natural, everywhere the same human, origin of virtue!

Augustine had recognized the *lex naturalis*, but had crippled and degraded it; for he had absorbed it entirely into the *lex divina*.

Now Abelard seemed about to treat the *lex divina* in the same fashion. He does not question the reality of divine grace, but he combines it with the law of Nature.[1] The religious character of Christian morality is, not indeed fundamentally and explicitly, but practically and *de facto*, questioned once more, by Abelard and other rationalists, e.g. by the author of the *Romaunt of the Rose* and translator of Abelard's correspondence, Jean de Meun, whom Dante doubtless knew.

But it is above all the increasing knowledge of Aristotle and the Arabian philosophers that threatens the doctrine of election and salvation by God's grace.

After the empire saw its theocratic semblance of holiness fade away in the struggle with the Church, it seemed as though the most brilliant of those emperors, Frederick II, wished to set upon his own head a worldly and philosophic crown. Aristotle and Averroës were the protégés of his court. To be an unbeliever and to be a Ghibelline were regarded in Italy, at the close of the Hohenstaufen period, as one and the same thing. Knighthood and the service of woman, ancient Greek, ancient Roman, Arabian, and Provençal art and science—all these forces refined and ennobled the long-suppressed sensuousness of man, and bade him gather courage once more.

Who could have suppressed such a mighty impulse toward worldliness? Only a few zealots denied or misinterpreted its moral value. The Church, unless it wished to risk its own influence, must come to terms with this new-born age, with this first Renaissance. It must offer a permanent place in its ethical structure to this pagan and lay culture.

Thomas Aquinas, the man who had secured recognition for secular science by the side of divine revelation, here also seemed able to establish the rights of the moral will by the side of divine grace.

The problem, to put it briefly, was to give adequate value to Nature's moral law without destroying the precedence of the divine law of grace. Between Augustine, who was inclined to sacrifice the first to the second, and the apostles of culture, who would give up the latter for the former, some middle ground must be discovered.

The simplest and most logical solution for Thomas would have

---

[1] If this is not the exact position taken in his writings, it is their marked tendency.

been to relate one ethical principle to the other, after the manner used to connect the two theoretical principles, reason and revelation. He would then have taught that by obedience to moral law man resists evil; by submission to the law of grace he devotes himself to the good. The first law is the negative and the second the positive side of one and the same principle. By asserting his own worth, by moral conduct, man satisfies his conscience and acquires inward harmony; by surrender to a higher power, by piety, he obtains the gift of grace, blessedness, and puts himself in harmony with the universe and with God. As the critical philosopher refutes error and the intuitive champion of the faith receives the truth, so man's character fights sin, and his piety receives the reward.

This simple wisdom speaks with mute, childlike eyes out of the depths of Dante's poem. Clearly and cheerfully it sounds in Virgil's words of farewell. Upon the top of the mountain he dismisses his protégé and pupil, who, perfectly trained by him, can pass out of toil and struggle into the realm of pious bliss.

> And said: "The temporal fire and the eternal,
>   Son, thou hast seen, and to a place art come
>   Where of myself no further I discern.
> By intellect and art I here have brought thee;
>   Take thine own pleasure for thy guide henceforth;
>   Beyond the steep ways and the narrow art thou.
> Behold the sun, that shines upon thy forehead;
>   Behold the grass, the flowerets, and the shrubs
>   Which of itself alone this land produces.
> Until rejoicing come the beauteous eyes
>   Which weeping caused me to come unto thee,
>   Thou canst sit down, and thou canst walk among them.
> Expect no more or word or sign from me;
>   Free and upright and sound is thy free-will,
>   And error were it not to do its bidding;
>   Thee o'er thyself I therefore crown and mitre!" [1]

Wonderful poetry, but—poetry, dream, faith, feeling. Nowhere in the *Commedia* is the scientific formula for this eternally true conviction to be found. St. Thomas, the philosophic authority of the poet, had not been able to discover it.

For Thomas, better qualified to draw distinctions than to solve problems, complicates, without answering it, the question of religious ethics.

---

[1] *Purgatorio*, XXVII, 127–142.

He divides the divine law of grace into an immediate and a mediate aspect, thus gaining by a clever stroke the advantage of having at his disposal three instead of two dimensions. He is then enabled to identify the *lex divina*, which operates mediately—that is, through Nature's instruments—with the *lex naturalis*, and thus assures to the latter both self-dependence and harmony with the *lex divina*. On the other hand, he can elevate the *lex divina*, which operates immediately—that is, through supernatural grace—as high as he pleases above the *lex naturalis*.

Unfortunately, the advantage is only one of appearance, and the confusion is increased. For as often as the effect of the *lex divina* is thwarted by that of the *lex naturalis*, there is not only a contradiction between the two laws, but an inner contradiction of the *lex divina* with itself. So in the Mosaic law, which is regarded as an emanation of the immediate *lex divina*, there are commandments that clash with the natural law of morals, and hence with the mediate *lex divina*.

Thus God appears at odds with Himself, and the oft-disputed question arises again as to whether He acts in accordance with fixed law and by necessity, or solely in accordance with His will. The foundation of the whole system is consequently imperilled, and with this last turn St. Thomas's ethical doctrine abandons the position of intellectual determinism, which we described above, and takes refuge, for good or for evil, in the mythical morality of the Nominalists.

This is the point where Dante must make his decision. He had the choice of three ways. First: to conceal and bridge over the gap by mystical ties and by logical subtleties, propping up the unstable partition between earthly morality and divine grace as well as he could. So Thomas had done. Second: to sacrifice boldly one of the two principles, and either, after the example of Augustine, the Victorines, and the Franciscans, to accept a supernatural and voluntaristic scope for moral action, or, following Averroës and the apostles of culture, to adopt a naturalistic and intellectualistic conception of it.

It sounds incredible, but Dante succeeded in travelling all three ways at once. On the theological and psychological side, his ethics is Thomistic; on the philosophico-historical and political side it is influenced by Augustine and the Franciscans, but betrays at the same time a vein of rationalism and intellectualism that points unmistakably to Averroës.

There can be but few examples of an ethico-political creed which, in so far as its philosophic sources are concerned, appears so comprehensive, many-sided, and contradictory, and on the other hand so compact, so direct and effective, as it wells from the inner spring of personality. Here streams from all directions flow into a broad basin; but, forced through a narrow metallic spout, they rise heavenward as one single, pure jet.

We shall consider briefly the three distinct phases united in Dante.

DANTE AND THE THOMISTIC ETHICS

The ethics of Thomas, as we have seen, falls into contradiction with itself. It could hardly be otherwise. For it absorbs with hardly any modification the empirical ethics of Aristotle, and then sets beside it, or rather above it, Augustine's mystical doctrine.

Precisely those conceptions of Aristotle which we qualified as most fruitful and promising are accepted only superficially and almost inadvertently. The doctrine that makes of the activity of the will the source of virtue and happiness is weakened and curtailed. There are indeed, according to Thomas, humanly acquired virtues, the four secular ones, and there is a humanly acquired happiness. Pure human activity is, to be sure, an ethical principle, but it was undermined by hereditary sin. So the inspired theological virtues (faith, hope, and charity) must help out the acquired ones; a supernatural Paradise must reinforce earthly happiness; and finally, our free activity must be supported by grace—indeed a twofold grace, one static, which disposes and prepares us, and one dynamic, which urges us on. Thus it appears that the acquired virtues are no virtues at all, that natural happiness is no happiness, and that moral action is no ethical principle.

Furthermore, even the most valuable forces of Christian ethics were grasped by Thomas only dogmatically and superficially. Paul's moral belief, hardened into the stern doctrine of predestination and softened into semi-Pelagianism, are left by Aquinas in a flabby and wretched condition. His ethics suffers severely from the influence of the past.

What we saw in the case of Dante is true in a higher degree of Thomas. He remained loosely and superficially dependent on his most important ethical authorities, Aristotle and Augustine. Only because he took neither of them seriously was he able to come to an understanding with both. The ethical side of his system is its weakest part, despite its fine distinctions, despite its psychological analyses, despite its masterly construction.

The weak mingling of cleverness and piety with which the contradictions of freedom and necessity of the divine will, and of human merit and divine grace, are patched together—that was the only thing which Dante could learn from Thomas, and most fortunately he learned it very incompletely.

In regard to this simple fact, modern investigation of sources, with its mass of comparisons, analogies, similarities, and correspondences between the works of Dante and those of St. Thomas, threatens to lead us astray, or what is still worse, to disturb our judgment with a false veneration for so-called sympathy and insight, that is, with intellectual prattling. It may be, and we concede it, that Dante studied the *Nicomachean Ethics* in Thomas's commentary. But even if he had memorized all Thomas's works that bear on ethical questions, he could have learned nothing, more than the mixture above described. For where there is nothing, even an emperor has no rights. Thomas was to him a channel or a water-pipe—of lukewarm water at that—but no original source.

To give an example, it is the spirit of Thomas that inspires the feeble demonstration by which the admission of two heathens into Paradise is justified. Fundamentally and truly, the Emperor Trajan owes his rescue to a mediæval legend, and the Trojan Ripheus owes his to a line of Virgil which has been interpreted allegorically.[1] But Dante takes delight in giving a scientific justification of this difficult case, and puts his masterpiece in the mouth of the heavenly imperial eagle:

> *Regnum coelorum* suffereth violence
>> From fervent love, and from that living hope
>> That overcometh the Divine volition;
> Not in the guise that man o'ercometh man,
>> But conquers it because it will be conquered,
>> And conquered conquers by benignity.[2]

[1] *Aeneid*, II, 426–427.   [2] *Paradiso*, XX, 94–99.

Thomas would have solved the riddle by a distinction between conditional and unconditional acts of God's will. Dante does it by some edifying tricks of speech to which a certain solemnity is not to be denied. But he too, the great poet, becomes petty the moment he goes into details and tells of a regular conversion and baptism of the two heathens. For without that it could not have come to pass. Of Ripheus it must even be said that the three allegorical women, that is, the inspired virtues, faith, hope, and charity, take the place for him of Christian baptism, which as yet was not. The weakness, which in this case is Thomistic, lies in the attempt to make the incomprehensible intelligible, and to account scholastically for the impulse of the poet's heart.

A similar example of Thomistic ingenuity meets us in the first Heaven of the *Paradiso*. We find there the blessed women who were prevented by external violence from fulfilling their monastic vows. Since their hearts were true to their pledge, their salvation is assured; but their place is the lowest in the heavenly kingdom, because they had not the courage to defy violence. Dante asks himself: How is it possible that they in spirit resisted, but yielded in fact? The will either is free or is not. The true answer in this case should have been: Dear friend, these souls were women. Do not measure their moral personality by that of a Mucius Scaevola. The Lord's sheep are of many folds. Dante, in fact, did intimate this, or a similar reply. It lies at the foundation of the order of his whole *Paradiso*, and it is a fine poetical touch that in the Heaven of good but inconstant will he presents to us only poor, oppressed, feminine creatures. But this silent poetical reply he spoiled by a Thomistic-Aristotelian, ethico-psychological distinction. He makes Beatrice instruct him thus: You must distinguish two kinds of will; the absolute will, which is free, and is not to be conquered by any human power, and the relative or mixed will, which in case of necessity commits a minor sin in order to avoid a greater one.[1]

Aristotle, in the course of his psychological observations, had discovered these fine distinctions,[2] but without following up their deeper significance and developing them into a fundamental separation of the moral from the political will. Thomas actually introduced these empirical conceptions into his metaphysical ethics, and like the semi-Pelagian that he essentially was, es-

[1] Cf. *Paradiso*, IV, 100–114.   [2] *Nicomachean Ethics*, III, 1.

tablished a distinction in the will of the unique Godhead similar to that which Aristotle had discovered in the actions of social man! The result of all this being that Dante's Beatrice also, in the heavenly Hereafter, makes a clever distinction between two moral forces, one "absolute" and one mixed.

Whoever takes the trouble to track down other and similar examples of Thomistic thinking in the *Divine Comedy* will soon learn that they are to be found chiefly in passages of inferior artistic merit. Scientific inadequacy coincides here with poetical deficiency.

And there is good reason for this. For what we characterize in ethics as Thomistic is not a special group of ideas or doctrines. These originate in the remoter past and are not shaped or re-shaped by Thomas, but merely put together. The true essence of Thomism in moral philosophy is dogmatism; therefore we find no view of his own, but only arrangements. It is the comparison or the uncertainty between a naturalistic and a supernaturalistic treatment of an ethical fact.

Thomas himself was hardly aware of the unsoundness of such comparisons. So he carried them out as best he could, honestly and resolutely. With Dante it is different. He did not indeed know, but he felt with unquestioning inward certainty, that the great problem was not solved by Thomas's fine distinctions. After his heavenly imperial eagle has spoken so cleverly, he is compelled to glorify, as he thankfully dismisses the subject, the impossibility of solving the mystery:

> O thou predestination, how remote
>   Thy root is from the aspect of all those
>   Who the First Cause do not behold entire!
> And you, O mortals! hold yourselves restrained
>   In judging; for ourselves, who look on God,
>   We do not know as yet all the elect;
> And sweet to us is such a deprivation,
>   Because our good in this good is made perfect,
>   That whatsoe'er God wills, we also will.[1]

No philosopher speaks thus. Thomas would not have been content with such darkness; in him the desire for investigation overcame all hesitancy. In Dante, however, reverence in the presence of mystery is greater than confidence in the solution. And often when this confidence fails him, the muse also deserts

[1] *Paradiso*, XX, 130–138.

him.   Precisely because his poetry is so austere and so sincere, we recognize by the tremor in his voice the slightest uncertainty in his view of the universe.

One of the most literary and least original inventions in the *Commedia* is the triumphal procession of the Church that moves from Heaven downward to the Earthly Paradise—rich and brilliant as a pageant and as descriptive art, but as inspiration conventional rather than personal and poetic.   And, in fact, what is hidden behind it?   The ethical Thomism, the indefensible, separation and the false mingling of the natural moral law and divine grace, is fully displayed in this great allegory.   But since Virgil has already crowned the moral man as pope and emperor over himself, what significance has this procession, this martial review, of mediæval authorities?

DANTE AND THOMAS'S POLITICAL DOCTRINE

When the question as to the relation of the human to the divine will becomes a burning one, when ethical Thomism enters politics and partisan strife, then Dante, with his firm, complete, passionate faith, hope, and hatred, must renounce Thomas altogether. For the latter had, simply and logically, derived an ecclesiastical political theory from his transcendental ethics.

But our poet learned that a man's books are something different from his political party.   From his party he could separate, and had separated himself; the books and the thoughts he could not so easily repudiate.   It was, as we have seen, the predicament of all who defended the secular state that they fought with weapons which their opponents had forged.

The most modern, double-edged weapon was prepared by Thomas toward the end of his life.   He was the first, so far as we know, to introduce Aristotle's *Politics* into mediæval political doctrine.[1]   In fact, despite his loyalty to the Church, under the immediate influence of this book he announced a new and positive justification of the secular state.   Aristotle's idea that man is by nature a social creature [2] Thomas was the first to

---

[1] Thomas's commentary covers only the first two books of the *Politics* and six chapters of the third.

[2] Social as well as political.   Thomas does not distinguish the two ideas.   Furthermore he interprets the moral purpose of the state, i.e., the perfect life, as something essentially technical or economic, for even in a state of innocence political organization would be necessary.

discuss seriously. He does not hesitate to abandon the doctrine of the sinful origin of the state and to admit that political rule would have arisen among men, even without sin. Natural dissimilarities, difference of sex, diversity of physical and mental capacity, and, not least, variety of economic needs, must under any circumstances have urged men to the formation of a state. Not the state, but only its degeneracy, was brought about by sin. Therefore the Church should not combat, but should watch over, the secular commonwealth.

But here we are threatened with a contradiction similar to that which we noted in Thomas's ethics, and which may rend his doctrine of politics also.

That is, if in truth the political structure of the state is no work of the Devil, nor yet God's direct creation, if it rather arises of necessity out of human needs and man's social life, then all political power, whether ecclesiastical or lay, must surely originate in human co-operation. For imperial and in general for all worldly power, such an origin from co-operation, or more accurately, from consent and assent, by contract and by choice, had been conceded long before Aristotle became known. But for the papacy the question might be a perilous one. Thomas, therefore, holds firmly to the directly divine source of the powers of the Church.

But in the year 1294, a remarkable incident occurred: Pope Celestine V abdicated. Boniface VIII was elevated to the tiara. But the foes of Boniface, with the intention of branding his election as irregular and of deposing him, attacked most violently the validity of Celestine's renunciation. In this connection they referred especially to Thomas's assertion of the plenitude and the inalienable nature of the pope's power.

But a disciple of St. Thomas, Aegidius Romanus (Egidio Colonna) undertook to defend the cause of Boniface. In his leaflet, *De Renuntiatione Papae*, he argued that in every kind of power the formal was to be distinguished from the material side. From the formal point of view all supremacy did, to be sure, come from God. That there should be an *ordo* of power is a divine law. But the content of such an *ordo*—that is, its *jurisdiction* through this or that person—can come into being only through human agency. The *ordo* is unalterable, the *jurisdiction* is transferable.

However, in another connection Aegidius himself identifies

the person of the pope not only with his office, but also with the Church (especially in his *De ecclesiastica sive de summi Pontificis Potestate*), and he even espouses the doctrine that the papal throne either receives a saint, or makes its occupant one. The first time he argued as a Conceptualist, the second as a Nominalist.

The writings of Aegidius show the fine distinctions and hidden contradictions of Thomas's political doctrines. This keen-witted publicist started off with his master's doctrines, but soon outgrew them and contradicted them. As instructor of the French crown prince, he composed his most widely read book, *De Regimine Principum*. Here as an Aristotelian empiricist he drew the picture of the modern dynastic territorial state. In the service of Pope Boniface, he wrote his great treatise on Church policy, *De ecclesiastica Potestate*, in which, as a Decretalist and Nominalist, he laid the foundations of papal absolutism. Finally in his *De Renuntiatione Papae*, he defended a strictly conceptualistic separation of *potestas* from *jurisdictio*, and developed the doctrine of the purely official character of the papal power, solely with apologetic intention, to be sure, and without realizing that he thereby ascribed the true *potestas* and sovereignty to the Church as a whole.

Like a sensitive weathercock, he turned in every direction that the Thomistic doctrine of politics could possibly take.

Dante knew this weathercock. It is not even improbable that he met Aegidius personally. But politically he was his avowed opponent. Whoever compares Aegidius's *De ecclesiastica Potestate* with Dante's *De Monarchia* will more than once wonder whether the treatise of the poet was written with direct reference to that of the Augustinian monk and in order to refute it. Like the *De ecclesiastica Potestate*, the *De Monarchia* divides into three parts. Just as Aegidius in the first part discusses the nature and purpose of papal authority, so Dante treats the nature and aim of imperial power. In the second part, Aegidius's argument that "all things temporal are under the dominion and power of the Church" corresponds to that of Dante that lay authority, throughout the world, belongs to the Roman emperor. Finally, in the third section, both Aegidius and Dante refute the several arguments of their opponents. If we go into details, we shall find in Aegidius a long series of theses, the immediate antitheses of which are to be found in the *De Monarchia*. In short, the shadow of Aegidius, though he is never named, haunts Dante's entire treatise.

It was long believed, and some believe it even today, that the *De Monarchia* is a polemic against Boniface VIII's famous bull *Unam Sanctam*, which he issued in November, 1302. But the latest investigations have revealed that Aegidius's treatise served as the foundation, and in part even as the model, for the papal manifesto.

Others believe that our poet knew and utilized the writings of those publicists who upheld the cause of the French king. Certainly these pamphlets bear a strong resemblance to the *De Monarchia*. But their points of contact could be explained by the identity of their opponent and by the intention to refute either Aegidius's treatise or the pope's bull. Furthermore, in the works of the French publicists, there is a feeling for *Realpolitik* and positive law that is completely lacking in Dante's treatise.

I should not, however, hold up the *De Monarchia* as a direct retort to Aegidius's *De ecclesiastica Potestate*. Our poet was not so petty as to write a special essay to refute a particular opponent, as Guido Vernani subsequently did in his invective against Dante's *De Monarchia*. In addition to Aegidius's writings, and perhaps the French, Dante also knew certain other works of Italian publicists of his day, and directed his attention to them in his polemic. It is, to my mind, highly probable that he had carefully studied the second important work on Church politics by an Italian disciple of Thomas, the *De Regimine christiano* of Jacobo of Viterbo. In particular, his metaphysical deduction of two powers from a single divine law could very well be directed against Jacobo's theological defense of one single power, which he based on the philosophy of law. That the treatises of Henry of Cremona were also known to him could hardly be questioned at the present day.

The *De Monarchia* is, moreover, not the only point at which Dante met Aegidius. The latter, as we saw, wrote a special work to defend the resignation of Celestine V. It is generally assumed that Dante condemned that renunciation as immoral, if not as illegal, in an obscure but powerful verse of the *Inferno*.[1] We also know that Aegidius, in the service of Philip the Fair of France, advocated most earnestly the dissolution of the order of Templars,

---

[1] *Inferno*, III, 59–60.

and thereby made a bargain for his own order (1307–1308). Dante has branded this action also in his *Commedia*.[1] Lastly, in his *Convivio* he refuted at much length the doctrine on the nature of nobility supported by Aegidius. In all these instances, however, Dante refrained from mentioning the name of his opponent.[2] Evidently he desired to oppose and strike his political views and intentions and not the man, whom he must have revered as an austere monk and as the most eminent disciple of Thomas.

Despite these notable differences, Dante had not been able, even in his political creed, to escape the scientific influence of the Thomists. This school of thinkers was broad and strong enough to include even such a determined foe of the pope's lay power as the Dominican John of Paris. What a critical jurist of this calibre had been unable to accomplish we can hardly demand of a poet and political dreamer like Dante. It was inevitable that he should accept without question all the Thomistic distinctions between divine, natural, and human law; the concepts of earthly and of heavenly bliss, as the purposes of the lay and of the ecclesiastical state; the monarchical ideal; the Catholic conception of world-rule; and, above all, the whole apparatus of theological and deductive argumentation. Regarded as logic, the *De Monarchia* is thoroughly Thomistic. Anti-Thomistic and anti-scholastic in tendency and in political faith, yet its formal conception, its arrangement, and its method are borrowed from Aquinas.

DANTE AND MYSTICAL HUMANISM

Yes, Dante even surpasses his master. At a decisive point, he argues more deductively, more theologically, than Thomas himself. Thence he glides through the scholastic into the mystical form of thought.

The point where the deviation occurs, the magnet which has disturbed the wonted paths of scholastic thought, is already known to us. Curiously enough, it is in itself not at all mystical or Christian; it is classical and especially Roman antiquity, the fundamental criticism of which we have already outlined in connection with mediæval philosophy.

Paganism then leads Dante, the political philosopher, into mysticism! This ancient Rome, this mighty world-empire, he

[1] *Purgatorio*, XX, 91 sqq.   [2] *Convivio*, IV, 24.

says to himself, hides such an abundance of ethico-political values that the so-called "acquired" virtues, or natural morality, would by no means have realized them. Here a divine miracle has intervened; here supernatural and inspired virtues have been active. Augustine could not make the development of the Roman state diabolical enough; Dante cannot make it sufficiently divine. Here the layman's delight in earthly life stands opposed to the world-denying faith of the monk. It is the enthusiasm of the youthful humanist in the garb of mediæval presentiment.

As natural science sprang from the mystical symbolism of numbers, so humanism arose out of a mystical philosophy of history. The spiritual interpretation of ancient history was a familiar habit of the Middle Ages. But in the second book of Dante's *De Monarchia*, in the words of the Emperor Justinian,[1] in the figure of the heavenly imperial eagle,[2] and in the second canto of the *Inferno*, we have no spiritual interpretation or altered valuation of antiquity, but a direct glorification, if I may so speak, a spiritual overvaluation, an idealization.

Yes, it is excessive glorification, for Dante and his age did not accurately and sanely grasp the true value of pagan culture. He can think of the Roman empire only in its connection with Christendom; he is no longer willing, however, to regard it as a devilish and profane thing, but as a divine, glorious, and holy preparation for Christianity.

Before he began his poetical journey into the next world, two other mortals, he tells us, had been there while yet in the body— Aeneas and Paul. For them alone had the divine mysteries been unveiled; they each had an epoch-making mission, Aeneas to shape events in preparation of the Roman empire and the papal throne, Paul to establish the Christian faith. Without especial divine illumination, neither the one task nor the other could have been accomplished. Upon a common holy ground, therefore, the warriors and statesmen of ancient Rome and the apostles and saints of the Catholic Church wander and meet.

But what is the nature of this broad and stable mystic ground? It cannot be a world-denying or perchance an Augustinian mysticism, but rather that Franciscan piety whose conciliatory tendency we have described in the section of this book that deals with the history of religion.

[1] *Paradiso*, VI.   [2] *Ibid.*, XVIII, 100 sqq.

It will be remembered that we characterized the figure of Bernard of Clairvaux as marking the transition from the ideas of Augustine to those of Francis. And, in fact, it is just after Bernard's death that mediæval piety feels itself drawn toward ethical and political ideals. Then, as we said, the struggle over the secularization of the Church begins. Even at an earlier period, humanistic ideas had become an effective weapon in this strife. Arnold of Brescia is the first and noblest to die the martyr's death. He is the forerunner of those romantic and truly Italian figures, of those humanistic mystics and mystical humanists, in whom the Renaissance and the Reformation are not yet distinguishable, in line with whom the Dantesque Virgil ideally stands—those scholars and artists like Petrarch, Cola di Rienzi, Pico della Mirandola.

THE FRANCISCAN IDEAL OF POVERTY

Ever louder, ever more strenuous, grows the demand for a new separation of state and Church, different from that for which Gregory VII and Peter Damian had struggled.

These men had joined battle with simony. But the persecution of the simoniacs turned out to be a disgraceful hunt for worldly possessions and for ecclesiastical rule. It must needs be so, said the disenchanted believers to themselves, for that persecution of the simoniacs was not indeed a bad but a halfway, lukewarm, and inadequate measure. Not simony alone, but every sort of worldly goods and worldly jurisdiction, is a weed in the Church's garden. The only question was whether such a tangled thicket could still be cleared without destroying the entire garden. Matters had gone so far that men could not but see danger in the very fact of possession.

The olden times were recalled when the Church was without possessions, and when, in the original congregation, all things were owned and enjoyed in common. Men's thoughts went back to the poverty of Christ and his apostles. "Through the Son of God," so Francis of Assisi taught, "who for our sake made Himself poor, poverty has become the royal virtue, and the seal of the elect." St. Francis took his place at Jesus's side. The idea that none save these two had truly accepted poverty was familiar in Franciscan circles. Dante repeated it, and he loved to emphasize this model of evangelical poverty, in contrast with the greed of the contemporary Church. It was one of the strongest and most popular trump cards.

Not only the edifying and sentimental, but also the moral and legal, condemnation of property could be brought forth again out of the traditions of the early Church. Even Basil the Great, Jerome, Ambrose, Augustine, and others, following the Stoics, had taught that all possessions and all natural utilities were common property. Only the encroachments of a few unrighteous men brought private property into existence and with it poverty and wealth. "Every rich man is either unjust or the heir of an unjust man," said an oft-repeated adage. "Wealth is robbery of the poor." All money transactions are sinful.

"Usury," declared Charlemagne in a capitulary of the year 808, "is the demand for something that was not given." To take interest on money lent was considered an outrage. Without doing any work, the lender enriched himself, exacting a profit out of something that belonged to all, this divinely ordered succession of time. There were only two sources of profit that were lawful and acceptable to God: natural matter and human labour. As the taking of interest could not fit into either of these two classes, Dante also treated "usury" as an offense against divine law.[1] From this we conclude that a positive and independent value was denied by mediæval ethics to economic life and property, as it was to the state. The chief principle of canon law was the common possession of goods. Hence it was only by way of concessions that the development of trade and banking could be tolerated. If moral reformers like St. Bernard and Peter Damian accepted Church property as permissible, indeed as sacred and inviolable, this was possible only because they beheld in the Church the personified community. As soon as regrettable masses of private property were accumulated in the world of the faithless, of the godless, and of the laity, sacred duty required the Church to counteract, atone for, and mitigate this robbery of the poor by gifts to the poor. In short, it was the task of the Church to offset the iniquity of private property.

Almsgiving was regarded in the mediæval ethics not as a deed of pity and piety, but purely as a matter of justice. The Church is the almoner *par excellence;* it manages and distributes among the poor the goods which come back to them by natural right.

[1] *Inferno,* XI, 94 sqq.

The patrimony of the Church is nothing other than the patrimony of the poor. "He who squanders it," cries Peter Damian, "crucifies Christ a second time and most cruelly wounds the Church, which is the body of Christ." [1] He thunders at the clergy who enrich their relatives with the possessions of the Church and turn over to some prosperous cousin that which belongs to a widow or an orphan.[2] In a similar spirit, and evidently against the same misuse, i.e. against the squandering of Church property, Dante utters a mighty word: "What else is it than tearing the cloth from the altar in order to decorate therewith the robber and his table?" [3]

Did Dante then regard Church property as sacred? A whole series of passages indicates that he did. In the *Paradiso* St. Bonaventura characterizes the revenues of the Church, the tithes, as the goods of the poor: *decimas quae sunt pauperum Dei*.[4] And St. Benedict preaches:

> But heavy usury is not taken up
> So much against God's pleasure as that fruit
> Which maketh so insane the heart of monks;
> For whatsoever hath the Church in keeping
> Is for the folk that ask it in God's name,
> Not for one's kindred or for something worse.[5]

And still more plainly in the *De Monarchia;* "Those especially raged, directed and imagined vain things against the Roman empire who call themselves the zealots of Christian faith. But they have no sympathy for Christ's poor who are cheated out of the income of the Church, while day by day something is stolen from the patrimony itself and the Church is impoverished. Meantime, these hypocritical zealots refuse to recognize the executor of justice (that is, the emperor, who should regulate the distribution of property)." [6]

On the other hand, we have seen that Dante denied the validity of the title by which the Church upheld its claim to temporal power. He regards the Donation of Constantine not merely as an act of injustice, but as a world-calamity.

> Ah, Constantine! of how much ill was mother,
> Not thy conversion, but that marriage dower
> Which the first wealthy Father took from thee.[7]

[1] *Epistolae*, Book V, 6.
[2] *Contra Inscitiam et Incuriam Clericorum*, Chapter 2.
[3] *Convivio*, IV, 27.
[4] *Paradiso*, XII, 93.
[5] *Ibid.*, XXII, 79–84.
[6] *De Monarchia*, II, 12.
[7] *Inferno*, XIX, 115–117.

Evidently two distinct trains of thought meet here. From the old Stoic and Christian doctrine which regarded all property as something unnatural and considered it as a nuisance, two conclusions could be drawn. First: since, unfortunately, private property has come into this sinful world, perhaps as a punishment for our sins, it can best be palliated through occasional and partial expropriations, through donations and alms; and can even be sanctified by the Church, the representative on earth of the principle of common property. Gregory VII, Peter Damian, and Bernard of Clairvaux acted in conformity with this view. Secondly: on no condition can there be private property among Christians! The Church must be the first to set the example of self-deprivation and communism. However the godless and the layman may traffic and trade, the Church must all the more avoid such defilement. This conviction was voiced in Italy by no one more passionately than by the Franciscans. It is their spirit that speaks in our poet when he deplores and curses the Donation of Constantine as a blot upon the Church; [1] and declares that the property of the Church is no longer sacred and inviolable, but deadly and iniquitous.

What we learned from the history of mediæval piety is confirmed anew: the discordant elements of the mysticism of Bernard are harmonized in Franciscan mysticism, and Dante stands midway between the two tendencies, uniting them. The canto of the *Inferno* which in the spirit of the elder generation of Bernard and Damian begins with condemnation of simony—"O Simon Magus! O his wretched followers!"—ends in the spirit of the Franciscans with a lament over the Donation of Constantine.

To be sure, it was a simple and logical matter to free the Church from all property and possessions. But it was not practicable. Even the most powerful supporters of the ideal of poverty, the Franciscan order, became hesitant and disunited at the first contact with actual conditions.

According to the strict rule, the Franciscans should have no possessions, either as an organization or as individuals. But as early as the middle of the thirteenth century they were burdened and enriched with numberless gifts and foundations. What was the result? A solution was found. In the year 1279, Pope Nicholas III decided that the disciples of St. Francis should not indeed

[1] Cf. also *Purgatorio*, XXXII, 124 sqq.

possess worldly goods, but could use them. In this manner, it was said, as users, not as proprietors, Christ and his disciples lived.

The distinction between ownership and usufruct was in the air, and gave satisfaction. This means of evasion, discovered for the Franciscans, proved practicable for the whole Church. The old reform declared that only the Church might have possessions, but the usufruct belonged to the poor. The new reform deprived the Church of ownership, but accorded it the usufruct.

How these two ideals, that all property should belong to the Church or should be secularized, impinge on each other, and how the earlier one promptly passes over into the later, can nowhere be better observed than in the continuation of the above-quoted lines of Dante:

"This impoverishment of the Church has not come to pass without the judgment of God, and justly, since, in the first place, the poor are not benefited thereby, though the possessions of the Church are their patrimony; and, secondly, since the empire, from which this possession is held by the Church, receives no gratitude. So it may well go back whence it came; it came with good intentions, it returns with bad ones; for it was well given, but badly owned. Yet what do priests care for that? What matters it to them that the wealth of the Church is dissipated, if only the riches of their kinsfolk be thereby increased?" [1]

In a later passage of the *De Monarchia*, we find that the poet has fully reached a new point of view. "The emperor could assign to the Church the administration (*patrocinium*) of a patrimony and of other goods, but the sovereignty thereof, whose unity tolerates no division, he must retain. The representative of Christ, for his part, could receive the patrimony not as possessor, but only as distributor of the income in the interest of the Church and of Christ's poor, as the apostles are known to have done." [2]

Neither in the original nor in translation does this passage yield a technically legal meaning. Dante's general idea is nevertheless clear. To him the emperor is the sole proprietor of the whole inhabited earth; all men's possessions are imperial fiefs. *Imperium* and *dominium*, sovereignty and property, public and private law, are in him united; for Dante thinks in terms of

[1] *De Monarchia*, II, 11.   [2] *Ibid.*, III, 10.

feudalism. The Donation of Constantine appears to him, therefore, improper; first, because the emperor may alienate nothing of his *imperium*, and secondly, because the Church may not own secular property. Only a mandate from the emperor or administration by the Church was possible. Furthermore, there was at that time in Italy no theory of government which elaborated the Franciscan idea of poverty into a clear-cut separation of Church and state. The first important attempts in this direction, by French publicists early in the fourteenth century, were hardly known to Dante, and certainly not seriously studied by him. Of Occam and Marsilius of Padua he surely knew nothing. So on the question of the separation only a certain tendency and mental orientation, no systematic political theory, is to be found in Dante's works. Whether he conceded to the pope, for example, only a *latifundium*, or, as Kraus thinks, a *temporale*, cannot be positively decided on the basis of his extant utterances.

Certainly the whole setting of his political theory is mystical and romantic. It gives not only to the political portions of the *Commedia*, but also to the poet's scientific work, the *De Monarchia*, a distinctly prophetic and Utopian tone, and transforms the scholastic and mediæval political doctrine into a sort of poetic prediction. The limits of concept are transgressed, and the contradictions which we have noted arise. A vague, unconscious, pressing mass of sacred and worldly dreams, of eschatological horrors, of evangelical longing for freedom, of vanished imperial glory and future rights of man, seethes in the fragile vessel of Thomistic scholasticism.

THE EMPEROR LEGEND

Who can bring out to clear light the suggestive and significant fables that once took refuge in the hearts of the humble Italian folk and of their beloved Franciscan brethren? Out of the depths of the soul, where hope and memory unite as legend, a poet is not wont to dip, for therein he was born. The nurse, the mother, the friendly friar, the playfellows, the many beloved faces that with glowing cheeks, with hesitant smile, with calm confidence, told such tales, are soon gone and forgotten like a childhood dream. Only the seed they strewed grows silently in the poet's heart, and one day, when he sings out his song to the world, or whispers it in soft tones, many a one recognizes his own dream.

Then comes the historian and says: It was a folk-song, a collective poem.

And even this most learned, boldest, most personal of poems, the *Divine Comedy*, is a folk-song. In fact it is so broad and collective a composition that one might in a certain sense call it an international folk-song.

The dream of the sunken imperial glory which in some future day, divinely transfigured and firmly rooted in earth, shall again assert itself and unite all mankind in peace, that dream which men call the mediæval emperor legend, was more real for the German than for the Italian people. To be sure, every race, yes, every party and every age, shaped anew its own emperor-legend. The one that reached our poet's ears has not yet been discovered. But valuable traces of it, as it seems to me, have gradually been brought to light.

There was current in Dante's day a tale of a mighty prince in Tartary, a Great Cham ("big dog," Italian *cane*) who rules over Asia, loves Christendom, lives in simplicity, craves not gold nor silver, is born in a land of felt huts, and one day shall subdue the whole Western world, crush all the petty tyrants, and build up an empire of universal peace.

This legend, perhaps combined with other fancies, may have been in the poet's mind when he made his Virgil prophesy the coming of a mighty hunting-hound (*Veltro*): [1] the envious and ravenous she-wolf, Avarice, will be tracked by the hound from town to town, back to Hell, and he shall be the deliverer of ruined Italy. Thus the last of the three puzzling and much-debated verses, *Inferno*, I, 103–105—

> He shall not feed on either earth or pelf,
> But upon wisdom, and on love and virtue;
> And his abode shall be twixt felt and felt.—

should be interpreted: "His abode shall be under humble felt."

Most scholars, on the other hand, think that *tra feltro e feltro* indicates the region between Feltre in Venetia and Montefeltro in the Marches; that is, the home of Can Grande della Scala, with whom the banished poet found refuge and protection, and to

---

[1] "The *veltro* was a heavily built dog, probably between our great Danes and the greyhound. Without doubt the *veltro* and *veautres* (Old French) are the same dog. They were strong enough to kill bears and wild boars."—R. T. Holbrook, *Dante and the Animal Kingdom*, New York, 1902, p. 118.

whom he dedicated his *Paradiso*. It is in fact not improbable that Dante also looked for the salvation of Italy to the young lord of Verona, a loyal Ghibelline who had helped him. But it might also well be true that in his mind the popular legend of the Tartar Cham mingled with his personal reverence and gratitude for the Veronese Can. In a harassed and hopeful mind there is room for every sort of fanciful expectation.

But if Dante should ever have given voice to the Asiatic dream of the future cherished by his fellow countrymen, it would still be far from proven that he sought his political saviour in the steppes of Tartary. The popular tale served merely to give a certain colouring to his political desires. If Bassermann is right, then in this passage the colouring is heathen and secular, such as might well be expected from the prophetic eye of Virgil. There can be no doubt, however, that in another passage the same wishes acquire a Christian and apocalyptic significance. On Beatrice's lips the "great dog" of the Orient has become a sacred number, and appears as a

> . . . Five-hundred, Ten, and Five,
> One sent from God shall slay the thievish woman,
> And that same giant who is sinning with her.[1]

The relation to the book of Revelation, especially Chapter XIII, is evident. Finally, in the highest Heaven, on the verge of space and time, these expectations lose all human and historical form, and are seen and defined only from the astronomical side of the movements of the heavens. Even before January, on account of the error contained in the Julian year, shall be pushed out of the winter—a period very indefinite and long to mortal comprehension, but brief for those in Paradise—the spheres of Heaven will roar loudly, and Fortune, the long desired, will put an end to the previous history of mankind, and guide all things for the best.[2]

There is in this ethical and political prophecy of the *Commedia* a mixture of popular tales and emperor-legends, personal experiences and courtly considerations, biblical, apocalyptic, astrological and mathematical speculations. And these last, which might be regarded as purely learned, were in Italy made familiar to all classes of society and to all political camps by the influence of Joachim.

---

[1] *Purgatorio*, XXXIII, 43–45.   [2] *Paradiso*, XXVII, 142 sqq.

PROPHECIES AND DOOMSDAY LEGENDS

The political prophecies of the Abbot Joachim of Flora, which found credence and imitation among the Franciscans, kept alive the apocalyptic mania of the order throughout the thirteenth and fourteenth centuries. Numerous new prophecies and commentaries in addition to the old ones appeared. At first this remained a fantastic and pedantic but essentially innocent diversion of religious idlers.

But when dissensions, quarrels, and strife began to shake the order, when, despite the conciliatory decision of Pope Nicholas III, the leading spirits assailed each other more and more passionately, until they parted over the fateful question of poverty—then these prophecies became a weapon of ineffective hatred. It is in a world of the imagination and in times yet to come that the defeated party, the strict spiritualists, avenge themselves on their victorious foes. The enemy was, primarily, the more liberal tendency of the conventualists, and with them the Roman Curia and the whole Curialist party, which sided with them. The friend and rescuer proved to be necessarily the temporal power, in so far as it was opposed to the pope—and more especially the German emperor. Thus it came about that the empire, long after it had been compelled to renounce its religious claims and influence on the Church, now at the close of the Middle Ages was once more summoned to a religious task, by the most renunciatory and most spiritual of all reforms.

It is true that the German rulers in the second half of the thirteenth century, Rudolph of Hapsburg, Adolph of Nassau, Albert I, who gave no attention to Italy and Rome, must appear to this party as shirking their duty. When Dante brands them as such,[1] he shows a "spiritualistic" Franciscan attitude.[2] Even so late as the year 1350, under the forged name of the most famous and most passionate Franciscan monk, Jacopone da Todi (ob. 1306), a prophecy was published that announced an emperor from Germany as the deliverer and Messianic prince of peace.

In the meantime, however, that is, in the absence of the em-

---

[1] *Convivio*, IV, 3. He refuses to recognize these three as emperors at all. This was a quite general feeling in Italy. Cf. also *Purgatorio*, VI, 97 sqq., and VII, 94 sqq.

[2] There were indeed also anti-imperial spiritualists. The condemnation of Celestine's retirement may be regarded in general as an indication of Franciscan spiritualism.

peror, the hopes of this party were practically diverted to other princes; for example, to Philip the Fair of France and, impractically, to a spiritual papacy, especially to a second advent of Francis.

A most important book, characteristic of the spirit of the age, was written by the leader of the spiritualists, Ubertino da Casale, in the year 1305. This is the *Arbor Vitae Crucifixae Jesu.* It demonstrates "that Christ lived in absolute poverty, that the rule and the spirit of St. Francis demand of his disciples the imitation of this perfect poverty, and that therefore, the laxer tendency of the conventualists and also the papal influence favourable to them [represented by Boniface VIII and Benedict IX] indicate a falling away from the idea of Christ." To give force to his reproof, Ubertino, using the gloomy colours of the biblical apocalypse and prophecies, painted a symbolic picture of the past and future fate of the Church.

Here, as in Dante, we find by the side of political despair and ethical hatred an expectation of the end of the world that was epidemic at the time. The numerous resemblances which may be pointed out between the *Arbor Vitae* and Dante's vision in the last cantos of the *Purgatorio* indicate, however, no direct dependence of the poet upon the monk. Similar states of mind and inclinations result in similar pictures. And as we know, nothing is more communicable than religious feeling and emotions.

From the appearance of Joachim's writings until late in the fourteenth century, all Italy was possessed with a mania for prophecy. Dante knew exactly what he was doing when he wrote his political epistles to the princes of Italy, to the cardinals, to the Florentines, and to Emperor Henry VII in that religious and prophetic tone that seems so strange to us today.

Apocalyptic visions of the destruction of the world and an ethical and religious renascence of the Church were not limited to spiritual Franciscans or to the enemies of the ambitious Boniface. Even the physician and favourite of this very pope, Arnaldo of Villanova, did not escape the Joachimistic disease. He upon whom this passion chiefly centred, Boniface the mighty pope, remained uninfluenced. "Why do simple folk expect the end of the world?" he is reported to have said. Dante was among these simple ones.

What sort of deliverer and reformer did he expect? Was it

one, or was it many? Was it an emperor, a pope, a monk? The question has been much debated, and will continue to be; for Dante himself did not exactly know. Do the prophets, pray, know what they foreshadow, and anxious people what they expect? The prophetic trend not only fails to unveil the future, but also runs a serious risk of darkening the present. So it fared with Dante. Mystical clouds of days to come darken his political doctrines, his philosophy of history, and his ethics. It is true that there is futurity, that is, foreshadowing of new and fruitful truths, in these clouds; but until they accumulate into a pouring rain and fall upon the earth, they only serve to darken the sun of reason.

As a political teacher Dante strove to separate the lay power of the emperor as sharply as possible from the spiritual rule of the pope. But in his enthusiasm for an independent secular organism, he forgets himself and assigns to his emperor spiritual traits, ecclesiastical tasks, divine missions, and even a reserved seat in Paradise.[1] As a philosopher of history, he distinguishes the heathen from the Christian world; his admiration for the ancient cradle of the empire, however, misleads him into mystical overvaluations; here too he forgets himself, and accords to the ancient Romans a superhuman distinction which should be granted, at most, to the people of Israel alone. So a prophetic mist hovers about the past also. Finally, as a teacher of ethics, he distinguishes bodily from spiritual, sensuous from supersensuous, love. But as a loving mystic—and now he is no prophetic or historical lover, but a real one—he spiritualizes and deifies sensuousness. In short, with his faith and hope he effaces the boundaries which his understanding had traced.

His love for Beatrice cannot be explained by Aristotle's or Thomas's influence. We shall see that it springs from an entirely different sentiment.

THE SPIRITUAL THEORY OF LOVE

In Dante's day and in the society in which he moved there was a developed, not to say a systematic, doctrine of the sensuously supersensuous or physical-spiritual love. It was a very remarkable and novel form of Platonism, which without any direct contact with Plato had taken shape under peculiar cultural

[1] *Paradiso*, XXX, 133 sqq.

conditions, as a mingling and compromise of various and opposed points of view and systems.

The earliest and vital germ of this doctrine, however, is not to be sought among the professional philosophers. These latter were clerics, and desired, at least in public, to ignore sensuous love altogether. Taught by Aristotle, Ovid, and the Church, they beheld in woman "only a fickle, unaccountable creature, incapable of education, controlled by evil impulses, who must be subordinated to man, for whose sake alone she exists. They saw in her only the Eve of the Old Testament, through whom man had become a sinner, without whom Adam would always have remained a saint, and the Atonement would never have been needed." [1]

The first who espoused the cause of the fair sex, and set rolling, as it were, the emancipation of woman, were knights. The noble lords north of the Alps had remained true and faithful to the old German feeling. Renunciation of the world had never entered their hearts. They were masters of the arts of eating, drinking, fighting, and loving heartily—and all without a particularly bad conscience. It was in vain that the Church forbade duel and tournament. Ambition, self-love, craving for fame, were mightier than the fear of the flames of Hell. In general, fear was contemptible.

In that land, however, where culture had made most progress, i.e. in Southern France, this knightly wilfulness, with its glorification of force and honour, rose out of the depths of impulse ever more clearly into consciousness.

So it was in Provence that the new spirit first took on the definite outline of a moral code. There first, partly from pleasure and love of beauty, partly from loftiness of soul and magnanimity, manly strength took up the defence of the weaker sex. Or, to look at it from the other side, woman's arts succeeded in securing a hold on man through his ambition and vanity, and in dictating to his warlike nature the laws of courtesy. Woman, whose mouth the mediæval Church had closed, became the aristocratic lady who set her claims against the commands of the Church. The service of woman took its place beside religious worship; woman's code of morals rivalled that of the Church.

[1] G. Gröber, "Die Frauen im Mittelalter und die erste Frauenrechtlerin," in the *Deutsche Revue*, December, 1902.

The most vital article of this code taught that love of woman and love-service lead man to moral dignity and to true chivalry. In the repetition, accentuation, and glorification of this dangerous maxim the minstrels of knighthood, the troubadours, found their chief delight.

At first they were content to exalt the beneficent influence of the service of woman on the external and social sides of man. If the knight is in love, he dresses better, rides better, smites better. But presently inward refinement took its place beside outward courtesy. This ethical code of a caste ceased to deal with worldly manners and began to consider the moral attributes of man.[1] As the caste was aristocratic, this spiritual deepening is nowhere more clearly mirrored than in the changing conception of nobility.

At first nobility of birth was regarded as the most important prerequisite for love and for the service of woman. Peasant and bourgeois knew not how to love. But as soon as the service of woman became fashionable, other people, bourgeois and even clerics, devoted themselves thereto, and it came to pass only too often that a lowly troubadour wooed a lady of higher station. The troubadours, with their outspoken inclination to casuistry, discussed such an occurrence under all its aspects, and the French André le Chapelain (Andreas), who toward the end of the twelfth century, in his *Tractatus de Amore*, recorded the rules of love-service, determined that it is no dishonour for man to love below his rank, but it does disgrace a lady, unless her low-born lover uplifts himself above his rank by personal nobility of soul. Nobility of soul thus becomes the direct rival to nobility of birth.

As in the course of the thirteenth century love-service and love-song make their way further and further into Italy, they find, especially in the centre of the peninsula, in Tuscany, a social life grown decidedly democratic: powerful cities and free bourgeois who are prepared to destroy the castles of the nobility in the open country, and to abolish their privileges within the cities. Taken out of the hands of feudal, serving, or wandering troubadours, this question of true nobility comes before the court of worthy and settled secretaries and notaries who have taken their courses in logic at Bologna. In such a court, naturally, feudal and hereditary nobility fares ill. It is thrown out, and only nobility of

---

[1] This influence is already noticeable in the troubadours, Marcabru and Bernard de Ventadour.

soul maintains itself; indeed it receives even a scientific definition, derived from Aristotle and Thomas.   Nobility of soul, we are taught, is an ethical condition, *habitus electivus*, a fitness or capacity for virtue.   So from this time it was not noble descent, but capacity for virtue, that was demanded as prerequisite for love-service.

This demand took for granted that true love-service and genuine love of woman lead to virtue.

In fact, we find in the troubadours of Provence the first germ of the maxim that sexual love is virtue.   And just as in the development of the problem of nobility a distinction had to be first made between aristocracy of blood and nobility of character, so in the question of love a preliminary division is made into sensuous and supersensuous love.   The troubadours were the first to bring a spiritual element into passion.   According to them it was the intellectual and sentimental element that constituted the very essence of love itself.   The churl in whom this element is lacking is unfitted for true service of woman.

To the extent that this spiritual element was more or less emphasized in relation to natural impulse, a higher or lower type of love was attained.   Courtly society was best aware of the means by which an æsthetic and sentimental enhancement of sexual love is assured; namely, by setting as many obstacles as possible between desire and fruition.   Unhindered intimacy, wedded life, can never lead to love, but only to friendship.   True love is—even for Dante!—outside of wedlock.   All such restraining emotions as jealousy, fear, defiance, and above all coyness, are a welcome spice in love-service, and are to be diligently sought after and, if need be, artificially created.

Love becomes an art, and its sentimental ennoblement soon leads to the distinction between mixed and pure love.   Pure love, so the French chaplain assures us, extends to the kiss, the embrace, *et verecundum amantis nudae contactum, extremo praetermisso solatio; nam illud pure amare volentibus exercere non licet.*[1]

By the later troubadours this *amor purus* is more and more exclusively favoured, and finally complete abstinence from physical enjoyment is required.   In Upper Italy, Sordello, a master

<hr>

[1] Andreas, *De Amore* (ed. Trojel, Hauniae, 1892), p. 182 sqq.   It was usual in love-service for the lady to grant her lover her company for the night, provided he did not go beyond a kiss.

whom Dante revered and loved, did more than all others to extend the vogue of this austere doctrine of love.

To a love so purified even the settled and honourable notaries in the Italian cities could give their allegiance.[1] If they recalled meantime their philosophic studies, they might even make the discovery that like the elevated conception of nobility, so too the new conception of love could be included without difficulty in the ethical system of the scholastics.

Thomas Aquinas taught that love pertains to that group of psychological faculties which are called appetitive in that it, too, strives for an end which is the good. In fact, we call love the inner motive principle of *appetitus*. So, corresponding to the triple division of our psychological powers, we distinguish (1) an *amor naturalis*, which, without perceptions and unconsciously, obeys the order of Nature; (2) an *amor sensitivus*, which is guided by the senses to a sensuous goal; (3) an *amor rationalis*, which is guided by reason. Love is the principle of universal motion. The stone that falls to earth obeys the *amor naturalis;* the beast that seeks its food or the continuance of its species, the *amor sensitivus;* man who uplifts himself to God, the *amor rationalis*.

But all *motus appetitivus* is reciprocal. It originates from a desirable object, which affects the soul and moves the desire; this, in its turn, struggles toward the object, strives to unite with it, and rests only when it reaches it. If we fix our attention on the first moment of this motion, that is, the action of the object on the *appetitus*, then love appears as *passion;* but if we fix attention on the second moment, the motion of desire toward its object, then love appears as *virtus*, as force or virtue. Hence, good is the object, and virtue the essence, of love.

But the common cause for all love is the similarity between the beloved and the loving being. The beings may be alike in two ways, actually or potentially, similar in their finished state or similar in their capacities. Actual similarity creates the love characteristic of friendship (*amorem amicitiae*), but potential likeness brings out longing.

From this it follows that those beings who stand on the same level with us, or beneath us, in the realm of the universe, we love predominantly with the *amor amicitiae*, for they all have, in certain respects, some likeness to us. But as for the higher beings,

[1] This does not mean that they abstained from eulogy of the *amor mixtus*.

for instance, the angels, since our similarity is only potential, our love toward them can only be that yearning which is longing. Downward, it is friendship and kindly feeling that draws us; upward, it is longing. To love one single human being with the upward-driving *amor rationalis* would be senseless.

But woman, who according to the Aristotelian and Thomistic doctrine is an inferior being, a male not fully developed, can be loved rationally only though friendship and kindly feeling, and irrationally only with the downward-urging desire of the flesh; but under no circumstances with that longing of the spirit that leads to Heaven.

Consequently, that spiritualized love for woman, as it was glorified with all the energy of their souls by the latest troubadours, according to the dominant philosophy of the day was a monstrosity. In view of this state of things, the love-serving notaries and bourgeois of the Italian cities became doubtful, bewildered, and of divided mind. The contrast between love of God and love of woman became a leading motif for their poems. The sober and conscientious ones among them, for example, Guittone d' Arezzo, stopped short and renounced the service of love. The most forceful and gifted among them, however, Guido Guinizelli, made his lady a higher being, a kind of angel. He fused the love of God with the love of woman, defended and explained the one by the other. In his famous poem, *Al cor gentil ripara sempre amore*, the new concepts of spiritual nobility as the preparation of that true service of woman and of that true devotion which uplift the lover to God are united, for the first time as far as I know, in a learned and yet lyrical presentation.

Dante knew and imitated this poem, probably composed during or about the seventh decade of the thirteenth century; and he expressly characterized its author, whom he considered the father of a new poetry and a new spirit, as his own father.[1]

The best that he has sung and taught concerning the nature of love and of nobility in his *Vita Nuova* and his *Convivio* he has inherited from Guinizelli. Whoever wishes to understand the evolution of Dante's Beatrice must make himself familiar with Guinizelli's epoch-making canzone. We offer here the most important parts.

[1] *Purgatorio*, XXVI, 91 sqq.

Love only in the noble (*gentil*) heart abides,
As in the verdant forest dwells the bird,
Love was not ere the noble heart was made
Nor noble heart created before love;
For when the sun appeared,
Then came the sunbeam too; and until then
The sun itself was not.
Alone in noble spirit doth love find
His true and only home,
As in the flame of fire the light is found. . . .

Though all day long the sun illumines the mud,
This still is foul and that its heat retains.
The proud man says: I by descent am noble.
Let none deceive himself
That save within the heart, nobility
Adorn the escutcheon
Where not by virtue is the heart ennobled.
On water plays the ray,
Yet in the sky abide both star and light.

God the creator in his angel's soul is mirrored
More clearly than the sunbeam in the eye,
That soul doth truly comprehend her lord;
From him she wins the power to move the Heaven.
Its orbit is completed
Accordant with her righteous God's desire.
So with the lovely dame:
She from her eye must the clear truth infuse
Into her lover's noble heart,
So that in serving her he weary not.

Beloved lady, when one day my soul
Before her God appears, then will He say:
"What! Art thou come throughout all Heaven to me
And tookst me for the likeness of thy love?
To me and to the queen
Of Heaven's realm who quelleth all deceit
Alone doth praise belong!"
Then must I say: "Oh, my beloved seemed
An angel of thy kingdom!
My love account not unto me as sin!" [1]

[1] The original may be found in all anthologies of early Italian poetry, such as
T. Casini's *Rime dei poeti bolognesi del secolo XIII*, Bologna, 1881, and English
versions are included in D. G. Rossetti's *Dante and his Circle*, London, 1900, and
L. de' Lucchi's *Anthology of Italian Poems*, London, 1922; the last also gives the
original.

This unique elevation or deification of woman created a school among the Italian troubadours, and Dante has given a name to this school, in which he claims membership. Even to this day it is called *il dolce stil nuovo*, "the sweet new style." [1]

THE FUSION OF MYSTICISM AND RATIONALISM

Where this charming style begins and where it ends is a question on which the critics cannot agree, for the spirit as well as the stylistic forms varied from one poet, yes, even from one poem, of this school to another. The lady, exalted even to a superhuman height, ceases, as it were, to keep her feet upon the ground, and is drawn hither and thither throughout the range of possibility, an airy creation. If the singer has scientific leanings, his lady becomes a mere concept and his song an allegory; to a devotee of religion, she appears as a saintly, angelic being, and he praises her in spiritual and symbolic eulogies; finally, he who is sensuously exalted transforms her into an inaccessible idealized body with inhumanly resplendent eyes, with incredibly golden locks, and an all too white and flawless skin. In Dante's *Convivio* we have the first, in his *Vita Nuova* the second, and in Petrarch's *Canzoniere* the third type of this superwoman. In the earlier days only the first two come into rivalry with each other.

Whoso wishes to know what view of life, what philosophic tendency, prevailed in the minds of Dante's contemporaries, should look into the love-poetry of the new style. For it is, on the one hand, sufficiently reflective to reveal its definite philosophic basis with certainty, and, on the other hand, sufficiently naïve not to excite suspicion as a deliberately falsified caricature of psychical conditions. From it we learn that men's minds were divided between Averroism and mysticism, and that Thomism, so far as it is distinguishable from the other two, had hardly anything worth mentioning to offer to a troubadour.

The unity and independence of the individual, for which, as we recall, Thomism had striven so ardently, are abandoned by this lyrical school. In the poems of the *stil nuovo* the question is never raised, which of the two lovers is to make conquest of the other. The man does not appear on the offensive, nor the woman on the defensive. The two are most widely separated. Neither reveals individual traits, neither acts like a human being. Rather

[1] *Purgatorio*, XXIV, 57.

the woman holds such a position toward man as the Averroistic universal reason to "possible intellect," or as the Queen of Heaven to her worshippers; that is to say, she either flashes into his brain as illuminating truth, or she pours heavenly sweetness into his heart. In short, her influence is magical and supernatural. The man, on his part, bears himself somewhat as befits the "possible intellect," or else like an entranced mystic, absolutely passive and receptive. If anything is going on within him, it is not he, his ego, but merely portions of him, his heart, his intellect, his eyes, his senses, his vital spirits, his memory, etc., that have aught to do or say. His whole psychic existence has in it something unnatural; at times it is a mere mechanism of forces, at others a magic world or a spiritual drama, but it is never a personal organism. Here also we recognize sometimes the Averroist, taking his soul apart as if it were a fragile toy, sometimes the mystic, boring blindly through his as if it were an unexplored and unending labyrinth of precious things.

Where the hero and heroine of the poem, the two lovers, do not rise to individual significance, it would be too much to expect it of their environment. As the mystic is aware only of the Divinity and of himself as its vessel, and the Averroist only of intelligence and of himself as its point of attraction, so the poet of the new style sees himself wholly alone with his lady. Jealousy and rivalry are excluded. The heroine has almost a retinue of attendants, even as the Godhead surrounds itself with heavenly choirs.

The only movement imaginable under these conditions—i.e. the isolation of the lovers, the superior position of the lady, and the greatness of the gap between them—is that the lady stoops to him without tarrying, and that the lover soars, but does not sustain himself aloft: a fugitive and miraculous approach. Even the action of the *Divine Comedy* falls within this scheme.

In fact, if we ignore single, unimportant details, we see a common spirit, a strikingly similar fundamental character, a kinship of soul in the love-poetry of the new style, in Franciscan mysticism, and in the naturalistic supernaturalism of the Averroists. This common trait may be characterized as the dreamy inclination toward the supernatural. It had a much greater hold on the minds of the period than did the sober spirit of Thomism. It was in fact so powerful that it drew together the two most diverse views of life in the Middle Ages, and the most opposite temperaments imaginable: intellectualism and mysticism, rationalism and faith in revelation, the Averroist and the Franciscan. Toward the close of the Middle Ages, the reciprocal approaches, the union and fusion, of these once irreconcilable extremes became more and more general. And now, when the extremes meet, the cycle of mediæval thought is completed. Mediæval philosophy, scholasticism, has not much more to say, for what it had striven to attain by means of logical distinctions and combinations has become, by practical means, a natural mood and a prevailing conviction; namely, the union and amalgamation of a speculation and a faith both oriented toward a future life.

In fact, if we study, in this connection, the *stil nuovo*, we are astonished at the ease and naturalness with which these troubadours glide from concept to angel, from allegory to symbol, from the wisdom of the schools to fantasy, from the soberest cleverness to yearning dream, as though they were all identical.

So there flourished, in the second half of the thirteenth century in Bologna, and especially in and about Florence, a school of poets whose obscure and learned stanzas today made them appear as exclusive and reserved Averroists, and who tomorrow could cast to the throng a simple folk-song, perchance a sensuous pastoral. Such a temperament was, for example, Guido Cavalcanti, the friend of Dante's youth; and the others who were not like him strove to be so. When they speak of their beloved, it sounds as if they were thinking, at one time, of the universal Intelligence of Averroës, which was actually glorified in two great Italian poems,[1] and, at another, of the Virgin Mary, as her praises are sung in the Franciscan lauds.

The Beatrice of the *Divine Comedy*, with a unique and an often careless naïveté, unites the utter devotion of the believing woman with the stilted didacticism of the masculine sage. This angelic creature under the hood of a doctor of theology is to our taste somewhat bizarre. Even the most matter-of-course seriousness with which she sets the philosophic pince-nez before her dreamy eyes cannot save her from the malicious smile of an attentive observer. Her contemporaries did not smile. They valued and admired Beatrice, because of this very two-sidedness,

---

[1] *L'Intelligenza* (author unknown), and the *Reggimento e costumi di donna* of Francesco da Barberino.

as the best and most complete child of her time. Even at the
end of the fourteenth century she is regarded by a Tuscan poet
and worshipper of Dante as the true representative of the complete union of poetry and science, of mysticism and rationalism.
The sturdy versifier constructs for himself a divine trinity, made
up of Poesy, Beatrice, and Theology:

> This is the holy goddess Poesy
> Who is so graceful, gentle, fair, and haughty,
> Or is she Beatrice? or is she rather named
> Theology? They are but synonyms
> Of one substance to the truthful fancy.[1]

The idea that the beloved is an actual human being must often
have threatened to disturb the poets of the *stil nuovo*. It was
for that reason that they gave such extraordinary prominence to
the death of their beloved. The three most important love-poets
at the close of the Middle Ages, Dante, Cino da Pistoia, and
Petrarch, lost their loves by death. That might well be something
more than chance. I am almost inclined to say that it was only
by their death, and because of their death, that Beatrice, Sel-
vaggia, and Laura became the beloved of their poets. Death
has become something lovable and is hailed as "noble death"
(*morte gentile*). Even so St. Francis regarded death as his brother,
and Averroës expected from death the union of his being with
the source of all knowledge.

It is hard for us to imagine how intimate death became to
these men of the later Middle Ages under the influence of Averroës
or Francis, how little colouring of penance and renunciation there
was in their longing for the other world, how completely, even
here below, the unattainable had become reality, and Heaven
their earth. This is not the place to illustrate with examples
from the history of customs, of art, and of literature this increasing immanence of the supernatural, this dissolution of mediæval
dualism into an uncritical, but extremely temperamental, syncretism. For us, those spiritual traits of the age by which the
chief motif of the *Commedia*, the Beatrice-cult, is to be explained,
hold the centre of the stage; that is, the love-poetry of the *dolce
stil nuovo*.

But the fact that not only there, but also in the remotest fields
of human thought and feeling, the same contact and fusion of

[1] Giovanni da Prato, in his allegorical didactic poem *Philomena*.

mysticism and rationalism is revealed, can be demonstrated by two notable passages from that work of our poet which he doubtless composed in the full maturity of his powers, in the later years of his life.

In the first chapters of the *De Monarchia*, Dante is in quest of the particular, peculiar purpose of a lay world-state. He seeks for it a task which is not subordinated to the mystical, super-mundane ends of the Church universal. And, lo! he finds no refuge outside of Averroës. To actualize the "possible intellect" in its widest extent, i.e. in the whole mass of humanity; to organize to its maximum the communication and realization of the superhuman universal intelligence; to make out of all mankind one single collective Averroist philosopher—that is the end and aim of all non-ecclesiastical political construction and effort.[1]

And in the last chapters of the *De Monarchia* it is argued that the secular power of the emperor proceeds from God Himself, without the intervention of the Church. And here the refuge is mysticism. For only Franciscan mysticism taught that the ordinary, natural, everyday intentions and occupations of mankind have their source in the living and omnipresent Creator. Only under the influence of the more or less pantheistic doctrines of the Franciscans could Dante seriously assert that natural man, just as directly as spiritual man, receives from the Deity the norm of his action, the rider (*cavalcatore*) of his will.[2]

So Dante, in his maturity, however mindful of the distinctions drawn by his master, Thomas, permitted himself to be driven into the nets of the Averroists first, and thereafter of the Franciscans, by the pressure of the new spirit and by the demands of life.

Nowhere else, it seems to me, has he parted to such a great extent and so unconcernedly from Thomas as at the beginning and at the end of his *De Monarchia*. In settling the date of the composition of the work, this point should be seriously considered.

THE MYSTICAL DOCTRINE OF THE LADDER OF THE SOUL

The contact and commingling of the worldly-superworldly contradiction of the soul, mentioned above, betrays itself not only

[1] However much Dante shrinks from an exact formulation of this thought, the passage *De Monarchia*, I, 3, cannot be made to yield any other meaning.

[2] Dante gives the emperor this name, *Convivio*, IV, 9. The same figure is elaborated in the *Purgatorio*, VI, 88–99.

in the character of poets and artists and in the logical inconsistencies of philosophers; its purest and most direct expression is to be found in the textbooks of the mystics.

To the mystics, everything religious, in fact all spiritual life, is nothing other than just such contact and fusion of contradictions, the immanent becoming of the transcendent and the objectification of the subjective.

For them the poles of religious life flow together from four directions to a mysterious central point. For Heaven and earth, God and Nature, or, from the ethical point of view, grace and merit, are so related that now grace comes to merit and now merit moves toward grace. These first two movements are like ascent and descent on a vertical line. Then will and knowledge, or, in ethical terms, active love and prophetic contemplation, unite, in such a way that at one time the light of knowledge comes from the warmth of the will; at another, warmth from light. These latter movements may be likened to a backward and forward horizontal motion. By such a compass-card the soul's mystic life orients itself, as we see in the works of Hugo of St. Victor, of Bonaventura, and of their disciples.

In our historical account, we have seen how the schoolmen's epistemological categories were effaced by these mystics, with their unbroken, gradual ascent from sensuous perception up to reason and revelation, and with an interpolated series of intermediate steps. These same men, in ethics, modified the rugged articulation of the scholastics by a vital ascent and a progressive interweaving of the natural and supernatural powers of the soul. They introduced into scholastic instruction the unrest of life and movement and treated the stones with Promethean fire until the scholastic dome, undermined by secret forces, slowly collapsed.

We possess two treatises by St. Bernard which aim from different sides at the same point: *De Consideratione ad Papam Eugenium* and *De Diligendo Deo*. The one describes the contemplative, the other the active, union of man with God. Beside the steps of knowledge, four steps of love arise. On the first, man appears as still captive and absorbed in carnal love of himself; on the second he attains to a selfish love for God; on the third he begins to love God for God's sake; on the fourth he effaces himself and loses himself wholly in Him.

What is marvellous in this typical story of the soul is, however, that the fourth step lies hidden in the first. How can man love man aright, if he does not love him for the sake of God? Self-love must be included in love of God. Since God is the cause of love, there is in reality only a single kind of love. *Causa diligendi Deum, Deus est; modus sine modo diligere.*[1] Accordingly there would be in reality no series of steps, and all the divisions and descriptions would serve merely to make the representation more easily intelligible. Just as self-love is but a form of love for God, so also all true knowledge is only a form of love, all genuine love merely a form of knowledge.

The contradictions that had run through all life and science flow back to their original source: the mystery of religion.

The more profoundly the mystics are convinced that religious life is a single, indivisible, incomprehensible mystery, the more do they nevertheless refine and multiply their psychological conceptual distinctions. Thus their view of man's relation to God passes gradually from an originally typical and naturalistic representation to one that is individual, contemplative, symbolic, and artistic.

In the writings of Richard of St. Victor the steps by which the soul rises to the knowledge and love of God become far more elaborate than in those of Bernard or Hugo. But even the most refined art of distinction soon becomes insufficient. In the conviction that even small and particular religious experiences contain in germ the entire mystery of the Godhead, he abandons the type and reaches out after the concrete, after examples, comparisons, likenesses, legends, tales of miracles, and the like. The impulse toward reality overturns or crushes the conceptual distinctions that had been discovered.

So, for example, Hugo of St. Victor fused the two fourfold series of the theoretical and the practical ascent of the soul into one. He wished to show that they mutually imply each other, and that it is erroneous to separate them. Therefore he welds them by a comparison to the Mosaic tale of creation. "In physical creation, as in spiritual life, there is a fourfold period or succession. On the first day light is created in the sinner's soul, and day is distinguished from night; he thus comes to a realization of his sinfulness, learns to distinguish good from evil, to love good and detest evil. On the second day the firmament is made within him, and

[1] *De Diligendo Deo*, Chapter I.

the upper and the lower waters are parted; that is, he is confirmed in his good resolutions, and begins to distinguish the impulses of the flesh from those of the spirit in such a way that they may not again be confused. On the third day the waters under the Heaven are gathered in one place; that is, the impulses of the flesh are held together, that they may not pass beyond the bounds of absolute necessity, and that the entire man may be restored to his original condition and directed in accordance with reason, so that the flesh be subject to the spirit, and the spirit to its creator. When man is thus re-shaped, he is worthy of the full light of the spiritual sun; his soul and all his yearnings are directed upward, and he receives within himself the ray of loftiest truth. He beholds the light no longer 'in a glass darkly,' but sees and feels it as it truly is; and this is the fourth day."[1]

Here the scheme of religious psychology is about to become a symbolic romance of the soul. With other mystics, Bonaventura, for instance, the succession of the days of creation becomes one of journeys. Genealogies, family trees, itineraries, ethico-religious circumstances, are constructed. In a treatise which is attributed, without justification, I think, to St. Bonaventura, in the *Diaetae Salutis*, it is shown how the soul, in nine days' journey, passes on from sin to repentance, to the Commandments, to the so-called resolutions, to the virtues, to the seven gifts of the Holy Ghost, to the seven beatitudes, and to the twelve fruits of the Holy Ghost; then on to the penalties of Hell, and finally to the blessedness of Paradise.

In short, all the precious stores of mystical figures gathered together from the past are thrown in with theological constructions and philosophic conceptions and more or less arbitrarily utilized. The purpose of these mystics is no longer scientific but edifying, in the widest sense of the word. Their intention is to edify the religious world and themselves. Hence a certain childish playfulness, coupled with a profound seriousness, pervades the writings of these men. Precisely because, for personal, arbitrary, and edifying motives, they appropriated all scientific discoveries and all dogmatic acquisitions—they endangered the objective and practical validity of these values.

Dante, too, utilized, in his *Divine Comedy* and for purposes of edification, the entire cultural wealth of the later Middle Ages.

[1] Quoted from Liebner, *Hugo von St. Victor*, Leipzig, 1832, pp. 227–28.

He, too, desires essentially nothing except to edify a religious world and to edify himself with it. We have seen that he found himself in a curious self-deception when he declared that his work was a moral didactic poem. The loftiest and profoundest sense in the service of which he shaped both his moral and his national intents is religious edification.

Subjective edification, or the realization of religious life in one's own consciousness, and personal religious experience, can never be derived from the history of culture. It has none of the so-called sources; it is itself a source. But objective edification does indeed have definite antecedents that can be thoroughly investigated. And in this external sense it will be appropriate to trace the essential motif of the *Divine Comedy* back to the mediæval mystics, especially Bernard of Clairvaux, the Victorines, and the Franciscans.

The mystics, above all, are responsible for the belief that certain men, in the living body and in a state of ecstasy, have been permitted to behold the future world of Hell and Heaven.

The mystics are the true architects of the mediæval vision of future life, the true practitioners of metaphysics. All philosophy, psychology, and ethics were recast, "lived through," and made actual by their inner activity. The schoolmen inquired: Where lies the peculiar nature of the will, of the intellect, of merit, of grace, of the natural and of the inspired virtues, etc.? All their labours were spent in the analysis and definition of concepts. But the mystics, in so far as they are pure mystics, do not investigate at all. They act and see to it that before our very eyes reason passes over into will, merit into grace, and the natural virtues into the spiritual ones. The concept of understanding, etc., is not an end, but an instrument, in their work; they are not interested in analyzing it; they want to experiment with it and connect it with other concepts. Their true goal is the artistic creation of religious life. They probe into all psychological combinations and associations out of which religious life springs. The most beautiful and typical examples of successful attempts, however, they offer to their auditors as a medicine for the soul. They pursue the religious life as an end in itself; they are specialists, virtuosos, and manufacturers* of religion, and are able to mould it out of every sort of psychic material.

But specialization carries its own penalties. All activity, be it art, science, politics, or religion, so soon as it is made an end in itself and does not work fruitfully in other fields, proves vain.

It would be a serious error to deny to the mediæval mystics any fruitful influence on science, morality, art, and social life. The purely edifying portion of their work, however, which interests us here, their tales of marvel, their ecstasies, their transports and visions of future life, considered scientifically and morally, are the least valuable and most ineffective of their achievements. That is why those men and those pursuits that produce no tangible result are called, in a derogatory sense, "edifying." Against such wearisome edification Goethe utters an angry word:

> He that has art and science too,
> Religion hath as well;
> He that hath neither of the twain,
> Religion hath no less!

Those pious treatises, those edifying itineraries, daily journeys and ascents of the soul, together with all the miracle tales, could be developed, if at all, only on the side of the arts and of poetry. In fact, the most important mystics, Bernard, Hugo, and Bonaventura, reveal, the moment they become edifying, an extraordinary poetical and artistic power.

Their chief subject, the ascent of the soul from earth to Heaven, or the gradual union of man with God, precisely because it was incapable of strict philosophical or moral treatment, was forced to take on an artistic expression. This tendency works itself out in the *Divine Comedy*.

The mystics led Dante on his way to art. Out of the bewilderment of speculation and of political strife, they facilitated his escape to poetry. When the whole life and thought of the Middle Ages was about to break up, they nourished our poet, drew him away from his scientific studies, turned his attention to new moral and political ideals, and gradually covered over his sharp contrasts with a wave of religious enthusiasm.

6. DANTE'S PERSONALITY

THE MYSTICAL LOVER

There is some ground for the surmise that Dante in early youth came into close relations with the Franciscans. His religious and political convictions and sentiments, which, as we

have seen, were closely allied to the tendencies of the order;
a tradition mentioned by the commentator Francesco da Buti
(1354-1406), and current in the Franciscan order; a passage,
somewhat dubious, to be sure, in the *Commedia* (*Inferno*, XVI,
106 sqq.), and finally, perhaps, the fact that the poet was buried
beside the Church of St. Francis in Ravenna—all seem to point
in that direction.

If it be taken for granted that Dante, perhaps at the age of
fourteen, was sent to the school of the Minorite Brothers in
Santa Croce in Florence, then this fertile conjecture serves to
throw light on many obscure points and inconsistencies in the
development of the poet's character. His upbringing in that
school would undoubtedly have tended to a one-sided development of feeling and of imagination. It would have given a fresh,
artificial, and somewhat perilous predominance to precisely those
powers in the soul of the young poet to which Nature had already
assured the ascendancy.

This error in education—supposing that it was committed—
avenged itself. An overheated monastic atmosphere of sensitiveness and dreaminess environed and weakened his all too emotional
spirit. And, lo! at the slightest contact with his troublesome
age, it took fire. A sensuous and supersensuous love, morbid,
intensified by fashion, took hold of him.

The story of this love he glorified poetically in the *Vita Nuova*.
Here, like Goethe in his *Werther*, he summed up a complete series
of inward experiences. Beyond this, the comparison with *Werther*
might be misleading. We will carry it no further, then, than to
say that the *Vita Nuova*, like *Werther*, is only with great caution to be utilized as an authority for the inner biography of
its poet. Its value for the outer life of Dante can never be fully
determined. Even the answer to the question whether his Beatrice
was actually the daughter of Folco Portinari and became the
wife of Simone de' Bardi will depend on the temperament of the
inquirer.

Vision and reality, things dreamed of and things experienced,
have been melted together in this enigmatic little book, and can
hardly be separated again.

If we consider the external circumstances and events therein
narrated, they present themselves as a meaningless and yet, no
doubt, deliberately planned series of the most diverse incidents.

A chance meeting of the poet with Beatrice—she is in her ninth year and is wearing a red dress—a second meeting, nine years later; she wears a white dress. But in reality, that is, apparently, the poet lauds not her, but another lady. The latter goes on a journey; a friend of Beatrice dies; Dante also makes a journey, evidently only in order to have a vision on the way. Barely returned, he again, for appearance' sake, sings the praises of another lady. Beatrice refuses him her greeting. Beatrice's father dies; Beatrice herself dies. It is not her death, but Dante's dream of her approaching decease, that is poetically elaborated. Another incipient attachment disturbs his remembrance of the dead. Finally, however, Beatrice is victorious; that is, not she, but her glorified image of light. No action: a dream, an intention, a wish, constitute the drama.

But if we study these events for their value as inner emotions, the book as a whole attains, as if by a magic touch, a certain unity that is perhaps not artistically moulded, but is evidently felt and intended; and its name is Beatrice. It is the beloved maiden's figure and the worshipful devotion of the poet modestly veiled and inwardly deepened. The many minor incidents, the apparent digressions, the death of her friend and of her father, everything that anticipates or distracts from Beatrice, is nothing but the external re-flux of pious love which circles about and within itself like a whirlpool, blurs the outlines of every vision, and dissolves all sensuousness. The apotheosis of woman is accomplished in symmetrical chapters, symbolically numbered. Her picturesque environment is merely the cloud on which she soars aloft.

Dante's true intention in this little book remains indeed an enigma. Investigators have not determined which of all his imaginable purposes deserves the preference. "Was it the wish to erect a monument to his dead beloved and at the same time to his own past youth? Was it not rather the desire to bring together a number of poems composed by him on various occasions, and to give them a higher significance, so as to entrust them under better auspices and with more dignity to posterity? Or again, was it the necessity to light a beacon for his own journey through earthly life, that should forevermore point out to him the haven in the recollection, in the idealization, or in the discovery of a source of happiness enjoyed and not wholly lost, which he might some day recover, as he eventually did in the

Commedia? Or, finally, was it all these various purposes inter-twined one with another?"[1]   We do not know.

A notable, attractive, and ingenious effort to explain the *Vita Nuova* as a composition that had sprung out of a social necessity has been made by Rudolf Borchardt.   He considers it a self-defence of the young poet who wished to regain his reputation, to restore his lessened importance, in an aristocratic, literary, and courtly circle of ladies and gentlemen.   If it be considered that in the *Convivio*, and even in the *Commedia*, the purpose of a social rehabilitation is active, we shall hardly venture, in the case of a man so sensitive about his honour as Dante was, to reject this surmise without full consideration.

If Dante's purpose was self-defence before the world, the actual inward result for him was a relapse.   His first contact with his age led to his flight from that age.   His sensuousness is not over-come, only mystically dulled; his self-love is not crushed, only religiously purified.   He studiously avoided coming to an under-standing with those passions which he was compelled to recognize later as the strongest in his nature: his pride and his sensuous-ness.   Inspired by uncontrolled sensuousness, he had been a dreamy worshipper,

> So not to venture on mere virtuous deeds.

His uncontrolled pride had made him choose as his lady-love an angel who lifted him above all mankind.

> . . . The pot,
> Itself of iron, would fain with silver tongs
> Out of the fire be lifted, so that it
> May fancy 'tis itself a silver pot.

The manner in which the Dante of the *Vita Nuova* treats his visions and the sacred mystery of his heart is neither altogether artistically naïve nor morally faultless.   There is something con-ventional in this youthful work, and for that reason it is passion-ately enjoyed by all modern æsthetes.

Only the theoretical, not the moral, inadequacy of his youthful dreaminess was recognized and overcome by the poet himself. He lit up the cloudy and shapeless desires of youth.   The hot surging of his blood he quieted, at least to some degree.   He had looked straight in the eye of that secret power which, at a certain

[1] Benedetto Croce, *The Poetry of Dante.*

period of life, lays hold on us all, and, half sexually, half metaphysically, bewilders and entrances us with the yearning for love
and death. He descended into the underworld of his own nature,
and more fortunate than Orpheus, released out of the struggling
night of impulses an ideal shape, the heavenly Beatrice.

To the man already growing old, she was a consolation and a
guiding star. In the *Vita Nuova*, he shaped for himself, out of
death and womanhood, a faith and a hope. And Beatrice again
saw to it that vulgarity and cynicism, the characteristic vices of
decadent mediævalism, were kept away from him.

Throughout the most important allegorical didactic poem of
France, the second part of the *Romaunt of the Rose*, there runs a
broad stream of filth. In it all the cynics of the later Middle
Ages, especially clerics and scholars, bathed at their ease. The
Romaunt had a wide circulation in Italy also. Toward the end
of the thirteenth century, a Florentine who called himself Ser
Durante reshaped it into a long series of sonnets. He gave more
space to the misogynous, unknightly, and obscene second part.
The attempt has been made to identify this Ser Durante with
our poet, whose first name is an abbreviation of Durante. Not
only philological but, I should suppose, humane considerations,
ought to protect the friend of Beatrice from such surmises.[1]

Not that we suppose cynical gestures to be inconsistent with
Platonic love. In the Italian poetry of the sixteenth century,
the two appear side by side. But with Beatrice they are utterly
inconsistent. She lives not only in the imagination but in the heart
of her poet.

The peculiar, dreamily religious character of this love, I know
not how to illustrate better than by a page from Carducci. Here
the poet supplements the historian: "In the canzones of the *stil
nuovo* there are strophes which I can only imagine as having
been composed between the solemn colonnades of the great
cathedrals, when the glow of the evening sun shines through the
stained glass windows, and grows pale before the ruddy flames of
the candelabra, while the fragrance of incense envelops the Holy
Virgin's altar; while the organ peals and women's silvery voices
fill the darkening aisles with melancholy chants. So Dante, no
doubt, beheld Portinari's daughter, veiled by a fragrant mist,

[1] One argument against Dante's authorship is the numerous and striking
Gallicisms.

her white forehead illuminated by the wavering light of the setting sun and the flickering candles, as she, kneeling upon the ground, uplifted her voice to God in plaintive tones of yearning. Then time and space vanished from him, and he beheld in his vision Paradise and Hell: and Paradise longed for her, Hell waited for him. Then he composed the solemn verses that ring like an early intimation of the *Divine Comedy*." [1]

> An angel of his blessed knowledge, saith
> To God: "Lord, in the world that thou hast made,
> A miracle in action is display'd
> By reason of a soul whose splendours fare
> Even hither: and since Heaven requireth
> Nought saving her, for her it prayeth Thee,
> Thy Saints crying aloud continually."
>   Yet pity still defends our earthly share
> In that sweet soul; God answering thus the prayer:
> "My well-belovèd, suffer that in peace
> Your hope remain, while so My pleasure is,
> There where one dwells who dreads the loss of her
> And who in Hell unto the doomed shall say,
> 'I have looked on that for which God's chosen pray.'" [2]

HIS MORAL ABERRATION

But one day Dante became untrue to his Beatrice. The sensuousness which he had silenced, not mastered, awoke and swept him off his feet. In his so called *Canzoniere* there is a group of poems that leave us no doubt. No matter how calmly and soberly we interpret them allegorically, their wording speaks louder. Whoso reads without prejudice the canzone *Così nel mio parlar voglio esser aspro*, feels that he is gazing into a furnace where behind heavy, creaking bars a hellish fire rages.[3] To be sure, we cannot, from the discordant sensuality of the language, draw an immediate conclusion as to behaviour, but there is some connection between the expression and the poet's temperament and experience. Dante was a sensuous nature: more we do not know. Nevertheless, in Dante-literature a great discussion has arisen over the interpretation of the questionable and mysterious

[1] Carducci, *Delle rime di Dante*, in *Prose di Giosuè Carducci*, Bologna, 1905, p. 83.
[2] *Vita Nuova*, first canzone, Rossetti's version.
[3] The sensuousness is most pronounced in certain poems addressed to Pargoletta and Pietra, which perhaps date from the same period.

love-adventures of the great man, over his marriage [1] and over his "aberrations." Since there is no evidence, erotic, soulful romances are constructed out of the varying and ambiguous materials of Dante's love-poetry—constructed and destroyed, only to be reconstructed and destroyed again.

We only know that Dante passed through a period of moral aberration, and it presumably occurred within a few years after Beatrice's death (in 1290). This is borne out by his friendship and his exchange of bitter and distasteful sonnets with the gourmand Forese Donati (ob. 1296). To this the reproach cast by his older friend, Guido Cavalcanti (ob. 1300), appears to refer, [2] not to mention the reproachful words of Beatrice in *Purgatorio*, Cantos XXX and XXXI. Reading between the lines, we can recognize there, and in other passages also, a mute, discreetly veiled confession of sensual sin.

But if Dante does not need to shrink from such confessions, he surely must have been free from unnatural sins or offences. The lust of the flesh is treated in the moral system of his *Commedia* as the first and easiest step into sin, and as the last and most serious hindrance to innocence. To be weak in this respect is, so to speak, the most natural and most general, and therefore the most pardonable and most lamentable, lot of men. Dante had experienced "original sin" in his own person, and at least for a time yielded to it with resignation:

> Even from my ninth summer have I been
> A loyal servitor of Love and know
> How he is wont both to restrain and spur
> With all the joy and sorrow he bestows.
> Whoso with sense and virtue strives with him,
> Is like a fool who hopes to drive away
> The furious storm wherewith the air is shattered
> Or would the lightning and the thunder bind. [3]

This experience, which he doubtless as a *mystical* lover had not yet had, he offers to his young friend Cino da Pistoia. He now first realizes that even in his youthful love for Beatrice there was a sensuous element. It lasted long, and a plunge into the

---

[1] About the year 1294, Dante married Gemma, of the famous Florentine family of the Donati. We know of four children whom she bore him.

[2] *Rime di Guido Cavalcanti*, the sonnet beginning, *Io vegno il giorno a te infinite volte*.

[3] *Canzoniere*, Sonnet CXI; *Io sono stato con Amore insieme*.

depths of "baser love" was needed before he gained this insight. Even after the visions of the *Vita Nuova*, even after the mystical Spring of love had withered, he repeatedly tried, as it seems, to blind his readers and himself.

In the *Vita Nuova* it was half childish faith, half literary imitation, that made him turn his love for a woman into a religious virtue. But in the *Convivio*, his mixture of love of woman and of philosophic study approaches ambiguity. To what extent he was conscious of it is hardly to be determined. He never wholly overcame it. A slight, barely noticeable, and certainly a dignified remnant of what we have called the moral illusionism of the Middle Ages, always remained in his mind. The belief that any natural fact, for example, the love of man for woman, can, by allegorical interpretation, that is, by a subsequent purely theoretical operation, be moralized, reappears even in the *Paradiso*, and transforms a loving woman into a teacher of theology.

With what efforts sturdy and conscientious investigators have tried to identify the *donna gentile* of the *Vita Nuova* with the *donna gentile* of the *Convivio!* In the former work she is a sympathetic, feminine creature, who stands at the window and weeps: here she is Philosophy, and Dante expressly assures us that the two are one and the same! I certainly would not assert that he wished to deceive us, but there is an ambiguity. It is the ambiguity of visionary mysticism which hovered over all mediævalism, and here, for once, becomes tangible.

And yet Dante has overcome, in another way, the dreamy deception which his eye never wholly pierced. His teacher and "father," Guido Guinizelli, the inventor of the spiritual conception of the love of woman, is seen by Dante in the fire wherein the lustful are purified. It is the same fire through which he himself must pass, and which, like a wall, parts him from Beatrice. And when he presently stands before her, on the crest of the Purgatorial mountain, something else still parts him from her; her own transformation. She is no longer the Beatrice of his youthful love. This she explains to her heavenly company, and pointing to Dante, the faithless, she declares:

> Some time did I sustain him with my look;
> Revealing unto him my youthful eyes,
> I led him with me turned in the right way.

> As soon as ever of my second age
> I was upon the threshold and changed life,
> Himself from me he took and gave to others.
> When from the flesh to spirit I ascended,
> And beauty and virtue were in me increased,
> I was to him less dear and less delightful.[1]

Here her appearance and her sentiments show a moral change and at the same time the continuity of her nature and spirit.

His feeling certainly guided him aright between ascetic renunciation and cynicism, for he was born "in the truth of the senses." With all its sensuousness his poetry maintains a high level of decency. He stands at an infinite height above the average of the Middle Ages. Not even the most delicate feeling of propriety could ever be outraged by this most passionate of all poets. It is true that in writing certain verses, he was not thinking of old maids who blush and schoolboys who laugh where there is no cause for blushes or laughter.

THE PATRIOT

However, such unfailing and natural propriety and tact does not come of itself out of "the truth of the senses"; familiarity with society is needed. Man must, without forgetting Nature, grow into culture.

But here the sharpest conflicts lurk. Human contacts alone can reveal of what stuff a personality is made up. One man is soft and adaptable, and that is a petty character. Another is hard, asserts himself and makes good, and he is a great, strong-willed individual. The third is still harder and—goes to pieces: he is a tragic hero. "There are two types of greatness. There are men of action, born to rule, who know how to bend and flatter in order to draw other men unto them. They keep their eyes fixed upon their goal, and yet they can show themselves in a thousand deceptive shapes. The common people no longer understand them, and call them weathercocks. They themselves alone are conscious of their inward consistency."[2] Such a man was Bismarck. If he was a man of the people, that does not prove that the people understood him.

"Dante had nothing of this statesmanlike greatness. He was

[1] *Purgatorio,* XXX, 121–129.
[2] Francesco de Sanctis, *Carattere di Dante,* in *Saggi critici,* 4th ed., Naples, 1881, 393.

not born to political leadership. He had in him more of Cato than of Caesar. Great men of this type are unfortunate from their birth. Every man admires them, no man follows them. 'Two men are just, but are not understood.' " [1]

In truth the poet's most loyal companions were misfortune and loneliness. He lost his mother early and had a stepmother. His father apparently died a shameful death as a heretic [2] (about 1280). Meantime Dante grew up—perhaps within monastery walls—to face his destiny. Not one word, in all his works, of his father's house. That father was apparently a banker, and must, as certain records of indebtedness show (1297), have left his financial affairs in a most ruinous condition. The oppressive contrast between an old and honoured family name and empty coffers might therefore early have weighed down Dante's spirit.

But his love and his youthful pride attached him to the world. He learned to ride, hunt, fence, dance, and draw, studied music, and became a love-poet. At eighteen (1283) he sent forth his first love-song. And just at that epoch, his home city was full of merriment and gaiety. The hostile parties, Guelfs and Ghibellines, had become reconciled and had made peace (1279). "In June of the year 1283," writes the chronicler Villani, "at the festival of St. John, when the city of Florence was happy, quiet, and at peace, and when the time was a most favourable one for merchants and craftsmen, and especially for the Guelf lords, in the quarter of Santa Felicità Oltr' Arno . . . a social union was formed, composed of a thousand people who, all clad in white, called themselves the Servants of Love. They arranged a succession of sports, merrymakings, dances with ladies; nobles and bourgeois marched to the sound of trumpets and music in wild delight to and fro, and held festive banquets at midday and at night. This Court of Love lasted nearly two months, and it was the finest and most famous that had ever been in Florence, or in all Tuscany. Jugglers and players came from all over the world, and they were received and entertained most heartily. It must be understood that this was the happiest time that the city of Florence and its citizens had ever known. It lasted until

---

[1] *Ibid.*
[2] I cannot indeed regard the source from which this surmise is drawn, the exchange of sonnets with Forese Donati, as a very clear one.

the year 1289, when the division arose between the 'great people' and the 'small people,' and later between the white Guelfs and the black ones. But there were at that time in Florence more than three hundred knights and many groups of cavaliers and lesser nobles, who held high festival at morn and eve, with many jugglers. At Easter time they gave away many garments of fur. So that from Lombardy and all Italy comedians and jugglers came flocking to Florence and were warmly welcomed. No stranger who had any name or dignity could pass through Florence without being entertained by the various coteries, in eager rivalry with each other, and escorted by them at need on horseback through the city and on his way."

And not only for the city, but for her greatest son as well, it was—I will not say the happiest, but the most delightful time. The remarkable combination of knightly splendour and sturdy bourgeois ability, this genuinely Florentine, democratically aristo-cratic manner of living, made a lasting impression upon him. It is not to be wondered at that he, full of such youthful memories, became a *laudator temprois acti*. In his *Commedia* he praises alter-nately the knightly courtesy and gallantry [1] and the civic sim-plicity and peace [2] of days gone by. In his youth he had indeed had both at once.

Enhanced by all the charms of lonely longing and glorified by the golden haze of memory, the fairest and most lovable of all cities, Florence, his home, rises before the eyes of the exile— "The lovely fold wherein a lamb I slumbered."

True even to the grave, he bore in his heart the best beloved of his youth, Beatrice and Florence. These are the two souls of his poem. It was the thought of Beatrice that made him under-take it. [3] The thought of Florence gives him the strength to complete it. [4]

He fought victoriously for Florence, as a soldier at Campaldino (June, 1289), perhaps also at Caprona (August, 1289). The perils of war, endured with his comrades, may have aroused his patriotism more than the enjoyment of the public festivals.

---

[1] Especially in *Purgatorio*, XVI, 115 sqq., and in the *Canzoniere*, Sonnet XCVI, *Perch'io non trovo chi meco ragioni.*
[2] E.g. *Paradiso*, XV, 97 sqq.
[3] Cf. the final words of the *Vita Nuova*, where the plan of the *Commedia* is an-nounced.
[4] *Paradiso*, XXV, 1 sqq.

THE CITIZEN

So, about the age of thirty (1295), he took a decisive step, and entered the political life of his native city. Florence was just then at the height of popular government. The struggle between Guelf and Ghibelline had been brought to an end by the fall of the Hohenstaufens. The wild and violent race of Swabian rulers and their feudal following was broken. With a mixture of disgust and admiration, the citizen of Florence, with his Guelf sympathies, recalled the gigantic shape of Frederick II, the bloody day of Montaperti (1260), and the terrible Ghibelline leader, Farinata degli Uberti. That haughty Church-hating generation, as the later Florentine was wont to regard it, that crew of desperate heretics, lives a poetic life in the flaming tombs of the *Inferno*.[1]

Florence, from her political and geographical position, naturally sided with the Guelfs. The nearness of the States of the Church, the economic rivalry with the Ghibelline city of Pisa, the close relations with Bologna, which was prevailingly Guelf, the hostility of Ghibelline Siena, which strove to block the path of trade toward Rome—made opposition to the emperor and alliance with the pope seem, again and again, the more profitable course.

Not that the Guelfs, in the Italian cities, were especially devoted to the cause of the pope, or the Ghibellines to that of the emperor. "The only goal before these local parties was the control of the community, from which one party strove to exclude the other. They called themselves Guelfs or Ghibellines according as they hoped to be supported in their political action by the pope or by the emperor. So they invoked their intervention and utilized their aid, as best they might, in their own interest. The moment pope or emperor, however, . . . set too high a price on their assistance, established his own sovereignty over the city-state, and attempted to involve the partisans in some strife that did not touch their selfish interests, opposition began, followed by open revolt and an allegiance, if possible, with the opposite party. . . . So we often see in the Italian cities—always for the sake of their own interests—the Ghibellines opposing the emperor, and the Guelfs at strife with the pope."[2]

While in such fashion the great lords of the city, divided into Guelfs and Ghibellines, strove for supremacy, the bourgeoisie

[1] *Inferno*, X.
[2] Salvemini, *Magnati e popolani in Firenze dal 1280 al 1295*, pp. 2–3.

had gathered strength as the fortunate third party. The sympathies of the mass of the people were with neither pope nor emperor, but were purely democratic. Step by step in the last decades of the thirteenth century they bereft the magnates of their power, now playing off the Ghibellines against the Guelfs, and now the Guelfs against the Ghibellines.

As this bourgeoisie gained the upper hand, it began to divide. First a distinction arose between the *popolo grasso*, the industrial and mercantile class, and the *popolo minuto*, the mechanics and shopkeepers. At the bottom, without legal rights, lay the *plebs*, partly skilled workmen, partly rustics.

While the conflicts between the magnates (Guelfs and Ghibellines) were chiefly caused by the ambition and desire for power of the great families, and usually took on the character of family wars and feuds, the strife between bourgeoisie and magnates was primarily determined by economic interests.

The land and the houses were in the hands of the magnates. On account of the astonishing increase in population—Florence numbered in the year 1200 about 10,000 inhabitants, in 1300 about 30,000, and in 1329 fully 90,000—the bourgeoisie was forced to struggle incessantly for reasonable food and rent prices, and to subject the magnates to taxation. While they were making every effort to free their labour and their money from the exactions of the feudal and aristocratic state, they became the pioneers of a civic and democratic culture. Without the victory of the Florentine bourgeoisie over the magnates the whole Italian Renaissance would be unthinkable. Democratic Florence is the "first modern city in the world,"[1] and the cradle of the Renaissance.

But every step forward in this struggle, each fresh political victory of the people, made it more and more clear that the reward fell to the rich and powerful, especially to the seven upper guilds, and that the lower guilds of the *popolo minuto* could only look on.

When, in consequence of this, the *popolo grasso* made common cause with the Guelf magnates, in order to break down the sovereignty of the Ghibellines, the *popolo minuto* also saw their own advantage, and attached themselves to the Ghibelline leaders.

After these latter, in the early eighties (1283), were defeated,

[1] Jakob Burckhardt, *Die Kultur der Renaissance in Italien*, Leipzig, 1904, I, 78.

and some of the rich citizens had themselves become magnates, the *popolo minuto* sided for the most part with the moderate magnates (or, as they were called after the year 1300, the white Guelfs), and the *popolo grasso* with the black Guelfs. Sometimes an opposite grouping occurred as a consequence of special conditions.

Such were the most important positions of the parties in the complicated and bloody family and class wars. "And from this partisan strife," such is the judgment of Machiavelli, the cleverest of Florentine politicians, "there resulted more murders, banishments, and destruction of families than ever in any city known to history. And truly, it seems to me that nothing quickened the vitality of this city more than partisan success. Even the greatest and most powerful city would have been ruined thereby. But ours seemed only to thrive better; so energetic, so ingenious, so courageous for their own greatness and that of their native city, were its citizens." [1]

The question has been, and is still, much discussed, to what class and to what party our poet belonged; but perhaps his misfortune sprang from the very fact that he himself did not rightly know, or wish to know.

The victory of the *popolo grasso* over the great lords was assured in 1293 by the so-called Ordinances of Justice. According to these ordinances, all the magnates who were members of no guild were excluded from a share in the government; that is, from the office of prior. Furthermore, the judicial proceedings against recalcitrants were simplified and made more severe. In the year 1295, the severity of the ordinances was somewhat softened in favour of the magnates.

The first political act of Alighieri known to us is his speech in favour of this milder procedure, made in the Grand Council of the republic. Presumably in the same year, he took advantage of it to have himself enrolled, as a mere matter of form, in one of the guilds. He chose the guild of the physicians and apothecaries—or the dealers in spices and drugs. He would probably have been ashamed, as the scion of an ancient family of Guelf magnates, to follow any such calling. He endured it only to make himself eligible for the highest office, the priorship. He thus, no doubt, found himself from the very beginning in a peculiar posi-

---

[1] Machiavelli, Introduction to his *Istorie fiorentine*.

tion, halfway between the two parties. The richest and most powerful among the magnates, who disdained to stoop to a guild, would regard him in his poverty as a renegade; and the people might be suspicious of him as a disguised magnate. He certainly had married a daughter of the most feudal family of all, the Donati!

In the ambiguous position in which his political ambition had placed him, he could at first maintain himself only by the aid of his personality and his extraordinary mental equipment. The very delicacy of his social and political position, which did not permit him to identify himself with any actual class and party, but compelled him to come to an understanding with all, may well have had a most stimulating influence upon him. Here perhaps he learned how to assert himself in the teeth of adverse criticism.

> What matters it to thee what here is whispered?
> Come after me and let the people talk;
> Stand like a steadfast tower, that never wags
> Its top for all the blowing of the winds.[1]

We must recall the strict and narrow social limitations, with all the hampering influences of class, guild, and descent. We must not forget, either, the suspicious nature of this democratic organization "where the personality of the rulers meant little or nothing," where the office of prior was vacated every two months, where the executive power (*podestà* and *capitano del popolo*) was not entrusted to a native Florentine at all, and where the decisions of the priors had to pass before no less than four deliberative bodies before they acquired validity. We shall then understand to what an extent the individual was exposed, in both his domestic and his public life, to the surveillance and censure of his fellow citizens. In such a milieu, in the midst of such witty, malignant, and reckless folk as the Florentines, a man might very quickly rise—and no less quickly fall. The temptation to rise to eminence, whether through high qualities or demagogic arts, was as great as the possibility of remaining there was small.

Dante yielded to the temptation as well as to the peril. He sacrificed himself to public life. In its public life, as in many other respects, mediæval Florence had a striking resemblance to ancient Athens.

[1] *Purgatorio*, V, 12–15.

In both cities, public and domestic activities were constantly running together. Private life, where people could find seclusion or repose, was unknown in these republics. A man with powerful inner aspirations has ever been unhappy in a community which makes exclusive demands upon him. Only clubmen and gregarious creatures can be comfortable under conditions that enable them to "devote themselves wholly to the cause." But great characters come to a tragic end like Socrates, or become contemplative Utopians and embittered satirists like Plato.

Dante's life encountered the lot both of Socrates and of Plato. More than one cup of poison was handed to him while he lived in his native city. With equanimity and dignity he drank them to the dregs. He made so little of it that naïve biographers could believe him to have been happy. Guido Cavalcanti was his dearest friend; Dante in his official capacity of prior must send him into banishment (June, 1300). Indeed, he may have been compelled to admit to himself that by this sentence of exile he sent his great friend to an untimely death. Corso Donati, the ambitious and scheming Guelf nobleman, becomes his deadly political enemy—and Gemma Donati is Dante's wedded wife! The pride with which he rejected an humiliating invitation to return to his native city made his children also homeless.[1]

So his character grows, and with it his unhappiness. Misfortune rises steadily against him and sweeps away with cruel strokes all that is near and dear to him—friend, wife, family, party, and fatherland—until finally he stands alone in his tragic greatness and is, as he himself has said, a party by himself.

The weak, tame thought that this greatness was nourished by the sacrifices of his friends and the tears of his loved ones probably never came to him. Or if it did, he put it aside.

> For evermore the man in whom is springing
> Thought upon thought, removes from him the mark,
> Because the force of one the other weakens.[2]

He was firmly convinced, if I am not mistaken, that this sort of human sacrifice befitted his moral dignity. He has described, in clear, calm words, just that magnanimity which he himself exemplified. "The great man always in his own heart deems

[1] At least, they were included in the reiterated decree of banishment of November 6, 1315.

[2] *Purgatorio*, V, 16-18.

himself great, and, on the other hand, the petty man rates himself more ignoble than he is. And as greatness and littleness must always have reference to some standard, compared with which the great man makes himself great and the small man small, so it comes to pass that the great man makes the rest ever smaller than they actually are, while the ignoble man makes them ever greater. And because man measures by the same standard both himself and his affairs, which are, so to speak, a part of himself, so it comes to pass that the great man deems his own interests more important and the interests of other men baser than they really are. But the ignoble man always believes his own interests are worthless and those of other men important." [1]

Such a type of greatness is always unsocial; for those who also have ambition, it must be first inconvenient, then burdensome, and finally insolent. It has no room for the much-praised Aristotelian civic happiness, for it is sufficient unto itself. How far it can carry one in a democratic environment is shown by an anecdote of Dante related by Boccaccio. When at a critical moment it was asked who should undertake the difficult embassy to Pope Boniface VIII (probably in the year 1301), our poet, who had been unanimously chosen therefor, is said to have remarked, after a moment's thought: "If I go, who remains? If I remain, who goes?" [2]—"As if he had been the only one fit for anything, and must make all others fit."

Thus are the greatest men struck blind. They tower above ordinary mortals, their sight fails them among the clouds on the dizzy heights, and they fall.

Just as Dante's love for the Florentine girl had grown greater than its object, so civic virtue in him became greater than his native city. He becomes, like Socrates, a citizen of the world, and can no longer understand the humbler aims and ways of his city.

THE PRACTICAL MAN AND POLITICIAN

As a politician Dante acted honourably, but perhaps not always tactfully. Not that his fellow citizens saw deeper or further than he. However high the average political intelligence was, mediæval Florence did not produce, so far as we know, a genius in statesmanship.

---

[1] *Convivio*, I, 11.　　　　　　　　[2] Boccaccio, *Vita di Dante*, § 12.

It would surely be a mistake to regard our poet as at all what the German Philistine calls an "idealist," awkward and helpless in everything that has to do with practical affairs. The little that we learn of his public conduct rather indicates the opposite.

He had a well-developed physique. By his presence of mind and energy he had, as he himself tells us, saved a child from drowning.[1] In April of the year 1301 he was in charge of the works for widening and rectifying a street in Florence. In numerous passages of his poem he reveals a surprising familiarity with technical details of the most varied arts, a fabulous topographical memory and sense of direction, and unusual exactitude in matters of mathematical geography. By the inventive ingenuity with which he carries out the construction of the three kingdoms of future life, he won an enthusiastic following even among those readers who were otherwise unable to appreciate his poem. Almost too large, too busy, too insistent, is the swarm of Dante-geographers, Dante-astronomers, Dante-mechanicians, architects, engineers, generals, and clock-makers.[2] So Dante must have had, like Goethe, an unusual eye for technical and practical matters.

The "struggle with the object" in which the choleric Swabian, Friedrich Theodor Vischer, bled to death, drop by drop, was silently and victoriously fought through by this deft Italian as merely something to be expected. There is a touch of Alberti or of Leonardo in his nature.

He could adjust himself not only to things but to men. Otherwise in the course of the Guelf military convention (*Taglia Guelfa*) the Florentines would never have sent him to conduct the negotiations at San Gimignano (May, 1299). The difficult mission to Boniface VIII, already mentioned, if true, may be claimed as favourable testimony to the diplomatic attainments of Alighieri. That as negotiator for Count Malaspina he was not unsuccessful is proved by documents (October 6, 1306). And even if the last undertaking of his life, the negotiations which he carried on with the Venetians on behalf of Guido Novello da Polenta, resulted negatively, that proves nothing against his capacity. The most striking evidence, however, of his profound insight into human

[1] *Inferno*, XIX, 16 sqq.
[2] In Italy alone there are three famous systems of Dantesque timepieces: those of Father Ponta (1845), of Professor Filippo Arci (1900), and of Lieutenant-General Ugo Pedrazzoli (1914).

nature, of his adaptability, and of his sympathetic comprehension of the most diverse temperaments, is given by the *Divine Comedy*.

How much, in his appreciation of practical worldly wisdom, he had learned from the golden utterances and examples of the ancients, has already been considered. Another important schooling for him may have been knighthood. As guest, as friend, as man of affairs, perhaps also as troubadour, the exile lived at the courts of knightly princes: the Scaligeri, the Malaspinas, the lords of Romena, of Polenta, and who knows where besides. And surely nowhere are prudence and worldly wisdom more useful than on the slippery ground of courts.

So it was certainly no lack of caution and experience that could account for his ill fortune. To put it crudely and flatly: he might well have become a good and successful politician, if he had wished it. He was not deficient in practical ingenuity; he merely lacked interest in the vulgar commonplaces of everyday life and had no will thereto.

By will I mean that inward impulse to power which cannot be acquired or renounced at pleasure. We either have it or we do not. Even the most gifted man is unable to accomplish aught of importance in any position unless he devotes himself to it without reserve and whole-heartedly. All else is not will, but mere fancy.

Dante tested himself, and was tested, in statesmanship, but with no great success. He had ambition, but not unconditioned love for political life. He could not be wholly absorbed by it; would not, had occasion demanded, have risked his soul for it.

When he began his political career, the ruling Guelf party had split into two sections; the merchants—half magnates, half bourgeois—and the Guelf nobility. Dante sided with the former, either for moral reasons, or because no other course was open to a man who had dropped from the class of magnates into the upper guilds. These white Guelfs were chiefly great capitalists, and Dante could hardly have felt himself linked to their cause by economic or other selfish interests. Hence his inclination to mediate between the two parties and to uphold the cause of justice.

There were then two great Guelf powers in Italy: the house of Anjou in Naples and Pope Boniface VIII in Rome. While the black Guelfs were trying to win over the pope to their side, the Whites, and above all Dante, thought it advisable to chal-

lenge the dangerous prince of the Church by refusing him the
military assistance which he demanded from the Florentines
against his enemies, the Colonnas. About the same time, by a
similar refusal, they antagonized King Charles II of Anjou.
Dante desired—and it was an excellent idea—to maintain the
independence of his city. But in that case he should have gone
over completely to the side of the pope's natural enemies and,
above all, the Colonnas. It does not appear likely that Dante was
ever able to adopt such a policy. He ignored the great economic
interests that were at stake. The threat of the *popolo minuto* to
abolish ecclesiastical privileges and especially tax exemption, and
the threat of the pope to destroy the credit of the Florentine
wholesale merchants throughout the Catholic world by excommunication—what was that to Dante? Furthermore Dino Com-
pagni, Dante's fellow partisan, has confessed, with childish
simplicity, all the compromises and hesitations of his policy.
The third Guelf power also, the King of France and his brother,
Charles of Valois, could not be won over to the side of the Whites.
When the latter prince, at the end of the year 1301, entered
Florence, nominally as a peacemaker between the two parties,
all was over for the Whites. Their leaders, including Dante, were
driven into exile.

Thus Dante's political experiment ended with the loss of his
home, his property, and even of his civic honour.[1]

He finally broke away even from his companions in misfortune,
whose violent efforts to return to Florence at any cost evidently
displeased him. From that time on he spent his life at the courts
of various princes. He was politically dead and was no longer
a member of any party, so that scholars always have a free hand
to brand him as Guelf or Ghibelline. I am even doubtful as to
his having been, before his exile, a white Guelf. It is well known
that the leaders of these Whites were the Cerchi, an upstart
family of bankers and merchants, newcomers in Florence, whose
political conscience was essentially their purse. How could a
Dante feel that he had any common interests with such people?
He could not suppress his contempt for these immigrant peasants
with their highly acquisitive instincts.[2] The soul of their politics

[1] He was accused by his enemies of fraud, extortion, and bribery; a charge
which we, in our present state of knowledge, have reason to regard as a political
manœuvre, hardly as a well-grounded moral arraignment.
[2] *Paradiso*, XVI, 52 sqq. and 65.

was industrialism, with which Dante had no sympathy. So, probably from the very beginning, he was on somewhat casual terms with the rest of his party, and therefore could not help them in their hour of need. On the contrary, it was in his misfortune, when their true nature stood revealed, "all ingrate, all mad and impious," [1] that he contemptuously turned his back upon them.

But his partisans had not deceived him; it was he who had deceived himself into accepting partisan loyalty.

In truth two views of the world, two historical periods, were here in contrast. In the depths of his soul, Dante was the paladin of the theocratic ideal. The Florentines were, in the full assurance of their instincts, practical politicians. To be sure, they too had had their compunctions; they too had to reckon with moral imponderables. But their scruples had been drowned in the blood of civil war and by the murderous extinction of families. Consider the countless deeds of horror when the Blacks and the Whites cut each other to pieces in Pistoia. And from Pistoia the Florentines took over, with the names, the partisan hatred and passion. And the imponderables, thanks to the example of the popes, men had long before learned to recast into quite ponderable and well-pondered political rhetoric.

The theocratic ideal still lived on among the Florentines and the Italians in general, but only as a convention; and as such it was discussed, praised, recognized, held in honour, but never taken seriously. A perusal of the political utterances of these groups, of the local chronicles and poems of the times, tends to show that the affairs of the world were by them observed and judged accurately, even though from a limited point of view; and that the martial poet, as well as the chronicler, "stands in the whirl of busy life, devotes his chief care to the interests of his own city; and his changing attitude toward passing events is determined by the variations of the intriguing policy of his city."

How differently was the world's history mirrored in the songs of the poets of chivalry, of the Provencal troubadours, or of Walther von der Vogelweide! These latter still believed in the theocratic ideal of the Middle Ages, whether they desired it to be realized through the emperor or the pope. They were still in-

[1] *Paradiso*, XVII, 64.

terested in world-politics. The shrewder bourgeois, on the other hand, cared only for the administration of his own little corner of the world. His life's mission was love for his home city and hatred of his rival neighbours; his loyalty was local patriotism and party spirit.

The fact that civic poets like Guittone d'Arezzo or Chiaro Davanzati, who were so profoundly under Provençal influences, go their own way in their political poems and suddenly become eloquent and original, is a striking proof of the openness and independence of their political conscience. And if we miss in them the broad outlook upon world-history of the troubadours, we discover, on the other hand, that they are able, within their narrower frame, to observe and judge political conditions far more accurately than the knights of Southern France, whose many-sided interests were by no means always accompanied by corresponding clearness of insight.

In short, instead of the knight's sentimental and personal attitude toward politics, we have among the Italian bourgeoisie, long before Machiavelli's days, a practical and utilitarian conception.

But Dante's political canzoni, in their spirit and style, are much more akin to the contemporary Provençal than to the Italian poems. For that reason Dante chose an Italian of Provençal spirit and of Provençal speech, the troubadour Sordello, as his critical and political guide through the valley of the duty-shirking princes,[1] and entrusted himself elsewhere to the first imperial poet of Rome, Virgil.

He seeks and finds the champions and true followers of his political creed in past ages and in foreign lands. But lo! there came a time when it seemed as though his romantic dream would be fulfilled.

In October of the year 1310, Henry VII, King of Germany, with a small army, crossed Mont Cenis, to seek in Rome the imperial crown. Since the death of Frederick II (1250), Italy had not seen a German emperor. The Guelfs had long rested easy in the assurance that there was to be no more imperialism. At most a French potentate, King Philip the Fair of France or King Robert of Naples, was still in a position to control the destinies of the peninsula. King Philip held even the pope in

[1] *Purgatorio*, VI and VII.

check, threatening him with a legal procedure against the memory
of Boniface VIII or with the scandal of the order of Templars.
In his dire need, Clement V rested his hopes upon the pious,
churchly, knightly, upright, and noble-hearted Count of Luxem-
burg, who now, as German king, in accordance with his promise,
was undertaking the march on Rome. Not in order to create a
Ghibelline power hostile to the Church, but to break down the
insolence and unruly behaviour of the French and of the Guelfs,
he had come as a protector and reformer of the Church, and, at
the same time, as her most loyal son, a new Charlemagne.

Perhaps no prince ever cherished so purely and sincerely in
his heart the ancient ideal of a peaceful, joint world-rule by
emperor and pope—the ideal of Peter Damian and of Dante.
"As the one God has arranged the heavenly hosts in grades, so
it is also His will that all mankind shall be divided into kingdoms
and provinces, and shall submit to one single ruler, so that they,
to the honour of Heaven's decree, may flourish in peace and
harmony, and be strengthened in love and faith. In the early
centuries the world-rule was insecure, and passed from hand to
hand, according as the peoples increased their distance from their
Creator; until He, in His wisdom and goodness, assigned it to
the Romans, so that where the apostolic seat of the pontificate
was destined to be, the loftiest throne of empire should also stand,
and so that on one and the same spot the power of the pontifex
and of the emperor should shine forth. The Son of God, as the
eternal pontifex, has instituted an eternal pontificate, and as
King of the Romans and Lord of Lords, has made all earthly
powers subject unto the empire." In such words did Henry
announce to the King of England his coronation as emperor.
And these thoughts were not mere rhetoric, but the guides of his
policy.

He, too, was a romanticist. He cared, as it seems, more for
the imperial crown and for its lawful title than for power.[1] But
just this idealistic and unpolitical spirit could not but win the
heart of our poet.

Together with all discontented and banished men, white Guelfs
and Ghibellines, Dante welcomed him with delight. He expected,

[1] He was, to be sure, from lack of dynastic power, because of the force of public
opinion, and as a result of the circumstances of his election, perhaps more than
all other emperors dependent on his legal title and on the ingratiating power of
the idea.

from the success of the emperor's cause, a remedy to the injustice done him, and a sort of Golden Age for all humanity.

Feverish excitement, eschatological feelings of revenge and hope, patriotism and prophetic spirit, measureless pride and devoted love, political dreams and moral enthusiasm, seethe in his soul. Now he must decide; now the day draws nigh when the two suns, Caesar and Peter, are to scatter all the clouds of malice by their united light, and to spread a golden sky of harmony and happiness over an agonized and bleeding Italy. Dante Alighieri, at his emperor's side, will ride in triumph through the gate of Florence, and civic and ecclesiastical virtues will march in with him!

At this moment of theocratic intoxication Dante flung into the world three Latin letters: one to the peoples and princes of Italy, one to the Florentines, and one to the emperor himself. Our philological criticism still utters a weak challenge to the authenticity of these convulsions of a Titanic soul and declares this most genuine bit of real life a forgery. I can see no sound consideration to militate against Dante's authorship.

Neither can I share, however, the æsthetic admiration felt by others for these letters. Precisely because they were written in impatience, in passion, and in wild excitement, they lack artistic finish. It is not poetry, but political rhetoric; it is not the style of our Dante, but that of an Old Testament prophet or a Joachim— or an imitation of them. The reader may judge for himself.

"Behold, now is the acceptable time when signs of consolation and peace appear. For a new day gleams forth, revealing the dawn in the east which already is dispersing the darkness of our long tribulation . . . and we, too, who spent a long night in the wilderness, shall behold the long-awaited joy, for a sun of peace is to come; and justice, which languished like the heliotrope bereft of its light, will revive again as soon as he sends forth his resplendent light. . . . For the strong lion of the tribe of Judah hath lifted up his ears in compassion, and, moved to pity by the lamentations of this universal thraldom, hath awakened another Moses who shall deliver his people from the oppression of the Egyptians and who shall lead them into the land where milk and honey flow. Rejoice, therefore, thou Italy, until now pitied even by the Saracens, for soon shalt thou be the envy of all mankind, since thy bridegroom, the solace of the world and the glory of thy people, even the most gracious Henry, our divine Augustus and Caesar, hastens to his nuptials." [1]

He threatens the Florentines who take up arms against the emperor: "What will it avail you to have girt your city with a rampart, to have fortified it with bulwarks and battlements, when, terrible in gold, the eagle shall swoop down upon you, which, soaring now over the Pyrenees, now over Caucasus, now over Atlas, sustained by the host of the heavenly spirits, once gazed down upon the vast seas in its flight." [2]

And to the emperor, who had to overpower the cities of Upper Italy—Cremona, Lodi, Brescia, Pavia—before he could venture southward, Dante gives, in somewhat the same language and with the same anxious expectation, his rash and dangerous counsel, advising Henry to leave his unconquered enemies behind him and to come in all haste to Florence.

"Art thou he that should come," [3] he writes to him, "or look we for another? Although the long-enduring, and violent desire, as is its wont, throws into doubt again what was sure and near at hand, yet we believe and hope in thee, declaring thee to be the minister of the Lord, the son of the Church, the champion of the glory of Rome. For I, too, who write both for myself and for others, beheld thee most gracious, and heard thee most clement as beseems imperial majesty, at the time when my hands touched thy feet, and my lips paid their tribute. Then my spirit rejoiced within me, when I said secretly within myself, Behold the Lamb of God which taketh away the sins of the world!

"But why this hesitation? . . . Dost thou linger in Milan through the Spring as through the Winter, thinking that thou shalt extirpate the venomous hydra by cutting off its heads? . . . What dost thou, the sole ruler of the world, imagine thou wilt have accomplished when thou hast set thy foot upon the neck of rebellious Cremona? Is it not likely that some unlooked-for madness will break out again in Brescia or in Pavia? . . . Dost thou not know, most excellent prince, and dost thou not descry from thy lofty watch-tower, where the little stinking vixen hides from its hunters? Verily, not from the rushing Po, not from thine own Tiber, doth that reckless creature drink, but its jaws poison even now the rushing stream of the Arno. Florence— canst thou not know it?—is the name of the baleful pest. She

[1] *Epistolae*, V. [2] *Ibid.*, VI, 3. [3] Luke 7:19.

is the viper that turneth against the vitals of her mother. She is
the mangy sheep that infecteth the flock of the Lord. She is the
unnatural Myrrha inflamed with passion for the embraces of her
father, . . . verily she too burns for the embraces of her own
father, she, Florence, when she wickedly and wantonly seeks to
compass a breach between thee and the supreme pontiff who is
the father of fathers. . . . But let the infuriate woman take
heed to the noose wherein she is entangling herself." [1]

Florence was indeed the soul of the Guelf resistance and was
weaving about the emperor's undertaking a net whose threads
ran to and fro between France, Rome, and Naples. With difficulty Henry obtained the crown in Rome (June 29, 1312); he
besieged Florence in vain (September-October, 1312); and while
he was preparing, with renewed strength and excellent prospects,
for a campaign against Robert of Naples, he was overtaken by
death on August 24, 1313, at Buonconvento.

For Dante it must have been a terrible disillusionment. Following the death of Beatrice and his exile from Florence, this was
the third and perhaps the heaviest blow. The band of imperialists,
white Guelfs and Ghibellines, dispersed, and again he stood alone
with his sorrow. Home was no longer to be thought of. The
Florentines requited his love for the emperor with a new edict
of banishment (1315). Cino da Pistoia lamented, in two eloquent
canzoni, the prince who had gone to his death for the ancient
imperial ideal. But Dante held his peace. Despair and longing
for death darkened about him.

> "How long," I answered, "I may live, I know not;
> Yet my return will not so speedy be,
> But I shall sooner in desire arrive;
> Because the place where I was set to live
> From day to day of good is more depleted,
> And unto dismal ruin seems ordained." [2]

But his energy soon revived. New hopes arise out of destruction, hopes that rest firmly upon the unshakable basis of faith,
forever young, forever old. Before God's face, in highest Heaven,
he sets the throne of his emperor:

> . . . of noble Henry, who shall come
> To redress Italy ere she be ready. [3]

[1] *Epistolae*, VII.　　　　　　　　　　　[3] *Paradiso*, XXX, 137–138.
[2] *Purgatorio*, XXIV, 76–81.

"Ere she be ready!" If Henry was not the appointed one, then shall it be another. Come he must, the imperial deliverer.

An incurable Utopian, with the changeless happy smile of the political dreamer, with the unbroken heart of youth, the cruelly tried, incomprehensible man sank into his grave (September 14, 1321).

THE POLITICAL TEACHER AND HIS SOCIAL TEACHING

Not until after his failures in the practice of politics did Dante devote himself to its theory. It was under the influence of his banishment that he composed the *Convivio*, which, though a work of moral philosophy, nevertheless contains in outline his theory of the state. It was under the pressure of Henry VII's unsuccessful march to Rome, if I am not mistaken, that the *De Monarchia* was written.

It may even be that a number of years elapsed between the emperor's death and the composition of this work. At least, the *De Monarchia* refers (I, 12), in the most authoritative manuscripts, more or less distinctly to *Paradiso*, V, 19 sqq. If this allusion be explained away as an interpolation, there still remains the cardinal fact that in the *Convivio*, the relation between state and Church, emperor and pope, had not yet become at all a problem for our poet, and that in the *Divine Comedy*, it was only treated and solved in general outlines, and that it is first fully discussed in the *De Monarchia*. Considering the completeness with which Dante usually recorded in the *Commedia* his most important convictions and acquisitions, we should certainly expect, if the *De Monarchia* were older than the poem, to find in the *Commedia* somewhat more instruction in the philosophy of law and somewhat more of distinctly scholastic political science than it actually contains. In the main, however, the poet holds to a prevailingly symbolic and figurative presentation of this doctrine. The *De Monarchia* is the first work to announce itself as a scientific survey of the state. "I desire . . . to set forth truths unattained by others." Furthermore, while some statements of the *Convivio* and of the *De vulgari Eloquentia* are expressly corrected or recalled in the *Commedia*, nothing of the kind occurs for the *De Monarchia*. The weightiest fact, however, seems to me to be that, as I have shown, Dante is nowhere further removed from

Thomas, has nowhere drawn closer to Averroism and, in particular, to mysticism, than in the *De Monarchia*.

So this essay must not be regarded by us as a sort of introduction to the *Commedia*, but as a subsequent, or perhaps contemporary, comment upon it, and should be so utilized.

Any references or allusions to a definite political state of things which would permit us to assign the *De Monarchia* to this or that year I have failed to discover, nor have others been more successful. I am still inclined to set the composition of the *De Monarchia* after, rather than before, that of the last cantos of the *Purgatorio*.

On the basis of the political experiences through which he had passed, and as *publicis documentis imbutus*,[1] Dante feels under obligations to write a treatise on the state. As a matter of fact he utilized his experiences, which had certainly been most thorough and sobering, in a purely negative fashion. He had not allowed himself to be converted, in real life, to *Realpolitik*, nor, in theory, to empiricism. The popes with their statesmen, and to a large extent the emperors with theirs, reveal themselves in fact as practical politicians, though their theories are idealistic and speculative; they seem to us, therefore, confused, sometimes even hypocritical. But Dante stands out in contrast to them, heroic, rigid, the most genuine, the most upright child of his time. Not only in his teachings but in his actions and in his sufferings he was a true citizen of the *civitas Dei*.

This unspoiled unity of life and of teachings, dimmed by no ignoble caution, enfeebled by no hesitancy, hampered by no weakness, enables and authorizes him to become the moral judge of his age. The test by which he measures is the eternal one of his conscience, and yet, at the same time, the contemporary one of mediævalism. Nature and history together laid it as a gift in his cradle. For it is an historical fact that the only law recognized by the Middle Ages as universal was natural right, or the divine moral law.

The relation might be expressed symbolically thus: The Middle Ages desired to incarnate their own political conscience—and created the absolutely moral personality of Dante.

In fact, of all that he thought and wrought, the theory most deeply rooted in his personal convictions and most firmly con-

[1] *De Monarchia*, I, 1.

ditioned historically is his state doctrine: Utopian, yet not invented; lived, yet not experienced. If it were not in existence, it could almost be deduced. For here Dante's character coincides with that of mediævalism. No theory of the state, neither Thomas's, nor Aegidius's, nor Occam's, nor that of the French, is so typically mediæval as Dante's. The logical contradictions that we have pointed out in it are inherent in the theocratic, papal-imperial system of Western Europe; they are not arbitrary errors, nor aberrations. The modern details which have been admired—desecularization of the Church, emancipation of the state, the moral nature and function of the state, ideals of freedom, peace, and justice—are likewise specific tendencies of the age, and no independent or meritorious discoveries of the poet. The table of contents of Dante's doctrine of the state will be found to be identical with our analysis of its sources. For sources and contents coincide. The artistic arrangement and presentation of the ideas is, to be sure, another matter.

Dante's political doctrines, like his piety, must be evaluated historically for what they are, not for what they produced. As a symptom they may be extraordinarily instructive; actually they remained without noticeable effects. In fact they stand so wholly apart from events that they cannot be characterized as either reactionary or progressive. The fact that they were condemned by the Roman Curia and refuted with some ability by an obscure monk named Guido Vernani cannot be claimed as a triumph. For this honour the treatise is indebted to the rare purity and simplicity with which it reflects the spirit of its age.

For it is a confession of faith, and it rests, untroubled by its own logical currents and counter-currents, on the foundation of conscience.

To take his share in public life was, for Dante, a matter of conscience. There can be no doubt whatever that he considered this participation a moral necessity for himself, as for every free citizen. If we may draw a conclusion from his silence as to father, mother, wife, and children, then it must even be assumed that public life appeared to him ethically more valuable than the family, even as the empire is higher than the city, the great groups higher than the lesser—and mankind as a whole, the community of Christian civilization or, as he was wont to say, the *humana civilitas*, higher than all political organisms.

Here two conceptions meet, which mediæval life, with its castles, city walls, monasteries, and churches, envisaged and defined otherwise than we of today: society and state. The state idea presented itself arrayed in stone and iron, but society was thought of under the monk's garb. Neither haircloth nor steel armour, however, befitted Dante's idea. His *humana civilitas* must establish itself on earth as world-empire, and become the state, while he hoped to establish the political powers upon civilization, and bid them maintain fraternal harmony. The *civitas Dei* and the *civitas terrena* were to be brought together on the soil of his *humana civilitas*. An ethical, humane, and modern conception of society arises out of Dante's mediæval theory of the state, to which the broken eggshells of theocracy and feudalism barely cling. The vital meaning of this conception could not be developed in a political treatise, in the *De Monarchia;* it could only be worked out in a prophetic poem. To that extent it may indeed be asserted that the *Commedia* marks an advance beyond the *De Monarchia.* But it is the lead of the dreamer over the teacher, from which no conclusions can be drawn as to the chronology of the works.

The *Commedia* has been recently characterized as "the lofty song of the city-state *(polis)* "; and, in truth, there is hardly an event in the complicated struggles between Guelfs and Ghibellines, pope and emperor, pope and France, white and black Guelfs, which does not find its echo in Dante's verses. Only a man who had been in the midst of this turmoil could depict it with such vividness. Indeed the closeness to actual events, to the dust of the battlefield and to the war-cries, obstructs the reader's higher view; and at the present day, it is precisely the "political" parts of the *Commedia* that most urgently need a commentary, and are the least accessible to our sympathy. But only out of this clashing confusion could Dante's dream of eternal peace arise, and the vision of the eternal "citizen of that Rome where Christ is Roman." [1] Hence the student and reader of today cannot hope, merely by the aid of contemporary documents, to trace the development of Dante from the Florentine partisan to the ethical teacher of society and the advocate of the *humana civilitas.* Unless we follow the poetical footprints of Dante's aspirations, we shall always go astray amid the contradictions of his political thought and action.

[1] *Purgatorio*, XXXII, 101–102.

NATIONAL FEELING

It is surprising how this statesman, with his theocratic, Utopian, and unhistorical faith, has been persistently claimed and glorified by the most serious Italian scholars as the champion of the national idea and the pioneer of Italian unity!

If the common people, especially the noisy defenders of national pride, write the mighty name of Dante Alighieri upon their banners as the *italianissimo*, the Germans may indeed smile, without, however, casting any stones. But when sound and able scholars who are wont to note the distinction between individual and race speak of their Dante as the awakener of Italian national consciousness, then we think there must, after all, be some truth in it.

Since, however, it is obvious that it was precisely the imperial and papal idea that delayed the advent of the national idea, the patriotic indebtedness to Dante is by no means a result of his politics or of his theory of the state. It lies chiefly in his literary activity, in his contributions to the Italian language and to Italian history; in short, in the artistic, philological, and humanistic side of his work. His nationalistic achievements are recorded in the history of literature, and they are his *De vulgari Eloquentia* and the first book of the *Convivio*. "Italy" is to him not a political, but a geographical, linguistic, and historical concept. It is "the fair land there where the *si* doth sound." [1] The land of the Apennines, the *terra latina*, or *italica*, *Scipionum patria*, etc.

The vivid representation, indeed, of the Italian landscape, of Italian speech, of Italian history, awakens in him—how could it be otherwise?—the emotion of love. So Italy becomes for him "the garden of the empire," [2] and the *Europae regio nobilissima*. [3]

That such a love for one's native land has nothing to do with national feeling can nowhere be more plainly seen than in that passage where it breaks forth most passionately:

> Ah! servile Italy, grief's hostelry!
> A ship without a pilot in great tempest!
> No lady thou of Provinces, but brothel! [4]

Just here, where those passionate tones resound with which the patriot for five hundred years has thundered against the

[1] *Inferno*, XXXIII, 80.
[2] *Purgatorio*, VI, 105.
[3] *De Monarchia*, II, 3.
[4] *Purgatorio*, VI, 76-126.

political mutilation of Italy—just here it is revealed that the horn which the poet blows is no national one. It is Roland's horn, prophetic of misfortune, with which the imperial paladin sends forth his appeal for help over the mountains to the deaf ear of the German emperor, of *Alberto tedesco.*

The Germans, who, like the Italians, had cultural unity before they became a united nation, are in a position to understand and to value from their own experience this unpolitical, idealistic, humane, humanistic, and romantic type of racial consciousness. Dante's love for the fatherland recalls that of the greatest German thinker and poet. It is, if I may so express myself, a more spiritual, nobler, therefore less jealous, and, alas! all too helpless form of love.

THE MORALIST

That the emperor is a foreigner and indifferent to the happiness of Italy hardly occurs to our idealist. He sees not the man but the office, and that not in its actual historical form, as a source of endless friction and struggle, but rather in its fundamental significance, as a moral imperative. He does not see— to use Machiavelli's words—"the immense difference between the way we live and the way we should live." [1] He does not wish to see it. Emperor and pope are to him two ethical categories: the former represents worldly or natural, the latter super-worldly or inspired, morality.

Accordingly, Dante's whole theory of the state turns not upon a political, but upon an ethical question. His purpose is to regulate not the means to the power, but the titles to the claims, of emperor and pope, and this, too, not on the ground of their actual material possessions, but on the basis of the unalterable logical relations of the two ethical categories which they represent. All historical evidences in the *De Monarchia* are external and secondary. They owe their existence to the apologetic attitude assumed by the author. But the fundamental motif rings out pure and clear: the emperor must bear that same relation to the pope which earthly happiness has to heavenly bliss, the natural will to grace, worldly to Christian virtue; in short, the relation of the body to the soul, or even of actions to intentions.

The attempt to deduce all political powers from ethical requirements is what gives to Dante's theory of the state its thor-

[1] *Il Principe*, XV.

oughly mediæval character, so completely in harmony with the conscience of his contemporaries. The fact that, properly speaking, it is not a political theory, but public and general ethics, is what makes it the typical state doctrine of the Middle Ages.

But is Dante's ethics quite as typically mediæval as his theory of the state? Does his personal conscience here also coincide perfectly with the general feeling of his time?

As far as his ethical system is concerned, I am unable to find, either in the *Convivio* or in the *Commedia*, any originality worth mentioning. Dominant throughout is the Catholic doctrine of the seven virtues and seven sins, that dogmatic and intellectualistic love-ethics which liberally made room, as we have seen, for Cicero and Aristotle beside Paul and Augustine. A certain freedom of choice which the system permits was utilized by Dante amply, but not to excess.

If he did take over the system, in the main, from the schoolmen, yet, on the other hand, the manner in which he worked out the gradual moral and religious ascent of man through sin and virtue had been anticipated, long before his time, by the mystics.

His ethical system then appears, if studied in the light of its sources, to be that of a moderate and orthodox eclectic. The best example of this attitude is to be found in the moral arrangement of the *Inferno*, where ecclesiastical, Aristotelian, and Ciceronian conceptions are set without question side by side.

Here Dante has actually created a new class: that of men morally insignificant, who are neither good nor bad.[1] Judged philosophically, it was the weakest invention that could be imagined. It is a sort of makeshift construction. Moral neutrality has never and nowhere in the world existed. To recognize indifference as a moral category in a system is to declare the inadequacy of the system itself, and is like trying to build something consistent out of deficiencies.

The morally indifferent, as recognized by the ethics of the Stoa and partially by that of the Church, cannot be adduced to excuse or explain the Dantesque category of the *ignavi;* for the *adiaphora* lie not within, but beyond, good and evil. Dante, on the other hand, evaluates the morally worthless, and creates a contradictory concept which gives weight to his invention if we consider it merely as a personal confession and as a poetic

[1] *Inferno*, III, 22 sqq.

creation. It is only to condemn and destroy it that he asserts the possibility of moral neutrality; only to silence it does he mention moral indifference.

Therefore, what psychologically and artistically appears to be one of the poet's most original characteristics shows, when considered logically, a lack of originality, and proves that he was not very seriously concerned in the scientific consistency of his moral structure.

HIS TEMPERAMENT

If Dante, then, is an eclectic in ethics, the reason for his attitude must be explained solely on grounds of temperament and character.

It will be remembered that, of all the moral ideals of antiquity, none was more attractive to our poet than that of the Stoics, and of those of Christianity, none pleased him better than the Franciscan.

These two, curiously enough, had little influence on his theory, but much on his character. Too little was known of the Stoa and too little of what could be obtained from the Franciscans was systematic enough to yield a ready-made doctrine of morals. Dante, therefore, was a born rather than a trained Stoic and Franciscan. Cato, as a representative of the Stoa, at the foot of the mountain of Purgatory, and St. Bernard, not indeed a Franciscan, yet enlightened in true Franciscan fashion, upon the last height of Paradise, testify by their remarkable and exceptional position to the poet's love for them both.

Stoic fortitude and pride, Franciscan humility and devotion, the extremest contrasts revealed in metaphysical ethics, strive with each other for his soul. But he, with the gigantic powers of his nature, embraces both and holds them fast.

Most of his readers are too narrow-hearted to take into themselves the full richness of his nature and to let it produce the same effect. Some comprehend best in him the gentle and amiable mystic, others the austere and confident judge. The latter prefer the *Inferno*, the former the *Purgatorio*, or perhaps the *Paradiso*. To cover the spiritual flight of the entire *Commedia* demands a rare breadth of wing.

It is in vain that De Sanctis admonished us: "The biographers always present to us merely one side of this character. Most of them make him defiant and vengeful. Others would justify him and prove to us how every least word of his harmonizes with historical truth and with justice; and when I read the biography written by Cesare Balbo, Dante gradually turns before my eyes into a pretty, amiable turtle-dove. Dante himself, however, is neither the one nor the other, but all of them together. A man of passion and force, an open nature that offers its whole soul to the passing impression of the instant: as terrible in wrath as he is tender in love. It would be a waste of time to seek for a logical connection in the midst of his invectives and appeals. The true tale of Dante's life can be written only by him who, placed above controversial grounds, refuses to be drawn to the partisan viewpoint of his predecessors, and gives us, not a left or right profile, but a full-face view—Dante in his completeness, in his painful shifts from love to hate, from wrath to despair; in his moods varying in colour but the same in intensity—and tells us how he composed the contrast of *Inferno* and *Paradiso*, portrayed Francesca and Filippo Argenti, Farinata and Cavalcanti, at one time calls his fellow citizens the beasts from Fiesole, at another lovingly beseeches them, 'My people, what have I done to thee?' Dante is so sympathetic that, as Francesca tells her story, he falls in a faint: and he is so savage that he can imagine, and depict with terrible detail, a human skull gnawed by human teeth." [1]

These contradictions seem to have been stamped even upon his features. [2] The thick sensuous underlip, upborne by the strong projecting chin, must have given him a wild appearance, but the backward-drawn corners of the firmly closed mouth and the hollow, deeply furrowed cheeks reveal the strength of a victorious will. The large, deep-set eyes and the finely-cut aquiline nose bespeak the entranced dreamer, but the knitted brow with its vertical lines and depressed eyebrows betrays the capacity for stern criticism and austere comprehension. The dark tint of his hair and skin, his bent shoulders, the meditative, almost gloomy expression of which Boccaccio tells us, would indicate an impratical dreamer or a seer, if it were not that his simple and

---

[1] Francesco de Sanctis, *Saggi critici*, p. 396 sqq.
[2] I follow the statements of Boccaccio, in his *Vita di Dante*, the youthful likeness by Giotto in the Bargello of Florence, and the wonderful bronze bust in Naples. Of course it cannot be determined to what extent these reveal to us the true Dante.

correct garb and cosmopolitan manners teach us otherwise. So many-sided, so rich, so powerful was his nature.

He belonged to that unspoiled race of giants in whom Nature could work without limitations, and whose downfall is told to us in Shakespeare's tragedies. Even the most passionate and original characters of modern times appear, in comparison with this mediæval Titan, somehow artificial.

Wherever we discover, under the paint and powder of modern Europe, a naked bit of emotional life, we are wont, in a droll mixture of sympathy and enjoyment, to praise the "delightful naïveté" of the person in question—thereby betraying our own insincerity.

The naïveté of Dante is not "delightful" in this sense. It is too mighty, too critical, too fully under control for that. The conflicts of his temperament with the world are neither petty nor foolish. In order to be able to smile at Dante's ambition, his political Utopia, his self-consciousness, his hate, his poetic vengeance wreaked on the contemptible world, or at his sensuousness and his erotic Utopia, from which Beatrice issued—in order to find all this delightful, one must be either a god or a beast.

To the ordinary comprehension, all these passions, offenses, and errors are so human, so natural, so dependent upon "original sin"—pride and lust!—that no man dare think of them as especially interesting. Furthermore, if the critics do catch Dante napping, it is such a great exploit, and they seem so clever, that one really must admire them.

But for his pride and ambition, Dante would never have plunged into politics; but for his sensuousness, he never would have found Beatrice. His love, however, moulded him into a religious man, his political struggle made him a moralist. Without *luxuria* and *superbia*, no *Divine Comedy*. It is because he is a complete man that his virtues are so indissolubly interlinked with his vices.

When he storms at his native city, we feel that he passionately exaggerates a deserved reproach; when he rails at his enemies, the note of moral indignation is heard in his personal hatred; and when in his pride he elevates himself above all his contemporaries, it is evident that the most sacred and most necessary of man's possessions, faith in oneself, has its share therein.

Faith, the support and measure of greatness in all personality, is his strongest quality. It gives him assurance, earnestness, success, and greatness in whatever he undertakes. It is the spiritual vitality which, like the physical, can be neither analyzed nor artificially created.

Let us say only this much, that this mystery, this strength of faith, is what makes the bodily and the spiritual physiognomy of Dante intelligible. The essence of the first we were able to detect in the remarkable union of dogmatic firmness and scientific curiosity, of religious zeal and calm intelligence. Dante is a philosophic believer, an investigating theologian. His steadfast belief in Christ does not prevent him from inquiring into His divine and human nature. His untiring doubt never shakes the moral foundation of his faith. He investigates not despite his belief, but because of his belief.

The practical manifestations of this faith now mark him as a Stoic, now as a follower of Francis.

We saw how the Stoic sage, with his pagan belief in the omnipotence of virtue, ran a double risk. He might, out of weakness, become a hypocrite, or, in persistency, lose hope. A man like Dante felt himself threatened only by the latter peril.

The Franciscan monk, too, with his belief in the omnipresence of God, suffered degenerating tendencies. His trepidation made him into a despondent penitent; his inordinate assuredness rendered him morally lax. Here again the danger lies in the direction not of deficient but of excessive confidence; that is, of moral laxity, against which Dante had need to be on his guard.

The priceless good fortune of his life, however, was that at the required moment the Stoic in him always came to the aid of the Franciscan, and vice versa. The Stoic rescued him from sensuous excesses, and the Franciscan from over-confidence. So, guided by two friendly powers of his own gifted nature, he passes strongly and calmly through the bewildering maze of life.

Near the end it seemed as though he almost ceased to notice the unhappiness of his lot in this world, the troubles and mortifications of his exile. He learned to stand "four-square against the blows of fate," *ben tetragono ai colpi di ventura*.[1] His eye learned to turn constantly inward and upward.

> Behind him, as an unreal semblance, lay
> That which doth bind us all—the commonplace.[2]

[1] *Paradiso*, XVII, 24.   [2] From Goethe's epitaph on Schiller.

In his last poems, the Latin eclogues, composed in correspondence with a young humanist, an Arcadian smile seems to flit over the firmly closed lips.

It is true, humour seldom lights up his soul, and his wit is rare. He was too fully impressed with the greatness and importance of his tasks and of himself to take either lightly. Stern vigilance over our nature brings out not the jester, but the jester's deadly enemy, the pedant. Yes, we can conceal it no longer, the great man wears a queue. If any one laughs at this point, we cannot help it. We would but offer the suggestion that in a man of genius even his pedantry becomes of interest, and that a wise man prefers to learn from it rather than make merry over it. We remind the reader that we found some scientific enjoyment even in the driest passages of the *Paradiso*. We would almost assert that a pedant, when he has grown so strong and vigorous, has some claim to our reverence.

Most pedants are tiresome and untemperamental. Dante is the liveliest and most temperamental of them all. He has no tendency toward indolence, sullenness, *acidia*, and mental sluggishness. Indeed he is so far removed from sloth, he is so fundamentally vigorous, that all feelings and sentiments of weariness appear in him as acute attacks and are instantly overcome. He does not give them time to become chronic. The slow and progressive soul-poisoning on which the romanticist so largely prides himself—melancholy, sensibility, world-weariness, wilful unbelief, resignation, self-torture, self-analysis, every sort of langour, and all luxurious ailments which have given rise to a hundred complacent names, are unknown to him. He gives his distress no space to develop into world-weariness; does not allow his wrath to degenerate into melancholy, his raillery into irony, or his tears into sentimentality. And in so hale a man, who at fifty-six felt younger than at twenty-six, should we not find a certain dignity even in his pedantry?

His perfect health made him, despite his piety, a man glad to be alive, an optimist—an heroic, not a bourgeois optimist. Hence his usual and, so to speak, innate disposition was classical Stoicism. Only a great crisis in his soul could awaken in him that Franciscan piety which revealed itself in occasional outbreaks. It is out of his profoundest inward experiences, loss of his early love and loss of his home, the terrible blow to his sensuous nature and the terrible blow to his pride, that the religious foundation of the *Divine Comedy* springs.

It is obvious that such a person could not adequately meet the needs of his convictions with the moral resources of Thomism. What was lacking in that system was, as will be remembered, the vigorous tension and clear illumination of the contrast between acceptance and renunciation of the world; between natural, pagan virtue, and Christian virtue. So a temperament like Dante's must appear at times not sufficiently practical, at times not devout enough, and hence he has, in both directions, gone outside of the system and taken what he needed, sometimes from the Averroists, sometimes from the Franciscans.

7. THE "COMMEDIA"

THE ALLEGORY OF ETHICAL POLITICS

The full comprehension of Dante's personality in its historical environment, and with its spiritual peculiarities, reveals the ethical and political significance of the *Divine Comedy*, which is in every way a personal poem.

A single example will show how closely the convictions and teachings of the individual correspond with the ethico-political character of the poem. We saw how Dante's political conscience was bound up with his ethical consciousness, and how in consequence his theory of the state is but an ethical treatise with legal and theological terminology, historical form, and political details. This is true of the *Commedia* also. The political theory is, therefore, included in and subordinated to the moral. While the Dante of the *Commedia* represents symbolically the ethical personality of man, he also stands for a political personality, the ideal citizen of a theocratic world-state; and while, according to the poet's own declaration, the didactic purpose of the poem is the uplifting of man out of his miserable condition into a state of bliss, the political purpose is also set forth; namely, his passage from political misery to an ideal polity. In short, political aims are not self-sufficient, but rather subordinate and incidental, and as such must originate from the central moral control of the social organism.

This point of view helps us considerably to give a political interpretation to the symbolic and allegorical side of the poem.

That is to say, the political information must be deduced from the ethical significance. As soon as we begin, by inductive methods, to assign this or that symbol to this or that definite political leader or event, the interpretation becomes uncertain and arbitrary, and no longer has any absolute validity, but, at best, an illustrative value. The *Veltro*, the *Dux*, the giant, the harlot, the griffin, the wagon, and all the other debatable symbols or allegories, are one and all primarily ethical and only secondarily political and historical characters. The results that can be obtained by the use of this method are not, to be sure, remarkably important or numerous, but they are demonstrably true. We would not, to be sure, disdain historical induction and illustration; but, on general principles, the bird in the hand is worth more than two in the bush.

THE DATE OF COMPOSITION OF THE POEM

The latter portion of this work will set forth in detail the manner in which the convictions, the character, the ethos, and the moods of our poet take shape in his poem.

Only one question still needs to be answered: When was the *Commedia* composed? Undoubtedly in Dante's intellectual and moral maturity. It was cast in a single mould, by a man in the fullness of his powers, and is thereby sharply contrasted with Goethe's *Faust*. Internal discrepancies, so-called sutures, which are to be explained by fresh experiences and altered convictions, no one has yet discovered in the *Commedia*. Its ethical structure presupposes two decisive experiences: the death of Beatrice (1290) and Dante's banishment from Florence in 1302. This, of course, does not exclude the possibility that a general plan of something like the *Divine Comedy* may date back to Dante's earliest youth. The literary and the ethical motivations are two different things. We are concerned at present with the latter only.

The question, however, whether this motive was presented by Dante's exile, or rather by the third decisive experience of his life, the death of Henry VII (1313), is worth investigating.

According to my view and to my presentation so far, this third event was the heaviest blow that befell Dante. Until then he had maintained his interest in Florentine politics and was still confidently hopeful. Only after the emperor's unfortunate expedition did the remote, world-embracing, theocratic dream acquire exclusive mastery of his soul. As long as a man keeps one eye fixed upon his home and only with the other gazes toward the divinely ordained world-state, he cannot write even the first canto of the *Inferno*. The poem cannot have been begun before the year 1313.

This conjecture, which is my conviction, can be rendered plausible by a series of external circumstances, but can be neither proven nor refuted with absolute certainty.

Above all, it is to be considered that the general scheme of the *Commedia* has not only ethico-political but also religious, artistic, and philosophical presuppositions. These are the *Vita Nuova*, the *Convivio*, and the *De vulgari Eloquentia*. With the first two we have already passed far beyond the limit of 1302 and have reached the years 1305 and 1308. But in the *Commedia* itself allusions are found to events the latest of which fall in the year 1316 and perhaps even in 1319; and what is especially important, the nineteenth canto of the *Inferno* contains a prophetic allusion to the death of Clement V (April 1314). He is the pope who at first made common cause with the Emperor Henry VII and later laid secret snares for him. In this passage Dante designates, not earlier, of course, than April 1314, the time and place of his punishment for this.

Philologists discuss the possibility that such passages are later interpolations. Dante would be capable of creating a special hell for Popes Boniface and Clement. But to take a cold revenge upon them subsequently and to thrust them, his deadly enemies, into the abyss through corrections, additions, and insertions—for that Dante was not sufficiently philological.

I close and confirm this argument with words uttered by a competent and lovable admirer and student of our poet—alas, prematurely removed by death—"The *Commedia* is the result of a spiritual revolution that begins with the year 1313 and which continues down to the year of his death, down to the last cantos of the *Paradiso*, more and more perfect, resplendent, and inspiring in the poet's life and in his work." [1]

[1] Kraus, *Dante*, p. 409.